The Management of
Tourism

To Alexa, Olivia, Robbie, Rosie and Matthew

The Management of
Tourism

Edited by
Lesley Pender and Richard Sharpley

SAGE Publications
London • Thousand Oaks • New Delhi

First published 2005

Reprinted 2006

SAGE Publications Ltd
1 Oliver's Yard
55 City Road
London EC1Y 1SP

SAGE Publications Inc.
2455 Teller Road
Thousand Oaks, California 91320

SAGE Publications India Pvt Ltd
B-42, Panchsheel Enclave
Post Box 4109
New Delhi 110 017

British Library Cataloguing in Publication data

A catalogue record for this book is available from the British
Library

ISBN-10 0 7619 4021 9   ISBN-13 978 0 7619 4021 0
ISBN-10 0 7619 4022 7 (pbk)   ISBN-13 978 0 7619-4022-7 (pbk)

Library of Congress Control Number: 2004094410

Typeset by C&M Digitals (P) Ltd., Chennai, India
Printed and bound in Great Britain by TJ International Ltd, Padstow, Cornwall

Contents

Part 2: Managing Tourism Businesses

List of Figures

List of Tables

ABTA	Association of British Travel Agents
ADA	Airline Deregulation Act 1978 (USA)
AEA	Association of European Airlines
AIDA	Attention, Interest, Desire, Action (model used in marketing)
AITO	Association of Independent Tour Operators
ARGE	Asset Revenue Generating Efficiency
ASSET	Association of Small-Scale Enterprises in Tourism
ATOL	Air Travel Organiser's Licence
BA	British Airways
B2B	Business to business
BCG	Boston Consulting Group
BTR	Bureau of Tourism Research
CAA	Civil Aviation Authority
CARTA	Campaign for Real Travel Agents
CEE	Central and Eastern Europe
CEO	Chief Executive Officer
CIRET	Centre International de Recherches et d'Etudes Touristiques
C-PEST	Competitors – political, economic, socio-cultural, technological environment
CPI	Consumer Price Index
CRM	Customer Relationship Management
CRO	Central Reservation Office
CRS	Computerised Reservations System
CSR	Corporate Social Responsibility
CS/D	Consumer satisfaction/dissatisfaction
DCF	Discounted cash flow
DCMS	Department for Culture, Media and Sport
DEAT	Department of Environmental Affairs and Tourism
DICIRMS	Destination Integrated Computerised Information Reservation Management System
DMO	Destination Marketing Organisation
DMS	Destination Management System
DVT	Deep-vein thrombosis

EC	European Community
EIA	Environmental Impact Assessment
EMS	Environmental Management Systems
EU	European Union

FMD	Foot and mouth disease
FTO	Federation of Tour Operators

GDP	Gross domestic product
GDS	Global Distribution System
GE	General Electric
GNP	Gross national product
GSA	General Sales Agents
GST	Goods and Services Tax

HDI	Human Development Index
HRM	Human Resource Management

IATA	International Air Transport Association
ICT	Information and communications technologies
IHEI	International Hotels Environment Initiative
ILG	International Leisure Group
ILO	International Labour Organisation
IP	Internet Protocol
ISO	International Standards Organisation
ITT	Information technology and tourism

LTV	Lifetime value

MBO	Management by objectives
MMC	Monopolies and Mergers Commission

NGO	Non-governmental organisation
NNP	Net national product
NPV	Net Present Value
NTO	National Tourist Organisations
NVQ	National Vocational Qualification

OECD	Organisation for Economic Co-operation and Development
OFT	Office of Fair Trading

Pax	Passengers
PLC	Product life cycle

PLC	Public limited company
PMS	Property Management System
ROCE	Return on capital employed
RPKs	Revenue passenger kilometres
RPMs	Revenue passenger miles
RTO	Regional Tourism Organisation
RWE	Real work environment
SARS	Severe Acute Respiratory Syndrome
SAS	Scandinavian Air Systems (airline company)
SICTA	Standard industrial classification of tourism activities
SMART	Specific, measurable, agreed with those who must attain them, realistic, time-constrained objectives
SME	Small and medium-sized enterprises
SVQ	Standard Vocational Qualifications
SWOT	Strengths, Weaknesses, Opportunities, Threats
TALC	Tourism area life cycle
TCAA	Transatlantic Common Aviation Area
TIM	Tourism income multiplier
ToMA	Top of Mind Awareness
TQM	Total Quality Management
TSI	Trading Standards Institute
VDU	Visual display unit
VSO	Voluntary Service Overseas
VTA	Virtual Travel Agency
WTO	World Tourism Organisation
WTTC	World Travel and Tourism Council
WWF(UK)	Worldwide Fund for Nature (World Wildlife Fund)

List of Contributors

Lesley Pender is a freelance lecturer and writer specialising in areas related to the travel trade and transport sectors of the tourism industry.

Richard Sharpley is senior lecturer in tourism, Hull University.

Tom Baum has taught extensively in tourism and hospitality education. He is a specialist in trends and developments in human resource management, education and training for tourism and has researched, consulted and published in this field in many parts of the world. Another major research interest is in the area of tourism and development in small islands and peripheral locations.

Tony Blackwood is a senior lecturer in the Division of Accounting and Financial Management in Newcastle Business School at the University of Northumbria. He specialises in financial management and has published research into tourism-related business activity in international tourism and business journals.

Dimitrios Buhalis is Director of the Centre for eTourism Research at the School of Management, University of Surrey. He regularly advises the World Tourism Organisation, the World Travel and Tourism Council and the European Commission in the field of information technology impacts on tourism. He has published widely in areas of tourism, including information technology.

Jackie Clarke is senior lecturer in marketing and tourism at the Business School, Oxford Brookes University. With a background in aviation and tour operating, her current research interests focus on tourist consumer behaviour and the interface between tourism marketing and sustainability. She is co-author (with Victor Middleton) of the third edition of *Marketing in Travel and Tourism* (3rd edition, 2001).

Keith Debbage is an associate professor of geography at the University of North Carolina at Greensboro, whose research interests include the airline industry, urban planning and tourism development. He received the Roy Wolfe Award from the Recreation, Tourism and Sport Speciality Group of the Association of American Geographers in 2002 for his outstanding research contributions in the field of tourism geography.

Frank M. Go is professor of tourism and head of the center of Tourism Management, Rotterdam School of Management, Erasmus University Rotterdam (email: FGo@fbk.eur.nl). Currently he is also a visiting professor in the Department of Tourism and Recreation at the University of Leuven, Belgium. His research interests include information and communication technology and tourism, networks, community, globalisation and branding. He is on the editorial board of several international journals and has written on widening participation in new media, which meets social inclusion objectives to connect individualised demand with distributed sources of supply in the global marketplace, following an integrated, sustainable tourism strategy.

Harold Goodwin is director of the International Centre for Responsible Tourism at the University of Greenwich. He has undertaken research for the Department for International Development on tourism, conservation and sustainable development, and pro-poor tourism. He co-founded responsibletravel.com and worked with the Association of Independent Tour Operators on responsible tourism. He now works on training with the Responsible Tourism Unit of the Federation of Tour Operators.

David Grant is professor of Law and Director of the Travel Law Centre at Northumbria University. He is editor of the *International Travel Law Journal* and co-author of *Holiday Law* (3rd edn, 2003). Until recently he was a member of the Air Transport Users Council (AUC) and chairman of Newcastle Airport Consultative Committee. Currently he is a member of the Air Travel Insolvency Protection Advisory Committee (ATIPAC).

Sandra (Carey) Gountas worked in the tour operations industry for some years before joining academia ten years ago. She taught tourism and marketing at the University of Hertfordshire before moving to Australia in 2000. She now works at La Trobe University in Melbourne. Sandra's current research is concerned with consumer satisfaction in service industries, particularly in the airline industry.

Michael Hall At the time of writing Professor Michael Hall was Head of the Department of Tourism, University of Otago, New Zealand and Honorary Professor in the Department of Marketing, University of Stirling in Scotland. He is co-editor of the journal *Current Issues in Tourism* and has written widely on tourism, environment policy and regional development-related issues.

Jithendran Kokkranikal is a lecturer in tourism at The Scottish Hotel School, University of Strathclyde. His main research and teaching interests are related to planning, tourist destination management, tourism in developing countries, and human resource issues in tourism and hospitality. He has also taught and researched tourism and related areas in India and Iran.

Ronald M. Lee is currently Distinguished Ryder Professor at the Faculty of Business at Florida International University, USA, prior to which he served as the Director of the Erasmus University Research Institute for Decision Information Systems (EURIDIS) in Rotterdam. He has a PhD in Decision Sciences from Wharton School, University of Pennsylvania, Philadelphia, USA (1980).

Lesley Roberts is senior lecturer in the Centre for Travel and Tourism at The University of Northumbria where she lectures in urban and rural tourism and in issues relating to tourism in diverse environments. Her research interests lie in wider economic, political and social implications of tourism development.

Antonio Paolo Russo is a visiting research fellow at Universitat Autònoma, Department of Geography, and lecturer in cultural policy at IULM University in Milan. He also collaborates with EURICUR (European Institute of Comparative Urban Research) at the Erasmus University Rotterdam. As a consultant he has collaborated with various international organisations, such as the International Centre for Art Economics, UNESCO and the Latin American Development Bank. His research interests range from tourism and regional studies to cultural economics.

Chris Ryan is Professor of Tourism at the University of Waikato, New Zealand, and Visiting Professor at the University of Northumbria. He is editor of *Tourism Management* and a member of the International Academy for the Study of Tourism.

David J. Telfer is an associate professor in the Department of Recreation and Leisure Studies at Brock University, Canada. He teaches in the areas of tourism planning and development, and heritage tourism. He has researched and published in the areas of the relationship between tourism and development theories, economic linkage of tourism with host communities, strategic alliances and rural tourism.

John Tribe is Professor of Tourism in the School of Management at the University of Surrey. His main tourism research interests and publications are in the areas of strategy, economics, sustainability, epistemology and education.

Since the early 1990s, there has been a dramatic expansion in the provision of travel and tourism courses at both undergraduate and postgraduate levels. Commensurate with this has been the rapid growth in the tourism literature, characterised in particular by a shift from more generalist books to specialised texts which focus on, for example, different sectors of the industry or various destinational contexts, or adopt a particular disciplinary approach to the study of tourism. Inevitably, perhaps, this increasing specialisation has diverted attention away from a more generalist perspective on travel and tourism, particularly within the context of contemporary management challenges and solutions. In other words, although 'tourism management' remains the focus of a number of books, less attention has been paid to the application of management theory and practice to this field.

This book attempts to meet this need. Aimed primarily at final year undergraduate and postgraduate students, it assumes a certain level of knowledge and understanding on the part of the reader, although relevant introductory sources for those new to the subject are given for each chapter. Structured around four principal themes, namely, the tourism system, the tourism business, the tourism environment and contemporary issues, each chapter highlights current challenges and appropriate management responses. At the same time, however, each chapter also provides suggestions for further reading that offer a more general perspective. Overall, the book aims to provide a comprehensive, up-to-date analysis of management issues relevant to travel and tourism.

We would like to thank all colleagues who have contributed to this volume. Our thanks are also due to Kiren Shoman and other staff at Sage for their help and support throughout this project while, last but not least, we would like to recognise the patience and understanding of our partners, Nick and Julia, during the writing of this book.

Lesley Pender & Richard Sharpley

PART 1: MANAGING THE TOURISM SYSTEM

1 Introduction

Lesley Pender

Chapter objectives

The purpose of this chapter is to establish a context for the consideration of the management of tourism businesses that follows. It introduces the tourism system and outlines the characteristics of tourism businesses. Having completed this chapter, the reader will be able to:

- recognise the debate that has surrounded definitions of tourism
- understand the tourism system
- recognise the variety and scope of tourism businesses
- appreciate the scale and significance of tourism at both global and local levels
- identify the important linkages between different types of tourism business
- understand the main implications of the service nature of tourism businesses

Chapter contents

Introduction: Aims and objectives of the book

This introductory chapter sets the context for the remainder of the book by illustrating the aims and objectives at the same time as providing relevant background information on tourism. The scope, scale and significance of tourism, as discussed below, make management issues highly important at every level in the system. It is the aim of this book to provide detailed coverage of the breadth of issues involved in the management of tourism businesses. It is hoped that the text will support the fundamental business management aspects while examining specific techniques required for the successful management of the broad spectrum of tourism businesses. The fundamental aim, therefore, is to consider and apply management concepts, philosophies and practices to the 'business' of tourism. This is something that few texts have addressed, as many have focused instead on the theories that have evolved within the tourism area. There has been a move away from more generalist research and teaching of tourism towards a more specific approach, as evidenced by the proliferation of more specialist journals. This book aims to develop some of these issues with a management focus in recognition of the increasing understanding and knowledge of tourism as a discipline.

Themes and issues relevant to contemporary management of travel and tourism are examined, with discussion and argument incorporated into the chapters. Each of the following chapters takes management as its starting point while assuming a degree of understanding and knowledge of tourism on the part of the reader. This primary management theme is reflected through a variety of perspectives on effective management within travel and tourism.

This chapter attempts to summarise the debate that has surrounded definitions of tourism and to extract from this the key elements that are important in terms of management. The chapter also identifies some of the key issues in relation to the study of tourism management, which later chapters go on to develop. It then considers the services nature of tourism businesses and the implications thereof. The chapter starts by outlining the scope, scale and significance of tourism.

The scope, scale and significance of tourism

Tourism is an economic activity of immense global significance. However, the precise measurement of travel and tourism has not always been easy. This stems in part from different definitions and methods of accounting adopted by different countries. Efforts by the World Tourism Organisation (WTO) and the Organisation for Economic Co-operation and Development (OECD) have helped in this respect, as discussed below.

Vellas and Becherel (1995) describe the WTO as the principal source of statistics on international tourism. According to the WTO, tourism is now the largest industry in the world. In 2000 an estimated 35 million UK tourists travelled abroad with expenditure reaching an estimated £15 billion, a 4% increase in expenditure on the previous year (Mintel, 2001). According to the World Travel and Tourism Council (WTTC), the travel and tourism economy, which includes the industry itself plus indirect activities, contributed 10% to global GDP in 2002 and 7.8% of global employment, amounting to 198,668,000 jobs, or one in every 12.8 jobs. In 2002 there were 702.6 million international tourist arrivals recorded worldwide. In the same year worldwide receipts for international tourism amounted to US$474 billion (€501 billion). WTO forecasts that international arrivals are expected to reach over 1.56 billion by 2020. Of these, 1.18 billion will be inter-regional and 377 million will be long-haul travellers (www.world-tourism.org/marketresearch/facts/highlights/Highlights.pdf).

Travel and tourism as a whole (international and domestic) is expected to generate US$4,235.5 billion of economic activity; that is, it is a US$4.3 trillion industry according to the WTTC (2002c). Travel and tourism is therefore a major activity by any standard. It is also an activity that impacts on many other areas, as the following discussion illustrates.

Demand for travel and tourism has grown at a faster rate than demand for most areas of economic activity. Tourism experienced sustained growth towards the end of the last century and this continues at the start of the new millennium. France et al. (1994) describe the increase in international tourist numbers since the end of the Second World War as dramatic: only 25 million international tourists were recorded worldwide in 1950 as against approximately 476 million tourists by 1992. They describe a pattern of moderately steady growth, with periods of interruption associated with particular events and economic downturns.

Tourism education has also been an area of significant development in recent decades. Masters programmes in tourism have been available in the UK since the 1970s and undergraduate degrees have been developing since the 1980s. Tourism has, in recent years, increased greatly in popularity as a subject of study at diploma, undergraduate and postgraduate levels. By the late 1990s some 64 undergraduate courses existed in the UK alone, accounting for an estimated 5,000 students enrolled in 1998. In addition to this were the many students studying tourism as an option on related courses such as geography. A further, more recent, significant development in this field has been the emergence of themed MBAs, such as those offered at Westminster and Bradford universities.

At an international level, according to Centre International de Recherches et d'Etudes Touristiques (CIRET), there are currently 543 academic institutions in 86 countries and 2,296 individual researchers in 95 countries specialising in tourism, leisure, outdoor recreation and the hospitality industry. CIRET has created directories of these on its website (http://www.ciret-tourism.com). Along with the growth in the provision of teaching of tourism and research in this area has been a growth of literature, as evidenced by new tourism collections and scientific reviews. CIRET's website also contains a thesaurus of more than 1,100 key words, a geographical index and access to the analysis of in excess of 116,974 documents of tourism literature, including books, articles and reports. Despite this growth in teaching, research and publications, tourism is still considered relatively immature as an academic discipline.

Tourism as an academic subject is offered within and often between a variety of broader fields of study, including economics, business and management, geography and the social sciences. The majority of tourism courses, however, are offered by schools of business and management. Their primary focus is on the scope and significance of tourism as a business. The approach taken by this book is in keeping with such courses. In research terms, tourism is a subject of many separate disciplines but also the subject of multidisciplinary and interdisciplinary research.

While early tourism had always been socially selective, according to several writers, including Urry (1990), it was in the second half of the nineteenth century, with the expansion of the railway, that there was an extensive development of mass travel by train. In the twentieth century the car and the aeroplane further democratised geographic movement. Certain destinations then began to become synonymous with mass tourism. Holloway (1994) details the origins of the mass tourism movement.

Definitions, concepts and structure of tourism

Mass tourism is therefore a relatively young phenomenon and, despite exceptional growth rates, is still characterised as immature, or only just reaching maturity, especially as a field of academic study. There have been definitional problems in relation to tourism and these in turn have led to measurement difficulties.

Different authors have taken different approaches when proposing definitions, but one thing that most seem to agree on is the difficulty they attach to defining tourism. Further difficulties exist in defining precise forms of tourism. Holloway (1994) describes as problematic establishing clear lines between shoppers and tourists, for example.

There is no universally agreed definition of the tourism industry. Indeed, there is no agreement that tourism can be described as an industry. Mill and Morrison (1998), for example, argue that it is hard to describe tourism as an industry given that there is a great deal of complementarity as well as competition between tourism businesses. They place definitions of tourism in context by highlighting the link between travel, tourism, recreation and leisure. However, they go on to describe this link as 'fuzzy' and to make the distinction that all tourism involves travel yet all travel is not tourism. Nevertheless, tourism is often described merely as an activity:

> Tourism is an activity. It is an activity that takes place when, in international terms, people cross borders for leisure or business and stay at least 24 hours but less than one year. (Mill and Morrison, 1998: 2)

The WTO's definition of tourism is now the one that is most widely accepted around the world. The definition, provided at the International Conference on Travel and Tourism Statistics in Ottawa in 1991, is

> The activities of a person outside his or her usual environment for less than a specified period of time and whose main purpose of travel is other than exercise of an activity remunerated from the place visited. (Chadwick, 1994: 66)

In the sixth edition of *The Business of Tourism*, Holloway (2002: 1) makes it clear that the definitional debates surrounding the concept of tourism are likely to rage on. He contrasts this with technical definitions: 'While it is relatively easy to agree on technical definitions of particular categories of tourism and tourist, the wider concept is ill-defined.' He concludes that to define tourism precisely in conceptual terms is an all but impossible task.

Finally, according to France (1994: 3):

> It is now commonly accepted that a tourist, as opposed to a day visitor, is someone who spends at least 24 hours away from home even though both categories of visitor might engage in similar activities. Although there is no generally accepted maximum time-limit for a tourist visit, it is normally accepted that a tourist is away from home for a relatively short period.

Debate has surrounded many of the aspects of definitions of tourism. For example, some have argued for the inclusion of day visitors in definitions, while others have argued against this. Similarly, some prefer to include business trips, while others exclude these. Arguments have also surrounded precise distances and purposes of visit to be included in definitions.

Cooper et al. (1998) are among those to distinguish between demand-side and supply-side definitions of tourism. Their discussion of each of these is summarised below.

Demand-side definitions

Both 'conceptual' and 'technical' demand-side definitions of tourism have evolved. In conceptual terms, tourism can be thought of as:

> The activities of persons travelling to and staying in places outside their usual environment for not more than one consecutive year for leisure, business and other purposes. (WTO and UNSTAT, 1994, also cited in Cooper et al., 1998: 8)

This definition covers the important elements of movement of people to, and their stay in, places or destinations outside their usual environment or normal place of residence or work. This movement is temporary and short-term. Destinations are visited for purposes other than taking up permanent residence or employment.

In technical terms, there has been a need to separate tourism from other forms of travel for statistical purposes. To count as tourism it is therefore necessary that an activity consists of a minimum length of stay (one night or they are termed day visitors or excursionists) and maximum length of stay (one year). There are also 'purpose of visit' categories, and a distance consideration helps to delineate 'usual environment'.

Supply-side definitions

There are technical problems in defining supply-side tourism as some businesses serve only tourists while others serve local residents and other markets at the same time. It is possible to classify tourism businesses according to whether they can survive without tourism (albeit in a diminished form) or not. This enables tourism to be gauged using standard industrial classifications (SIC). Indeed, the WTO has published a 'standard industrial classification of tourism activities' (SICTA) in an attempt to overcome the lack of an agreed definition. Once again, both 'conceptual' and 'technical' viewpoints can be taken in relation to supply-side definitions of tourism. Conceptually, the industry is made up of all firms, organisations and facilities designed to meet the needs and wants of tourists. The industry is discussed more fully below.

Given the heterogeneous nature of tourists, it is important that they too can be classified in a variety of ways. The most obvious distinction is that between domestic and international tourists. This has something in common with the WTO's distinction between three basic forms of tourism:

- domestic – travel by residents within their own country;
- inbound – travel by residents from overseas into a country; and
- outbound – travel from the generating country to another country.

A number of key aspects to many of the definitions of tourism can therefore be identified. First, day visitors or excursionists are not tourists because, by definition, an overnight stay is required. Secondly, the stay should not be too long (less than a year is often given as a maximum), and finally, tourists should not be earning while at a destination. However, these aspects are not accepted by all.

Holloway (1994) suggests that it is all but impossible to define tourism conceptually in precise terms. Technical definitions for statistical purposes are, he believes, less problematic, as long as there is clarity regarding what the data comprise and as long as one compares like with like.

It is not only in definitional terms but also as an activity that tourism is misunderstood. Indeed, Cooper et al. (1998) describe a series of myths about tourism and counter these with realities. It is worth noting the following points here:

1. Rather than being predominantly international, the majority of tourism involves people travelling in their own country with journeys mainly by surface transport as opposed to by air.
2. Tourism is not only about leisure holidays but also includes business, conferences and education as purposes of visit.

Finally, it is worth noting that, for the purposes of definitions, tourism can be seen as a form of recreation but it is clearly not all recreation. Tourism is often described as merely one aspect of leisure. This does not, of course, account for business travel.

The tourism system

That tourism spans a variety of fields of business and study has already been discussed. This has clear implications for the provision of organisational frameworks for tourism.

Figure 1.1   Basic tourism system

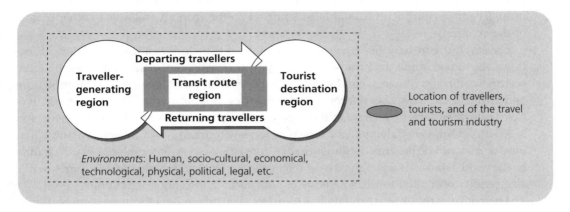

Source: Leiper (1990b)

Many different frameworks have been developed in relation to particular orientations as well as some which offer a more holistic view. While these approaches are adequately covered elsewhere in the tourism literature, it is important to illustrate one such system here. Leiper's basic tourism system (see Figure 1.1) has been seleced for both its enduring popularity and its ease of understanding. Leiper first offered this model for consideration in 1979, although it has since been updated.

The three basic elements included are the tourists themselves (the actors in the system), geographical elements (traveller-generating regions, tourist destination regions and tourist route regions) and the tourism industry (those businesses and organisations involved in the delivery of the tourism product). Interaction between these elements is in terms of transactions and impacts. It is important to highlight the relationships, especially in academic circles where subject divisions are often created that prevent a full appreciation of relationships and transactions.

Leiper suggests that the tourism industry consists of 'all those firms, organisations and facilities which are intended to serve the specific needs and wants of tourists' (1979: 400). Similarly, Henderson (1994) argues that the travel and tourism industry exists as a broad network of commercial and non-commercial organisations linked together by the common objective of servicing the needs of travellers and tourists. These descriptions of the industry are consistent with many others. Despite such consensus in general terms, less agreement surrounds exactly which firms, organisations and facilities are included in tourism.

Tourism is a complex phenomenon. It is a multi-sectoral, multifaceted business and this in itself creates difficulties when attempting to generalise about the management of tourism businesses. It is multi-sectoral because it encompasses different industrial sectors. According to Lickorish and Jenkins (1997), tourism is an activity which cuts across conventional sectors in the economy, requiring inputs of an economic, social, cultural and environmental nature. This accounts for tourism's multifaceted nature. The same authors highlight the lack of a common structure that is representative of the industry in every country. In particular, they argue that the amorphous nature of the tourism industry makes it difficult to evaluate its impact on the economy relative to other sectors of the economy.

Clearly, tourism activities cover a variety of sectors, including accommodation, attractions, the travel trade and transport. Henderson (1994) points out that some of these sectors within the industry can be seen as independent industries. The accommodation and airline sectors are also referred to as industries in their own right, for example. It is necessary therefore to recognise the extent and nature of involvement in travel and tourism, yet this is not always easy. One way to view tourism is as a collective activity that may or may not be described as an industry, consisting of various sub-sectors which may be industries in their own right. These may or may not also operate outside tourism. It is also worth noting that tourism consists of both social and economic activities.

The complexity of tourism has led to many disciplines developing an interest in it. Integrative approaches to the study of tourism are, however, more holistic and can lead to a better understanding of the phenomenon. Particularly in academia, it is often the case that a narrow view of tourism is taken. Marketers, for example, may focus on the service nature of tourism while economists may view it as an industry.

The impacts of travel and tourism

Travel and tourism has many positive benefits, including that it is, for some countries, the main source of job creation and revenue. However, there are many negative consequences of tourism, including the often-cited destruction of both the environment and the traditions of local populations. Vellas and Becherel (1995: xxii) go as far as to describe international tourism as 'undeniably one of the most influential phenomena (possibly even the most influential) in the economic and social development of our society'.

The economic impacts of tourism for tourist-receiving areas can be hugely significant. Indeed, some destinations depend on tourism for their income. Such income is generated from a number of sources, including wages and salaries of those in tourism-related employment. A well-recognised phenomenon in tourism is the tourism income multiplier (TIM), whereby tourists' expenditure in an area is re-spent by recipients, so augmenting the total. The factor by which tourist expenditure is increased in this process is the multiplier (Holloway, 1994). Also important to tourist-generating and receiving areas is the creation of jobs. Tourism can greatly influence a country's balance of payments. Money spent by tourists overseas acts as an invisible on the balance of payments account of the country visited and a debit against the home country account. Any money spent overseas is an import to the generating country and an export to the receiving country (Holloway, 1994).

The social and environmental impacts of tourism are now very well documented, as are suggestions for the minimisation of the negative consequences of tourism. Chapter 18 on the environmental impacts of tourism particularly illustrates how the debate has moved on in this area of tourism management.

Key themes

There now follows a brief introduction to some of the key themes covered in this book.

Integration

Integration between businesses is a hugely important concept, particularly for the larger travel and tourism organisations. Integration refers to formal linking arrangements between organisations which can occur both across the chain of distribution (horizontal integration) and down the chain of distribution (vertical integration). There are many examples of both forms of integration from the travel trade and transport as well as from the accommodation sectors of the tourism industry. Vertical integration can be both backward and forward along the chain of distribution.

Burns and Holden (1994) describe vertical integration – the business phenomenon whereby firms seek to control various stages of production, delivery and marketing of their products – as something of an established practice within the production of mass tourism. The importance of integration is highlighted in many of the chapters that follow, particularly in Part 1 of the book, which concentrates on the industry. Arguments in favour of integration are that it leads to cost savings, and therefore to price reductions, and that it leads to increased control and therefore to quality improvements. On the other hand, it can be argued that consumers suffer from reduced choice and possible price increases as a result of integration:

> Just as the great meat-packing companies take live cattle into their slaughter houses and find a profitable use for every part of the resultant carcass – be it bones, hooves or meat – so do the great tourist conglomerates try to control as many stages as possible as their clients are separated from their money in the course of a holiday. ... Until the passenger leaves his hotel and ventures into the local restaurants, all his money may have been going into a single company. That is integration at its clearest. (Turner and Ash, 1975: 107–8)

Pender (2001) takes an in-depth look at integration in the tourism industry.

Globalisation

Tourism, for obvious reasons, is generally thought of as an international business despite the fact that much of it takes a domestic form. Indeed, there are strong factors in favour of some of the larger tourism organisations becoming global businesses. This does not merely require organisations to operate across national frontiers. Transportation companies doing business across national frontiers are operating internationally but, in order to be classified as 'global' organisations, businesses need to be operating in all four hemispheres, according to Lovelock and Yip (1999). Further, simply operating globally does not mean that a company has a global strategy. Research into global strategy for service businesses in general is still at an early stage. Tourism, however, is now frequently described as a global industry (Meethan, 2002b). Indeed, this is a recurring theme throughout this text. The importance of globalisation to many tourism businesses (e.g., large international hotel chains) cannot be overstated, while at the other end of the spectrum it can be meaningless to many small, locally-based tourism businesses. Even for some of the larger tourism organisations, barriers to globalisation exist. International airlines, despite the large part they play in facilitating global business for so many different types of organisation, are currently prevented from operating globally themselves (see Chapter 3).

Globalisation is a recurring theme throughout this text. The increasing power of organisations that follow strategies of global expansion is evident in the industry, yet the tourism industry remains one characterised by small businesses (some of the implications of this small business environment in terms of human resource management (HRM) are discussed in Chapter 6). Indeed, the legacy of small-business thinking can often be seen in the management of tourism businesses. This, in itself, is unsurprising given that the industry is characterised by a proliferation of small companies. The way in which the tourism system has evolved has only compounded this aspect of the industry.

Information and communication technologies

The impact of information and communications technologies (ICTs) on travel and tourism has been huge in the last few decades. Most areas of management have been greatly affected by developments in ICTs and some aspects of tourism have been completely changed as a result. Several chapters in this book concentrate on different aspects of these developments.

Crises and disasters

The tourism industry has a history of being highly reactive to short-term local and international events. It is nevertheless an extremely resilient industry. A further hugely significant influence on tourism is therefore the occurrence of disasters and crises. Very recent examples were the outbreak of Foot and Mouth disease in the UK, the SARS outbreak and the war in Iraq. Chapter 19 highlights some of the disasters and crises that affect tourism and explores the potential for developing effective crisis management plans in tourism destinations.

A number of themes can thus be seen to be significant to the current-day management of tourism. These issues which were introduced above are also covered in relevant chapters and a summary of their importance is provided at the end in the conclusion.

Management issues

Tourism businesses in the past were seldom at the forefront of strategic management. Some of the reasons for this are obvious given their small size, geographical fragmentation

Table 1.1   Differences between services and physical goods

Physical goods	Services
Tangible	Intangible
Homogeneous	Heterogeneous
Production and distribution are separated from consumption	Production, distribution and consumption are simultaneous processes
A thing	An activity or process
Core value produced in a factory	Core value produced in buyer–seller interactions
Customers do not (normally) participate in the production process	Customers participate in the production process
Can be kept in stock	Cannot be kept in stock
Transfer of ownership	No transfer of ownership

Source: Grönroos (2000: 47)

and the general nature of management training that predominated in some sectors of the industry, which prevented the introduction of new ideas or experience from areas outside tourism.

That tourism is service-based is an important aspect in terms of management. Few physical products are associated with the industry and this greatly influences how tourism should be managed. It is often argued that a good manager should be as skilled in managing services as physical goods. This requires an appreciation of the characteristics of services as these influence the way in which services should be managed.

The nature of services

As was seen to be the case with tourism, 'services' have no agreed definition. Grönroos (2000), however, summarises the most frequently mentioned characteristics of services (see Table 1.1). He identifies three basic characteristics for most services:

1. Services are *processes* consisting of *activities* or a *series of activities* rather than *things*.
2. Services are at least to some extent *produced* and *consumed simultaneously.*
3. The customer *participates in the service production process* at least to some extent (Grönroos, 2000: 47, original italics).

Grönroos therefore concludes that the processes of services form their major feature, and that the problems associated with services stem from these characteristics. This is especially true in respect of marketing. Intangibility leads to difficulties in image creation, for example. The lack of transfer of ownership can act against customers purchasing a service. A main difficulty is that of providing an identical service experience from one encounter to the next (heterogeneity). Another particularly difficult aspect to manage is the mix of customers using a service at any one time as they may affect one anothers' service experience. As services are processes consisting of activities which are produced and consumed simultaneously (inseparability), quality can be difficult to manage and traditional marketing approaches need to be altered to take account of this (Grönroos, 2000).

In addition to the characteristics of services, the following aspects are important in relation to tourism.

■ *Complex product.* The tourism product is often said to be complex. This stems from the fact that there is input from various service suppliers into the total tourism product. An overseas holiday, for example, may consist of services provided by a number of different suppliers both in the home country and the destination to be visited, such as a travel agent, a national or local tourist office, a handling agent, a transfer company, an airline, rail or coach company, an airport, coach or railway station and an accommodation provider, as well as restaurants, shops and so on. All play a part in providing the total holiday experience.

■ *Complex industry.* As mentioned above, the tourism industry is characterised by a number of different suppliers and tourists themselves often have little understanding of the different roles performed by each, let alone the relationships between these players. Formal or informal linkages between organisations are often not recognised by travellers.

■ *Fragmented industry.* The tourism industry is characterised by a proliferation of small companies spread over vast geographical areas.

Structure of the book

This book is divided into four sections relating to specific areas. Part 1 is concerned with 'Managing the Tourism System' and covers accommodation, airlines, airports and international aviation, tour operations management and tourism distribution. Clearly, this section is not able to cover the many different types of organisation involved in tourism in detail. For example, only airlines are covered in relation to the transport sector. This form of transport has been selected for the many interesting challenges facing the sector and the relevance of the strategies being pursued by airlines and airports. Part 2 looks at 'Managing Tourism Businesses' and covers the functional areas of management, including human resources management, marketing management, strategy, finance and the law. Part 3 focuses on 'Managing Tourism in its Environment' including urban tourism, managing the countryside, managing tourism for development, and site and visitor management at natural attractions. Finally, Part 4 covers 'Contemporary Issues in Tourism Management', including the role of government in the management of tourism, information and communications technologies (ICTs) for tourism, destination marketing and technology, tourism and the environment, international tourism and the management of crisis, ethics in tourism management, and managing the heritage enterprise for liveable host communities. A general concluding chapter then follows.

Conclusion

This chapter has introduced tourism and outlined some of the characteristics of tourism businesses while highlighting the variety and scope of these businesses. The problems of definition have been discussed, as has the scale and significance of tourism. The chapter briefly considered the implications of the service nature of tourism businesses for management, before outlining the structure of the book.

Discussion questions

1. Examine the definitional problems in relation to tourism.
2. Explain arguments both for and against describing tourism as an industry.
3. Consider the characteristics of services as they influence the management of tourism businesses.

Suggested further reading

Grönroos, C. (2000) *Service Management and Marketing: A Customer Relationship Management Approach*, 2nd edition. Chichester: John Wiley & Sons.

Lickorish, L.J. and Jenkins, C.L. (1997) *An Introduction to Tourism*. Oxford: Butterworth Heinemann.

Mill, R. and Morrison, A. (1998) *The Tourism System: An Introductory Text* (3rd edition). Dubuque, IA: Kendell/Hunt Publishing Co.

2 The accommodation sector: managing for quality

Richard Sharpley

Chapter objectives

The purpose of this chapter is to explore the need for appropriate quality management policies as a principal management challenge within the accommodation sector of the tourism industry. In particular, it argues that it is essential to focus attention on an organisation's human resources as the fundamental element in quality service provision. Having completed this chapter, the reader will be able to:

- appreciate the range of management challenges relevant to the accommodation sector
- recognise the importance of quality management to the continuing success of accommodation facilities
- identify and consider human resource policies appropriate to the development of quality management programmes

Chapter contents

Introduction: quality and the accommodation sector

Accommodation is, 'by a long way, the largest and most ubiquitous sub-sector within the tourism economy' (Cooper et al., 1998: 313). Not only do most, if not all, tourists require overnight accommodation during their journey through, or stay in, a destination, but also spending on accommodation usually represents the most significant

Table 2.1   Tourism expenditure in the UK as a percentage of the total (1999)

	Overseas visitors in UK	Domestic visitors	All visitors
Accommodation	33.3	34.0	34.0
Eating out	20.6	26.0	23.5
Shopping	26.0	13.0	18.9
Travel in UK	9.2	19.0	14.7
Services	7.1	1.0	3.4
Entertainment	2.9	6.0	4.4
Other	0.9	1.0	1.0

Source: BHA (2001)

element of total tourist expenditure. For example, over one-third of all tourism expenditure in the UK is typically accounted for by spending on accommodation (Table 2.1). In other words, the accommodation sector is a fundamental element of the domestic and international tourism industry. Indeed, it is generally the case that accommodation facilities are provided, usually on a commercial basis (although private tourism facilities, including second homes, timeshare and visiting friends and relatives, represent an important sub-sector of tourist accommodation) wherever tourists venture.

Immediately, however, three points must be stressed. First, and quite evidently, the accommodation sector of the tourism industry is enormously fragmented and diverse. Thus, although hotels are the 'most significant and widely recognised form of overnight accommodation' (Holloway, 1998: 143) – and, of course, are themselves highly diverse in terms of size, style, location, ownership and the type, variety and level of services provided – a multitude of other types of accommodation are available. These include bed-and-breakfasts, self-catering apartments, home exchanges and camping, as well as transport-based accommodation, such as cruise liners or train accommodation. Inevitably, such heterogeneity means that different forms of accommodation face different management challenges. For example, the problems facing the management of a resort-based hotel dependent upon a seasonal, tour-operator controlled market are different from those of, say, inland resorts such as the European Center Parcs group or an hotel operating principally in the MICE (meetings, incentives, conventions and exhibitions) market.

Secondly, tourism accommodation is a sub-sector of the international hospitality industry. Hospitality, according to Jones (1996: 1) is 'made up of two distinct services – the provision of overnight accommodation for people staying away from home, and the provision of sustenance for people eating away from home'. Of course, the former is not a prerequisite for the latter; the provision of food and beverage hospitality is as much concerned with local consumers as it is with visitors. Equally, the two services (accommodation and sustenance) are often provided within a single context (the hotel) and it is not surprising, therefore, that much of international hospitality literature focuses specifically upon the international hotel industry (e.g., Teare and Olson, 1992; Jones and Pizam, 1993; Kotas et al., 1996; Knowles, 1996, 1998). Importantly, however, the structure, nature and operations of the international hospitality industry are dynamic and subject to a variety of economic and cultural forces, not least the process of globalisation (Go and Pine, 1995). Thus, despite the heterogeneity referred to in the previous point, most accommodation providers also face a similar set of challenges, though in varying degrees, and the management of tourism accommodation in particular should not be divorced from the international hospitality sector of which it is a part.

Thirdly, and perhaps most significantly, accommodation is not only a constituent element of the tourism *product* but also of the tourism *experience*. That is, accommodation provision represents more than the tangible elements of a room, a bed, a meal and so on; it is also concerned with meeting guests' needs and expectations. In some instances, this might be incidental to the overall tourism experience, such as a night at an airport hotel where cost and accessibility to the airport terminal may be important factors. In other instances, accommodation services might be synonymous with the overall tourism experience, as in the case of all-inclusive centres, such as the Sandals resorts in the Caribbean, where accommodation represents, in effect, the entire holiday experience. In either case, however, the challenge is to recognise guests' needs and expectations and to implement appropriate management policies and practices to ensure that these are satisfied.

Importantly, common to all of these issues is the notion of quality. In other words, and as this chapter argues, the principal challenge facing the accommodation sector of the tourism industry is the need to manage for quality service provision. There is, of course, nothing new in this. As Johns (1996) observes, 'service quality has been a major preoccupation of the hospitality industry' since the early 1980s and much research has been undertaken into service quality in general (Grönroos, 1983; Parasuraman et al., 1985; Brogowicz et al., 1990) and quality management in hospitality in particular (Gilbert and Joshi, 1992; Lockwood et al., 1996; Olsen et al., 1996; Harrington and Lenehan, 1998). However, as discussed in more detail shortly, there are three principal factors that justify a specific management focus on quality:

- The tourism industry is, from both an organisational and a destinational perspective, becoming increasingly concerned with the provision of quality tourism experiences.
- A fundamental influence on the nature of tourism experiences is the quality of the service provided at the point of delivery or 'moment of truth' (Hope and Mühlemann, 1998).
- Accommodation/hospitality operations are subject to a variety of external forces; quality, however, remains under the control of management.

Additionally, according to Jones and Lockwood (1989), the management of hotels in general is concerned with three main components, namely, the workforce, the assets and customers, 'the combined interaction [of which] focuses on the key result area of managing quality' (Jones and Lockwood, 1989: 30) (see Figure 2.1 below). The purpose of this chapter, therefore, is to explore the importance of quality management in the provision of tourism accommodation services, focusing, in particular, on the issue of appropriate human resource management policies in the commercial (primarily hotel) sector. First, however, it is useful to review the challenges typically faced by accommodation providers.

Figure 2.1   Managing hotel operations

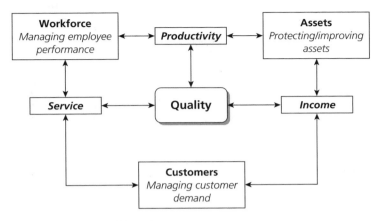

Source: Adapted from Jones and Lockwood (1989)

The accommodation sector: overview and challenges

As already observed, the accommodation sector of tourism is complex, diverse and fragmented. It comprises not only the well-known national and international hotel chains – often referred to as the international hotel industry (see TTI, 2001) – but also a myriad of different forms of accommodation in both the commercial and non-commercial or 'quasi-commercial' (e.g., youth hostels or YMCA facilities) sectors. In fact, although much attention is paid in the literature to the international hotel industry, in particular with respect to its dynamic structure and various business development processes, such as franchising, management contracts and acquisition, and competitive strategies, such as branding and distribution, it is the non-chain sector that is collectively more significant in the tourism context. That is, although the overall proportion of hotel rooms held by major hotel corporations is on the increase, 'the bulk of hotel accommodation around the world remains in the hands of individual owner-operators or small, privately owned companies (TTI, 2001: 77). For historical and other reasons, such as land shortages and planning restrictions, this is certainly the case in Europe, where just 15% of hotel rooms are part of corporate chains. Conversely, in the USA, arguably the birthplace of the chain hotel, the figure is 70%, with many of the world's best-known groups represented (although, frequently, the parent company is less well known – for example, both Sheraton and Westin are owned by Starwood). Table 2.2 lists the world's top ten hotel groups and Case Study 2.1 reviews the French group Accor.

Nevertheless, hotels, whether private/independent, members of a consortium, such as Best Western, or part of an internationally recognised chain, such as Marriott or Holiday Inn (the latter owned by the UK-based Bass), face a number of common challenges. These are primarily related to the typical features or characteristics of hotel operations.

Table 2.2 Top ten hotel groups worldwide (2001)

	Hotel group	Rooms	Hotels
1	Cendant Corp. (USA)	539,836	6,429
2	Bass Hotels & Resorts (UK)	496,005	3,092
3	Marriott International (USA)	404,792	2,223
4	Accor (France)	389,437	3,488
5	Choice Hotels International (USA)	349,392	4,371
6	Hilton Hotels Corp. (USA)	314,629	1,867
7	Best Western International (USA)	307,856	4,066
8	Starwood Hotels & Resorts	225,540	733
9	Carlson (USA)	122,774	677
10	Hyatt Hotels (USA)	85,777	199

Source: Adapted from TTI (2001)

Case Study 2.1   The Accor Group

Accor is, in terms of number of rooms, the world's fourth largest hotel group. It also has substantial interests in other sectors of tourism and leisure; its co-ownership of Carlson Wagonlit Travel, for example, means that, with a global network of more than 5,000 branches, it is among the world's largest travel agency operations. However, not only is the Accor name largely unknown among tourists but also it is probably true to say that few, if any, of its hotel brands enjoy widespread recognition outside France, where the company is based.

Accor was founded in 1967 with the opening of the first Novotel in Lille. As the company expanded in the following years, it continued to operate under the Novotel name, although the Ibis and Mercure brands were added during the 1970s. In 1980, by which time the group boasted some 280 hotels and 35,000 rooms, the Sofitel chain was acquired through a merger with Jacques Borel International. In subsequent years, further brands have been added to the Accor portfolio. The Formule 1 budget hotel brand was developed during the early 1980s and the company's presence in the budget end of the market

was further strengthened in 1990 with the purchase of the Motel 6 chain in the USA. More recently, in 1999, the company also acquired the Red Roof Inns chain in the USA and a number of national and regional chains in Europe. It also expressed an interest in purchasing the Granada-Compass group in 2000, although the deal was not followed through.

Accor currently has eight core brands, along with a number of sub-brands. Table 2.3 lists the company's principal brands.

Table 2.3   Accor core hotel brands (1999)

Brand	Hotels	Rooms
Sofitel	135	24,186
Novotel	318	48,553
Mercure	562	60,236
Ibis	502	51,430
Etap	202	14,839
Formule 1	322	23,460
Motel 6	808	86,228
Red Roof Inns	330	37,325

As already observed, many of these brand names remain unfamiliar. For example, Sofitel, the company's top brand, is similar in size to Inter-Continental, but the latter is much more widely known internationally. Conversely, Novotel enjoys better brand recognition. However, this general lack of international recognition is less of a problem than might be imagined as the company's strength undoubtedly lies in the economy/budget end of the market. The Formule 1 (rated by Accor as 'zero' star, and offering few facilities) and Etap brands are the two principal products in Europe, while Motel 6 competes in the roadside inn market in the USA. Together, the budget and Motel 6 brands generated over 44% of turnover and 67% of profits in 1997 (TTI, 2001: 170). Indeed, it is at the economy end of the market that the company sees most potential for the future. For example, early in 2002 it was announced that Accor was considering the possibility of establishing a chain of backpacker hostels in Australia, representing a move into the 'true' budget tourism market.

Common features of hotel operations

The hotel industry is, of course, a business – the purpose of managing commercial accommodation facilities, whether a 200-room hotel or a small bed-and-breakfast operation, is to make a profit and/or to provide a return to investors. However, it is also a business that possesses certain characteristics which represent common management challenges (see Jones and Lockwood, 1989).

- An hotel is a major investment. Whether building new, refurbishing an existing hotel or converting a property originally built for another purpose, the level of investment is such that significant levels of return are required to justify it.
- Although hospitality is a service with its own set of challenges, the physical structure or 'plant' (reception area, the bedroom, dining/bar areas, etc.) is a vital contributor to an hotel's success. Therefore, ongoing investment in improving/updating this may be required.
- Most forms of accommodation are characterised by spatial 'fixity', that is, they occupy fixed locations within environments which may change. There is therefore the need to adapt to the changing environment.
- Hotels typically suffer from high fixed costs as a proportion of total operating costs. Thus, the level of business must at least cover such fixed costs plus relevant variable costs. As a result, however, the external economic environment has a significant influence on profitability. Indeed, in general, it has been found that in times of boom the hotel sector outperforms the economy, whereas during recession it suffers disproportionately (Knowles and Egan, 2001; TTI, 2001).
- The core product – selling bedrooms – is perishable, that is, an unsold room is business lost forever. Thus, a principal management task is to optimise profitability by balancing occupancy levels with room rates. In the case of resort hotels contracting blocks of rooms to tour operators, this may be less problematic – lower margins will be achieved but occupancy may (depending on the nature of the contract) be guaranteed.

Conversely, city hotels with a significant level of 'walk-in' business have to employ sophisticated yield management systems.

■ Branding has become an increasingly important strategic tool for gaining competitive advantage within the hotel industry (Rounce, 1987; Slattery, 1991). It is seen as an effective means of gaining customer loyalty, of matching the product to specific customer needs (Accor's Formule 1, for example, is a strong brand in the budget hotel market) and for increased profitability per room. Even independent hotels, which rely on their individuality (as distinct from the homogeneous chain brands) for their business, must, in a sense, have a brand image. Thus, management must ensure that the product/service is commensurate with their brand, either matching the group/consortium requirements or, in the case of independent businesses, their self-imposed brand.

Many of these challenges focus upon the need to maximise occupancy levels at rates which optimise earnings, although other factors, such as employee productivity and reducing fixed costs, are also important considerations in improving profitability and return on investment. The ways in which high occupancy levels are achieved depends, of course, on the nature/location of the business. However, as the following section suggests, not only does the management of both demand and the other aspects of hotel operations depend ultimately upon quality management, but also there are strong arguments for a more general focus on quality as the principal management challenge in the provision of accommodation services.

Tourism accommodation: the role of quality

As observed above, Jones and Lockwood (1989) suggest that there exist three key, interdependent areas of hotel operations which are of concern to hotel management. These are the customers, the workforce and the assets of the business, from each of which key management 'result areas' may be identified (see Table 2.4).

Each of these areas of management activity is, in itself, complex and, at the same time, related to the other components. For example, managing customers is concerned with managing both demand and supply. That is, an appropriate and constant volume of business must be attracted to maintain occupancy levels and to generate required levels of income. Equally, the supply (assets) must be managed effectively (e.g., the number, type and standard of rooms in an hotel) to ensure that demand is satisfied.

Table 2.4 Key components of hotel management

Key component	Key result area
Customers	Ensuring customer satisfaction
Workforce	Maintaining employee performance
Business assets	Protecting assets from threat

Source: Adapted from Jones and Lockwood (1989)

Similarly, managing the workforce is concerned with a variety of issues that relate not only to employees themselves (that is, maintaining or improving performance through appropriate human resource policies), but also to customers (meeting expected levels of service) and to assets (achieving levels of productivity that contribute to required profits and returns on investment).

A full consideration of these hotel-specific management tasks is beyond the scope of this chapter. The important point, however, is that quality is of central importance. Customer satisfaction (hence, maintaining demand, occupancy and profitability) is dependent on expectations of service levels (that is, quality expectations) being met. This is only likely to occur if, first, employees provide the quality of service that is expected by customers and that is commensurate with the brand or image of the hotel and the quality of its assets and, secondly, if the quality of the assets meets customer requirements and expectations. In other words, the quality of the customer experience is dependent upon the tangible quality of the hotel product and the manner in which services are provided to the customer at the point of delivery.

Beyond the specific challenges of managing hotel operations, a broader focus on quality management in the provision of accommodation can be justified for a number of reasons. First, research has shown that, in general, a relationship exists between quality and an organisation's longer-term business success; product or service quality is an essential ingredient for return on investment and market share (Langer, 1997: 28). More specifically, in the context of tourism, the following points can be made:

- The nature of tourism demand has, in recent years, undergone a significant transformation, manifested not only in the arguable emergence of the so-called 'new' tourist (Poon, 1993) seeking alternatives to the traditional sun-sea-sand, passive pleasure-seeking holiday, but certainly also in the increasing demands on the part of tourists for quality and value for money. As tourists have become more experienced and sophisticated, they are no longer willing 'to compromise themselves to a mediocre service' (Kandampully, 1997: 4).
- Tourists are more aware of their rights as consumers and, as a result, are more confident in claiming compensation for poor quality. Thus, investing in quality may lead to significant cost savings in the longer term.
- In an increasingly competitive environment, tourism businesses are 'striving to move towards a new model based on competitive advantage based on quality' (Harrington and Lenehan, 1998: 1). The same is true at the destinational level; many tourist destinations, particularly those in highly competitive markets, such as the Mediterranean summer sun market, are seeking to develop 'quality tourism' both to gain competitive advantage and to achieve higher returns from tourism (a 'quality' tourist being synonymous with a higher-spending tourist). Central to such quality tourism, of course, is the need for quality accommodation services.
- In some contexts, particularly within European package holiday operations, greater legislation and regulation imposed upon the industry are obliging many organisations to focus on quality.

Figure 2.2 The total tourism experience

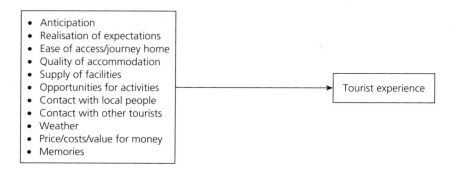

- Anticipation
- Realisation of expectations
- Ease of access/journey home
- Quality of accommodation
- Supply of facilities
- Opportunities for activities
- Contact with local people
- Contact with other tourists
- Weather
- Price/costs/value for money
- Memories

Tourist experience

Secondly, the overall tourist experience is, in general, multifaceted, and hence difficult to manage. That is, the total tourism experience comprises a variety of tangible and intangible elements (Middleton, 1988), as shown in Figure 2.2. Inevitably, some elements of the total tourism experience, such as the weather, are uncontrollable. However, not only is accommodation frequently central to the tourist experience, particularly in the context of holidays, but the provision of accommodation services is controllable. Implicitly, therefore, managing quality in accommodation may contribute significantly to the overall tourist experience.

Thirdly, and related, a principal characteristic of all services, including tourism accommodation, is their 'inseparability', that is, services are contact-dependent – their production and consumption cannot be separated. Therefore, the nature of the tourist experience may be determined by the quality of delivery at the so-called 'moment of truth', when the service is produced/consumed. Of course, the tangible quality of the service (the quality of the bedroom, of a meal, etc.) is of equal importance; good service in a restaurant, for example, will not compensate for poorly cooked food. However, as this chapter now suggests, given the above justification for a management focus on quality in the provision of accommodation services, that focus should principally be upon what Witt and Mühlemann (1994) refer to as the 'human aspects of the delivery system', or appropriate human resource management for service quality.

Tourism accommodation: managing for quality

An understanding of the dimensions of quality management within a service environment in general, and within accommodation provision in particular, is provided by the well-known and widely cited theoretical service quality models. These are based primarily upon the notion that a gap exists between quality as perceived by the producer and quality as perceived by the consumer. Nightingale (1985), for example, argues that the gap between these two perceptions of quality represents a lack of service quality that should be addressed by the producer. Similarly, the concept of a gap between perceived and expected service on the part of the consumer also underpins the two principal schools of thought with respect to service quality.

Figure 2.3   A model of service quality management

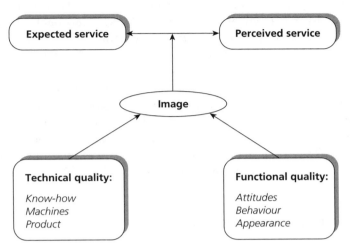

Source: Adapted from Grönroos (1983)

According to the North American school, exemplified by the work of Parasuraman et al. (1985) and Brogowicz et al. (1990), a number of discrepancies between the expected service on the part of both the provider and receiver and that actually delivered leads to unsuccessful service delivery (for a discussion, see Gilbert and Joshi, 1992). For example, Parasuraman et al. (1985) suggest five such gaps:

- a gap between consumer expectations and management perceptions of quality;
- a gap between management perceptions and service quality specifications;
- a gap between service quality specifications and service delivery;
- a gap between service delivery and external communications, such as promotional materials; and
- a gap between perceived service and delivered service.

According to Parasuraman et al. (1988), the identification and measurement of these gaps, through instruments such as SERVQUAL, may provide the basis for developing quality management strategies designed to achieve greater fit between expected and perceived service (Tribe and Snaith, 1998).

The so-called Nordic school (Grönroos, 1983) also argues that consumers' image of service quality is determined by the gap between the expected service and that which they perceive they experience. However, this image is a function of two elements – the *technical* quality of a service, such as the quality of the meal provided, and its *functional* quality, that is, the way the service is delivered. A simplified version of this model is provided in Figure 2.3.

Implicit in this model is the position that service quality may be improved by focusing on elements of functional quality, such as the behaviour and attitudes of staff. Indeed, it has been argued elsewhere that the factor linking all models of quality management – as well as methods of operationalising quality, such as Total Quality Management – is people (Hope and Mühlemann, 1998). This is not to say that other elements of quality management, such as product/technical quality and quality measurement issues, are less relevant (Witt and Mühlemann, 1994). However, it is generally accepted that 'the key variable in quality improvement has been a company's human resources' (Horney, 1996: 70); that is, the success of any quality initiative depends upon the willingness and ability of staff to respond and adapt to demands for increased quality in the delivery of services. In other words, positive attitudes on the part of employees are not only vital to organisational success in general (Hofmeyr, 1997), but to customer satisfaction in particular (Snipes, 1999). The question is then: what human resource policies and other management activities are required to develop a culture of quality service provision within the accommodation sector?

Human resources and quality management

The relationship between human resource policies and quality management is addressed at length in the literature, an excellent overview being provided by Hope and Mühlemann (1998). Typically, the importance of building a culture of service quality is accepted, the foundation being provided by a variety of human resource policies which, overall, seek to develop a trained, stable and appropriately rewarded workforce that collectively works towards the achievement of the organisation's quality objectives. More specifically, it is suggested that integrating service quality into an hotel's culture and operations may be achieved through a number of human resource policies. These include:

1. *Selection*. It is important to implement recruitment and selection procedures that identify potential employees who will not only have a natural disposition towards service provision, but who will also fit in with and respond to the organisation's service culture.
2. *Training and development*. A key element in quality management is appropriate staff training and development, focusing not only on key technical and interpersonal skills, but also on organisational culture and objectives.
3. *Empowerment*. Given the heterogeneous nature of service 'encounters', employees should enjoy the freedom to react appropriately, to apply creativity to their work and to apply problem-solving skills without constant recourse to supervisors or managers.
4. *Teamworking*. According to Hope and Mühlemann (1998: 379), 'everyone within an organisation should have a common goal; meeting customer requirements'. Mutually-supportive teamworking can be effective in this context.
5. *Rewards*. Extrinsic rewards (pay, promotion) and intrinsic rewards (recognition, feeling valued) are important means of encouraging desired behaviour on the part of employees.

To this list should be added the requirement of research into employee attitudes (see Horney, 1996). That is, it can be argued that an understanding of employees' attitudes towards their work and, in particular, to service quality, is an essential prerequisite to any quality management programme. Only when such knowledge has been generated can appropriate training programmes, reward schemes and other policies be developed. However, there is little evidence of such research within the literature and, certainly in the case of broader quality tourism development programmes, little if any attention is paid to the role of the accommodation sector in general or to employee attitudes in particular. As Case Study 2.2 shows, this may have serious implications for tourism development at the destinational level.

Case Study 2.2   Hotel employee attitudes in Cyprus

Since the early 1980s, tourism development policy in Cyprus has implicitly focused upon the development of so-called up-market tourism. The explicit objective of the latest strategy for 2000–10, however, is the development of quality tourism, the overall purpose being to re-position the island as a 'quality' destination. Not surprisingly, the strategy builds upon the island's deserved reputation for high standards of hospitality and service and focuses on issues such as core markets, product development, marketing, and so on. However, little or no attention is paid to the role of hotel employees in the development of quality of tourism, a surprising omission given the centrality of the accommodation sector to the Cypriot tourism product and the prevailing challenges facing the island's tourism industry (see Sharpley, 2001b). Therefore, research into hotel employee attitudes in Cyprus was undertaken by the author during 2002.

Based upon a self-completion questionnaire centred around a 40-item, 5-point Likert scale, the survey sought to elicit employee attitudes towards a range of issues regarding their work, but specifically focusing on seven attitudinal themes related to motivation, quality and service provision, namely:

- reasons for working in hospitality;
- job security/prospects;
- empowerment/teamwork;
- job conditions/rewards;
- job satisfaction;
- motivation;
- guests' attitudes and service provision.

The survey revealed a number of important issues. The majority surveyed had worked in the industry for at least five years, and many over ten years, and most believed that they would continue working in hotels. However, a significant proportion felt they were likely to change jobs in the near future (an unsurprising finding given the highly regulated work conditions imposed by collective agreements negotiated with the powerful trade unions), while a majority also believed their jobs to be insecure. Thus, prospects for developing a culture of quality service faced an immediate hurdle of relatively high employee turnover.

There were two dominant reasons for working in the industry: earnings (again as a result of union power, Cypriot hotel employees are well paid in comparison to those in other countries) and 'meeting people'. The desire to work in the service sector was less evident, although most respondents recognised the importance of providing a good service within their job context. Most felt well rewarded financially for their work, to the extent that higher pay was not considered an important motivator, but intrinsically felt undervalued and unrecognised by management. Thus, although most felt that they were part of a team and enjoyed working in a friendly atmosphere, they had not experienced empowerment. Many also wanted more training and more support from management, while working hours and shift patterns were an increasingly disliked aspect of the job.

Importantly, a gap was identified between guests' and employees' expectations of appropriate service levels, the most frequent agreement to the statement 'guests expectations of service are too high' being, surprisingly, in the five-star hotel group. There was also a strong belief that guests were becoming more demanding, while dealing with unhappy or difficult customers was a principal dislike of the job. Thus, although most respondents revealed a positive attitude towards providing a service to their customers, perceived excessive demands and an unwillingness to attend to problems represent significant barriers to improving levels of service quality.

Importantly, the survey revealed overall that the co-operation of hotel employees cannot be taken for granted in any 'quality tourism' development policy in Cyprus. In other words, there is an important role to be played by the Cyprus Tourism Organisation in developing industry-wide training schemes, establishing quality service benchmarks, providing liaison between the employers and the unions and, more generally, undertaking research into employee attitudes. Equally, the research suggested that hotel management should support the quality tourism strategy through developing training programmes, attempting to minimise staff turnover, developing a sense of empowerment and involvement among their staff, while more generally embracing a culture that recognises and rewards achievement and, finally, seeking ways of overcoming the problem of anti-social hours and shift patterns to improve work conditions.

Conclusion

The accommodation sector is a fundamental element of the tourism industry, while the accommodation experience is, frequently, central to the overall tourist experience. The sector is also diverse and fragmented, yet collectively faces a number of common management challenges. In particular, all providers, from small independent operations up to multinational chains, need to maximise their profit through the effective management of demand, employees and the physical product (assets) and, as this chapter has suggested, the management of quality is a key issue from the point of view of individual businesses or destination management. In particular, attention should be paid to the role of employees, although the need to understand employees' attitudes is frequently overlooked. Therefore, research into employee attitudes should be considered a vital element of quality management in the accommodation sector.

Discussion questions

1. What are the principal management challenges and issues facing operators in the accommodation sector and what role can quality management play in addressing them?
2. What is the relevance of Total Quality Management to the accommodation sector?
3. Typically, the accommodation sector is characterised by high staff turnover and low wages. To what extent does this represent a barrier to the implementation of quality management programmes?

Suggested further reading

Gilbert, D. and Joshi, I. (1992) Quality management in the tourism and hospitality industry. In C. Cooper and A. Lockwood (eds), *Progress in Tourism, Recreation and Hospitality Management* (Vol. IV). London: Belhaven Press, pp. 149–68.

Harrington, D. and Lenehan, T. (1998) *Managing Quality in Tourism: Theory and Practice.* Dublin: Oak Tree Press.

Hope, C. and Mühlemann, A. (1998) Total quality, human resource management and tourism. *Tourism Economics*, 4(4): 367–86.

TTI (2001) *The International Hotel Industry* (3rd edition). London: Travel & Tourism Intelligence.

3 Airlines, airports and international aviation

Keith G. Debbage

Chapter objectives

The purpose of this chapter is to explore how the main contemporary, competitive strategies and management challenges faced by the international airline industry and airport authorities can impinge on tourism development processes. Having completed this chapter, the reader will be able to:

- understand the historical tensions engrained within the aviation industry
- appreciate the argument that strategic alliance networks are strategic responses to restrictive regulations and the forces of globalisation
- appreciate the interrelated nature of airline–airport management issues

Chapter contents

Introduction

Air transportation is an essential ingredient of tourism development, especially at an international scale where destination choice may be more constrained by time, cost and accessibility factors. In many cases, air transportation becomes the only reasonable transportation alternative. For example, many significant international tourism destinations in the relatively isolated 'pleasure peripheries' of the Caribbean and the South Pacific are highly dependent on international tourist arrivals by air. The competitive management strategies of the air transportation industry can have profound implications on the indigenous travel industries of these sorts of island destination. Even major tourism destinations in Northwest Europe and North America have depended to some extent on the development of the jet engine and wide-bodied aircraft because transportation innovations like these essentially ushered in the era of mass tourism in places like Florida, Greece, Hawaii and Spain.

In the past few decades, the contemporary air transportation industry has experienced radical shifts in the regulatory regime that once set airfares and authorised air routes, and these changes have implicitly shaped the flow of tourists from origin to destination markets. The deregulation of airline markets in the USA and the European Union (EU), the development of international 'open-skies' agreements between countries like the USA and The Netherlands, and the emergence of powerful strategic alliance networks between carriers have all increased airline management's freedom to restructure route networks, as well as increasing the overall level of competitive volatility in the air transport industry. In contrast, the acute capacity constraints that exist at nearly all major European and American airports – due to a lack of runway space and terminal congestion – have substantially curtailed tourist flows in certain contexts. It is in this way that the success and failure of resort destinations can be partially explained by the management decisions made by airline executives and airport authority directors with regard to such matters as route networks and runway/terminal expansion schemes.

Despite the obvious synergies and interconnections that exist between international aviation and the international tourist industry, it is often the case that the air transport–tourism connection is not well co-ordinated or well understood. Even though air transport frequently acts as the crucial link between tourist-generating and tourist-receiving countries, it is usually relegated to a minor place in tourism studies, although this is slowly changing (Britton, 1991; Wheatcroft, 1994; Page, 1999; Debbage, 2000, 2002). In contrast, most of the transportation studies literature discusses only indirectly the movement of tourists, even though we have seen an explosion of new transportation-related journals in recent years (e.g., the *Journal of Air Transport Management*, the *Journal of Transport Geography*, and *Transportation Research F.*).

The purpose of this chapter is to remedy this 'gap' in the literature by exploring how the main contemporary, competitive strategies and management challenges faced by the international airline industry and airport authorities can impinge on tourism development processes. Overall, the chapter is structured in the following manner. First, a brief description of the critical role that international air transportation plays in shaping the tourist product is provided. Next, the chapter provides a succinct overview of the historical tensions that are ingrained within international aviation with respect to the often contradictory forces of deregulation and protectionism. The historic development of 'open-skies' markets in the USA and the EU, and the simultaneous proliferation of restrictive bilateral air service agreements elsewhere are then discussed. The chapter then argues that strategic alliance networks, like the Star Alliance anchored by United Airlines and Lufthansa, are strategic responses to both the ongoing restrictive, bilateral regulations that govern much international aviation, and the more general forces of globalisation. It is suggested that an under-appreciated management issue in international aviation revolves around the thorny issue of airport capacity constraints, especially as it relates to terminal capacity and the finite number of airport runway slots available at most major international airports. Particular attention is paid to the interrelated nature of these airline–airport management issues through a case study of recent negotiations involving the US–UK aviation bilateral access rights to Heathrow Airport, and its impact on the Oneworld Alliance network anchored by American Airlines and British Airways.

A recent survey of air travel by *The Economist* magazine highlighted the bewildering array of policy issues impacting on air transportation. According to *The Economist* (2001: 4), 'it is a puzzling paradox that an industry which has done so much to foster globalisation has itself been stuck in a regulated environment with a purely national ownership structure and protectionist trade rules'. This chapter attempts to shed some light on this paradox as it relates to the management of tourism.

Air transport and tourism

It has long been recognised in the tourism literature that transportation is an important facilitator of travel and tourism. Transport is widely viewed as the key element that matches tourist demand (origin) with tourist supply (destination). Consequently, much of the tourist transport literature has conceptualised the relationship between tourism and transport in terms of accessibility (Miossec, 1976; Lundgren, 1982; Inskeep, 1991; Gunn, 1994). Others have examined the important role that new breakthroughs in transport technology (e.g., the railway, the jet engine and the automobile) have played in influencing the historical evolution of mass tourism (Gilbert, 1939; Robinson, 1976; Thurot, 1980; Holloway, 1989; Mill, 1992; Prideaux, 1993, 2000). For example, in the nineteenth century, the construction of the railroad network in the UK facilitated the development of coastal resorts that were tied to major metropolitan centres by fast and economical rail links. During the twentieth century, the private automobile accelerated the spatial diffusion of tourism due to the flexibility offered by automobile touring relative to the scheduled, fixed routes provided by rail transport. By the 1970s, the civilian air transport industry had matured and Boeing launched the highly successful wide-bodied 'Jumbo Jet' 747, which ushered in an era of mass intercontinental travel. Wide-bodied jets made it possible to transport large numbers of tourists at high speed in relative comfort, and they also partly triggered the rapid growth of the tour operating industry. Tour operators began block-booking large numbers of airline seats and offering packaged vacations incorporating flight arrangements, accommodation and sightseeing tours in all-inclusively priced travel deals. In effect, the earth shrank for the tourist as previously distant exotic islands were now within reach in terms of travel time and economic costs.

Theoretical travel models that attempted to conceptualise these dynamic shifts in the geographic pattern of origin–destination tourist flows have been conceived by a number of researchers (Campbell, 1967; Yokeno, 1974; Miossec, 1976; Greer and Wall, 1979; Thurot, 1980; Britton, 1982; Lundgren, 1982). Although the majority of these models stressed the key role transport networks played in shaping the tourist product, few of them explicitly commented on the way in which the competitive strategies of either the airline industry or airport authorities might inhibit or facilitate destination development. Such an oversight is crucial because 'if the ability of tourists to travel to preferred destinations is inhibited by inefficiencies in the transport system, … there is a likelihood that they will seek alternative destinations' (Prideaux, 2000: 56).

One of the most profound influences on the overall efficiency of the air transport system has been the radical shift in government transport policy since the 1970s towards deregulation, liberalisation and privatisation. We now turn our attention to an analysis of air transport policy and its implications for tourist travel patterns in two regions of the world that have been at the epicentre of regulatory reform in international aviation – the USA and the European Union.

Air transport policy: competing philosophies and the emergence of contestability

Traditionally, air transport policy has affected the tourist transport system in a number of ways, although much of the debate has tended to centre on two competing management philosophies: a public interest or interventionist philosophy and a free-market or price-efficiency philosophy. Historically, interventionists have justified the regulation of air transport markets on the grounds that it served a larger public interest by ensuring market stability, maintained safety standards, protected the public from monopoly exploitation, and provided a comprehensive network of services for air passengers (Button and Gillingwater, 1983; Button, 1989; Button et al., 1998; Page, 1999). In contrast, free-marketers believed that competition and the price mechanism were the best way to achieve efficient access to air transport and travel. Competition is generally accepted as being good for the air transport industry because it encourages airlines and airports to be cost-efficient, thus driving down prices and expanding output (Kahn, 1988; Morrison and Winston, 1995). The difficulty with this approach was that the neo-classical idea of perfect competition as a benchmark goal did not seem to match an industry where many suppliers were certainly not small (e.g., American and United Airlines) and where many routes were most efficiently served by, at best, two different air carriers that often tacitly 'price-colluded'.

It was the development of the theory of contestable markets in the 1970s that eventually provided the intellectual justification for the US Airline Deregulation Act of 1978 (Baumol et al., 1982; Bailey and Baumol, 1984; Baumol and Willig, 1986). Contestable conditions were theorised to arise not simply through the existence of classical perfect competition but from the *potential threat of competition*. Deregulated airline markets were believed to be contestable and, thus, easy to enter, because aircraft were mobile at a relatively low cost – the 'capital on wings' rationalisation. Contestability theorists believed that even city-pair markets with only one airline serving the route would remain competitive simply because airlines not currently in the market might conceivably enter if the incumbent carrier charged too high an airfare on any given route.

In October 1978, US President Carter signed the Airline Deregulation Act into law, based, to some extent, on the intellectual rationalisation of contestable markets. The ramifications for the travel and tourism industry were immediate and substantive.

US-style airline deregulation

The size of the air transport market in the USA, and its early progress to more deregulated markets, has resulted in the USA often being seen as a benchmark in judging how market forces shape the international airline industry and its related travel patterns and route networks (Button et al., 1998). The centrepiece of this liberalisation process was undoubtedly the Airline Deregulation Act (ADA). The 1978 Act essentially removed economic regulation of scheduled passenger interstate aviation in the USA, although it is important to note that air safety issues and anti-trust matters remained, respectively, under the regulatory jurisdiction of the Federal Aviation Administration and the Departments of Transport and Justice. Essentially, the ADA removed federal regulations relating to market entry (by 1982); route competition, levels of service, and pricing policies (by 1983); and free exit from a route. The Civil Aeronautics Board itself ceased to exist in 1985 under the so-called 'Sunset Clause'. The overriding theme of the Act was that competitive forces would facilitate an efficient and well-managed air transportation system within the USA.

Industry opinion is divided on how airline deregulation affected competition and airfares but the impact on accessibility levels for tourists and its impact on the industrial structure of the airline sector was, nevertheless, both dramatic and profound. During the early 1980s, 'no-frills', low-fare, new entrant airlines began to take advantage of the new freedoms offered by the ADA by providing new routes in specific geographic markets and targeting primarily non-business travellers. The initiation of discount service by low-cost carriers, of which People Express, New York Air and Air Florida were only the best-known examples, helped to pull down overall fare levels, thus elevating the propensity to fly in certain geographic areas and radically altering overall travel patterns. For example, between 1978 and 1983, the number of scheduled carriers in the USA increased from 36 to 123 (Brenner et al., 1985) and the proportion of travellers utilising discount fares increased from 15% in 1976 to 90% by 1987 (*Economic Report of the President*, 1988).

The deregulated airline market and the 'boom' economy of the early to mid-1980s also triggered the economic expansion of the lodging industry, and airlines like People Express helped reshape origin–destination tourist flows in significant ways. By 1983, People Express was offering 125 daily departures to almost 3 million passengers out of a previously under-utilised Newark hub with services to the northeast USA and various non-traditional Florida markets (e.g., Jacksonville, Melbourne, Sarasota and West Palm Beach). Without deregulation, it is doubtful that the level of low-fare service available at People Express destinations would have been at comparable levels. It is in this way that air transport management decisions can play a fundamental role in shaping the geography of origin–destination tourist flows.

By the mid-1980s, the major incumbent carriers began to react more aggressively to competition from the fledgling new entrants by utilising a three-pronged competitive strategy involving the following:

- more sophisticated pricing policies;
- the development of hub-and-spoke systems; and
- the development of a more assertive merger and acquisition policy.

First, the major carriers began to develop more complex yield management pricing strategies based on the powerful computer reservation information systems technologies that were being developed by large incumbents like American (i.e., Sabre) and United (i.e., Apollo). The ability to manage effectively the pricing mix of a large number of airline seats on hundreds of different routes allowed the incumbent carriers to initiate and respond more effectively to price and entry competition from the new entrants. The majors began to cut prices only where the low-cost airlines challenged them on routes central to their operating strategy, while healthier profit margins and high passenger load factors (i.e., the percentage of the seats filled) were maintained on less competitive routes. Several new entrants alleged that, in some instances, illegal predatory pricing strategies were being implemented by the larger incumbents, but the Reagan administration of the mid-1980s remained ambivalent about abrogating the central tenet of government aviation policy – that prices and services should be determined by the forces of market supply and demand.

A second key element to the 'new' competitive strategies of the mid-1980s was the rapid development of comprehensive hub-and-spoke systems, especially by American Airlines at Dallas–Fort Worth Airport, United Airlines at Chicago's O'Hare Airport, and Delta Airlines at Atlanta and Salt Lake City. The major carriers rapidly developed hub-and-spoke networks in the mid-1980s to internalise and benefit from network-based externalities and economies of scope. A hub increases geometrically the number of city-pair markets served, which can greatly enhance the chances of achieving high passenger load factors. Additionally, the economies of scope and scale generated by extensive hubbing complexes confer upon the dominant carrier a sustainable competitive advantage and a geographic monopoly power (Pustay, 1993; Debbage, 1994). The hubbing airline tends to have access to a large number of gates and landing slots, thus making it difficult for any other carrier to challenge it competitively. The enormous market power of the so-called 'fortress hubs', where the dominant carrier controls 60% or more of all enplanements (Table 3.1), has also resulted in higher fares than normal and a lack of competition in some markets that was not anticipated by some of the supporters of deregulation (US General Accounting Office, 1990, 1996, 1999).

Finally, a third crucial development in the 'new' competitive strategy of the larger, incumbent carriers was a policy of industrial consolidation exemplified by the 'frenzy' of mergers and acquisitions that occurred during the mid-1980s. Many of the major carriers eliminated competition by simply 'buying-out' some of the more competitive new entrant airlines. The consolidation undertaken from 1985 to 1987 (Table 3.2) remains one of the most significant structural changes in the industry's history and seemed more

Table 3.1 Principal hub cities for the major US airlines (1999)

US airline	Hub cities	Market share of enplanements at airport (%)
Alaska	Seattle/Tacoma	30.0
	Portland	21.5
American	Dallas/Fort Worth	63.7
	Miami	61.1
	San Juan	47.4
	Chicago – O'Hare	31.6
America West	Phoenix	40.9
	Las Vegas	18.0
Continental	Houston – Intercontinental	76.6
	Newark	59.1
	Cleveland	41.0
Delta	Atlanta	76.2
	Cincinnati	72.8
	Orlando	31.4
	Salt Lake City	68.5
Southwest	Oakland	68.9
	Chicago – Midway	46.1
	San Jose	34.5
	San Diego	32.0
Northwest	Minneapolis/St Paul	74.5
	Detroit	70.8
	Memphis	65.5
TWA	St Louis	73.3
	New York – Kennedy	16.5
US Airways	Charlotte	80.7
	Pittsburgh	74.7
	Philadelphia	60.2
United	Denver	66.1
	San Francisco	55.5
	Chicago – O'Hare	48.5
	Washington – Dulles	47.9

motivated by notions of scale economies or market control than by network extension. For example, in 1986, TWA's acquisition of Ozark Airlines and the merger of Republic Airlines and Northwest Airlines saw only limited network expansion. Exceptions to this rule included the purchase of Western Airlines by Delta Airlines, which provided Delta with a national route network focused on Atlanta and Salt Lake City (and later Cincinnati).

Not surprisingly, passenger market share held by the larger carriers became substantially more concentrated. In 1987, the five largest systems accounted for 71.5% of total revenue passenger miles or RPMs (i.e., the number of passengers times miles flown) compared with 54.4% in 1985 (Table 3.3). Throughout the 1990s, concerns have

Table 3.2 Acquisitions and mergers involving US airlines (1985–87)

Year	Month		Airline	
	Acquisition	**Merger**	**Surviving**	**Acquired**
1985		May	Air Wisconsin	Mississippi Valley
	June		Southwest	Muse Air
	November		People Express	Frontier
1986		February	Piedmont	Empire
		February	United	Pan Am – Pacific
	February		People Express	Britt
	May		People Express	Provincetown-Boston
	July		Presidential	Key/Colgan
		August	Northwest	Republic
		September	TWA	Ozark
	October		Texas Air Corp.	Rocky Mountain
		October	Texas Air Corp.	Frontier
	November		Texas Air Corp.	Eastern
	December		Delta	Western
	December		Alaska	Jet America
	December		Alaska	Horizon Air
	December		Texas Air Corp.	People Express
1987		February	Continental	New York Air
		February	Continental	People Express
		February	Continental	Frontier
	April	July	American	Air Cal
	May		World	Key
	May		Midway	Fischer Brs. Aviation
	May		US Air	PSA
	November		US Air	Piedmont

Note: An acquisition is where an acquired airline continues operations as a separate entity while a merger involves an airline becoming an integral part of the surviving airline's operations.

been voiced that industrial concentration has diminished competition and lessened the benefits that deregulation has provided for the public. However, a major study for the Brookings Institution by Morrison and Winston (1995) found that US fares are overall lower since the airline industry deregulated in 1978, and the level of competition on routes is comparable to conditions in 1978.

By the end of the 1990s, the US airline industry appeared to have found a natural equilibrium where seven major carriers – United, American, Delta, Northwest, Continental, US Airways, and Southwest – funnelled 635.4 billion RPMs through essentially 30 hub cities (Table 3.1 and Figure 3.1). By 1999, the five largest carriers accounted for 72.5% of all RPMs – a marginal change in market share relative to 1987 (Table 3.3). Essentially, the national fabric or network of origin–destination links by air had been established, thus predetermining the travel options by air for large numbers of tourists. Crucial in this equation was whether a potential tourist was at a spoke or hub city origin given the dramatic differences in the level of connectivity by location, and the range of fares available to the leisure or business traveller at hubs *vis-à-vis* spokes.

Table 3.3 Percentage of US airline market share ranked by revenue passenger miles, (1985, 1987 and 1999)

1985		1987		1999	
Airline	Market share (%)	Airline	Market share (%)	Airline	Market share (%)
American	13.3	Texas Air System	19.0	United	19.2
United	12.5	United	16.7	American	16.9
Eastern	10.0	American	14.1	Delta	16.1
TWA	9.6	Delta	11.7	Northwest	11.4
Delta	9.0	Northwest	10.0	Continental	8.9
Pan Am	8.1	TWA	8.3	US Airways	6.4
Northwest	6.7	US Airways	7.3	Southwest	5.6
Continental	4.9	Pan Am	6.6	TWA	4.0
People Express	3.3	Southwest	1.7	America West	2.7
Republic	3.2	America West	1.5	Alaska	1.8
Others	19.4	Others	3.1	Others	7.0

Figure 3.1   Enplaned passenger volume by metropolitan area (2000)

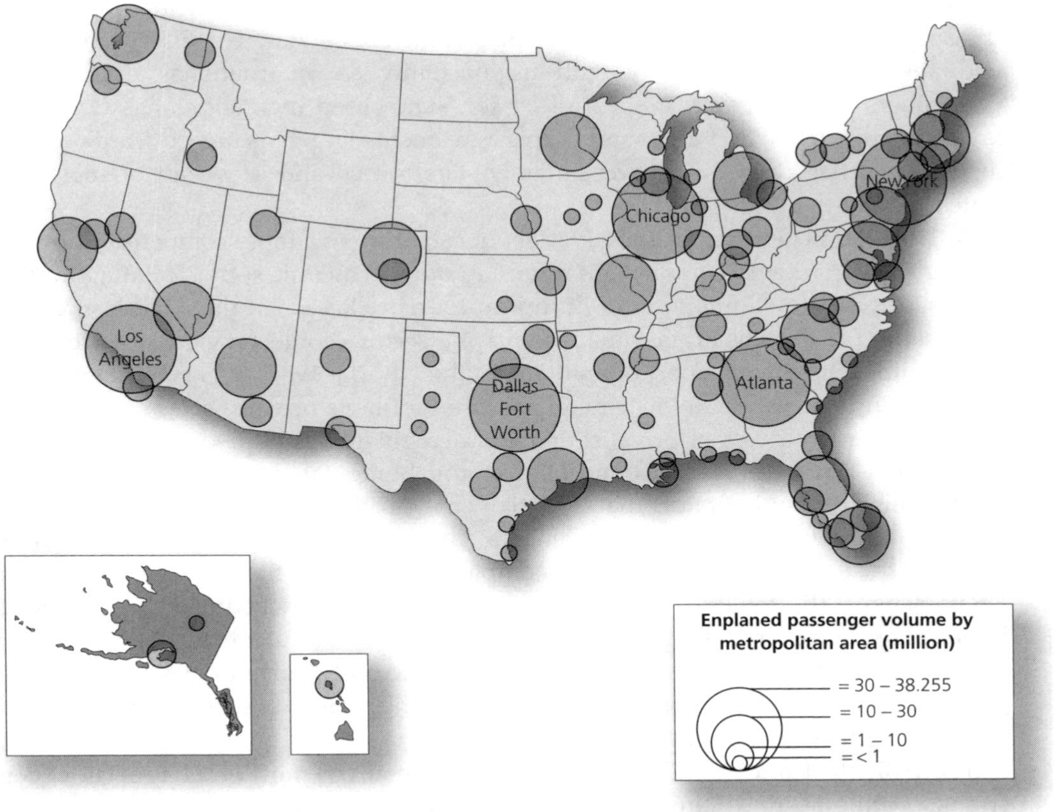

Enplaned passenger volume by
metropolitan area (million)

= 30 – 38.255
= 10 – 30
= 1 – 10
= < 1

Source: Federal Aviation Administration (2000)
Map by: C. Woodey & G. Nuyda

While US airlines found relative regulatory stability amid dramatic change (especially after September 11, 2001), the focus of regulatory reform switched from the US experience to the collective multilateral initiatives of the European Union which gradually phased in a series of three aviation packages in 1987, 1990 and 1993 that radically liberalised the EU air transport market.

European-style liberalisation

According to Button (1996: 279), 'the traditional picture of European aviation is one of institutionalised cartelisation and collusion'. Part of the reason for this is that, although a Common Transport Policy for the EU was established under the 1957 Treaty of Rome (which first created the European Community), aviation was initially excluded. Subsequently, each member state essentially regulated its own domestic aviation markets while a system of aviation bilateral agreements governed international air transport links between each respective pair of member states. The EU has also never had a single regulatory body with responsibility for international air transport. Consequently, a regulatory regime of *ad hoc*, state-based regulations has flourished, favouring restrictive and anti-competitive agreements largely geared towards protecting national flag carriers that were mainly state-owned and in receipt of substantial state subsidies.

In 1986, the EU initiated discussions about establishing a more competitive, internal air transport market to complement reform in other economic sectors relating to trade and tariffs, and to stimulate intra-European tourism. Based on the American experience, some EU officials argued that the private sector should be viewed as the main panacea for efficient transport operations. In the UK, the 1987 sale of the state-owned airline, British Airways, and its emergence as a profitable private sector company was seen as an early success of privatisation and deregulation. Coupled with this was the existence in Europe of a robust and less rigorously regulated charter airline industry run by low-cost tour operators that essentially met north–south tourist traffic demands. In 1985, 42 of the 162 million passengers carried by the European Civil Aviation Conference countries were by charter compared to three of the 356 million domestic US passengers (Button et al., 1998). However, although non-scheduled charter airlines offered low fares for leisure travellers, they were less useful for business travellers who required scheduled, frequent connections between the major cities of the tourist-generating countries (e.g., London, Paris, Rome) rather than non-scheduled connections to sun-spot cities on the Mediterranean rim.

The 1987, 1990 and 1993 EU Aviation Packages removed most of the regulatory constraints acting on intra-European air transport relating to fares, frequency of service, market entry and capacity constraints. By the late 1990s, the regulatory framework in the EU became even more liberal than the regulatory conditions prevailing in US domestic aviation. Since 1997, EU airlines have been able to operate between points within an EU country besides the home country (commonly referred to as cabotage). Cabotage within the USA is prohibited by law, meaning that it is illegal for a foreign carrier to operate only on a domestic route within America. In contrast, it was now possible for an EU-based carrier, such as British Airways, to operate solely inside France on, for example, the Paris–Marseilles route.

The theoretical and management implications of EU liberalisation on tourism were supposed to include cheaper fares and greater choice in terms of the destinations served as competitive fares encouraged the proliferation of new carriers, like Ryanair and easyJet, and expanded capacity. However, empirical evidence now exists which suggests that EU member states still enjoy significant control over their own domestic markets and that air carriers are not fully utilising their new cabotage rights (US General Accounting Office, 1993; UK Civil Aviation Authority, 1998; *Aviation Week and Space Technology*, 1999). According to Caves (1997: 125), there is little evidence of lower fares in the EU, possibly because 'there has been so little new entry on dense routes'. An in-depth assessment of EU liberalisation by the UK Civil Aviation Authority (1998: 6) concluded that 'no fundamental restructuring of the European airline industry has yet taken place', even though the market has been 'freed from the strait-jacket of the Chicago-based bilateral system'. The 1944 Chicago Conference on Civil Aviation established the existing bilateral system of international aviation, which has historically tended to favour restrictive and protectionist measures in order to protect vulnerable national flag carriers from competition.

Within the EU, national pride appears to continue to play a prominent role in the air transport market, despite recent liberalisation measures. For example, in 2002, a plan to replace bankrupt Sabena Airlines with a new flag carrier was largely supported by the Belgian government, despite Sabena's massive losses over several decades and the small size of the Belgian market. Ironically, Belgium is home to the European Commission (EC).

The EU has also yet to fully reconcile the conflicting goals of ensuring a competitive industry within Europe relative to the global competitive positions of EU carriers. If the EU is now a fully unified and liberalised market similar to the US domestic market, then external relations and the negotiation of aviation bilaterals with non-EU member states should fall under the rubric of the European Commission (the executive body of the EU) and not individual member states. In 2002, the European Court's Advocate General asserted that bilateral agreements between EU and non-EU countries were contrary to Community law and compromised deregulation in the EU's single market (*Aviation Week and Space Technology*, 2002). Bilateral agreements have traditionally mandated that participating airlines be owned substantially by nationals of the home country – the so-called 'nationality clause'. However, the European Commission Vice President Loyola de Palacio has suggested that the 'unlawful nationality clauses' in bilateral accords are contrary to the spirit and goals of the 1957 Treaty of Rome. Resolving the extra-territorial issues is crucial given the fundamental role the EU–North America and EU–Asia markets play in determining the overall health of the international tourist industry. For example, the North Atlantic has traditionally been the busiest tourist market in the world, accounting for one-quarter of all international tourist arrivals.

Proposals for a Transatlantic Common Aviation Area (TCAA) have been sponsored by the European Commission and the US Department of Transportation, but many issues still need to be sorted out before a full 'open-skies' accord across the North Atlantic is signed. Some of the thorny issues facing TCAA policy-makers include harmonising regulations governing airline computer reservation systems, code-sharing agreements, airport slots, state aid, anti-trust rulings and cabotage. If the TCAA were to become a reality, the geography of origin–destination tourist flows could be reconfigured on a grand scale and the mobility levels of individual tourists could be greatly enhanced. For example, if the TCAA were to be approved, airlines like Virgin Atlantic could set up a domestic airline in the USA and Southwest Airlines could provide service to non-traditional markets in the EU that are currently under-utilised.

Strategic alliance networks

As the domestic airline industries in North America, the European Union and Asia simultaneously deregulated and consolidated, the larger carriers began to seek out strategic alliances with overseas partners in the form of joint marketing programmes, code-sharing arrangements, joint computerised reservations systems (CRS) operations, joint frequent flier programmes, cross-holding arrangements, and minority ownership. The various alliances have not included outright mergers or acquisitions because traditional bilateral air service agreements typically prohibit majority ownership and/or impose caps on the extent of equity involvement by foreign airlines in domestic carriers. Nationalistic pride in the national flag carrier and the fact that some airlines are still partially or wholly owned by the national government make all-out mergers or acquisitions even less likely.

For these and other reasons, airlines have instead developed 'strategic tie-ups' with functionally related foreign airlines in what appears to be an 'end run' around the constraints imposed by the current regulatory system. Globally-based alliance networks offer several competitive advantages, including improved access to other continents, complementary route networks, valuable runway slots and terminal gates at otherwise gridlocked hub airports, and the development of a domestic feeder network in another country. Because cabotage is prohibited by law in the USA and only available to EU-based carriers within the European Union, most sustainable alliances include at least one major US and EU airline. Also, it is becoming clear that a small number of key alliance groupings are dictating the types of structural change that may occur in the industry in the decade ahead.

Currently, there are four major global groupings (year of formation in parentheses) (Tables 3.4 and 3.5), including the Star Alliance anchored by United Airlines and Lufthansa (1997), the Oneworld Alliance involving American Airlines and British Airways (1998), the Sky Team Alliance incorporating Delta and Air France (1999), and the KLM/Northwest 'Wings' Alliance (1992). Each of these four major alliances also involve other major carriers, although the membership status of these airlines is volatile and rapidly changing. In 2000, these four alliance groupings accounted for 55% of the world's revenue passenger kilometres (RPKs) and included most of the world's top 50 passenger carriers with a few exceptions (e.g., Japan Airlines and Southwest Airlines have yet to join a major alliance grouping).

In the early years, allegiance to any one alliance tended to be weak with a high level of shifting partners during the 1990s. Since 2000, a measure of stability appears to be emerging. According to Oum and Zhang (2001), membership in these alliance groups is likely to become increasingly stable as the cost of separation becomes prohibitively high and the option of finding appropriate alternative groupings continues to diminish. Some industry observers consider the Star Alliance to be the strongest alliance grouping, especially given the anti-trust immunity granted to the United Airlines–Lufthansa alliance in 1996 by the US Department of Transportation. The immunity was granted virtually coincidentally with the signing of an 'open skies' bilateral agreement between the USA and Germany. Similar immunities have been granted to both the KLM/Northwest

Table 3.4   Major airline alliance groupings (2002)

Star Alliance	Oneworld Alliance	Sky Team Alliance	Wings Alliance
United	American	Delta	Northwest
Lufthansa	British Airways	Air France	KLM
Air Canada	Aer Lingus	Aero Mexico	
Air New Zealand	Cathay Pacific	Alitalia	
ANA	Finnair	CSA Czech	
Ansett Australia	Iberia	Korean Air	
Austrian Airlines	Lan Chile		
British Midland	Qantas		
Lauda Air			
Mexicana			
SAS			
Singapore			
Thai			
Tyrolean			
Varig			

Table 3.5   Market share of major alliance groupings

	1998			2000		
Alliance	RPKs billions	(%)	Alliance	RPKs billions	(%)
Star Alliance	428.0	16.3	Star Alliance	647.0	21.4
Oneworld Alliance	415.7	15.8	Oneworld Alliance	488.0	16.2
Wings	287.0	10.9	Sky Team	301.0	10.0
Atlantic Excellence/ Qualiflyer	259.3	9.9	Wings	223.0	7.4
Total	1390	52.9	Total	1659	55.0

alliance in 1992 and the Delta–Air France alliance in 2001. In both cases, the respective national governments also approved open skies agreements (i.e., US–Netherlands and US–France) in tandem with the granting of anti-trust immunity.

US anti-trust laws are designed to prohibit anti-competitive behaviour and thus bar closely co-ordinated joint action by two different airlines on route selection, capacity measures, pricing and purchasing. Anti-trust immunity allows alliance partners to more closely control and co-ordinate prices/schedules, pool revenues and costs, and set capacity together. It is widely perceived that an open skies agreement has become a pre-requisite for the USA to grant anti-trust immunity to proposed alliances between US airlines and foreign airlines. Consequently, immunised alliances have a major competitive advantage over non-immunised alliances. In mid-2002, Oneworld remained the only worldwide alliance without anti-trust immunity across the Atlantic. We now turn to a case study of the Oneworld Alliance to better understand how these complex management issues play out in international aviation.

Case Study 3.1 The Oneworld Alliance conundrum

The Oneworld Alliance was founded in the late 1990s, but attempts by the two core members – British Airways and American Airlines – to strengthen the Oneworld partnership have faced significant regulatory hurdles. The core of the regulatory conundrum has revolved around two major sticking points.

1. The USA has not been willing to approve anti-trust immunity for the American Airlines–British Airways alliance without a revised US–UK open skies bilateral agreement to replace the currently restrictive Bermuda II bilateral agreement – so-called because it succeeded a 1946 bilateral negotiated at a Bermuda conference. Under Bermuda II, only two airlines from each country – American, United, British Airways and Virgin Atlantic – can fly between Heathrow Airport and the USA. The US government would prefer to see more US airlines, such as Continental, Delta, Northwest, and US Airways, in the US–Heathrow market.
2. The UK has not been willing to agree to an open skies arrangement without an anti-trust immunity agreement that is acceptable to British Airways. The substantial slot divestitures required of British Airways to encourage new entrants at Heathrow Airport (Table 3.6), and the inability of British Airways to offer a service wholly within the domestic US market (i.e., cabotage) have been major stumbling blocks for British Airways and the UK government. Additionally, the UK government has wanted some relaxation of the restrictions on foreign ownership of US carriers. The US government restricts overseas investment in a US

carrier to 25% of the voting shares of the airline's stock. In the USA, the Department of Defense has consistently opposed any change to the law largely for national security reasons.

Table 3.6 Proposed slot divestitures at Heathrow Airport for British Airways

Government Agency or Airline	Year	No. of weekly slots	No. of daily US–UK roundtrips
UK Office of Fair Trading	1997	168	12
EU Competition Commissioner	1998	266	19
US Department of Justice	1998	336	24
Northwest Airlines	2001	448	32
Delta Airlines	2001	504	36
US Department of Transportation	2002	224	16
American Airlines– British Airways	2002	126–140	9–10

Given the ruling by the European Court's Advocate General in 2002 that bilateral open skies agreements ran contrary to Community law, it would appear that the 'window of opportunity' for the USA and the UK to negotiate an innovative Bermuda III agreement has significantly diminished. For example, future negotiations with the US government may be conducted by the European Commission instead of the UK government. For the British Airways–American Airlines partnership and the Oneworld Alliance, it may mean that its largest aviation market across the Atlantic will remain one of its most strictly regulated. In the immediate future, it is possible that British Airways may resurrect negotiations with Dutch airline KLM, although the US government has already indicated that the US–Netherlands open skies agreement will not extend to a KLM–BA partnership.

Potential remedies may include the approval of a multilateral TCAA and the completion of a fifth, new terminal at Heathrow Airport. But, in many respects, either option may be more complex and difficult than the recent regulatory hurdles that the Oneworld Alliance has been unable to clear. Although a TCAA may ultimately open up the North Atlantic market, it may also, ironically, undermine the recently formed alliances between European Union and US airlines. Additionally, the sceptical position of the US Department of Transportation on the matter does not bode well for an early resolution to the numerous problems facing any TCAA proposal. As for the Heathrow Terminal 5 project, it has already been subject to the longest enquiry in British planning history and the government plans to impose substantial limits on Heathrow's annual flight traffic in order to mitigate noise pollution.

All these regulatory and infrastructural constraints can profoundly impede tourist flows and the entire process of tourism development. For example, 'BA and AA combined carry 60% of all US–UK air traffic and 70% of all flights between London and New York, as well as 25% of all traffic between the US and Europe as a whole' (*Air Transport World*, 1997: 55). A better understanding of the key management issues facing airlines and airports in the international aviation industry can only heighten the awareness of tourism practitioners to the impact of air transportation on the economic performance of key tourism suppliers (e.g., hotels, restaurants, major attractions, tour operators and travel agents).

Conclusion: the aftermath of September 11, 2001 and future directions

In recent years, the international airline and airport industries have experienced structural instability and dynamic change in both the marketplace and the regulatory regimes that govern airline competition policy. These changes have been compounded by the dramatic events of September 11, 2001, when terrorist attacks on New York's World Trade Center and the Pentagon subsequently triggered unprecedented downturns in air passenger traffic. During late 2001, US carriers laid off over 100,000 airline employees and trimmed seat capacity by 15–20% in an attempt to better match system capacity with the precipitous drop-off in passenger volume. Many airlines experienced record net losses, including United Airlines which reported $1.16 billion in losses for the third quarter of 2001 – the worst quarterly performance in the airline's 75-year history.

Given these sorts of losses, the US government swiftly passed the 2001 Air Transportation Safety and Stabilization Act, largely to provide the US airline industry with $5 billion in direct, taxpayer-financed aid and $10 billion in federally-guaranteed loans. Despite the massive cash infusion from federal government, the US airline industry still reported net losses of $7 billion for 2001 (in stark contrast to the $6 billion of announced profits in 1997). By 2002, both US Airways and United Airlines had filed Chapter 11 bankruptcy protection and it appeared that the geography of air travel had been fundamentally altered. Demand for air travel was substantially down, and United Airlines and American Airlines reported combined net losses of $6.7 billion for year end 2002. Expensive airline hub systems came under closer scrutiny. US Airways and Delta both announced in 2004 that their operations in Pittsburgh and Dallas-Forth Worth, respectively, would be discontinued as all US carriers looked for ways to save money.

The elevated uncertainty and volatility in the US air transport market in the early 2000s exacerbated the competitive pressures faced by the entire airline industry world-wide. For example, in late 2001, the European Union and the Association of European Airlines (AEA) expressed deep concern about the 'anti-competitive' nature of US federal aid to US carriers. Transatlantic traffic for AEA members dropped 35% below the previous year's levels in the weeks immediately after September 11, and concerns were raised that US carriers might offer unrealistically low airfares across the Atlantic that were, in part, subsidised by the $15 billion US aid package.

Predicting future outcomes amidst such turbulence is a difficult topic. However, one clear outcome is that the international air transport industry will continue to play a sub-stantive role in shaping the tourist industry in the years ahead. Access to international flight connections and an international airport are crucial components in the devel-opment of most international tourism markets. For these and other reasons, tourism policy-makers need to be more acutely aware of the significant management challenges facing the international air transport industry if they wish successfully to co-ordinate destination development and develop new tourism markets. Key to such an awareness is a familiarity with the radical shifts in the regulatory regimes that essentially govern competition in international aviation.

Future trends are likely to include continued globalisation through alliance forma-tion and share acquisitions as more regions of the world deregulate and liberalise their respective national air transport markets, particularly in Asia and Latin America. A small number of mega-carriers are likely to emerge, centred around three or four alliances. Each alliance network will probably be anchored by a trio of major carriers, one each from the USA, the EU and Asia respectively. Each alliance will also likely be supported by numerous junior partners, serving niche markets that the anchor carriers have traditionally either underserved or ignored.

The pressure to reduce costs will also likely force airlines to outsource many more activ-ities (e.g., baggage handling, food and catering services, airplane maintenance and leasing, etc.) and develop 'virtual' airline strategies more focused on the core business of serving the air passenger largely through more sophisticated information technologies. A key component of this strategy will be the development of ever more complex computerised reservations systems (CRS) and yield management software applications. Additionally, web-based applications incorporating online booking and e-ticketing (e.g., Orbitz) will allow the airlines to better customise the product to more fully serve the needs of business or pleasure tourists who choose to travel by air to reach their destinations.

The collective end result will be the dissolution of the protectionist era and aviation bilaterals as the air transport industry implements more progressive multilateral solutions, such as the TCAA, and national governments increasingly recognise that increasing airline competition can boost tourism by lowering the overall cost of air travel.

Perhaps the greatest competitive challenge in the coming decades will be developing innovative management solutions that essentially allow the existing liberalisation of air services 'in-the-sky' to be complemented by similar levels of reform 'on-the-ground'. Regulatory reform in the airport industry has traditionally lagged behind that experienced in the airline industry, and this has emerged as an increasingly thorny problem as airports across the world begin to experience acute congestion levels (excepting the two or three quarters after September 11, 2001).

Other than the obvious solution of building new airports and runways (a lengthy and time-consuming process), more attention will undoubtedly be focused on improving the management of existing runway slots and terminal gates in an attempt to squeeze more capacity out of existing airport terminals. Both the UK and US governments are becoming increasingly preoccupied with such matters and it is not unreasonable to assume that innovative solutions to the airport congestion problem will emerge from these familiar centres of regulatory reform in the international air transport industry.

Discussion questions

1. It is widely speculated that in the aftermath of the financial losses of September 11, 2001 the airline industry may be faced with another round of consolidation. How can governments avoid anticipated market dominance by one airline group without re-regulation, and what would be the best solution for tourism policy-makers and practitioners?

2. Since 2001, US 'hub-and-spoke' network carriers have trimmed capacity significantly while 'point-to-point', niche-market carriers like Southwest Airlines and JetBlue have introduced low-fare services in markets left behind by the bigger carriers. What are the long-term implications of this restructuring, and how will it reshape the geography of origin–destination tourist flows?

3. What are some of the best solutions for 'squeezing' more capacity out of the congested international gateway airports like New York's JFK and London's Heathrow? Why is this such a crucial question for the tourist industry?

4. Are we likely to see more airline alliances in the next decade, and what are the pros and cons of international alliance networks?

5. For emerging tourism markets in less developed countries, how do national governments embrace the open competition offered by liberalised air transport markets without sacrificing the national flag carrier?

6. Is it reasonable to expect the multilateral systems of governance adopted by the EU to mature into the TCAA? If so, would a global competition authority be needed to assess the trade-offs associated with a more competitive air transport industry, particularly with respect to market power abuses and predatory behaviour arising from increased industrial concentration in some hub airports?

Suggested further reading

Button, K.J. and Stough, R. (2000) *Air Transport Networks: Theory and Policy Implications*. Cheltenham: Edward Elgar.

Button, K.J., Haynes, K. and Stough, R. (1998) *Flying into the Future: Air Transport Policy in the European Union*. Cheltenham: Edward Elgar.

Doganis, R. (2001) *Airline Business in the 21st Century*. London: Routledge.

Hanlon, P. (1999) *Global Airlines: Competition in a Transnational Industry*. Oxford: Butterworth Heinemann.

Page, S.J. (1999) *Transport and Tourism*. Harlow: Addison-Wesley Longman.

Wheatcroft, S. (1994) *Aviation and Tourism Policies: Balancing the Benefits*. London: Routledge.

4 Tour Operations Management

Sandra (Carey) Gountas

Chapter objectives

The purpose of this chapter is to examine the current situation in the tour operations industry, analyse strategic approaches and question the industry's interactions with and impact on its consumers. Having completed this chapter, the reader will be able to:

- recognise current issues in the dynamic tour operations industry
- identify strategic approaches adopted by the sector
- appreciate the sector's interaction with and impact on its consumers

Chapter contents

Introduction

The tour operating sector of the travel and tourism industry is an important but frequently overlooked influence on many issues relating to tourism studies. Marketing, tourism planning and development, financial management and consumer behaviour are among those areas to feel such influence. Tour operations forms a dynamic industry sector characterised by expansion, intense competition, mergers and acquisitions, all of which have been pivotal to industry development and product offerings over the past 20 years. Many operators have looked to other countries for business expansion. There have been several mergers and take-overs between tour operators in the UK, Germany, Scandinavia and elsewhere in Europe, which have brought both advantages and disadvantages for many industry players. This chapter examines each of these aspects of the industry.

Many issues emerge when one starts to unravel the industry structure and consider its ramifications, and it is impossible to cover all of them in depth here. This chapter will focus on the current situation in this dynamic industry, analyse strategic approaches and question the industry's interaction with, and impact on, its consumers. The operational methods and considerations vary throughout the world, but as the majority of tourists continue to be generated from Europe, this area, most specifically the UK, will be the focus for discussion.

The UK tour operating industry

For several years, the UK travel industry has been characterised by intense competition which has resulted in many mergers and acquisitions. However, the 'real' balance of power has changed very little in the past ten years. In spite of more than 1,000 operators being registered with the Civil Aviation Authority's Air Travel Organiser's Licence (ATOL), the top ten companies hold around 65% of total capacity with 53% held by the top four: Airtours Travel Group (My Travel Group plc), Thomson Group (TUI UK), Thomas Cook Group (JMC Holidays Ltd) and First Choice Holidays Group. The sector can therefore be seen to be highly polarised and the dominance of the largest four groups has long been the cause of general concern for the future of the industry and consumers' interests. The discussion has focused mainly on the difficulties that small, independent companies face for mere survival, healthy competition, directional selling through vertical integration and concern for the 'sustainable' and 'fair' development of destinations.

Table 4.1 illustrates the size of these main players in the UK tour operating sector, showing the number of passengers authorised by the largest ATOL licences at December 2002. The percentage change to these figures from December 2001 is also given.

Although the Civil Aviation Authority (CAA) gives the figures in this format, it should be noted that Unijet Travel Ltd is part of the First Choice Group. Therefore, the First Choice Group ranks as the third largest operator in the UK. Table 4.2 shows the size of the total passenger market carried under all ATOL licences for the years 1999–2001.

While passenger numbers carried is highly important to tour operators, another important measure in the industry is that of revenue earned. Table 4.3 shows the total revenue earned under all ATOLs over the same period as covered by Table 4.2 (1999–2001).

Although there has been a general increase in holidays sold, there has been variation in the rate of growth over recent years: 'The volume of holidays sold in summer 2001 was 5% higher than in the previous summer and it represented a fifth successive summer of volume increase' (CAA *ATOL Business*, http://www.caa.co.uk). The overall increase to September 2001 was 6.3%, which was mostly due to a better winter season

Table 4.1   Passengers authorised by largest licences at December 2001

Licence holder	Passengers licensed		% Change
	Dec. 2001	Dec. 2000	
1. Thomson Holidays Ltd	4,050,000	3,907,245	4
2. Airtours plc	4,019,853	3,591,050	12
3. JMC Holidays Ltd.	2,850,055	2,836,191	1
4. First Choice Holidays & Flights Ltd.	2,098,790	1,888,008	11
5. Unijet Travel Ltd.	1,092,712	1,000,435	9

Table 4.2   Passengers carried under all ATOLs

Year to September	Passengers (million)	Change over last period	
		(million)	(%)
1999	26.3	1.7	7.0
2000	27.5	1.2	4.7
2001	29.2	1.7	6.3

Source: CAA ATOL

Table 4.3   Revenue earned under all ATOLs

Year to September	Revenue (£bn)	Change over last period	
		(£bn)	(%)
1999	11.0	0.8	8.2
2000	12.1	1.0	9.3
2001	13.1	1.0	8.2

Source: CAA ATOL

than the previous year. Even so, the increase in summer 2001 represented a smaller percentage on growth than in the previous year. There was also a reduction in yield with the average price increase below the rate of inflation. At the time of writing there appeared to be a decrease of between 10 and 20% in forward bookings for summer 2002. This is attributed to the effect of the terrorist attack on America on September 11, 2001.

Table 4.4 presents an overall picture of the top four operators' activities at the time of writing. The main purpose the table serves is to illustrate the vastness and complexity of the industry. These main operators have spread their portfolio of business units into seven major areas that may be described as: aviation, UK-based tour operators, European-based tour operators, operators based outside Europe, cruising, retail in the UK and elsewhere, which includes travel shops/agencies, call centres and Internet sites,

Table 4.4   The 'top four' UK tour operators' businesses

My Travel Group plc (formerly Airtours plc)	TUI UK (formerly Thomson Travel Group)	First Choice Holidays plc	JMC Holidays
Aviation: Airways UK, My Travel	Britannia	Air 2000, Viking Aviation	JMC, Condor, Sun Express, Thomas Cook, Airlines
UK-based tour operators: Airtours, Aspro, Direct Holidays, Panorama, Jetset, Manos, Bridge, Cresta, Tradewinds, Eurosites	Thomson Holidays, Portland Holidays, Austravel, Jetsave & Jersey Travel, Tropical Places, Something Special, Villadeals, OSL, Simply Travel, Headwater Holidays, Magic Travel Group, Spanish Harbour Holidays, Crystal Holidays, Thomson Worldwide, Thomson Australia, Thomson Breakaway, Thomson Ski, Lakes and Mountains	First Choice, Unijet, Falcon, JWT, Eclipse, 2wentys, Ski, Lakes and Mountains, Flexiski, Citalia, Hayes & Jarvis, Sovereign, Meon Villas, Longshot	JMC, Neilson, Sunworld Ireland, Thomas Cook, Holidays, Club 18–30
European-based tour operators: Ving, Always, Spies, Tjaereborg, Sunair, Trivsel, Globetrotter, Marysol, Travel Trend, Gate Eleven, Bridge, Skibby, Gullivers, Itaka, FTi Touristik, Air Maritime, Seereisen, Club Valtur, LAL Sprachreisen	Budget Travel, Fritidsresor, Star Tours, TEMA, Sportresor, Hassen Matkat, Finnmatkat, Prisma	Marmara, Etapes Nouvelles, Tourinter, Blue Lagoon, Nazar, Taurus, Bosphorus, I Viaggi del Turchese, Sunrise	Air marin, Aldiana, All Seasons, Aquatour, Belvilla, Bucher Reisen, Havas Voyages Vacances, Kreutzer Touristik, Neckermann Reisen, Pegase, Style, Sunsnacks, Terramar, Vakantie Direkt, Vrij Uit
Operators based outside Europe:		Signature	Thomas Cook, North America
Cruising: Sun Cruises, Acquasol		Encore Cruises, Sunsail, Stardust Platinum, Crown Blue Line	
Retail: Going Places, Travelworld, Late Escapes, Holidayline, Go Direct, Ving, Spies, Tjaereborg, My Travel, Reisewinkels	Lunn Poly, Team Lincoln, Travel House Group, Sibbald Travel, Callers Pegasus, Manchester Flights, Glasgow Call Centre	Travel Choice, Bakers Dolphin, Holiday Hypermarket	Thomas Cook Travel Shop and Travel Agencies Worldwide, Neckermann Travel Agencies, Touristique, Havas Voyages, Holiday Land, Marlin Travel
Other services: Tenerife Sol, Globales, My Travel Money		Suncars Flexi Conference	Thomas Cook Exchange

and other services such as finance and hotels. Obviously, the top four are trying to ensure that their interests in any aspect of the chain, in any area, are not being strangled by their competitors.

Figure 4.1   The tour operating value chain

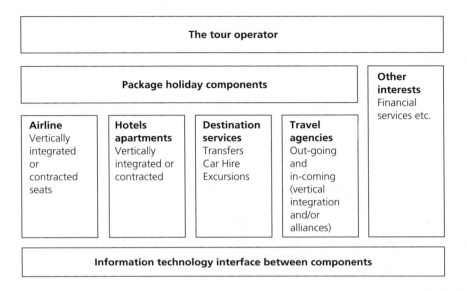

The tour operating value chain

A useful method of analysing the process of value creation in an industry is Porter's (1980) value chain. While this book's coverage of the value chain continues in Chapter 5, it is useful to consider the application of this to a large tour operator here. The tour operating value chain for a large operator is shown in Figure 4.1. As previously mentioned, the top four operators have dominated the industry, with some changes in volume, for several years. This has caused concern and public discussion among smaller independent operators, many of whom are members of the Association of Independent Tour Operators (AITO). Noel Josephides of Sunvil Holidays, former chairman of AITO and current deputy chairman, is widely known as a champion of the independent operators, quality products, consumer choice and destination sustainability. He acknowledges that the market today has changed due to a large portion of the UK tour operators now being German-owned.

In response to a possible merger between Airtours and First Choice at the end of 2002, Josephides said: 'If we are going to have a powerful UK player (in the global market), then providing it looks after our interests we would find it difficult to object. It makes little difference if there are three major players in the market or four'. He said that AITO would be looking for assurances that availability of third-party flying would be maintained from Gatwick airport and that there would be no exclusivity deals between the new larger operator and hotels (*Travel Weekly*, http://www.travelweekly. co.uk, 14 December 2001). On this basis, AITO was prepared to drop its objections to the merger. This would seem to indicate that the smaller, independent operators have

Table 4.5 Group assets

	Tui AG	Thomas Cook AG	My Travel Group PLC	First Choice
Turnover (2001)	Approx. €22bn	Approx. €8bn	£ 4,434.80m	£ 2,396.10m
Travel agencies	Over 3,700	3,600	2001	Approx. 337
Tour operator brands	81	30	Over 100	More than 30
Customers	Approx. 22m	Approx. 14m	Approx. 15m	Approx. 5m
Hotels	285		125	
Hotel beds	Over 150,000	73,000	N/A	N/A
Cruise Ships			4	
Aircraft	88	85	49	29
Workforce	Approx. 70,000	Approx. 28,000	Approx. 27,900	Approx. 14,000

conceded that they cannot compete with the large operators head-on, but are looking for a more co-operative working arrangement than has been the case in the past. Table 4.5 illustrates the might of the larger groups. One only needs to look at this table briefly to appreciate AITO's fears. Obviously, if My Travel Group and First Choice were to merge, their joint assets would provide a stronger rival for Tui AG and exceed those of Thomas Cook. A combined company would have a larger number of tour operators attracting the full range of market segments from mainstream, specialist and cruising.

Tour Operators' Strategies

Given the dominance of the larger groups in the UK tour operating industry, it is worth considering their operation in a little more detail. Larger companies look to multi-business involvement as a way to create synergies that outweigh the costs of managing a large, complex organisation: 'Synergies occur when firms are able to productively share resources among two or more businesses (also referred to as economies of scope)' (de Witt and Meyer, 1998: 412).

There are both costs and benefits for large operators. Among the obvious benefits are sharing of knowledge, expertise, reputation, staff and tangible assets. Yet problems may occur due to broad span-of-control issues that may mean that consistency of product delivery is difficult to ensure. For example, most of us have experienced different levels of service at different travel agents within the same chain.

Bigger companies tend to resemble large machines with each part contributing towards the optimum working of the other parts. This often results in a degree of regimentation that reduces the organisation's responsiveness. This can also cause conflicts in organisational cultural values between merging or acquired firms. Smaller organisations have greater control over staff, working relationships in smaller operators tend to be closer to management, there is greater information dissemination through the company and better service quality, but smaller companies obviously lack the benefits of larger organisations' competences.

The paradox of responsiveness and synergy is sometimes referred to as the *portfolio* versus *core competence* perspectives (de Witt and Meyer, 1998). This concept emphasises that firms that are operating independently, whether as a small company or as a business unit which is part of a larger corporation, have a greater ability to respond to competitors, greater cash flow optimisation, and an autonomous decision-making ability with greater diversification possibilities. The downside is that competence development and building tends to be slower than that of larger companies.

Industry-specific concerns affecting strategic decisions

The Federation of Tour Operators (FTO) draws attention to the underlying complexities of the industry that affect strategy development. 'Planning, negotiating, contracting, marketing and successfully administering a package holiday is a complex management task and takes place over a long period of time' (FTO, http://www.fto.co.uk). The FTO's fact file refers to price setting and brochure printing taking place over a year in advance. These days, this is somewhat of an understatement, with planning taking place up to two years in advance. The FTO says: 'we can think of no other consumer industry or service which has to fix prices so far ahead' (ibid.). This practice implies a great deal of risk. Consider the issues beyond the control of the operator that may affect their business: competition, mergers and acquisitions, political changes, war, terrorism, economic recessions, outbreaks of disease to cite but some of the disasters that may affect even the best-laid plans. The September 11, 2001 terrorist attack on America, and the ensuing loss of passenger bookings and staff redundancies, is a good example of this, albeit an extreme one. As, at the time of the disaster, the summer season had only a few weeks left to run, the full impact was not immediately apparent. However, tour operators responded by maintaining increased fluidity in their planned, future capacity. Chapter 19 examines many of the crises that have impacted upon the tourism industry in detail, together with suggestions for their management.

> The successful organization of the future will be customer-focused, not product- or technology-focused, supported by a market-information competence that links the voice of the customer to all the firm's values-delivery processes. Successful marketing organizations will have the skills necessary to manage multiple strategic marketing processes, many of which have not, until recently, been regarded as within the domain of marketing. (Webster, 1997, cited in Hooley et al., 1998: 3)

The above statement reflects the position often discussed by marketing academics that there is a need to move towards a more customer-focused orientation. In the case of tour operating, this is true for some consumers and some organisations some of the time. However, it is impossible to make a broad brush statement that any one approach to marketing strategy is the best. Companies serve different purposes for their clients in a plethora of circumstances and need to take the marketing approach that is best suited to their mission and goals, and also more or less meets their customers' needs. It is naïve to suggest that a perfect condition is ever likely to exist.

As previously mentioned, the fierce competitive nature of the industry means that mere survival is often the prime concern. For many organisations the customer is important, but the focus is on strategic positioning that will ensure a competitive edge. Quality and customers' needs may be somewhat compromised (this issue will be discussed in more detail in a later section).

Hooley, Saunders and Piercy (1998: 4) cite Doyle's (1997) claim that 'relatively few companies have succeeded in moving beyond the "marketing" trappings of advertising, short-term sales growth and flamboyant innovation to achieve the substance of a robust marketing strategy that produces long-term performance and strong shareholder value'. Corporate development strategy typically takes one of two directions – expansion or diversification. In the case of the major tour operators a mixture of both approaches has been used.

Expansion strategies

There are three main expansion strategies:

- *Market penetration.* This involves an increased share of an existing market through tactics such as advertising, TV programme sponsorship, cutting costs and prices, and other promotions. Many of these are very familiar to tour operators' consumers.
- *Product development.* This is normally concerned with developing product-line extensions or new products. A tour operator may decide to offer all-inclusive holidays, cruises, etc., in addition to the usual hotel packages. Another development which is increasingly common is offering financial services to facilitate payment for holidays or sales of items such as beach bags and towels.
- *Market development.* This focuses on the development of new markets for existing products and often involves expansion into global markets. This method is becoming easier with free trade agreements and easy electronic communication through the Internet.

A combination of product and market development is seen through horizontal integration where a company seeks to increase its product portfolio through merging with or acquiring another company. This concept was introduced earlier in this chapter. The large tour operators have all used this approach to increase their appeal to a broader range of consumers. For example, First Choice's Independent Travel Specialist Business section includes 'up-market' companies such as Meon Villas and Hayes and Jarvis. Airtours moved into cruising and now own four cruise ships. Mergers and acquisitions accelerated from the late 1980s and early 1990s. During that period, many well-known brands were gradually subsumed into the 'parent' company's brand and were eventually lost, for example, Horizon, Sunmed and Wings, to name but a few.

The aim of buying up other operators was mostly to increase capacity. This aim was also fulfilled through the demise of companies such as International Leisure Group (ILG) in the early 1990s. Although increased capacity was achieved by this method, brand power was undermined and clients who had strongly identified with an 'up-market' operator were alienated.

During the past ten years the approach has changed to a mixed segmentation strategy, which usually maintains the brand name of the original company and, hopefully, its regular client base. This strategy means that previous limitations on holidays offered, and so their appeal to the full range of consumer, are reduced. The operator hopes to buy the goodwill and trust of a new market without having to go through the costly development stages. This situation makes the job of small independent operators increasingly difficult as they must look for more and more innovative ways to differentiate themselves.

Diversification strategies

There are four main diversification strategies:

- *Vertical integration: forward integration.* The larger tour operators have bought and/or created retail agencies. The obvious advantage with this is that it allows a stronger influence on consumers' choices. This is done primarily in two ways. First, brochure racking space in the retail outlet is dominated by the associated tour operators' brochures. Clients will usually examine an average of between five and 15 brochures that will be pivotal in their decision-making process (Carey and Gountas, 1999). Secondly, with around 1,000 tour operators in the UK, the average client is unlikely to be aware of the majority of companies and the proliferation of choice is extremely confusing. Therefore, trust is often placed in the advice of relatives and friends, and sometimes in the advice of travel agents themselves. Although there seems to be a suspicion of tour operators and associated agents, the retail outlets are used as a point of convenience (Carey and Gountas, 1999). In fact, the distribution chain is set up in a way that leaves the consumer with little choice but to use an intermediary for their booking, thus ensuring some control over the information and advice that are readily available to clients.

  The issue of directional selling has often been raised in the travel trade press and frequently denied. However, personal experience would suggest that it does occur and is likely to continue whether or not the practice is in the best interests of the client. Electronic means of retailing travel products are now firmly in the supply chain, with Internet access to bookings as well as the emergence of large call centres. These aspects are covered more fully in Chapters 5 and 17 of this book.
- *Backward integration.* Backward integration means that a business moves up in the chain to acquire a supplier. This gives organisations easier access to resources and tighter control on the availability of these resources to the competition. For example, tour operators that are vertically integrated with airlines will receive preferential rates and allocations on flights. Since the flight component comprises a large part of the cost of the package, the advantages of this type of integration are obvious.
- *Related diversification.* This is where a company acquires or creates another business that does not have products or customers in common with its current business but that might contribute to internal synergy through the sharing of facilities, brand names,

Figure 4.2   Porter's elements of industry structure

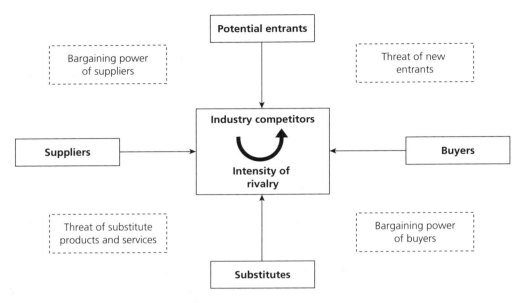

Source: Porter (1980)

research and marketing skills (Walker et al., 1999: 47). This might be illustrated with some operators' move into sectors such as financial services.

■ *Unrelated diversification.*   Obviously, this indicates diversification that has nothing in common with the existing business. This type of diversification in the tour operating industry is quite rare, although there have been examples of various banking and other financial institutions either taking over or becoming a major shareholder in a tour operator.

The key issue, as always, is competition, and Porter's five forces model (Porter, 1980) helps to highlight some salient issues (see Figure 4.2). The elements of the five forces model are shown in Table 4.6.

Some authors consider that Porter's five forces model fails to take into account modern business conditions (Thurlby, 1998). However, as with any model or theoretical framework, if we use Porter's model as a guideline to be adapted as appropriate for the situation or conditions that we wish to analyse, it provides a useful basis for understanding the salient characteristics of the tour operating industry. It is important to remember that the key issues and determinants within Porter's model should not be treated as a discrete list, but viewed as a dynamic with covariance among its components. The level of relevance of individual components depends on the nature of the industry and its prevailing conditions.

It is easy to see that with the dominance of the four larger operators the *entry barriers* would be prohibitive for most companies other than those of a highly specialist nature.

Table 4.6 Elements of the five forces model

Entry barriers	Rivalry determinants
Economies of scale	Industry growth
Proprietary product differences	Fixed costs/value added
Brand identity	Intermittent overcapacity
Switching costs	Product differences
Capital requirements	Brand identity
Access to distribution	Switching costs
Absolute cost advantages	Concentration and balance
Proprietary learning curve	International complexity
Access to necessary inputs	Diversity of competitors
Proprietary low-cost product design	Corporate stakes
Government policy/other legislation	Exit barriers
Expected retaliation	
Determinants of supply power	**Determinants of substitution threat**
Differentiation of inputs	Relative price performance of substitutes
Switching costs of suppliers and firms in the industry	Switching costs
Presence of substitute inputs	Buyer propensity to substitute
Importance of volume to supplier	
Cost relative to total purchases in the industry	
Impact of forward integration relative to threat of backward integration by firms in the industry	
Buyer power–bargaining leverage	**Buyer power–price sensitivity**
Buyer concentration versus firm concentration	Price/total purchases
Buyer volume	Product differences
Buyer switching costs relative to firm switching costs	Brand identity
Buyer information	Impact on quality/performance
Ability to backward integrate	Buyer profits
Substitute products	Decision makers' incentives

Source: Porter (1980)

The four larger operators dominate both supply, particularly airline seats, and distribution, through their integrated chains. The larger operators' strategy of mixed market segmentation, acquiring companies from the full range of product offerings – flight only, basic packages to popular destinations, age and life-cycle targeted products, special interest, 'up-market' brands, cruises and more – means that they are able to compete with almost all other companies on all levels. The mergers between UK companies and foreign organisations provide greater financial security as well as cost advantages and leverage related to bulk buying. The travel industry has always been subject to conditions beyond the control of the operator, as previously mentioned. The larger operator which has the support of its associated companies is likely to be in a better position to survive downturns in booking patterns.

The tourism industry has grown rapidly since the advent of mass travel in the 1960s and it continues to grow steadily, albeit at a slower rate, with new markets constantly developing. Even so, there is still greater supply than demand. This is evident if we compare the number of seats that organisations are licensed for in any given period and the actual number of passengers. The fact that National Tourism Organisations are so desperate to attract new business that they are willing to give incentives to tour operators confirms this point. These conditions characterise the *rivalry determinants*.

The concentration and balance of the four larger operators is overwhelmingly powerful for the majority of other operators. The larger companies have always used very aggressive rivalry tactics and continue to do so. Creating awareness of small companies can be problematic. In ongoing research conducted by Gountas and Gountas (1998–2002), consumers consistently claimed to deliberately resist advertising. In fact the outdoor advertising campaigns of a major operator were completely unnoticed by the sample. Carey and Gountas say, 'TV advertising was considered to be most effective in increasing company awareness. It also seems to have an effect on supporting a positive image of the company' (Carey and Gountas, 1999: 73).

Given the extremely high cost of TV advertising in the UK and throughout most of Europe, this means that smaller, independent companies cannot consider this medium. Also, there would be a high level of wastage for companies with a niche appeal. So for these companies, building on existing relationships, word-of-mouth recommendation and working with associations such as AITO and the Campaign for Real Travel Agents (CARTA) are probably the only solutions.

The most important threat to small independent operators in the UK is now whether their interests will be overshadowed and/or controlled by groups owned by German shareholders which is the concern expressed by AITO's deputy chairman, Noel Josephides.

Of course, we must consider that 35% of volume is controlled by 99% of industry. If size is important, and the discussion indicates that in competitive terms it is, we would need to consider that many of the 99% carry very few passengers and some even operate just one trip per year. Most companies within the 99% do not pose any threat to any brand under the auspices of the main four. In fact, the first 40 licence holders on ATOL's list include several companies that are owned by the first four.

Transport and accommodation are the two essential components of a package holiday. Porter identifies supplier concentration, volume, costs and vertical integration as critical aspects of *supply power*. The larger groups have the power to control the majority of leisure air traffic through their own airlines, thus severing any possibility of serious threat from any other operators who offer flights as part of the package.

Tour operators' investment in accommodation is a fairly recent practice, which is perceived as a threat by other accommodation suppliers. This, added to the oversupply of accommodation that exists in most destinations, means that suppliers are very aware of their weak position. A Greek hotelier with more than 20 years' experience put it simply: 'We need the business, they (the tour operators) know that and we have to co-operate with them. If we don't, they simply go elsewhere. There's always another hotel who will sign contracts at lower rates.' For obvious reasons, the hotelier wishes to remain anonymous.

In most industries the *threat of substitutes* is ever present. The proliferation of choice available to the package holiday consumer would suggest that this is a threat. The reality is that, in true terms, this threat exists only for smaller independent operators in a significant way. The threat for larger operators is much more complex and much depends on the consumer's access to information and distribution. In theory, the consumer/buyer has the power to switch. Brand awareness is the issue here. For instance, if a buyer switches from Magic of Spain to Spanish Harbour Holidays, do they consciously recognise or consider that they are switching brands but not parent? Do they care?

It could be said that buyers have the ultimate *power* as they decide whether to buy, what to buy and when to buy. The reality is that the intricacies of the industry are confusing for many consumers and the main advantage of package holidays is the convenience factor. Bearing this in mind, it is difficult to envisage a time when the concept of the package is abhorrent to enough people to have a real impact on volume. Porter identifies the ability to backward integrate as being a key factor in determining the *buyer's power*. The issue of backward integration and its implication for the industry were discussed earlier.

Price sensitivity is a fundamental concern for tour operators, whether it is at the supply or buyer end of the chain. The already low profit margins and other financial management issues referred to earlier would suggest that there is little room for manoeuvre in terms of further lowering of costs or selling prices. Let us now turn to pricing strategies.

Pricing strategies

It cannot be said that a state of *pure competition* exists in the travel industry. Buyers and sellers in the travel industry most certainly affect each other and the industry as a whole through their individual activities. The tour operating sector can currently be described as *monopolistic competition* as it has many buyers and sellers offering a range of products and prices competing through branding and product and price differentiation strategies. However, the dominance of the four large groups indicates a move towards *oligopolistic competition* with a few sellers controlling the majority of the market (Kotler and Armstrong, 1999).

Most companies are under great pressure to produce desirable results for shareholders, hence the emphasis on financials such as pre-tax profit. Most company reports highlight only those accounting ratios that give a favourable impression of the company's performance. In the case of tour operations, acid test and gearing ratios applied to the majority of annual accounts would give rise to concern if normal financial management rules were applied.

To cope with the conditions highlighted above, most firms employ a mix of strategies that are trying to balance price–quality perception – the impression of good value with a 'fair' comparison to competitors in a highly price-sensitive market.

Tour operators have to manage complexities not experienced by other consumer industries and in addition accept a low return on turnover at 2–3% in order to remain competitive. According to the Civil Aviation Authority's Air Travel Organiser's Licence (UK) statistics, the average cost of a summer holiday, originating in UK, in 2001 was £441. This means a margin of just £8.

The revenue and volume figures show that the competition between the big operators continues to be intense.

Low-cost pricing strategies have prevailed in the UK for as long as most tourists can remember. Competition based on aggressive pricing has often been the precursor of turbulent industry conditions, typified by the 'boom and bust' of several operators, including the ILG group in the 1990s. British consumers enjoy lower package holiday prices compared with other European countries for a number of reasons:

- The UK has fewer restrictions on night flying than other countries, such as Germany, which allows greater use of aircraft. The average UK charter airline (or leisure airline as they now prefer to be called) operates an average of three return flights per day as opposed to two round trips per day from Germany.
- Flights from Scandinavia to popular destinations are longer.
- The season for UK consumers tends to be longer and with larger allocations than some other European countries which enables more favourable accommodation and resort services contracts.
- Differing booking patterns increase or decrease the risk to tour operators. British operators have gradually encouraged consumers to book earlier with a number of incentives, thereby reducing uncertainty. This again is reflected in the accommodation contract terms. (FTO, http://www.fto.co.uk)

Accommodation contract terms are affected by volume, season and 'what the market can bear'. This obviously depends on the economic conditions in the country that the tourists originated in, what has been acceptable as a price range and the past behaviour of the market. For example, an hotelier in Athens may have contracts with tour operators from UK, France, Germany, Scandinavia, the USA and Japan. The room rates will depend on past and predicted future trends that will take into account volume, season, whether there is valuable traffic during traditionally low booking periods, length of average stay, average 'extras' spend per client, whether the contract has any guarantee or is a 'sale or return' basis and what the other competing hotels are doing.

Price setting is a perennial headache for tour operators. Taylor (1998), in his article which takes a game theory approach to tour operators' price setting, states:

> The moves in the game are that operators first choose capacity for their whole range of package tours with a high degree of commitment, and then set brochure prices. Prices will be interdependent across each of the operator's range of packages because of the allocation of fixed costs, but will also embody some probabilistic element resulting from expectations about other operators' prices and quantities. This makes each operator's pricing behaviour similar to that of bidders in a sealed-bid auction, or rather, a large number of simultaneous sealed-bid auctions. (Taylor, 1998: 31)

Taylor argues that the operator is price setting with incomplete information about the competition's prices and quantities. Although tour operators insist, in theory, that their own contractual arrangements remain confidential, each one has a vested interest in finding out accurate information about other tour operators' contracts. This covert practice is simply part of gathering intelligence to support decision-making. How successful an individual negotiator/contractor will be in acquiring 'confidential' information will depend on the force of his/her operator in the marketplace, personal skill, and other tactics best left unmentioned!

Industry-specific issues such as exchange rates and fuel costs compound the precarious nature of forecasting and forward planning. Most tour operators try to obviate the negative effects of unfavourable fluctuations through the practice of 'hedging' or buying forward. This obviously needs a great deal of skill as overestimation is a very costly business. Forecasting allocation requirements is essential to operations, yet the aforementioned extraneous conditions often strike without warning and render business conditions chaotic and unpredictable.

The pricing structure of a package offered by a large, integrated operator has some inherent differences that influence all other strategic, product development and marketing decisions. The major differences are:

- The larger the operator, the greater the opportunities for economies of scale in supply-side contracts that will be reflected in competitive pricing at the consumer end. This synergetic advantage can be applied to the full product range, that is both the 'mass' and specialist product ranges across seasonal fluctuations.
- The small independent operators' supply contracts are more likely to include fewer blocks of non-returnable components. While this allows them to dispense with unused supplies without cost, it weakens their bargaining power. This is reflected in higher prices to clients.
- The large operator buys large blocks of supplies (accommodation, airline seats) over long periods of time, for example, perhaps spanning several seasons. Although there is a price advantage, this means that there are few variable costs in the costing. The mostly fixed-cost scenario creates an enormous pressure to sell through any pricing strategy necessary. This has resulted in *discount pricing* and *fluid pricing* strategies which have attracted considerable concern and criticism from other industry players and consumer watchdogs.
- Over the years there has been a move away from late discounts towards early booking discounts. For many years consumers had become 'conditioned' by experience to expect heavy discounts for late bookings. This practice created an unrealistic notion of what comprises 'value for money' for the British holidaymaker. It also caused insecurity and cash flow problems for organisations.

Most tour operators have tried to ameliorate this effect by offering early booking discounts and severely cutting last-minute discounts in order to 'retrain' the public. The Trading Standards Institute (TSI) has urged the tour operating industry to avoid 'discount madness'. Bruce Treloar, of Trading Standards Central, has said: 'Travel firms use this bait and trap mechanism, whereby the discount lures customers in but then they find there are certain restrictions. They are offered a slightly higher price and by then they think they have gone this far so they may as well take the holiday at that higher cost' (Treloar, http://www.tradingstandards.gov.uk, 29 December 2000).

- The Trading Standards Institute has serious concerns about fluid pricing. This technique means that prices are raised and lowered according to demand and may change daily.

Those who have enjoyed a discount in the past may be supportive of discount strategy, but a downside, according to the Trading Standards Institute, is that there are sometimes cases of artificially high prices shown in brochures so that discounts look even more attractive. In a press release issued on 7 March 2002, Trading Standards said that 'Holiday brochures are giving consumers no meaningful way of comparing prices and there is still a blatant lack of transparency in pricing'. Fluid pricing appears to be a direct breach of the 1992 Package Travel Regulations, as there is no accurate price in the brochure upon which consumers can rely.

The brochure is the operators' main selling tool and the TSI considers that the complicated pricing structures that may include supplements for room types, occupancy, flight times, etc., means that consumers have trouble working out the actual cost of the holiday. The TSI believes that this confusion also impairs the consumer's ability to compare prices between operators. The TSI's press release of 7 March 2002 states: 'The TSI believes all these measures are intended to confuse consumers, who already have real trouble in working out the actual price they will end up paying for their holidays. The deliberate lack of transparency is something the TSI, along with other consumer bodies, has campaigned hard against for many years.' Neither is the aforementioned array of supplements popular with the TSI. According to Bruce Treloar: 'It would seem tour operators continue to be intoxicated by that heady cocktail of misleading consumers to calculate the cost of their holiday, or compare prices between operators.'

A report in *The Independent* on 11 July 2002 indicates that the battle between the TSI and many operators is far from over. The number of supplements seems to be increasing. One complaint to the TSI claimed that a brochure advertised an apartment with a pool but when the customer came to book, the travel agent said there was a £20 supplement per person to swim! Such conditions have prompted a rise in complaints to the TSI from 12,551 in 2000 to 28,502 in 2001. The conclusion of this analysis is that the might of the larger companies is so great that the 'war' between the independents and integrated operators no longer has any relevance to the overall structure of the industry.

The Consumer

Hooley, Saunders and Piercy (1998) refer to a survey of major British companies that found evidence that many paid 'lip service' to customers' needs rather than real commitment:

> One hundred per cent of a sample of senior management from *Times 1000* companies said that customer satisfaction was their real measure of success. In fact, most measure performance by short-term financials like pre-tax profit, and only 60 per cent use any form of customer-based criteria to evaluate staff performance. (Hooley et al., 1998: 4)

This shows that there is a conflict between the principles companies *think* they should hold as their credo and what *actually* happens. Many organisations notionally believe in consumer research and conduct it to a limited extent. Research is often used to 'measure' consumers' reactions to advertising, new products or crisis situations such as September 11, 2001. However, well thought out, continuous, long-term research focusing on all aspects of performance, evaluation and satisfaction is frequently haphazard and inconsistent to the point that it becomes relatively meaningless.

The quality and level of consumer research among tour operators is very variable. Most, at least, conduct customer satisfaction questionnaires either on return flights or in the resort. These questionnaires are often administered through large marketing research companies. Tour operators cut costs by allowing the inclusion of so-called 'lifestyle' questions that will provide the marketing research company with information on general product preferences that can be sold to companies in other industry sectors. The questions that directly relate to the tour operator are often limited and provide little scope for the type of analysis that would yield in-depth information about their clients. Rather, the questionnaires give an overall snap shot of performance. Some operators conduct additional qualitative research to support their marketing mix decisions.

> Seventy per cent of executives said that the customer was their first or second priority. At the same time less than 24 per cent believed management time spent with customers was important and only 34 per cent saw it as important to train staff in customer service skills.

Again, we see contradictions between principle and practice. Qualitative research, in the form of focus groups (Carey and Gountas, 1999), indicated that some tourists feel that tour operators underestimate their intelligence and ability to evaluate marketing strategies. The consumers interviewed cited good customer care and service as the most important feature of an operator. 'The overseas representative's service is the most memorable aspect of the overall performance' (Carey and Gountas, 1999: 73). This expressed the need to feel secure and confident with the operator's problem-solving actions if necessary.

As the operator's overseas representatives are often the clients only face-to-face contact with the company, it is understandable that they are key to consumer satisfaction and company image. There are several websites which carry consumers' holiday feedback that attest to this. Sadly, many of the comments allude to the lack of concern, care, knowledge and experience of overseas representatives.

Perhaps the larger operators would claim that they build relationships with their clients through brand identity strategies and service provision but the scale of their businesses obviously means that the specific interests of all consumers cannot be catered for. Hence, the popular analogies which refer to the hoards of package holiday tourists.

A Thomson Holidays' statement 'Your holiday, your choice – the future of package holidays', dated 30 April 2002, says that more flexibility and choice is the key behind Thomson's new range of holidays for summer 2003. Thomson's managing director, Chris Mottershead, said:

Shoppers today appreciate choice. You don't just buy a coffee these days; you buy a latte, a cappuccino or an espresso. It's the same with cars or new homes and we believe the same applies to holidays. People will customise the holiday to suit their needs and they won't have to pay for anything they won't use. (http://www.tui.com)

Thomson Holidays are offering a range of optional services such as in-flight meals, transfers and pre-bookable seats, to name a few that carry supplements. According to the statement, this move is responding to customers' wishes which research revealed, and yet the use of supplements and complicated pricing structures is the cause of an enormous amount of complaints to TSI discussed earlier.

Finally, there is little evidence to suggest that most operators really behave any differently from the large companies in the survey discussed by Hooley, Saunders and Piercy (1998), and does it *really* matter to the consumers? By and large, package holiday-makers moderate their expectations according to their past experience and knowledge of the industry and believe that they are realistic in their analysis of what represents good value for money and acceptable levels of product offering (Carey and Gountas, 1999). In spite of attention drawn to consumer complaints through various watchdogs, the author's recent research, yet to be published, suggests that most holidaymakers feel adequately satisfied with the product they have bought.

Case Study 4.1   First Choice – stuck in the middle?

Background

In terms of Group Assets, First Choice currently stands as the fourth largest tour operator in the UK, although the company's annual turnover and customer base are considerably less than the three leaders (see Tables 4.4 and 4.5). The business, now known as First Choice, started in 1973 and traded as Owners Abroad for many years (http://www.firstchoice.co.uk). Under the umbrella name of Owners Abroad, the company acquired/merged with a number of other tour operators, such as Falcon, Sunmed and Sovereign, until 1994 when the company was restructured and re-branded as First Choice. The years between 1994 and 2000 constituted a recovery period, during which the company grew through a strategy based on acquisition, distribution and supplier relationships that resulted in a fully vertically integrated company.

First Choice's most recent acquisitions have been niche market and specialist operators, such as Hayes and Jarvis, Meon Holidays and Flexigroup. First Choice's portfolio now includes more than 30 tour operator brands. The new distribution strategy saw the development of regional and out-of-town holiday hypermarkets and travel agencies, bringing the total to approximately 337.

The year 2000 saw much consolidation within the European tour operating industry. First Choice did not participate in the mass-market consolidation of its competitors but set out to differentiate the company from the main competitors' strategies. It focused on diversification from the mainstream, with the acquisition of specialists and strategic alliances with companies such as Royal Caribbean Cruise Lines. There were developments in Canada and Europe also, which have strengthened the company's product offering and increased its attractiveness to its rivals.

Other operators' attempts to buy First Choice have so far been unsuccessful.

Current strategies

First Choice Group Managing Director, Peter Long, gave the analysts' presentation on current and projected performance in December 2002. (This can be viewed on the First Choice website: http://www.firstchoice.co.uk). To summarise, Peter Long drew attention to the First Choice business model which differs from those of its competitors in several ways.

First Choice has a policy of tight capacity management which is implemented in conjunction with pricing strategies which aim to increase profitability without over-dependence on early booking discounting. The strategy is driven by greater flexibility, particularly supply chain contracts, and higher containment of losses during the shoulder and low booking seasons. The company continues to focus on the development of its specialist products. In some areas, such as the marine division, First Choice enjoys an unrivalled position. The distribution strategy includes further development of e-commerce by increasing the breadth of the online product offering. The group's airline is following the strategy of increasing flexibility and a range of services such as scheduled and 'no frills' services.

Overall, the key to the future for First Choice seems to be in cutting cost bases through all links in the group's chain, differentiation through niche and specialist markets and in creating relationships which move away from the dependency on vertical integration that is typical of other operators. Peter Long is convinced that the company will be able to meet today's challenging circumstances positively.

The future

In future, tour operating will be shaped by the activities, mergers and acquisitions of the larger companies only. Smaller independents will only survive if they form alliances with suppliers, each other, independent distributors or if their product offering is highly specialised, appealing to small niche segments of the market.

In the short term it seems likely that the battle among the larger operators for market share will continue and the smaller independents will have no respite from their perpetual struggle to survive. Presumably, existing competition legislation will prevent more mergers that compromise the consumer's interests.

For a more creative view of the future of travel, see TUI AG's web page 'Visions of the future' at http://www.tui.com.

Conclusion

This chapter has examined some of the main issues currently impacting on the outbound, as opposed to the inbound and domestic, tour operations sector of the tourism industry. The implications of polarisation within the UK market, whereby there are a few dominant companies and many more smaller players, was considered. Tour operator diversification, which has met with differing results, was also discussed. The tour operating market, in the UK at least, is often described as mature and has reached a degree of saturation. Overseas expansion has therefore been a recent strategic focus for many of the larger tour operators and so this too received attention. Indeed, take-overs were shown to have led to a very different tour operating business from that which existed in the past. Other aspects covered in this chapter included the tour operating value chain and the consumer.

Discussion questions

1. Discuss integration within the tour operations sector from the point of view of the consumer.
2. Examine pricing issues faced by tour operators.
3. Is First Choice currently 'stuck in the middle'?
4. Is First Choice successful in its differentiation strategy?

Suggested further reading

Carey, S. and Gountas, Y. (1999) Changing attitudes to 'mass tourism' products: the UK outbound market perspective. *Journal of Vacation Marketing*, December: 69–75.

Pender, L.J. (2001) *Travel Trade and Transport: An Introduction*. London: Continuum.

Taylor, P. (1998) Mixed strategy pricing behaviour in the UK package tour industry. *International Journal of the Economics of Business*, 5(1): 29–46.

5 Managing tourism distribution

Lesley Pender

Chapter objectives

The purpose of this chapter is to examine the main issues confronting managers in relation to tourism distribution in a highly competitive environment. Having completed this chapter, the reader will be able to:

■ identify particular problems in relation to the distribution of tourism products and the major issues confronting tourism managers in relation to distribution
■ recognise how change within the tourism industry and its environment has impacted upon tourism distribution
■ appreciate ways in which appropriate distribution channels can be selected and managed more effectively

Chapter contents

Introduction: the importance of successful distribution in tourism

Taking a management perspective, this chapter aims to outline the main challenges in relation to the distribution of tourism products and to examine some of the means by which such challenges can be met. The chapter starts by looking at the reasons why the successful management of distribution is important in tourism, before considering particular problems in relation to the distribution of tourism products. This leads to a consideration of the tourism industry and its environment, and in particular to change in this environment. The focus then turns to a more detailed examination of the application of distribution theory by tourism businesses in light of these changes. The chapter primarily explores ways in which the choice of distribution alternatives can be addressed and, once selected, how these can be managed more effectively. Developments in the area of distribution are highlighted, together with their implications.

Both theoretical and practical perspectives on the management of tourism distribution changed markedly during the last two decades of the twentieth century and this is reflected in the literature. In part, this has stemmed from developments in both the broader area of services marketing and in the field of information and communications technologies (ICTs). In line with other areas of tourism management, a number of issues have increased the complexity of managing distribution. Particularly significant for distribution has been the emergence of new channels. Together with altered power structures, these have led to changed priorities in terms of distribution. These issues are addressed later in this chapter.

Distribution has become far more important in terms of managerial decision-making in recent years. This has, in part, resulted from the influence that this area of marketing can have on profitability and competitiveness. Indeed, for many tourism businesses distribution has become a critical aspect of strategic management. Distribution is also a vital link in the tourism system itself. The distribution function delivers both messages and services to the tourism market and in this way links tourism supply and demand. The reasons for the importance of successful tourism distribution are briefly outlined below.

1. *Narrow profit margins.* Many tourism businesses make only small profits yet distribution costs can be high and so distribution is an area where managers look to make savings where possible.
2. *Highly competitive sectors.* Several sectors of the tourism industry are highly competitive and distribution has become an area of competitive advantage for some companies.
3. *Intermediary power.* Intermediaries can have a powerful influence over consumers and their decision-making, so where middlemen are used, careful management of this aspect of the marketing mix is important.
4. *The global marketplace.* The challenges posed by the global marketplace offer further incentives to manage distribution appropriately. With new and often disparate markets now available, tourism marketers need to consider effective ways of reaching them.
5. *Perishability of the product.* A more traditional reason for the importance of successful management of the distribution function relates to the perishability of the tourism product and the associated requirement to remove any excess 'stock' at the last minute.

6. *Information intensity*. Tourism is highly dependent on information provision to aid the decision-making process for consumers and this partly helps to overcome difficulties stemming from the intangibility of the product (see below). It is important that information reaches consumers in appropriate ways at appropriate times. The importance of information in tourism distribution is discussed in more detail later.

Successful distribution is therefore highly important in tourism yet this is not always easily achieved, as the following discussion highlights.

Problems in relation to the distribution of tourism services

A number of factors make the distribution of tourism services especially problematic. The main ones are listed below.

1. *Intangible product*. When a tourism product is purchased the consumer does not receive a tangible product. Rather, it is a service that is offered for consumption. It is impossible to see, feel or taste tourism products prior to their purchase. As a result, tourism marketers are often portrayed as being challenged with selling 'dreams'. While this applies to some tourism products more than others, it leads to difficulties as it is merely information about tourism services that can be distributed in advance of participation in the service delivery.
2. *Expensive and high-risk product*. For many consumers, holidays represent a costly purchase with financial risk attached to their consumption. There is also inherent risk in purchasing a product that it is not possible to see in advance, let alone try out. This is clearly linked to the intangibility factor described above.
3. *No stock holding/display by middlemen*. Travel agents and other middlemen do not purchase stock. Only information is provided at the point of purchase. The risk remains with the producer rather than the distributor. The only display that is possible is that of brochures or other information relating to the product.

There are therefore strong arguments for the careful management of the tourism distribution function. This challenge has been greatly aided in recent years by the development of electronic distributive techniques, which have enhanced opportunities to reach both new and old markets in new ways. At the same time this has increased the profile of distribution as an aspect of marketing. Electronic methods of distributing tourism products are considered in some detail later in this chapter, but first the view that information plays a pivotal role in the distribution of tourism products is explored further.

The role of information in tourism distribution

Recent changes in society have, according to O'Connor (2001), highlighted the importance of getting appropriate information to consumers as they search for detailed information in an attempt to minimise the gap between their expectations and subsequent experience. Indeed, O'Connor goes as far as to claim that those suppliers who best satisfy consumers' information needs are those most likely to be selected and subsequently booked. However, he also states that information alone is not enough and that a booking mechanism is also required.

Paradoxically, information not only aids the selection process but can also compound the difficulty of choice. It does, however, provide reassurance against the risk inherent in some tourism purchases. Management of the information flow is thus a crucial aspect of tourism distribution.

Intermediaries in tourism

The tourism industry has traditionally been characterised by its use of intermediaries. Travel agents have long been the friendly face of travel distribution. Their estimated share of the UK tourism market is shown in Table 5.1. Despite the dominance in the past of travel agents as middlemen to the tourism business, other types of intermediary have also come to be associated with the industry, for example hotel marketing and booking schemes, travel clubs, incentive travel organisations and sales representatives. More recent developments have included the ICTs such as the Internet, computerised reservations systems (CRS) and global distribution systems (GDS). Taken together, these represent a greatly increased choice of distributive methods than was available in the not so distant past. We will return to some of these forms of distribution later.

Arguments both for and against the use of intermediaries have been postulated in the literature. Christopher (1992), for example, discusses these in general terms while Pender (1999) examines tourism with reference to the use of travel agents as middlemen. There are, however, problems associated with the use of middlemen. Controlling distribution, for example, has been a major issue for principals in the tourism industry. The more an organisation uses intermediaries and the more distant these are from the organisation, the more difficult it can be to control them. Cost issues have also emerged as some principals within the tourism industry have adopted a low-cost strategy and shown a preference for direct sales (any sale made without the use of an intermediary service can be said to be a direct sale).

Distribution channels

Tourism distribution channels link the different combinations of travel organisations involved in moving tourism products from producer to consumer. Clearly, the number and types of distribution channel used differ between organisations and by country. Channel choices in the tourism industry are influenced by factors such as the nature of the tourism products to be distributed and the levels of public sector involvement in tourism distribution. National Tourist Organisations (NTOs), for example, will have their distribution choices influenced by government structures. Levels of public sector involvement can vary greatly.

Relevant comparisons have been made between tourism distribution channels and those in the manufacturing industries (see for example Renshaw, 1997). There has,

Table 5.1   Estimated share of the UK tourism market accounted for by travel agents by value (1997)

	Travel agents (%)
Domestic tourism	11
Outbound tourism	38
Total	49

Source: Key Note Market Review (1998)

however, been little detailed consideration of the application of the theory of channel management to tourism businesses. The tourism literature is now addressing this gap.

While distribution is relatively simple for smaller tourism businesses such as those offering a single service, either directly or through one type of intermediary to one type of customer, most of the larger tourism organisations have more complex distribution strategies. Indeed, many larger tourism organisations use a variety of distribution methods. Typically, these reflect the different market segments that the organisation aims to attract.

Much has been written about dependencies between the different members of distribution channels in general and this literature is no less relevant in relation to tourism distribution channels. For example, many destinations and tour operators depend upon staff knowledge and enthusiasm, and the selling skills of travel agents, while travel agents themselves depend on tour operators for advertising, staff training, brochures and computerised reservations systems. Specialist tourism product providers have, as we have seen, fewer options in terms of distribution. Case Study 5.1 outlines distribution channels used by the independent tour operator Mark Warner.

Case Study 5.1   Mark Warner and the distribution of the specialised holiday product

Mark Warner has been operating for 28 years as an independent tour operator specialising in the following areas:

Market Specialisation	*Product Specialisation*
Adults only market	Winter ski holidays
Family market	Summer beach resorts
The product	(including watersports and other sporting activities)

Mark Warner summer resorts are all situated within a prime Mediterranean or Aegean beach setting and are for the exclusive use of Mark Warner guests. The 'package' sold includes free watersports activities, including both sailing and windsurfing with free tuition, award-winning childcare (free for children over two) and a children's listening service in the evenings, as well as tennis, aerobics, aqua aerobics, canoeing and volley ball, among other sports. Most activities are available at most resorts. Flights, accommodation, transfers, the use of swimming pools and all meals are also included in the price of a

Mark Warner holiday. Three of the beach resorts are reserved exclusively for adults at certain times of the year. Mark Warner holidays and flights are ATOL protected by the CAA and the company is a member of AITO.

Distribution

75% of guests come to Mark Warner by personal recommendation or through repeat bookings. The company produces two main brochures each year – the beach resort brochure for summer and the ski brochure for the winter season. Each brochure contains a brochure request postcard for readers' friends. The brochures are attractive, clear and informative.

Previous and existing customers are contacted regularly by mail in the form of newsletters and late availability fliers. The distribution of information about developments at resorts, snow conditions, etc. help to act as stimuli to motivate bookings. Sending this information out at different times helps Mark Warner to reach customers at appropriate points in any pre-booking consumer behaviour. Attempts are also made to foster good relations with these clients through pricing initiatives such as early booking offers or frozen price offers for previous customers. All of this helps to promote a 'club like' relationship with the customer.

Mark Warner also makes extensive use of the Internet to contact customers and potential customers. Email messages are sent providing details of late offers and other special offers. The company's website (www.markwarner.co.uk) offers potential customers the opportunity to view details of each of their chalet hotels, and for some properties their 360-degree viewer offers views of the bedrooms and public areas. While customers could not at the time of writing make bookings directly via the Internet, current updating of systems should mean that this will be possible for the 2004 summer season.

In addition to the more 'direct' forms of distribution outlined above, bookings can also be made via travel agents. Brochures are automatically sent to agents who regularly sell Mark Warner's holidays. The company also responds to requests for brochures from agents who are less familiar with their products, where, for example, a customer has made an enquiry to the agent who has then contacted the company. In such circumstances a brochure may be sent to the customer's home address and/or to the agent. Agents make bookings in writing either by completing a booking form or by providing some other form of written confirmation. Bookings are therefore not made using CRS. However, Mark Warner does have its own in-house reservations system.

Channel management issues

Rosenbloom (1987) adopts the term 'channel manager' to describe anyone involved in making distribution channel decisions, regardless of his/her job title. This is a useful approach, especially when considering the smaller organisations where formal roles may be less clear-cut. Bateson (1991) is among those who have moved the debate regarding channel management into the services arena. He describes the broadening of distribution channels to include more than the physical distribution characteristics that dominated the field in the past. The general literature highlights other channel management issues, including channel design strategies, member selection (i.e., the choice of middlemen), the management of conflict, the evaluation of member performance, power and the management of multiple channels.

Channel design

Channel design can cover a variety of variables. Light (in Bateson, 1991) suggests the following:

- the number of intermediaries;
- the types of intermediary;
- the allocation of value adding functions among the channel participants;
- the kinds of material and technological support that the participants use; and
- the service itself – its elements and the dimensions of those elements.

Member selection

A number of factors influence the choice of middlemen, including the company marketing/distribution strategy, the customers to be targeted, the products themselves, costs and market characteristics. The latter might include the type and size of market, the distribution of customers, customer purchasing power and patterns, etc. Field sales forces can help companies such as airlines and shipping companies find new channel members.

The management of conflict

Conflict between different organisations within the distribution chain can occur. Indeed, a degree of conflict is almost inevitable where intermediaries are used, and it is necessary to manage this in an appropriate manner. The interdependence of channel members, who can have incompatible aims can influence levels of co-operation and so result in channel conflict. It is important to acknowledge and identify the causes of conflict, which can operate at different levels. It is also important to recognise that not all such conflict has negative effects. Therefore, acceptable levels of conflict should be set.

Evaluating member performance

The evaluation of channel member performance is increasingly important for cash-constrained organisations within the tourism industry, including those organisations that have had their public sector resource allocations reduced. The instigation of performance measurements by some tour operators, for example, has led to a withdrawal of certain companies' brochures from particular travel agents' shelves. Organisations must ensure that the evaluation criteria they select (e.g., selling skills and attitude) are suited to the organisation's needs.

Power in distribution channels

The major tour operators display a large degree of control over sales outlets and other distribution channels in the UK. They even have a dominant position when it comes to price bargaining with resort hoteliers and this, in turn, can influence customer choice as it leads to standardisation in order to keep prices down. The control brought by ownership of multiple travel agents in the UK by major tour operators is discussed in Chapter 4 and is covered more fully by Pender (2001).

Poon (2001) describes the power of important suppliers relative to most travel agencies as overwhelming. This she attributes to the fact that suppliers pay the agents while consumers are told that the services of the agent are 'free'. Agents therefore carry little risk in terms of inventory. Poon also suggests that agents are still dependent on the airlines for much of their revenue and that supplier power advantage also stems from the GDS. Despite both this and the fact that airlines have greatly reduced the payment of commissions to travel agents, airlines have little, if any, pricing power over GDS – the middlemen that they themselves created (O'Toole, 2002).

Managing multiple channels

O'Connor (2001), writing about distribution in relation to hotels, points to the difficulty of managing multiple channels. He describes the importance of consistency of offerings across channels as customers increasingly visit multiple sites and undertake comparison shopping. Price differences or other inconsistencies of offering across different distribution channels without good reason can alienate the customer.

Distribution channels can be independent organisations and their management requires a level of interaction between different players in the system, as was seen earlier. A particular issue in terms of services, stemming from their intangibility, is the impact that channel choice can have on cost and perceived value as customers tend to look for clues from these. The channel itself can have the power to influence travel decisions. For example, an up-market agent dealing with high-class products may, for some consumers, appear to offer security against the risks inherent in tourism purchases.

Research has been conducted to identify the optimal means of organising and managing distribution channels, and has identified the behavioural concepts of dependence, co-operation, power and conflict as having an impact on channels of distribution (Ujma, 2001). These aspects were introduced above. The skills of co-operation, co-ordination and the management of integration are particularly necessary in operating such channels. Stern et al. (1996) have described issues involved in the management of interdependent institutions and agencies.

Industry restructuring and its effect on the management of distribution

As suggested above, a great deal of change has been occurring in the tourism distribution environment and reasons for this include: (1) increased levels of integration leading to consolidation in the industry and different ownership profiles (i.e., acquisitions, networks, mergers, consortia); (2) exponential growth in the use of electronic media; and (3) the fact that tourism organisations are becoming more international. These factors all point to a restructuring within the tourism industry in recent years. This section continues with a brief consideration of the management implications of such changes.

Integration and consolidation

A major change factor experienced within the industry has been the consolidation of travel agencies into larger groups and consortia. Take-overs, mergers and acquisitions have all contributed to this process. This has arguably been one of the strongest factors to influence the shape of the industry, in particular affecting domestic market shares and helping to forge international expansion. An objective of vertical integration has long been to control distribution. Principal chains have therefore taken over travel agents and so mass market tour operators have become powerful intermediaries while smaller independents often find it difficult to obtain distribution through their outlets.

Travel agencies themselves have often changed as a result of this trend towards consolidation. Although smaller agencies are still important, there are now far fewer of them and they are less influential. The ownership profiles of tourism distribution companies are also becoming increasingly international as a result of merger activity and this aspect is considered in more detail below.

A great deal of integration has occurred among organisations that are involved in the manufacture and sale of travel products and this has led to yet more change. These formal linking arrangements can be seen to occur both across and down the chain of distribution. Pender (2001) discusses the reasons for such integration in travel and tourism as well as the outcomes in some detail. It is worth noting here, however, that the extent of integration has been such that there are large tour operators now linked to major travel agency chains yet these linkages are not always recognised by customers. Smaller travel agents often find it hard to compete in this environment of ever larger tour operators owning travel agency chains and becoming increasingly global, and so many have joined consortia or become franchisees.

The growth of electronic media

The tourism industry has been affected more than most by information and communications technology (ICT). Indeed, a major aspect in the restructuring of the industry has been the new technology-based entrants into the travel distribution business. For example, a number of capabilities are offered to airlines by GDS, including economies of scale that individual airlines would struggle to achieve and seamless sharing with alliance partners (see Chapter 16). Particularly significant in terms of distribution, however, has been the emergence of new virtual intermediaries, including lastminute.com, which was set up as a travel company selling late holiday deals online.

Increased competition is paradoxically accompanied by more evidence of co-operation between tourism organisations. This is in part driven by the requirement to offer a range of products through electronic means of distribution. Virtual alliances are therefore being formed to meet consumer demand for complete product offerings online. Once again this points to a restructuring stemming from the fragmented nature of the industry.

Barnett and Standing (2001) believe that consolidation offers greater opportunities for improved access to the necessary skills and resources to develop an effective online presence. They assert that 'the rapidly changing business environment, largely brought about by the Internet, will require companies to quickly develop new affiliations and alliances, have access to new products and be creative in their thinking' (Barnett and Standing, 2001: 150).

Internationalisation

In the past decade there has been a significant shift towards cross-border operations in the travel distribution industry. Mergers and acquisitions have been greatly responsible for the internationalisation of the industry. Dominant international groups have either emerged or consolidated their positions within Europe where international expansion of the major tour operators has been great. In the UK, for example, Thomson Travel Group, which has long been a main player in the industry, is now under German ownership. This change in the industry (introduced in Chapter 4) has in part been fuelled by the larger organisations outgrowing their domestic markets. The growth in electronic media has also influenced the ability of larger airline carriers and groupings of carriers working together to distribute their services on a global basis.

Especially in the growth area of business travel, it is becoming important for specialist business agencies to have a global presence. As business travel becomes more multinational there is a need for more global business travel agencies. This could negatively influence the competitiveness of smaller companies.

Stemming from these changes in the distribution environment are further related issues, including the implications of the increased use of technology, new competitors, different customer requirements, changed prices, 24-hour distribution, equality of access to remote suppliers (such as destinations) and changed bargaining power in supplier relations.

Management implications

Poon (2001) is among those authors to suggest that changes in the sector are forcing a number of travel agents to re-evaluate their traditional role. Providing customers with added value and fee-based services have become relevant issues. Some of the implications of the changed distribution environment are challenges common to all types of organisation, while others are specific to the tourism organisation.

Management challenges for the traditional middlemen, travel agents, include the development of new skills, investments in technology and the creation of sustainable competitive advantage. Travel agents represent a key influence in the tourism marketing system and so marketers need to develop an understanding of factors that can influence travel agency recommendations (Hudson et al., 2001). Despite this, surprisingly little research has been conducted on this intermediary in the tourism industry. This is despite the fact that the distribution of inclusive tours has come under close government scrutiny, with directional selling being a concern of the Monopolies and Mergers Commission (MMC), now the Competition Commission. Even the outcomes of this scrutiny have been debated by some (Pender, 2001).

Poon (2001) has looked at alternative services to travel agencies, describing many of these as having offered only partial substitutes in the past. For example, airline consolidators became suppliers to the travel agencies. Hotel reservations services and cruise-only companies similarly have focused on limiting their product line, unlike Internet travel agencies which can be considered to be more complete substitutes.

Despite the above, there remains potential for yet more structural change in the industry, leading to further implications for management. Particularly threatening to travel agencies are prospects of continued disintermediation by primary producers and the emergence of new virtual intermediaries, as described by Barnett and Standing (2001). The term 'disintermediation' refers to the effective removal of middlemen from the chain of travel distribution. There is increasing evidence of suppliers selling direct to the consumer and so 'cutting out the middleman' (see Pender, 2001). Further significant moves have led to the increased speed and convenience of reservations and payments, as well as worldwide access to reservations systems. It is not only the supply side that is changing. Customers themselves are becoming far more sophisticated and often more demanding.

According to Mintel (2000), in the space of a decade the economic dynamics of business travel distribution have changed drastically. The relationship between travel agents and their clients has changed as travellers or their travel arrangers can book flights and hotels independently without losing value for money. Where travel agents used to work on a commission basis and could offer cost savings due to their buying power, they are now increasingly becoming vehicles for corporate travel policies paid on a fee basis. Indeed, as many as 90% of Carlson Wagonlit Travel's 2,000 corporate clients pay a management fee.

There is general agreement in the literature (Pender, 1999; Poon, 2001) regarding the sorts of strategy that travel agencies should be pursuing in the competitive environment. Market specialisation, product specialisation and information provision in particular have received a great deal of attention. Increased opening hours, the sale of non-core products, better service provision, more innovation and the development of strategic alliances with other agencies and suppliers offer further possibilities for some. Barnett and Standing (2001) reach similar conclusions in relation to online developments favouring product specialisation (whether by market, destination or activity) or information specialisation.

Value chain approaches

The value chain is an analytical tool, described by Porter (1987), which traces the process of value creation in an industry through understanding the role of each player in the industry. Poon (1993) applied this theory to the tourism industry, describing six primary activities and five support services which all create value (Figure 5.1). The travel agent clearly adds value through his/her role in customer services, including information processing, counselling travellers and preparing itineraries. Tour operators similarly control a number of activities along the value chain, as was shown in Chapter 4, and where vertically integrated this can include the distribution function. Davidson (2001: 81), discussing business travel, expresses the view that 'rapidly, the agent's contribution to the value chain is becoming less about sharing commission and issuing tickets and more about providing strategic advice about supplier selection and managing travel policies for clients'.

Relationships with intermediaries in tourism have changed greatly in recent years, particularly as airlines and other principals have forged ahead with cost-cutting programmes. This is likely to continue in the short term, at least as organisations become more selective in the management of their distribution.

Outsourcing distribution in the airline industry

Airlines such as British Airways have opted to outsource core systems, including inventory, in-house reservations and departure control systems. These systems were previously viewed as key areas of differentiation for the organisation. A downturn in business, however, has prompted airlines to turn fixed information technology (IT) costs to variable costs by handing control of these systems to global distribution systems (GDS). Airlines are not alone in pursuing this strategy. Banks have also favoured outsourcing certain aspects of their business. Other examples can be observed in the hotel industry. O'Connor (2001) describes the outsourcing of hotel companies' central reservations functions, which require a transaction fee to be paid per call answered or reservation processed. This option can therefore become expensive as the volume of bookings through this channel increases.

Keen to avoid disintermediation, Amadeus, Europe's largest GDS, is attempting to reposition itself as a 'technology business partner' for airlines. It provides:

Figure 5.1 The travel and tourism value chain

PROFIT   MARGIN

PRIMARY ACTIVITIES

Services on site	Transportation	Wholesale packaging	Retail distribution	Marketing & sales	Customer service
• Airport transfers	• In-flight service	• Brochure production	• Travel Agency Management	• Frequent flyer/Customer loyalty programmes	• Complaint management
• Selection and control of third-party services	• Gate operations	• Brochure distribution	• Assortment strategies	• Advertising, PR, promotions	• Direct mail
• Repair & maintenance	• Baggage handling	• Commission negotiations	• Brochure display	• Marketplace representation	• Key account management
• Tours & attractions	• Ticketing	• Package pricing	• Information processing	• Sales aids, trade shows	• Guest questionnaires
• Car & craft rentals	• Yield management	• Holiday packaging	• Reservations, confirmations	• Co-op advertising	• Client database management
• Health & beauty	• Seat pricing	• Inventory control	• Ticketing	• Familiarisation trips	• Itinerary development & management
• Sports	• Schedule management	• Travel agency training	• Customer advice	• Sales	• Vacation follow-up
		• Reservations and information handling			• Client advice

SUPPORT ACTIVITIES

Firm infrastructure	General management	Planning & finance	Strategic alliances	Mergers & acquisitions	Deregulation	Diagonal integration	Quality management
Human resources development	Recruitment	Training & education	Staff motivation	Salary & benefits	Staff turnover	Labour negotiations	Staff development
Product development	New Alliances & destinations	Yield management	New services & facilities	New markets	New market segments	New routes, hubs & spokes	Improved delivery of services
Technology and systems development	Computerised reservations systems		Research & development	New systems & procedures	Energy management	Engineering safety & security	Telecommunications & entertainment
Procurement	Equipment & supplies		Fuel, food, beverage	Contracted services	Professional services	Other services	Real estate & buildings

Source: Poon (1993: 211).

- a fast track to Internet sales;
- the capability to handle multiple sales channels;
- seamless sharing to alliance partners; and
- economies of scale that individual airlines would struggle to achieve.

Already airlines including British Airways and Qantas have handed over significant amounts of their commercial systems to be run by Amadeus (O'Toole, 2002).

Managing hotel reservations systems

Marketing and booking systems, also known as 'listings', essentially aim to take reservations on behalf of member properties. While hotels in some such schemes have been through a rigorous selection process and meet exacting standards, others offer far less reliable measures for consumers. Like many other distribution mechanisms, these options can be expensive, with annual fees plus commission to pay (sometimes per booking received). They can also be restrictive if membership prevents a hotel from using other schemes. Other mechanisms that require less commitment are the many directories and guides that are available. This area of distribution may become subject to more regulation in the future.

Managing the costs of distribution

Distribution costs in the tourism industry are high and so reducing these has necessarily become a key management concern. The effectiveness of GDS at reaching the travel agent market, for example, has to be measured against its high capital and transaction costs. O'Connor (2001) describes the transaction cost of electronic distribution as potentially problematic due to the number of intermediaries. A central reservations system (CRS), a switch company and a travel agent may all facilitate a booking and so wish to be compensated. EasyJet is one of several airlines to manage distribution costs effectively (see Case Study 5.2).

Case Study 5.2   EasyJet cuts the costs of airline distribution

Distribution is one of the main areas in which low-cost carriers, also known as 'no-frills' or budget airlines, have attempted to make the major cost savings that they can reflect in their prices. The means by which they have achieved this are examined here using easyJet as an illustration. EasyJet began business in November 1995 and quickly became a strong competitor to flag carriers. The following are some of the company's easily identifiable marketing and operational characteristics:

- one type of aircraft;
- point-to-point operations;

- short-haul travel;
- no in-flight catering;
- rapid turnaround times;
- high aircraft utilisation; and
- low distribution costs.

Low distribution costs, can be achieved for a number of reasons and these are now examined.

Cutting out the middleman

Methods used to cut distribution costs include cutting out the middleman. Budget airlines encourage the direct purchase of tickets, for example by telephone or online. Not all low-cost carriers sell direct to consumers but a high proportion of seats on 'no-frills' carriers are sold in this way, so removing the necessity to pay commission to travel agents. Unlike some, including the American carrier, Southwest Airlines, easyJet has avoided using travel agents altogether. Instead, the company has relied exclusively upon direct sales. EasyJet started with 16 reservations agents (all teenagers) operating out of the company headquarters, easyLand. In addition to English-speaking agents, there were French, Spanish and Dutch-speaking reservations agents based in Luton. Reservations agents were solely paid in commission.

Alternative channels used in the early days

This system was initially backed up with the extensive use of advertising and public relations. According to Sull (1999: 25):

> Because easyJet completely eschewed travel agents, the company relied heavily upon a variety of alternative marketing channels to raise awareness among potential customers. The company spent up to 8% of revenues on newspaper, magazine and radio advertising

to reach customers directly. The company also actively sponsored special promotions, such as providing a dedicated phone line for fans of London's Tottenham Hotspur football (soccer) team.

This initial strategy was aimed at making the market comfortable with direct sales. As demand grew, expenditure on advertising was cut. This use of promotional channels to back up distribution strategy serves to illustrate very well the overlap that exists between different components of the marketing mix.

Rejecting CRS

Budget carriers tend not to use CRS. Fees charged by these systems can be excessive for airlines operating on thin margins as a flat rate is charged regardless of the type of ticket being sold. Budget carriers tend not to want to entertain such high distribution costs per ticket. EasyJet avoids these costs, preferring to encourage consumers to use the Internet. Indeed, the company has used differential pricing in an effort to increase Internet bookings.

Ticketless travel

In addition to cutting out commission to middlemen, ticketless travel also increases productivity by freeing up check-in staff as well as removing the actual cost of the ticket. EasyJet are fully ticketless. Instead, a reference number is issued and the passenger merely shows identification at the airport.

Lack of interline agreements

Low-cost carriers also keep costs down through the lack of ticket and baggage interline agreements with other airlines. This helps budget airlines such as easyJet to maintain simple booking systems.

Removing tickets, travel agents (and their commissions) and global reservations systems from their distribution strategy enables savings of around 25% of the cost of a flight. This clearly helps easyJet to undercut major carriers and compete more effectively in the competitive airline environment that now exists in Europe.

Sources: Feldman (1997) and Sull (1999)

Commission capping

Commission capping is one means by which savings in the cost of distribution are being made. Poon (2001) discusses the reduced levels of commission being experienced by travel agents, referring to IATA's estimation that selling costs have become the biggest cost for international airlines with distribution accounting for 23% of their members' operating costs, including 11% for commission and 4% for CRS charges. IATA also believes that Europe will follow the US example of commission capping, which has been estimated to be saving their airlines US$1 million a day. Poon (2001) states that seven US carriers have joined forces to cap travel agency commissions at $50 for domestic round-trip tickets costing over $500 and $25 for those costing over $250. This would prevent commission on high-priced tickets subsidising the high volume, low commission business of low-cost competitors and is estimated to save the seven carriers a considerable amount in commission payments. Many of the largest business travel agents have been quick to restructure their remuneration from a commission basis to a management fee-based payment in response to commission capping. This is a development that seems likely to continue.

Conclusion

A number of issues can be identified in the services marketing literature that are relevant to the management of tourism distribution yet are outside the scope of a chapter of this length. These include empowerment, customer orientations and service quality approaches. Harrington and Power (2001) discuss these in some detail, providing an illustration of the application to tourism of the well-known Servqual model which helps companies to anticipate and measure customer expectations. This reflects the development of tourism distribution as a management area. The literature is now encompassing these developments and becoming more specialist, while at the same time offering broader perspectives on tourism distribution. Buhalis and Laws (2001), for example, consider distribution channel analysis for leisure and business travel, and highlight questions of ethics and sustainability in relation to distribution. The growing literature on distribution theory reflects the increased importance of this area of the tourism marketing mix.

Managers at all levels in the tourism industry need to recognise the expanding choice of distribution routes now available and how best to manage them. A network of mutual dependencies can be seen to link tourism distribution channel members. Technological advances have undoubtedly helped to increase the popularity of distribution as an aspect of tourism marketing. The application of services marketing theory to the tourism distribution area has also helped to move this field forward both as a practical area of business management and as an academic subject. Further research examining the management of the distribution function in tourism is now likely and would complement these two developments.

Discussion questions

1. To what extent do you agree with the view that airlines should nurture technology partnerships with GDS rather than continue to manage them as an intermediary? Why?

2. Compare and contrast two different distribution forms for each of the following:

   - a small independent tour operator;
   - a fully integrated mass market tour operator;
   - a low-cost airline;
   - an owner-managed small resort hotel; and
   - an international hotel chain.

3. Examine the role of information provision in the distribution of tourism products.

Suggested further reading

Buhalis, D. and Laws, E. (2001) *Tourism Distribution Channels: Practices, Issues and Transformations*. London: Continuum.

Pender, L.J. (2001) *Travel Trade and Transport: An Introduction*. London: Continuum.

PART 2: MANAGING TOURISM BUSINESSES

6 Human Resource Management in Tourism

Tom Baum and Jithendran Kokkranikal

Chapter objectives

The purpose of this chapter is to examine a number of key themes in the strategic management of human resources in tourism. Having completed this chapter, the reader will be able to:

- identify characteristics of tourism as they impact on the management of human resources
- appreciate the impacts of globalisation and the development of ICTs on human resource management (HRM) in tourism
- recognise the importance of quality, cultural context and the emergence of aesthetic labour in the management of human resources

Chapter contents

Introduction

The human resource dimension is one of the most important elements of any industry sector, none more so than in a service sector such as tourism, which is characterised by high levels of human involvement in the development and delivery of services or vacation experiences. Whatever means are employed to deliver tourism services to the customer, the role of human intervention (as individuals and groups) is almost universal. In this context, the management of employees is a critical function and one that, ultimately, determines whether a tourism organisation is competitively successful or not. Highly successful tourism organisations, particularly in the luxury end of the marketplace, invariably place considerable emphasis on the engagement, education and empowerment of their employees at all levels to deliver services that define or differentiate the organisation from others in the field. At the same time, parts of the tourism sector, alongside other parts in the economy, are making increasing use of technology substitution and the creation of an e-service environment, within which human mediation in the service process is reduced or eliminated. Electronic ticketing and check-in with airlines and hotels are examples of this process at work. However, effective organisations do use technology substitution in selected areas of their service delivery systems in order to focus the quality human touch in other areas, where it is, perhaps, more important.

In an era of increasing emphasis on quality, the delivery of service quality in tourism, and the human support such service demands, can be looked upon as a competitive opportunity and strategic issue. The role of human resources and its efficient management in creating quality has been widely recognised as one of the most important elements in improving an organisation's competitiveness. At the same time, the tourism industry worldwide is characterised by ambiguous attitudes to investment in human capital, inflexible employment practices and an unsustainable approach to human resources development (Jithendran and Baum, 2000). Often perceived as operational considerations (Baum, 1993), the management of human resources in tourism can be described as an example of *adhocism*. It is also an area of activity that has repercussions far beyond the operational domain in organisations and clearly impacts on the marketing and financial effectiveness of tourism organisations.

This chapter will address a number of key themes in the strategic management of human resources in tourism. We will attempt to give the reader a flavour for the strategic issues and concerns which underpin each area, while at the same time recognising that each of the issues identified merits fuller consideration. The reader will have the opportunity to delve deeper into each topic, as appropriate. The themes are:

- the characteristics of tourism as a sector and their impact on the management of human resources;
- tourism's image as an employer;
- skills shortages in tourism;
- education and training in tourism;
- flexibility and innovation in the management of human resources;

- recruitment, retention and turnover;
- rewards, benefits and compensation;
- managing quality through human resources;
- the impact of globalisation;
- cultural contexts;
- the emergence of aesthetic labour; and
- the impact of information and communications technologies (ICT).

The characteristics of tourism as a sector and their impact on the management of human resources

In many respects, our consideration of this relatively wide agenda relating to human resources in tourism is predicated upon the first theme, that of the impact that tourism's characteristics as a sector have upon the management of human resources. It can be argued that virtually all the challenges faced by the sector are a consequence of the structure and operating features of tourism. Therefore, we will concentrate on this aspect in order to set the scene for the others.

The big challenge in tourism is that it is difficult to define the typical travel, tourism and hospitality organisation. This is, in part, because tourism is an amalgam of sub-sectors such as transport, accommodation, attractions, services and tourism facilitation, each of which consists of a number of different groups. For example, the transport sub-sector includes organisations that operate airlines, railways, ferries and cruise ships, bus and coach companies, care hire and taxis as well as organisations that provide infra-structure for these – airports, bus terminals, ports. It also covers private transport by car, bicycle and on foot. In addition to this diversity within each sub-sector, tourism organisations vary according to size (from major multinationals to micro, one-person businesses), ownership (public, private) and location (local, national, international).

Tourism organisations also vary greatly across national boundaries. There are some emerging global or multinational companies in tourism, and the sector is affected by trends towards globalisation in business, for example, the major airline alliances such as Star and Oneworld. However, the vast majority of operators are greatly influenced by the political, economic, socio-cultural and technological context within which they are located, generally at a national or local level. They are subject to variation as a result of differing political conditions, varying company and consumer laws and the influence of cultural considerations, for example, attitudes to alcohol in Islamic countries.

Tourism organisations also operate within a highly volatile demand environment, primarily exhibited through seasonality (Baum and Lundtorp, 2001) but also through demand fluctuation within the week (business hotels and airlines at weekends face a major downturn) and within any working day. This characteristic demand curve imposes significant constraints on the management of human resources within tourism and underpins many of the issues faced within the themes that we address later in this chapter.

Tourism organisations belong within the service sector of the economy. They are, therefore, very different in the way they operate and how they are organised from organisations which focus on the processing and production of manufactured goods. There are particular features of service organisations, and the services that they provide for their customers, which differentiate them from the manufacturing sector. These features establish the parameters within which people work and are managed in tourism. The characteristics of tourism service operations include the following features.

■ *Most tourism services include a significant intangible component.* Most services are intangible in that you do not receive something physical or tangible in return for your money. You are buying an experience and the evaluation of this experience may include a strong subjective element as well as aspects that you can judge objectively. The punctuality of an airline's service can, generally, be measured objectively, while the quality of the service offered on board is much more subjective. The human contribution to the delivery of both tangible and intangible aspects of tourism services is core.

■ *Tourism services cannot be inventoried.* If left unsold, the sales opportunity for a service is lost. A hotel room left unsold overnight or an empty seat on a theme park ride is lost revenue and an opportunity that can never be recouped. In other words, services cannot be inventoried or stored in the manner that many non-perishable manufactured goods can be held in a warehouse until trading conditions become more favourable. This reality has a major impact on how service organisations, especially those in the tourism sector, organise themselves, particularly with respect to sales and marketing. This feature induces a constant level of stress into tourism operations and this impacts upon employees in that they are constantly required to respond to short-term sales requirements. The operation of effective yield management systems by, for example, the low-cost airlines can reduce this pressure on the individual to a considerable extent.

■ *Tourism services are time dependent.* Tourism services are frequently prepared/produced, served and consumed almost simultaneously, frequently within sight of, and possibly with the participation of, the customer in a way that is infrequent in manufacturing. The human contribution within this process is critical.

■ *Tourism services are place dependent.* Many tourism services must be offered to the customer where they are required. Delivery and production cannot take place remotely or in a centralised location. Hotels must be located where people want to stay and not where it suits the hotel company. The emergence of e-technology means that this consideration is no longer as absolute as it once was. Sales/reservations, customer services departments (call centres) and financial processing operations are examples of service functions that are no longer location dependent. As a result, many European and North American companies are locating these functions off-shore, in countries such as India where language barriers do not exist and where technology literacy is high. Place dependency impacts on the recruitment and welfare of tourism employees in that they are frequently recruited within the local host community of the tourism operation. This local dimension has implications for skills and training within the workforce and, in some cases, the ability of tourism organisations to deliver some of their services.

- *Consumers are always involved in the production process.* Simultaneous production and service inevitably involve the customer in aspects of the production process, overtly in the case of self-service facilities or restaurants where there is the opportunity to barbecue your own fish, but also in a more general sense. Fellow customers, whether friends or strangers, are part of the atmosphere or ambiance that we buy into when we go to a restaurant or attend a concert.

- *Tourism services cannot be quality controlled at the factory gate.* Tourism services are difficult to standardise because they generally require a high level of human intervention for their delivery and are, thus, subject to variability because of the human element. As a result, you cannot return or substitute a service which has been unsatisfactory in the way that you can seek to exchange a faulty good such as an umbrella or personal stereo. Once your experience of a service is concluded, the provider can seek to compensate you for a bad experience but cannot replace the experience.

- *A different concept of marketing is required for tourism services as a total organisational function (relationship marketing).* Most staff in a tourism organisation have the opportunity to work in direct contact with the customer or operate in very close proximity to customer service points. This means that the marketing role is the responsibility of all tourism staff in the organisation and cannot be confined to a dedicated marketing unit.

- *There is a human role in tourism service delivery or mediation which creates a degree of uncertainty and unpredictability.* Human behaviour, whether staff or customer, is unpredictable although good management and effective training should minimise this unpredictability among employees in good organisations. Human interaction at the point of production and service inevitably produces an element of uncertainty that is not faced on the factory floor in manufacturing or, at worst, can be eliminated through effective quality control.

These characteristics of services in general apply within the tourism sector in particular and contribute to the manner in which tourism organisations are structured and operate. They influence the operational culture of organisations and also how they market their services, how their finances are structured and, in particular, the management of people within organisations.

Tourism's image as an employer

Tourism employment is varied and includes many types of work, ranging from the routine (gardening, cleaning, retail) through to the technological (aircraft and theme park ride maintenance) and senior managerial (corporate executives in multinational organisations). It is therefore difficult to generalise about the sector's image as an employer. There is a tendency and danger to assume that its image is determined by lowest common denominator so that tourism is labelled with the image of routine, hospitality work in hotels and restaurants. However, tourism does have its glamour end in terms of work with airlines, in tour guiding and in the heritage sector. Tourism work, generally, does suffer from a lack of mystique brought about by the ease of access to the tourism production environment. Unlike factories, we can walk into and witness tourism operations in action on a daily basis and this certainly undermines the sector's image. This is compounded by the fact that tourism, for some of the structural reasons addressed above, is seen in some countries as a sector of low pay and transitory work (Wood, 1997). In some cultures, tourism is seen as a frivolous activity which does not merit serious career consideration and this undermines its attempts to recruit quality entrants.

Skills shortages in tourism

Baum (2002) has explored skills in tourism and concluded that the nature and relative level of skills in the sector are determined by the social, economic, political and technological context within which they operate. To talk of tourism as a low-skills sector has some validity in the developed world, but is meaningless in many developing countries. Likewise, to talk about absolute skills shortages in tourism is something which has relevance in the developed world. In most developing countries, there is no shortage of labour but the skills base that exists in the economy may not be tuned to effective tourism work. In developed countries, skills shortages exist as a result of the image problems that the sector has, demand factors such as seasonality and changes in the technical focus of education and training programmes within the college system.

Education and training in tourism

Education and training for tourism has developed, historically, over a period in excess of 100 years, with the burden of investment, in most countries, shared between the public sector (schools, colleges, universities, training boards) and private enterprises. The traditional focus was on the development of technical skills in core tourism areas and this remains the rationale and priority of programmes in many countries. Recognition of the need to complement technical with generic skills has emerged over the past two decades and is well represented in subject benchmarks for the sector in the UK (QAA, 2000). Investment in skills development in tourism is frequently justified on the basis of the small business structure of the industry and its geographical fragmentation. Yet the nature of investment has been such that the prime beneficiaries of public education in tourism and training through the training boards in the UK up to the early 1980s were and continue to be the major companies, organisations which, arguably, can cater for their own skills requirements. However, the case continues to be made for investment in skills development for tourism. Thomas and Long (2001) note what they see as a critical role for supported skills development in areas of economic regeneration if the benefits of new tourism employment are to assist the local community's employment needs.

If the argument that tourism work is essentially low-skilled in nature is sustained, questions must be asked about the level of public investment in skills development that has been targeted at the sector over the past 100 years. This analysis would draw upon Ashton and Green's (1996) critique of the economic benefits of vocational education. However, if tourism skills are recognised as rather more contextual in nature, such investment may be justified although the predominantly technical emphasis of much of its delivery may not.

The development of skills to meet the needs of various stakeholders in tourism is frequently seen as a partnership between the industry and the educational/training providers, with each playing a complementary role. The extent of their respective involvement depends upon the objectives and level of training as well as upon the system in which such training is located. Guerra and Peroni (1991) note a relatively homogeneous tourism industry in Europe but point to considerable diversity within the educational and training systems that operate alongside the industry, reflecting differences in national vocational education systems as well as diversity in the status and focus of tourism at a national or regional level. This diversity is clearly reflected in the structure of tourism skills programmes in different European countries. Within the German apprenticeship system, apprentices spend the majority of their training time in the workplace with a short, normally eight-week, release period to college within any one year. By contrast, NVQ and SVQ training in the UK is predominantly within the so-called 'real work environment' (RWE) of the college, with only limited formal and assessed exposure to the industry during the programme.

Higher-level education and training for tourism, and tourism generally, maintain a clear commitment to the development of skills designed to complement more generic educational and business development objectives. Gillespie and Baum (2000) consider the changing role of practical, vocational education within tourism degree programmes and note substantial retrenchment but not the elimination of this process. Busby (2001) analyses the content of tourism degrees in the UK and concludes that what he describes as vocationalism is a strong feature in provision. Such vocationalism includes the development of specific skills in tourism and travel-related areas and, Busby argues, these elements play an important role in ensuring the employability of graduates.

Flexibility and innovation in the management of human resources

The management of human resources in tourism is underpinned by traditions of authority and directive leadership. However, recognition of the importance of what Bateson and Hoffman (1996) call 'boundary-spanning roles' in tourism has led to a re-evaluation of the roles and responsibilities of frontline staff in many tourism organisations. Innovation in the management of people has accorded greater responsibility and authority to all staff on the basis that they play an important part in relationship marketing. This is reinforced by their key role in ensuring customer satisfaction and means that such responsibility is critical if they are to do their jobs in a manner that is responsive to customer needs and solves customer problems in a spontaneous and timely manner. Innovative responses see management relinquish many of the overt vestiges of authority through processes of empowerment (Baum, 1995) whereby boundary-spanning staff are given the role and authority to handle customer-related problems as they arise and as they see fit. Boundary-spanning, which involves employees undertaking totally different functional roles, for example operational versus relationship marketing, is now becoming increasingly common in the service sector.

Such innovation in the management of human resources requires considerable investment in the recruitment of appropriate staff and their training in both hard competencies (the ability to deliver the product component) and in soft competencies, such as judgement, complaints handling and problem-solving. Such skills demands may be incompatible with the realities of a seasonal tourism business facing high labour turnover and offering little in the way of competitive remuneration.

Recruitment, retention and turnover

The mobility of staff within tourism is a direct factor of the wider environmental, structural and sectoral operating characteristics that we have addressed above. Sectors of tourism in some countries (particularly developed ones) face ongoing challenges to recruit appropriate staff, skilled and unskilled, to key positions in the industry. They also face challenges with respect to retaining these staff once they are recruited, and reducing what can be very high rates of labour turnover. The impact of variable demand (seasonality), issues of remuneration (see below), unsociable working conditions and generally negative perceptions of the sector for employment contribute to problems faced in this regard. Tourism is also an industry that is seen to be highly reactive to short-term local and international events in terms of its willingness to retrench staff in order to meet short-term financial requirements. The impact on travel and transport sectors in the immediate aftermath of events on September 11, 2001 is a major case in point. Potential employees may not wish to risk their long-term security in an employment environment that is perceived to be unstable.

At the same time, the small business environment within tourism means that the recruitment process may not always be conducted in such a way as to ensure the selection of the best and most suitable employees for the job. Limited credence is given to the outcomes of formal education and training while opportunities for workplace development are limited. As a consequence, the recruitment technique of internal promotion is not as widely used in tourism as it could be.

Rewards, benefits and compensation

The popular perception of the tourism industry in many developed countries is that of relatively poor pay (Baum, 1995; Wood, 1997). This is a reflection of a number of factors:

- perceptions of tourism work as synonymous with the large but not necessarily typical hotel and catering sub-sector;

- the low-skills environment of many jobs within tourism;
- limited workplace organisations in some tourism businesses, although this is not true of, for example, the traditional airline sector;
- seasonal and part-time work;
- the grey or 'tipping' economy within many tourism operations, undermining core remuneration;
- trends to de-skill work in tourism through technology substitution;
- accessible employment to the majority of the population through seasonal and other temporary work.

At the same time, tourism can offer highly remunerated and high-status employment within, for example, airlines. In the developing world, tourism employment may be highly prized, and its remuneration, relative to local conditions, is competitive with other opportunities in the economy. The experience of newly industrialised states such as Malaysia, Singapore and Taiwan, however, is that as the economy develops, the attractiveness and competitiveness of remuneration in tourism declines, presenting a real challenge to the sector in meeting its employment needs.

Managing quality through human resources

The importance of quality in the tourism industry has already been well established (Mahesh, 1993; Baum, 1997). The tourists of today are quality conscious, and the trend towards authentic experiences suggests that the provision of quality products and services is essential for the tourism industry to survive in an increasingly competitive international market (see Chapter 2). As a service industry, quality in tourism depends upon a range of human skills during the service encounter, recognition of which has resulted in the adoption of concepts such as managing 'moments of truth' (Carlzon, 1987) and developing a 'spirit of service' (Albrecht, 1992). Carlzon describes 'moments of truth' as the points of contact between the customer and employee of the company, and argues that these are the critical occasions which determine a customer's satisfaction in a service encounter. As Berry (1995: 89) observes, 'customers may not give extra credit to businesses for doing what they are supposed to do, rather they attach higher value to those that surprise with unusual caring, commitment, and resourcefulness during the service encounter'. Human resource management obviously plays a crucial role in developing quality service. The criteria of good, perceived service quality identified by Grönroos (1988) further underlines the important role of human resources in delivering service quality (Table 6.1). These criteria are professionalism and skill; attitudes and behaviour; access and flexibility; reliability and trustworthiness; recovery; and reputation and credibility. Most of these elements belong strictly to the human resource domain, but they are also relevant to the service quality in the tourism industry, especially professionalism, skills, attitudes and behaviour. As Poon (1993: 258) argues, 'while quality is a key determinant of competitive success in the travel and tourism industry, the key to quality in the travel and tourism industry is its human resources'. With the

Table 6.1 Criteria of good perceived service quality

No	Designation	Description
1	Professionalism and skill	Customers see the service provider as knowledgeable and able to solve their problems in a professional way
2	Attitudes and behaviour	Customers perceive a genuine, friendly concern for them and their problems
3	Access and flexibility	Customers feel that they have easy, timely access and that the service provider is prepared to adjust to their needs
4	Reliability and trustworthiness	Customers can trust the service provider to keep promises and act in their best interests
5	Recovery	Customers know that immediate corrective action will be taken if anything goes wrong
6	Reputation and credibility	Customers believe that the brand image stands for good performance and accepted values

Source: Grönroos, 1988, adapted by Johns, 1996: 15

increasing emphasis on quality, service industries such as tourism need to consider service quality as a competitive opportunity and a strategic issue (Gamble and Jones, 1991; Rapert and Wren, 1998). The efficient management of human resources has been widely recognised as one of the most important methods of improving quality (Horney, 1996: 70), and competitiveness.

The impact of globalisation

There are three kinds of globalisation: technological globalisation, political globalisation and economic globalisation. Globalisation makes distance a relatively insignificant factor in that it establishes long-distance economic, commercial, political and socio-cultural relations. It is more than simply a way of doing business or running financial markets – it is an ongoing process. Modern communication systems make the process easier. For example, the British and American service sectors are increasingly dealing with their customers through call centres in India. Another major manifestation of globalisation is the increasing power of global business corporations which follow a strategy of global expansion.

Globalisation has definite influences on human resource management. The changing labour markets reduce the number of low-paid jobs for the poorly educated while simultaneously increasing the number of low-paid jobs for the better educated (Lubbers, 1998). These trends create a mismatch between available labour and labour for which a demand exists. Job seekers with a lack of vocational training are more frequently excluded from job opportunities. At the same time, because of globalisation, the supply of labour from less developed countries affects the global labour market and especially those who have relatively limited skills to offer, as they are likely to be marginalised by more qualified and cheaper migrant job seekers. This results in a situation where only the most competitive can retain their position in the labour marketplace.

From the organisational perspective, globalisation creates what are called 'postmodern organisations' (Bergquist, 1993), which have the following characteristics. They emphasise moderate size and complexity rather than large-scale bureaucracy. With clear and strong mission statements, they accept increasingly diffuse and weak organisational boundaries and roles, easily opening up to external influences. The reign of market leaders is often short and turbulent. Knowledge workers have the upper hand and leadership is preferred to management. In order to meet the turbulent conditions they strive to adopt flexible structures and methods. Communication is dominated by the use of electronic media, and information and expertise are given as much importance in the organisation as capital.

The globalisation of business firms has a number of implications for human resource management (Schwella, 2000). Knowledge and skilled workers will become increasingly mobile so that recruitment will be from a global pool rather than a national or local pool. Employers who are unable to provide competitive packages will be confronted with an increasing shortage of these types of worker. In order to recruit new employees from a global pool, employers will have to use global media rather than local or national media. The information technology (IT) capacity and the extent to which workers who possess the knowledge and skills to be competitive in a global sense are connected to the new media will enhance their recruitment. Face-to-face testing and interviewing will be used less due to long distances and possible cost factors, and will be replaced by electronically mediated selection procedures. Appointments will be made on the basis of internationally acceptable contract laws and agreements, and remuneration and benefit levels will become increasingly standardised across national boundaries.

The major factors driving globalisation of the tourism industry are the liberalisation of air transport, the liberalisation of trade in services, economic integration, and the emerging power of information and communications technologies (ILO, 2001a). Besides increasing the power of the multinational tourism businesses, and being a potential threat to indigenous, small and medium-sized tourism businesses, globalisation tends to generate further homogenisation of tourism products. Globalisation has also created 'high-skilled' tourists (Richards, 1995), who are better informed, more experienced and quality-conscious.

A major consequence of globalisation in tourism is the issue of matching employee skills with changing industry requirements. The traditional practice of employees learning a majority of skills on the job and gradually progressing to senior positions is threatened by the rapid technological changes and the need to respond to the changing service requirements. Employees at the operational and managerial levels are now required to be more flexible. According to Becherel and Cooper (2002), globalisation has major implications for human resource management in tourism. These include:

- the need for different skills and competencies so that employees are able to deal with the widespread use of technology, especially the Internet;
- dealing with employment-related consequences of mergers and strategic alliances;
- issues of the relocation of employees, and understanding the social and cultural sensitivities of those working away from home;

- new forms of tourism, utilising natural and cultural environments, that create a demand for indigenous employees who can deliver high-quality and original products and services;
- meeting the needs of highly skilled tourists who are more experienced and demand higher-quality products and service.

Cultural contexts

Cultural, national and ethnic diversity is increasingly becoming a major feature of the workforce in the global tourism industry (Baum, 1995). Labour mobility within the regional associations such as the European Union has major implications on the tourism industry. Globalisation and the increased integration of the global economy tend to have a positive effect on labour mobility. Demographic changes, especially the increase in the average age of citizens and the low population growth in the developed world, make the movement of labour from developing countries to the developed ones inevitable. In the next few decades such demographic changes are likely to be a major issue in maintaining sustainable productivity levels in developed countries. In order to maintain the present standard of living and therefore the current size of workforce, they will need an annual inflow of millions of migrant workers. Countries such as UK have already started changing immigration rules to attract skilled labour from other countries in a number of sectors (e.g., education, information technology and the health services). The hospitality sector in many countries in Europe and America has traditionally been the first stop for immigrants seeking employment. The tourism industry in many European tourist destinations (e.g., Santorini in Greece) is heavily dependent on migrant workers from Eastern Europe and North Africa.

A major challenge resulting from these changes is the need to manage a culturally heterogeneous workforce. Human resource managers in the tourism industry have to deal with multiculturalism, multinationalism and multi-ethnicity in the workplace. They need to be sympathetic to, and sensitive of, individuals' or groups' origins and background. According to Baum (1995: 176), issues include:

- where a business in the tourism industry receives guests from countries, cultures and ethnic backgrounds that are different from that of the dominant culture in which the business is located (e.g., Japanese visitors staying in a Paris hotel);
- where guests are from a different culture, nationality or ethnic origin from that of the workforce (e.g., in a Chinese restaurant staffed by immigrant Chinese workers and catering for local demand in, say, Bucharest, Oslo or Rome);
- where a varying proportion of the workforce in a business or department are of different cultural, national or ethnic origins from that of the dominant local culture;
- where the management of the tourism/hospitality business is from a different culture or ethnic background from that of the majority of the workforce.
- where the corporate culture of the tourism business is significantly different from that normally prevailing in the country or community in which it is based, which would mean that although there is little or no distance between the management and operational

staff in terms of their original culture, corporate norms create new divides which must be addressed.

These situations are likely to create misunderstanding, conflict and discriminatory behaviour in the relationships between managers, staff and, indeed, guests. Multicultural management, which is about anticipating potential problems in the inter-relationships of different customer and employee groups, and instituting positive measures to avoid their occurrence (Baum, 1995), is an essential skill that human resource managers in the tourism industry require in an era of 'cultural globalisation'.

The emergence of 'aesthetic labour'

Warhurst et al. (2000), in their pioneering research on the service sector labour trends in Glasgow, identified a relatively under-appreciated and unexplored form of labour, namely 'aesthetic labour'. Aesthetic labour has been defined as 'a supply of embodied capacities and attributes possessed by workers at the point of entry into employment' (Warhurst et al., 2000: 1). 'Looking good' or 'sounding right' are described as the obvious manifestations of aesthetic labour, which can be a major variable in ensuring service quality in the tourism industry. With the tendency within the global economy to restructure towards services, including tourism, employers are increasingly on the look out for employees with a new set of skills for delivering higher-quality service interactions – 'moments of truth'. In other words, employers are increasingly looking for workers who can portray the firm's image through their work, at the same time appealing to the senses of the customer.

The emergence of aesthetic labour means that human resource managers have to develop these skills and attributes through the processes of recruitment, selection and training, transforming them into competencies and skills which are aesthetically geared to producing a higher-quality service encounter in which style is a major component. Recruitment and selection is the obvious starting point for incorporating aesthetic labour into the human resource management of the tourism sector. Organisations now have to look for the 'right' sort of appearance and disposition. Many employers in the tourism industry are now putting more stress on the right personality than the skills, the rationale being that the technical skills can be developed through training.

Another implication of aesthetic labour on human resource management is on training and development practices. The overemphasis on personality and appearance at the expense of technical skills in recruitment and selection means that organisations have to train the 'desired person' in the appropriate technical skills once they have entered employment. External consultants are employed to give grooming and deportment training, which include sessions in hair cuts/styling and 'acceptable' make-up, individual make-overs, how men should shave and the standards expected in relation to appearance (Warhurst et al., 2000). Another method of employee training is role-playing, which is used to impress upon employees the importance of their own aesthetic skills and attributes from the customers' perspective. Role-playing is also used to develop skills and attributes that enable employees to differentiate and better serve customers. Warhurst et al. (2000) argue that organisations are increasingly aware of the possible competitive advantage to be gained by utilising aesthetic labour, which in turn has implications as to who is allowed to present the public face of the organisation. Being a major service industry, aesthetic labour has significant implications for human resource practices in the tourism industry.

The impact of information and communications technologies

Information and communications technologies (ICTs) have changed the ways in which the tourism industry is organised and managed. The tourism industry is confronted with changes in its distribution, marketing and working systems. Buhalis (1998) argues that the ICT-based interaction between customers and service providers reduces transaction costs, creating a process of disintermediation. Internet-based intermediaries facilitate direct interaction between tourists, tourist destination managers and service providers. The provision of better quality information and direct interaction with service providers are likely to change the behaviour and requirements of tourists. ICTs can transform the tourism business's relations with its customers, improving the scope to provide tailor-made products and services. The use of ICTs can, in turn, help tourist destinations to enhance their capacity to compete with other destinations and respond to market forces. As far as human resource management is concerned, ICTs can help managers to introduce new processes and organisational structures. ICTs also contribute towards the reduction of hierarchical structures within business organisations, allowing employee empowerment and greater development of capabilities for individual workers.

Specific human resource management issues resulting from the application of ICTs include developing the skills and efficiency of the workforce, increasing expenses on training and development and increasing the quality of, and participation in, training systems. According to the World Travel and Tourism Council (2002), the role of human resource managers is likely to be affected by ICTs in a number of ways. Human resource managers are likely to be a centrally located source of deep expertise that line managers can access electronically from wherever they are working that day, something that is made possible by the improvements in computer systems. With improved decision support systems, human resource managers will have more time and resources to deal with strategic human resource issues. ICTs can also help develop efficient electronic recruitment systems that pre-select applicants.

The spread of ICTs in the tourism industry and the likely disappearance of many service providers have major ramifications for human resource management in the form of handling potentially large-scale redundancies. While it represents a major loss of comparative advantage in developing countries, downsizing workforces creates new functional challenges for human resource management. The employee welfare functions of organisations are likely to regain importance when they are faced with retrenchment of employees. The development of innovative severance packages and counselling services are likely to assume more importance as a human resource management practice. This will also have an impact on tourism's image as an employer, making it increasingly difficult to attract quality employees.

Case study 6.1   Pret a Manger

Pret a Manger[1] was created in 1986 by two entrepreneurs, Julian Metcalfe and Sinclair Beecham, who recognised a gap in the market and sought to change the world of fast food to incorporate their innovation. Metcalfe and Beecham acquired the Pret a Manger name from a bankrupt café in Hampstead to open their first Pret a Manger sandwich shop in central London. From these beginnings the company has expanded rapidly and currently has over 120 shops and a workforce of approximately 2400.

Everything about Pret a Manger emphasises a simple, no-nonsense approach, e.g. the minimalist interiors coated in a metallic covering. As well as aiming for a distinctive high quality approach to the product Pret a Manger also aims to offer a 'successful employment formula – a fun working environment, rewards, openness and career opportunities'. Seemingly, this approach has been successful. Recently the company was voted 34th in *The Sunday Times* list of top UK employers, *100 Best Companies to Work For 2002*, a publication based on employee feedback, including a confidential questionnaire sent to 250 employees in the company. Equally, *Fortune* magazine has latterly rated Pret a Manger as one of the top ten places to work in Europe.

Quality and service have always been core values and workers are given a card of 12 key points for 'great' production and service. The 12 key points are given to employees to ensure that certain standards are adhered to and a quality service provided. For example, sandwiches should be 'picture perfect' and employees should aim to present themselves in the 'style' of a Pret Ambassador.

There are standard requirements for the service offer. Although employees have a certain amount of freedom to interact with the customers in their own way, there are certain procedures that need to be followed such as repeating the items, asking customers if they would like a coffee, whether they are eating in or taking away, and so on. From joining the queue, customers are to be served by Team Members within 90 seconds in a friendly and individual way and for tea and coffee orders it has to be within 60 seconds.

Although a quick service is considered a high priority the company focuses on recruiting staff with personalities so that they can talk to customers during the service provision. Standardisation only goes so far and it is important for the employees not to be entirely scripted as one manager explained, 'we specifically ask them to thank the customer for coming in and specifically to make a parting comment.

We don't tell them what they should say'. The friendly staff at Pret are more redolent of an example of the good service usually found in excellent restaurants rather than the robotic smile of the normal fast food operators.

With high standardised operations across the company it would be expected that employees have little room for empowerment. However, the discretion afforded to employees seems to be greater than that found in most fast food companies. The managers at Pret appear to give their employees a degree of empowerment and especially when dealing with complaints, they feel that staff can rectify the situation themselves if it is relatively minor. Similarly staff can discard substandard ingredients or even completed but unsatisfactory sandwiches. Staff are also encouraged to 'up sell', with employees expected to encourage people to buy products using their own style and approach.

There is also less external control over employee performance, although there is tight control over the output there is scope for employees to be empowered. Such empowerment as does take place is through commitment and is largely focused on gaining commitment to the company's definitions of service quality through the detection and replacement of service faults and customer complaints.

Therefore Pret a Manger fits best within a service that is highly standardised with relatively low levels of intangibility in the service offer. And Pret's human resource formula seems to be a major factor in ensuring high quality of its services, despite the obvious limitations of being a fast food service.

[1] In line with the company's own description of themselves the case study will use the full title of the company and its shortened name of Pret, which is used throughout a number of company documents.

Source: adapted from Nickson, D., Baum, T., Losekoot, E., Morrison, A. and Frochot, I. (2002) Skills , Organizational Performance and Economic Activity in the Hospitality Industry: A Literature Review. ESRC Centre for Skills, Knowledge and Organizational Performance (SKOPE), Research Monograph No. 5, Universities of Oxford and Warwick: SKOPE.

Conclusion

In this chapter, we have attempted to touch upon some of the key human resource issues that impact upon tourism operations at a strategic level. Inevitably, in so doing, we have had to make judgements about the issues that are addressed and, therefore, have omitted significant areas.

Human resource concerns in international tourism remain among the most intractable for managers in the sector. While the focus of concern varies considerably from sector to sector and within different cultural contexts, the substance of these concerns shows amazing similarities throughout the world. There are no simple answers to many of the challenges that we have outlined here. However, it is essential that any discussion of tourism management issues considers those relating to the management of people.

Discussion questions

1. Examine the causes and effects of the globalisation of tourism businesses on the HRM function.
2. What are the implications of aesthetic labour for human resource practices in the tourism industry?
3. Discuss the impacts of ICTs in relation to the management of people.

Suggested further reading

Bateson, J.E.G. and Hoffman, D.K. (1996) *Managing Services Marketing: Texts and Readings* (4th edition). Fort Worth, TX: Harcourt Brace.

Baum, T. (1993) *Human Resource Issues in International Tourism*. Oxford: Butterworth Heinemann.

Becherel, L. and Cooper, C. (2002) The impact of globalisation on HR management in the tourism sector. *Tourism Recreation Research*, 27(1): 3–16.

Schwella, E. (2000) Globalisation and human resource management: context, challenges and change. *Administratio Publica*, 10(2): 88–105.

7 Marketing Management for Tourism

Jackie Clarke

Chapter objectives

The purpose of this chapter is to examine tourism marketing management in the context of services marketing. Having completed this chapter, the reader will be able to:

- appreciate the challenges faced by marketers of travel and tourism today
- recognise issues stemming from strategic–tactical tension
- understand the marketing process and appreciate the need for a marketing plan

Chapter contents

Introduction

Marketing as a management discipline offers the tourism manager that essential outward focus and receptivity to consumer needs that facilitates organisational success in the competitive environment of global tourism today. Oft-cited definitions of marketing include the following:

> Marketing is the process of planning and executing the conception, pricing, promotion, and distribution of ideas, goods, and services to create exchanges that satisfy individual and organizational objectives. (American Marketing Association)
> Marketing is the management process for identifying, anticipating, and satisfying customer requirements profitably. (UK Chartered Institute of Marketing)

> The marketing concept holds that the key to achieving organizational goals consists in determining the needs and wants of target markets and delivering the desired satisfactions more effectively and efficiently than competitors. (Kotler, 1991: 16)

The reader will see that marketing is about achieving organisational goals through understanding and responding to consumers and marketplace conditions. Importantly, these goals need not be profit-related and, thus, the practice of marketing in tourism has spread from the commercial tourism industry to sectors and sub-sectors not traditionally associated with the discipline. These include public sector museums, national parks, charities responsible for heritage conservation, and so forth. For some organisations, the practice of 'marketing' encompasses no more than differing forms of communication or promotion. This, however, is to misunderstand the scope of the discipline and its strategic dimension. Indeed, marketing may be better explained as a way of doing business, rather than as a 'stand alone' discipline (see Hooley et al., 1998).

The marketing processes and decisions vary to the extent of their formality; a micro-business in rural tourism, for example, has very different structures and style for managing marketing than the multinational tour operating and aviation conglomerate. A micro-business may have no written marketing plan (unless a loan is needed), while the multinational may have written strategic and campaign plans by brand, product or key segment. However, they may be equally foresighted (or not) in their strategic marketing thinking. And marketing is invariably results-driven.

In academia today, the marketing discipline has matured to embrace a multitude of research streams, as evidenced in the many marketing journals and echoed eventually in the marketing texts (see, for example, Enright (2002) for a discussion of the development of marketing thought). Practical 'how to do marketing' texts, such as McDonald's (1999) well-established book on creating marketing plans, rub alongside postmodern critiques (Brown, 1993, 1995, 2001). There is also a large number of texts and journals on each of the sub-topics of marketing; these include consumer behaviour, marketing research, advertising, communications, public relations, strategic planning and branding, as well as marketing permutations, such as relationship marketing, interactive marketing, database marketing, environmental marketing, and macro marketing – the lists run on. There are also texts concerned with identified sectors. Here, our natural focus is travel and tourism, although most marketing academics would place this within the services marketing remit.

In practice, successful marketers in one sub-sector of tourism can transfer to other sub-sectors with ease; their value is recognised. Chiefly, this comes down to their ability to handle the practical implications of the characteristics of tourism within marketing decision-making. These characteristics of perishability, variability, inseparability and intangibility will be familiar to the tourism student, but they are worth repeating here as they are the root cause of many of the areas of emphasis that emerge when marketing is applied to travel and tourism (see Table 7.1).

The so-called service characteristics outlined in Table 7.1 were very much the topic of discussion in the pre-1980s journal literature in services marketing (Brown et al., 1994). They have also long been accepted as the part-rationale for the emergence of

Table 7.1 The characteristics of tourism

Perishability: The inability to store the product for sale at a later date. Each product exists only at a single point in time, so failure to sell by that point in time results in lost revenue too. A plane leaving at 09.05 with 20 empty seats means that the revenue from 20 products will never be realised.

Variability: Tourism is a product high in human contact. Each experience element relies on human interaction between user and provider staff (and equipment/processes), so that each incident is intrinsically unique. The fact that much tourism marketing effort is made to iron out performance variability through employee training and procedures does not annul this essential tendency towards variability.

Inseparability: The fact that the consumer has to interact with the tourism provider or destination in order to experience the product at all. Sometimes called 'simultaneous production and consumption'; in other words, until the consumer uses the product, the product doesn't actually exist (merely the *capability* to produce it).

Intangibility: The tourism product cannot be inspected by the human senses at the point of sale (although surrogates for the product can be, of course). A popular phrase, 'tangibilising the intangible', again sums up practical marketing effort to eradicate this characteristic. Intangibility may not overly bother the consumer with brand or product experience.

service marketing theory within the marketing discipline. Understood as they are, they will, therefore, be woven into the explanations rather than providing the focus of this chapter.

To these four characteristics should be added the cost structure of tourism businesses. This consists of *high fixed costs* and *low variable costs*, relatively *fixed supply capacity* in the short term, and *complementarity* between the different tourism elements. Moreover, no single tourism organisation exists in isolation – from the user's perspective, the vacation experience (if we are referring to leisure tourism) consists of meals, transport, accommodation, sight-seeing, activities, and so on, all rolled into one, seamless experience (see Middleton and Clarke, 2001). Therefore, Buttle's (2001; see also Hooley et al., 1998) argument that modern marketing consists of networks of organisations (suppliers, intermediaries, partners, etc.) competing against other networks is pertinent for tourism. Witness the co-operation between components in a given destination, or the composition of players in aviation-led loyalty schemes, such as the Oneworld and Star Alliances (see Chapter 3).

A single chapter in a text such as this can do little more than give a flavour of the management of the discipline as applied to tourism. Therefore, throughout the chapter, areas of difference and of emphasis, both within the marketing theory and as exhibited in marketing practice, form the guiding principle – just how might marketing for tourism vary from marketing *per se*? And why? With what results? The chapter first addresses the topic of consumer behaviour before moving on to examine the problem of handling day-to-day tactics without losing sight of the strategic direction (a marketing dilemma typical throughout travel and tourism organisations). This section is supported by a short, practical task for the reader. Certain aspects of the marketing mix are then identified and elaborated upon before attention is turned to the marketing process and the marketing plan. Finally, the chapter highlights the role of branding within many of the larger tourism organisations and destinations.

At the core lies consumer behaviour

At the macro level, the modern tourism consumer of the developed world is a confident and experienced traveller – there are now second-, third- or fourth-generation tourists from the postwar years, 'broken in' as children to the overseas vacation, with levels of affluence, life opportunities and personal mobility that are incomparable to previous generations. Alongside increases in life expectancy, with the older generations enjoying good health for longer, lie increases in quality life expectancy. At the same time, new markets are opening up, including Eastern Europe, Asia and the Pacific, and most notably China, which looks set to dominate the international tourism scene within 20 years (WTO, 1997). There is also evidence of changes in leisure time patterns and holiday entitlement versus actual uptake (see WTO, 1999a, for a thought provoking study). Tourism is therefore a 'moving' market in a very real sense. Changes in consumer behaviour require corresponding changes in product offers and product portfolios. For example, inclusive tours are not required to 'hand-hold' the virgin user. Instead, the focus is on convenience for time-crushed purchasers and on niche products that answer specific higher-order needs (skill development in a pursued hobby, for example). These macro trends are the aggregate results of the behaviour of multitudes of individuals.

Understanding individual consumer behaviour is basic to the practice of marketing and borrows, in particular, from the disciplines of economics (price elasticity, demand forecasting, etc.), sociology (reference groups, social class, family, etc.) and psychology (motivation, attitudes, perception, learning, personality, etc.). On to these fundamentals, marketing researchers have built, for instance, loyalty theory (e.g., Dick and Basu, 1994) or consumer satisfaction/dissatisfaction theory (CS/D) (e.g., Fournier and Mick, 1999), with all specialisms contributing to a fuller knowledge of consumer behaviour. In practical terms, much of what marketers understand of their consumers is distilled into the segmentation structure that they use (see Case Study 7.1).

Case Study 7.1   Segmentation in the Museum Sector

Museums in the United Kingdom follow a pragmatic approach to segmentation, and tend to use basic socio-demographic variables for the task. Often the segment types are reflected in the ticketing structures of those museums charging entrance. The segmentation structure might be summarised as:

- Admission visitors
  - General visitor (see below)
  - Education
  - Special interest

- Non-admission visitors
  - Function/venue
    - Business/corporate
    - Leisure/celebration
  - Shop/café only

- Loyalty scheme members
  - Corporate
  - School
  - Education

The general admission visitor may be further segmented using one or more of the following variables:

- 'Distance' from museum

  - Local residents
  - Catchment area 1 hour to 1 and ½ hours drive time
  - Domestic tourists
  - International tourists (by country of origin)

- Lifestage

  - Families
  - Senior citizens
  - University students, etc.
- Group size
- Sales promotions/initiative respondents

Source: Clarke and Elwin (2002).

Early effort in mapping complex consumer behaviour was directed towards the generation of complex flow diagrams of decision processes. These 'grand' models of consumer behaviour were particularly prevalent in the 1960s and 1970s, examples including the Nicosia model (1966: cited in Chisnall, 1985); the Andreasan model (1965: cited in Chisnall, 1985); Engel, Kollat and Blackwell (1968: cited in Chisnall, 1985, and subsequently updated; e.g., Engel et al., 1993); and Howard and Sheth (1969 and subsequently updated; e.g., Sheth et al., 1999). Tourism researchers conducted similar exercises, although a little later. Examples include the Schmoll model (1977: cited in Cooper et al., 1998); Woodside and Lyonski (1989); Woodside and King (2001); and Um and Crompton (1990). At the heart of these models lies the simple purchase decision process (see Figure 7.1) which, allowing for change of label, runs from problem recognition by the individual consumer through to post-use evaluation, with both internal and external factors influencing each of the stages. Moutinho (1987) was one of the first to publish a dedicated paper on tourism consumer behaviour, culminating in a model within a generic marketing journal. This paper is worth reading as a summary of the interlinking elements that help to explain why tourism consumers make the decisions they do. The models of tourism consumer behaviour have, perhaps inevitably, attracted criticism (Gilbert, 1991; Decrop, 1999; Hudson, 1999). For example, it is argued that the models focus on individual decision-making, when group decisions, with all the complications of negotiation and compromise, are more prevalent in tourism decision-making.

With due allowance for certain segments and/or tourism products, tourism decision-making is generally characterised by high-risk, high-involvement and extensive problem-solving behaviour. Typically, then, we might expect a given tourist to exhibit an active search for information, a bias towards personal information sources and a longer decision time than for low-involvement goods. The product is intangible at the point of sale, exacerbating any feelings of uncertainty, and the long time gap favoured by tourism producers (for better management of perishability) between purchase and usage may contribute to consumer feelings of post-purchase anxiety regarding the correctness of their purchase decision. Of course, there are tourism experiences that exhibit other behavioural patterns, such as the impulse purchase of the last minute holiday, the frequently purchased airline ticket or the business-to-business (B2B) decision – it is always a matter of examining the segment in question as well as the tourism product

Figure 7.1   The simple purchase decision process

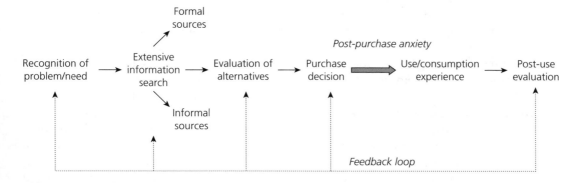

itself. It should also be remembered that the prevalent pattern of decision-making in leisure tourism shows 'one' major decision made in the country of origin, supported by a series of sub-decisions (e.g., which restaurants or which attractions?) made during the extended consumption experience at the destination.

Essentially, all tourism marketers want to know consumer information pertaining to 'who, what, when, where, how and why' type questions in order to usefully segment their markets. Advancements in database technology have considerably aided this process in recent years, particularly in respect of the frequent user, as captured by loyalty schemes.

Managing the strategic–tactical tension

Practical success revolves around managing the strategic–tactical tension. Sometimes labelled as 'demand–capacity management', skilful marketers in tourism are endlessly balancing their time and resources between short-term demand–capacity requirements and long-term brand development and strategic direction. Much of the tourism marketer's energy focuses on stimulating last minute sales to fill remaining capacity; remember the service characteristics of perishability, relatively fixed capacity and high fixed costs. Stelios Haji-Ioannou, founder of the low-cost airline easyJet, frequently talks of the number of seats in each plane (fixed capacity) being fundamental to paring down unit costs (essentially addressing high fixed costs) and being central to his strategic thinking for the success of the no-frills airline. Extra seats over and above his competitors give easyJet its basis for competitive advantage.

The combination of perishability, fixed capacity and high fixed costs serves to beef up profits or plummet losses in a way not experienced by the marketer of physical goods. As a consequence, tourism marketers need to pay close attention to demand patterns. For example, the development of yield management systems in aviation is rooted in the analysis of historic sales data that allows predictions to be made for a given route and timing, so that overbooking percentages and price alterations can be made on a continuous basis with a degree of confidence unimaginable in previous decades. Developments in information technology have allowed capacity for production to be inventoried for distribution and the tracking of subsequent sales. It is therefore no surprise that many sub-sectors in travel and tourism have invested heavily in information technology (see Chapter 16). For the marketers of physical goods, their antennae have no need to be so finely tuned to daily, weekly and seasonal demand patterns, while product storage and a more generous cost structure lessen the problem. On extreme occasions, of course, tourism is vulnerable to sudden external events, such as terrorist attacks or the natural disasters. These events, due to the inseparable nature of the product, by necessity send marketers into tactical overdrive. But even on an everyday basis, much of the tourism marketer's time will be taken up with tactical decision-making, using classic tools that include price discounting and sales promotions. Over the strategic time frame, however, the marketer may find that overuse of discounts and sales promotions has damaged the values of the brand that the organisation is nurturing. The most valuable tourism marketers are those with the ability to handle the ever-present tactical detail, create the space for strategic thought and planning, and then reconcile the tensions between the two.

Case Study 7.2 is a simple illustration that constitutes a task for the reader, and should ably demonstrate the problems of filling last minute capacity and the impact on revenue, as well as the mix of segments targeted and the impact on revenue. It is left to the reader's imagination to scale up the problem into aviation, cruise ship or tour operation, and to reflect on the merits of IT systems that inventory capacity and sales in real time.

Case Study 7.2 Working with Fixed Capacity of a Perishable Product: The London Eye

The London Eye, a giant wheel offering the 'passenger' a birds-eye view of London, has 32 capsules, each carrying up to 25 passengers, which, when the rotation cycle is brought into the calculation, gives a maximum hourly capacity of 1,500 passengers. The attraction is closed from 1 January to 27 January for annual maintenance, and is also closed on Christmas Day (25 December).

The winter season runs from 28 January to 30 April, and from 1 October to 31 December. It is open from 9.30am to 8.00pm.

The summer season runs from 1 May to 30 September. It is open from 9.30am to 10.00pm.

The pricing structure is as follows:

Price category	Individual	Group
Adult	£9.50	£8.55
Child (under 16)	£5.00	£4.50
Senior citizen	£7.50	£6.75
Registered disabled	£7.50	£6.75

1. Calculate the maximum number of visitors that the London Eye can take during a day in the summer season and in the winter season. Assuming that 100% of capacity is sold, what is the

maximum revenue that the Eye can achieve for each day?

2. Now see what happens if you sell only 70% of your capacity over one week in the winter season. How much of your maximum revenue have you 'lost'? As a perishable product, there is no way of retrieving this.

3. It is unrealistic to assume that you will sell all your capsule space to individual adults. Imagine that over one week in summer, 20% of your market are individual adults, 40% are children, 10% senior citizens, 5% registered disabled, and 25% are school groups. How much revenue have you 'lost' from the maximum? It is

realistic to assume that in the trough and shoulder periods, you will need to target different segments, including the group market, in order to fill your capsules. Try altering your portfolio of segments, and your percentage of capacity sold, and see what happens to your revenue.

Source: Adapted from MSc International Travel and Tourism Management exercise, Oxford Brookes University (Clarke). Drawn from information www.londoneye.com and Jenkins (2000). NB: Information has been simplified for ease of exercise. See end of chapter for answers.

Stirring around the marketing mix

With a heritage going back as least as far as McCarthy in the 1960s, the four Ps of the marketing mix – product, promotion (communication), price, and place (distribution) – are the sticking point of marketing knowledge for most non-marketers (McCarthy, 1960; see also Blois, 2000). They are no more than labels for categories of different types of decision that marketing managers of any product take on a regular basis. Middleton's (1988) analogy of a car – that is, the centrality of co-ordinating wheel, gear-box, accelerator and brakes to drive in the desired manner – explains the concept effectively. Within services marketing, Booms and Bitner (1981) added to the classic four an additional three: process, physical evidence and participants.

- *Process.*   Or the service delivery process through which the service product is actually experienced. Includes reservations, queuing, flow paths, service recovery from service failure, complaint management systems, etc.
- *Physical evidence.*   Or the methods used to tangibilise the service to the consumer, at the point of sale, during consumption (the servicescape), and remotely (website, telephone, invoice, etc.). Includes uniforms or dress codes, signage, equipment, colour, lighting, textures, use of sound – essentially any appeals to the senses. Some think of it as the equivalent of 'packaging' for physical goods.
- *Participants.*   Include the consumer, the frontline and the backstage employee, any intermediaries or third parties, and elements such as participant recruitment, appraisal and motivation.

As a result, there is now a greater necessity for working closely with human relations and operations departments, and a correspondingly greater emphasis on internal marketing (where employees form the target audience) than might be found with physical goods marketing. Again, the roots lie with the characteristics of inseparability, intangibility and variability. (One of the best texts to explore the ideas of process, physical evidence and participants is Zeithaml and Bitner, 2000). It can be argued that the additional three Ps can be subsumed into the traditional mix; there is certainly overlap, for the categories are not discrete, but then neither are the original four. I return to my point that it is a matter of convenient labelling of decisions.

The next four sections dip into the marketing mix and extract examples of where and how decisions for marketing managers of tourism might be particularly important. It cannot be comprehensive, merely illustrative, but it does serve to highlight typical experiences in tourism marketing that are not so commonplace within generic or, indeed, physical goods marketing.

Product

At its simplest, a product is an offer of a bundle of benefits that meets consumer needs – a service is as much a product as a physical good. The tourism or destination experience is often described as an amalgam of products. Whereas commercial organisations have full control over product decisions (within the regulatory framework), destination organisers are more commonly in the position of responsibility without the authority. As a result, cajoling, mediating and co-ordinating different interests are commonly part and parcel of the marketing task. For commercial organisations, the gathering of data about consumer behaviour is easier than for destinations (bar the inclusive resort) – for the destination, calculation of 'sales' and market share data is somewhat problematic.

Products, product categories and brands are believed to move through the product life cycle model (PLC), a framework which may be familiar to the tourism student through Butler's (non-marketing) research on the destination/resort life cycle. In practice, however, the PLC model has its limitations for tourism over and above those for physical goods. The difficulty of accurate data collection is, for example, one of a number of challenges. Therefore, more useful are the ways of thinking about product portfolios, such as product line widths, lengths and depths or, perhaps, some of the well-documented strategic models, such as the Boston Consulting Group matrix or the General Electric model (see Hooley et al., 1998).

As an inseparable and variable service, *quality* becomes a product management issue of some importance for tourism marketers. Systems for quality control have to operate in real time as tourists interact with service providers. However, there is also a genuine opportunity to recover a poor experience as it occurs, an opportunity not available to physical goods manufacturers. The overlap between marketing functions, operation functions and human resource functions comes to the fore very strongly. For example, a blueprint (or logical flow diagram) of the consumer experience may be used (perhaps divided by key segments) to highlight critical incidents, potential failure points, recovery actions, and discrepancies between consumer and employee perspectives. Adoption of a policy of frontline employee empowerment (or, indeed, the opposite approach of formal scripting) or training in customer care are examples from the overlap with human resources. All fall, arguably, under the remit of product management, as do, of course, the ubiquitous product capacity decisions (see 'Managing the strategic–tactical tension' section above, p. 105).

Communication (promotion)

The word 'promotion' has overtones of propaganda, whereas 'communication' more naturally suggests a two-way flow of messages. Communication tools today seek to gain feedback from the target audience through, for example, the website address and direct telephone numbers on advertisements, responses to sales promotions, the design of monitoring and evaluation mechanisms within communication campaigns. Compared to physical goods, it can be argued that, due to the intangibility of the product, it is easy and tempting to over-promise in tourism advertisements. However, setting up heightened expectations of the product in the mind of the consumer that cannot then be consistently delivered is detrimental to positive word-of-mouth recommendation and to the brand, and should be avoided. Because of the nature of tourism as a group experience, precise targeting of the audience for communication is, perhaps, more important than it might be for physical goods; the behaviour of one consumer has repercussions for the satisfaction of another consumer experiencing the product at the same time. Inseparability and the high-contact nature of tourism also make it advisable to treat the employee as a secondary audience for all forms of communication. The Air Malta campaign on the London Underground in 2002 which (above the photograph of a beautiful air stewardess and a background picture of a picturesque harbour) stated '34 times a week and no headache' probably did little for employee morale and motivation. Yet these are the frontline staff delivering much of the product experience.

The communication mix includes advertising, public relations (including publicity, sponsorship and crisis management), sales promotions (including point-of-sale merchandising), personal selling, printed literature, websites, direct marketing, and physical evidence and participants. These are co-ordinated into specific campaigns. The communication mix is controlled by the marketing manager, while expertise in media buying, creative strategy or any given communication tool may be bought in from external agencies. Informal communication channels through reference groups and opinion leaders are also important, particularly in tourism, but the marketing manager has no direct control over these and can only seek to influence them. In practice, the balance of usage between public relations and advertising by tourism organisations may be tipping towards the former. In particular, tourism is more intrinsically newsworthy than many physical goods, while, being exceptionally vulnerable to external events, crisis management assumes importance in tourism.

The rising costs of advertising, ICT developments and the international nature of many markets may also contribute to the reduction in emphasis on advertising. Printed literature in its many forms is probably used to a greater extent in travel and tourism than for many goods and services. The printed piece (be it leaflet or brochure) acts to provide detailed information, support product positioning and, frequently, to offer a booking mechanism. The extent to which printed material may be usurped by website development remains to be seen. Printed literature can also be designed to enhance the actual product experience by facilitating usage of, say, an attraction by the provision of maps, opening times, location of facilities like restaurants, toilets, First Aid points and so forth, and by providing a standardised 'welcome' upon entrance to the site (see Middleton with Clarke, 2001, for discussion of printed literature).

Sales promotion, in all its guises, is a popular communications tool for generating last minute purchase of unsold capacity or stimulating demand in the trough or shoulder periods. Again, however, the marketer needs to weigh the pros and cons of short-term price discounts against those of temporary added value. The merits of the first lie in the rapid response of price-sensitive consumers (particularly when allied to IT distribution channels), but adding value may be more beneficial for building and supporting brand values.

Price

Not all tourism products carry a monetary price to the consumer. Religious buildings, museums, national parks (depending on the country), shopping malls or natural attractions may not levy a compulsory fee to the user, although some encourage donations. But for most tourism organisations, managing price is critical.

First, it is important to remember that price actually equates to cost in consumer parlance, cost including time and effort spent, as well as money. Money-back guarantees can be built into tourism products to provide reassurance of delivery standards, but time-back guarantees? The temporal risk to the consumer of mis-spending precious holiday entitlement must not be overlooked. Given the intangibility of the product, price is often cited as being perceived by the consumer as a tangible clue for product quality.

The cost structure of high fixed costs and low variable costs gives great flexibility to the marketer when juggling tactical price cuts. Marginal cost pricing is very much favoured, the approach being to cover the low variable cost element and then build in (and here lies the flexibility) a contribution towards the fixed cost or profit (depending on the breakeven point). Discretionary pricing, where prices alter by segment, time or place of purchase, is also a common tool, though utilised more at the strategic level. Lower prices for early booking (increasing the gap between purchase and consumption) or entrance to attractions according to student, local resident, unemployed or senior citizen status are widely used methods; the skill lies in successful ring-fencing to ensure only those consumers who qualify benefit, thus preventing revenue dilution. A humorous example, but one that makes the point, is the experience of Caledonian MacBrayne, a ferry company running services between the Hebridean Islands and the Scottish mainland. The company introduced a fare for crofters taking livestock to market – £2.35 per sheep. Ordinary fares were £104 return for a driver and car, with an additional £29 per extra passenger. A large number of cars could be spotted with a sheep in the back and bulging suitcases on the roof, only to return two weeks later with an unsold sheep, and a driver with a suntan. Canny crofters were leaving the sheep with friends and going on holiday at a saving to themselves of over £100 on the crossing. The company hastily tightened up its ring-fencing policy.

On a more serious note, the combination of fare structure and tactical, discount pricing can result in very complex price structures. A typical scheduled airline will have thousands of different prices, and each person on a given flight may have paid a different seat price to everyone else. The attractiveness of discounting prices as a response to unsold capacity can trigger price wars and train the consumer to think in terms of booking as late as possible for the best price deals (something most tourism providers would prefer to avoid). The results of all this can be damaging to brands and to perceptions of product quality.

Distribution (place)

Attributed to Conrad Hilton, the phrase 'location, location and location' as the crux of tourism 'place' has a lot to answer for. Although highly relevant to the micro location of tourism retail outlets, individual attractions (where impulse purchasing behaviour may be particularly important) and products at the leisure end of the spectrum, the phrase has served to overshadow the vital importance of creating methods by which the potential consumer can purchase a tourism product *ahead of consumption*, increasingly through technology available at the home or workplace. For the destination, the airline or the tour operator, the key is to provide efficient 'pipelines' (Middleton, 1988) for both early and last minute purchases. Online distribution technology operating in real time integrated with systems that inventory product capacity and sales is a powerful tool for generating the often crucial late sales. Website developments have revolutionised the use of direct marketing by travel and tourism providers, from small and medium-sized enterprises (SMEs) to the multinationals. For the SME, bound by inseparability and limited resources for reaching consumers, the Internet has opened up new international markets at affordable cost, allowing them to play on the global tourism stage. Traditional print (brochure, leaflet) commonly double as purchasing mechanisms through tear-off booking forms. Advertisements carry website addresses and direct booking telephone numbers. Conventional 'high street' travel agents scrabble to meet the challenges of retaining increasingly IT-savvy consumers. Distribution may not be the 'sexy' body of marketing, but it is where the present battles are fought, and where the foresighted tourism business can gain advantage over a seemingly entrenched competitor. For the marketer interested in destinations, World Tourism Organisation (2000) on ICT is still an informative read.

The marketing process and the marketing plan

The marketing process can be considered as the 'analysis, planning, implementation, and control' of marketing (Kotler, 1991), whereas the marketing plan is the accepted

Figure 7.2   A comparison of strategic and annual marketing plans

	Strategic marketing plan (3–5 years typical)	Annual or tactical marketing plan (1 year)
Typical line of marketing research or use of marketing information systems	Situation analysis *macro* *micro* *external* *internal*	Summary of *situation analysis* *SWOT*
	Forecast/prognosis	Target segments
	Key factors for success and distinctive competencies	Annual marketing objectives *in SMART format*
	SWOT analysis	Product *[objectives]* *strategies* *tactics*
	Target segments *including profile*	Price *[objectives]* *strategies* *tactics*
	Positioning statement *including positioning map*	Distribution *[objectives]* *strategies* *tactics*
	Marketing objectives	Communication *objectives* *strategies* *tactics*
	Strategies [which may be categorised as *product* *price* *distribution* *communication]*	Monitoring, evaluation and control *including budget*
	Evaluation and control *including budget*	

Source: Adapted from Godfrey and Clarke (2000: 126, Table 7.1).

output, commonly (though not exclusively) in written format. The marketing process is ongoing, but the written marketing plans cover different time scales designed to dovetail into one another. The strategic plan (see Figure 7.2 for typical components) creates the overall goals and direction for the series of tactical (often annual) plans.

As already suggested, in large travel and tourism companies, marketing plans may be written for specific brands, key segments or products, and some tactical plans may take the form of an integrated communications campaign focusing on a shared message: Spain's 'everything under the sun', or 'passion for life', or Champney's 'Mind, Body, Spirit' (see Middleton with Clarke, 2001). (For the development of strategic marketing thinking, Hooley et al., 1998 is an informative read.)

Branding as a focus for marketing effort

Perhaps one of the most noticeable differences between large travel and tourism organisations and micro enterprises (or even destinations) is the ability to develop strong brands. Many of the wished for brands are little more than logos and names – there is scant awareness among potential consumers or other stakeholders in the marketplace, and the logos carry no meaningful values for consumers to identify with. Destinations, particularly those at a local level, find it particularly hard, possibly due to the limited resources and control those responsible have for engineering the desired images. Readers can probably recall their own examples. Some may take a form of 'brand franchising' (or using a name/symbol recognised in another product category to provide 'instant' awareness and value for the consumer). Examples may include the use of authors' names (in the UK, Catherine Cookson Country or Captain Cook Country), or characters from novels (in the UK, Tarka Country). Efforts to brand sustainable tourism schemes and ecolabels have met with limited success and much consumer confusion (Synergy, 2000). Yet branding may offer distinct advantages for travel and tourism in, for example, countering the effects of intangibility and variability or facilitating precise segmentation, or by providing a focal point for the integration of producer effort (thus aiding internal marketing) (see Clarke, 2000 for discussion).

It is worth noting that some of the most interesting and successful brands in travel and tourism today are, in fact, a type of corporate branding, whereby the values of the brand are not fixed to a given product but transfer freely from product category to product category. The Virgin brand carries its values to different sectors where it feels it can challenge established yet sleepy competitors. The easy group follows a similar approach. Among the niche brands, it is possible to find plenty of strong examples of lifestage brands (or brands that are designed to attract consumers in a given life-cycle stage, which they subsequently outgrow or move on from); brands such as Club 18–30 (for singles), Saga (for older vacationers), or Sandals (geared to couples) speak to distinct and recognisable consumer life-cycle stages.

For many large tourism organisations, branding is the culmination of marketing effort. Davidson (1997) uses the analogy of a branding iceberg – the consumer is aware of the 'tip' of marketing activity above the 'waterline', but is unaware of the sheer bulk of activity that is hidden from them. This author prefers to use the analogy of a spider's web (see Figure 7.3), a strong, yet flexible, intricate pattern of activity suspended from the three strands of strategic thinking, environmental analysis and competitive networks, with the spider as marketing manager, weaving, moving and co-ordinating (and occasionally taking out a competitor). But all the strands of the web run to and from the centre – the brand.

Figure 7.3 The branding web for tourism

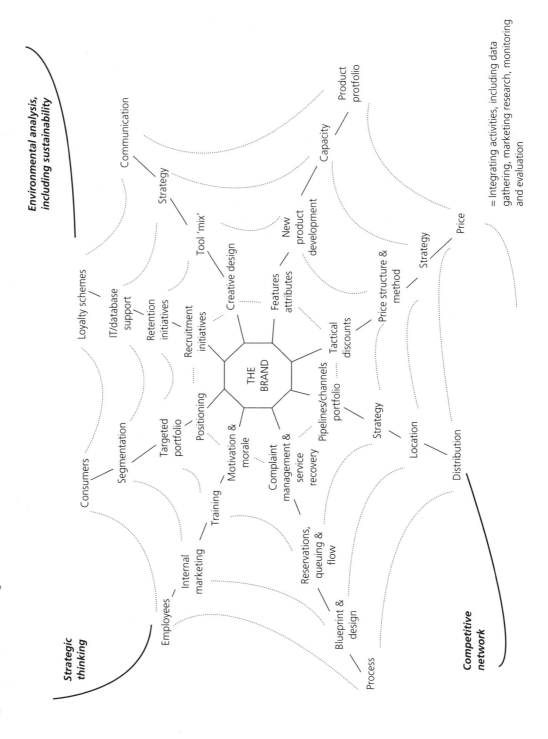

Strategic thinking

Environmental analysis, including sustainability

Competitive network

Employees

Internal marketing

Consumers

Segmentation

Loyalty schemes

IT/database support

Communication

Targeted portfolio

Positioning

Retention initiatives

Recruitment initiatives

Strategy

Training

Motivation & morale

Creative design

Tool 'mix'

Features attributes

New product development

Product portfolio

Capacity

THE BRAND

Complaint management & service recovery

Pipelines/channels portfolio

Tactical discounts

Price structure & method

Strategy

Price

Reservations, queuing & flow

Strategy

Location

Blueprint & design

Distribution

Process

= Integrating activities, including data gathering, marketing research, monitoring and evaluation

A brief probe into the loyalty question

Most loyalty schemes are 'owned' by single brands or by a collection of brands (for schemes such as Oneworld or Star Alliance). The development of consumer loyalty schemes within travel and tourism is a natural extension of lifetime value (LTV) thinking, consumer retention, and the necessity of capturing information about frequent users. Certain tourism sectors, such as many destinations and attractions, may find loyalty scheme efforts move against certain consumer tendencies to move on to 'something new' – for example, tourism connected to exploration and discovery of the previously unvisited. For those sectors where loyalty schemes appear attractive (aviation, tour operation, cruise operation, inclusive resorts, hospitality brands, and so forth), the accumulation of consumer benefits may represent a considerable future liability. They generate repeat purchase (of varying patterns, depending on consumer membership of rival schemes) but do not necessarily foster the attitudinal side of the loyalty equation (as argued by Dick and Basu, 1994). Loyalty programmes require strategic thought and careful attention to detail if they are truly to be the valuable assets portrayed in magazine articles and case studies.

Conclusion

This chapter set out to give a flavour of some of the challenges faced by marketers in travel and tourism today, and links these challenges back to the underlying characteristics of the product. The discussion questions below give the reader an opportunity to further develop and explore some of the ideas introduced within the chapter, and the final question allows the reader to marry (or, indeed, divorce) knowledge of sustainability within the tourism literature to the ideas being highlighted within generic marketing. No single source can present the reader with a solid appreciation of the marketing task, but the recommended reading given here and the references used within the chapter should provide the reader with stimulating and useful material with which to further their marketing knowledge.

Discussion questions

1. How and why might the marketing practice for a destination differ from the marketing practice for a commercial tourism company? How and why might the marketing practice for a small or micro enterprise differ from the marketing practice for a large international tourism company?
2. How far do you think tourism destinations and tourism organisations are competing in a global marketplace? What evidence (and contra-evidence) do you have to support your argument?
3. If tourism marketing is about the consumption of experiences, what role (if any) does marketing have for sustainability?
   [Students interested in developing these ideas may like to read Kilbourne (1995) and van Dam and Apeldoorn (1996) for a perspective on the discussion within the marketing (as opposed to tourism) field.]

Suggested further reading

Enright, M. (2002) Marketing and conflicting dates for its emergence: Hotchkiss, Bartels, the 'Fifties School' and alternative accounts. *Journal of Marketing*, 18(5–6): 445–61.

Hooley, G.J., Saunders, J.A. and Piercy, N.F. (1998) *Marketing Strategy and Competitive Positioning* (2nd edition). London: Financial Times/Prentice-Hall.

Middleton, V.T.C. with Clarke, J. (2001) *Marketing in Travel and Tourism* (3rd edition). Oxford: Butterworth Heinemann.

Moutinho, L. (1987) Consumer behaviour in tourism. *European Journal of Marketing*, 21(10): 5–44.

World Tourism Organisation (1999) *Changes in Leisure Time*. Madrid: WTO.

World Tourism Organisation (2000) *Marketing Tourism Destinations Online. Strategies for the Information Age*. Madrid: WTO.

Zeithaml, V.A. and Bitner, M.J. (2000) *Services Marketing: Integrating Customer Focus Across the Firm* (2nd edition). London: Irwin McGraw-Hill.

Answers to Case Study 7.2 Working with Fixed Capacity of a Perishable Product: The London Eye

1. Winter season: 10 ½ hours × 1,500 (hourly capacity) = 15,750 pax, giving a maximum daily revenue (15,750 × £9.50 of individual adult) of £149,625. Summer season: 12 ½ hours × 1,500 (hourly capacity) = 18,750 pax, giving a maximum daily revenue (18,750 × £9.50 of individual adult) of £178,125.

2. Over one week in winter season, potential maximum revenue £149,625 × 7 = £1,047,375 (representing 110,250 pax). At 70% this means only 77,175 pax, giving a revenue of £733,163, representing a 'loss' of £314,212 over the one week.

3. Potential maximum revenue for one summer season week is 131,250 pax × £9.50 = £1,246,875. 20% individual adults (26,250 pax/£249,375 revenue), 40% children (52,500 pax/£262,500 revenue), 10% senior citizens (13,125 pax/£98,437.5 revenue), 5% registered disabled (6,563 pax/£49,222.5 revenue) and 25% school groups (32,812 pax/£147,654 revenue), giving a total revenue of £807,189. In other words, a drop of £439,686, or 35%, just from a given segment mix (and assuming 100% of capacity sold!).

8 Strategy for tourism

John Tribe

Chapter objectives

The purpose of this chapter is to provide an overview of tourism corporate strategy. Having completed this chapter, the reader will be able to:

- appreciate the importance of both mission and stakeholders
- identify the techniques of strategic analysis and choice
- appreciate the processes of strategic implementation

Chapter contents

Introduction

This chapter provides an overview of tourism corporate strategy. Without strategy, organisations are susceptible to strategic drift – a consequence of failure to monitor and respond to the changing external environment. Organisations which do not use strategic planning tend to make *ad hoc* decisions and be reactive rather than proactive to events. The absence of an effective strategy can result in corporate failure as exemplified by Debonair, the Luton-based low-cost airline which ceased trading in 1999. So what is strategy? According to Johnson and Scholes (2001: 10, original emphasis), 'Strategy is the *direction* and *scope* of an organisation over the *long term*: which achieves *advantage* for the organisation through the configuration of *resources* within a changing *environment*, to meet the needs of *markets* and to fulfil *stakeholder* expectations'. Athiyamen and Robertson (1995) found 'a level of commitment to strategic planning in the tourism industry at least as strong as that in the manufacturing sector'. Their study restricted its research to large tourism firms. However, use of the strategic approach is not confined to large firms and may be undertaken by the whole range of organisations in the tourism sector.

In the UK, the tourism industry consists of some 127,000 businesses, 80% of which have a turnover of less than £250,000 per annum (http://www.culture.gov.uk/tourism/). These private sector organisations range from small and medium-sized enterprises (SMEs) which are particularly important in this sector, such as family-owned guest houses, to large plcs and multinationals such as Six Continents plc. But tourism organisations include those which are not for profit (e.g., Tourism Concern) as well as public sector organisations (such as the English Tourism Council) and departments within the government (the Department for Culture, Media and Sport (DCMS) is the government department responsible for tourism in the UK). In addition, destinations and Trade Associations, which are not single organisations but rather represent a coalition of interested parties, commonly take a strategic approach. For example, Zhang (1999) describes a strategy for the development of tourism for Altay Prefecture, Xinjiang, China. Finally, strategies are formulated to achieve goals at a more general level, for instance sustainable tourism. For example, Hosni (2000) outlines a strategy for sustainable tourism development in the Sahara. Because of the complexity of organisations, coalitions and themes involved in tourism, Tribe's (1997: 13) definition of strategy is an appropriate one for this sector: 'Strategy ... [is] the planning of a desirable future and the design of suitable ways of bringing it about.'

There are four key elements of corporate strategy:

1. *Mission*: This determines what an organisation is trying to achieve and provides the aim and direction for strategy.
2. *Strategic analysis*: This provides information to an organisation regarding the strengths and weaknesses of its internal resources and the opportunities and threats evident in its external environment.
3. *Strategic choice*: This is where an organisation generates, evaluates and chooses an appropriate strategy.
4. *Strategic implementation*: This shows how an organisation puts its strategy into practice.

Mission and stakeholders

It is difficult for an organisation to formulate a strategy without a clear idea of its overall aim. The mission of an organisation can be thought of as what the organisation is trying to achieve; what its purpose or aim is and where it is trying to head in the medium to long term (David, 1989). For example, the mission statement of Six Continents plc is:

> Six Continents aims to create long-term sustainable growth in shareholder value through developing and strengthening the leading brands within its core businesses of high-growth

international hotels and high-return restaurants and pubs. Six Continents is deploying its strong management, global infrastructure and substantial financial resources to drive superior returns from the expansion of its proven brands. (www.sixcontinents.com)

A mission statement should be a succinct, achievable, visionary statement that looks to the future and describes the main aim of the organisation. The Six Continents plc mission statement is typical of those of profit-making organisations with its emphasis on shareholder value. Not-for-profit organisations such as Tourism Concern have missions that encompass different aims:

'Tourism Concern campaigns for a tourism industry that is

- Just: yielding benefits that are fairly distributed;
- Participatory: involving local people in its development and management; and
- Sustainable: putting long-term environmental and social benefit before short-term gain. (www.tourismconcern.org.uk)

In this case it is ethical considerations, rather than profit, which guide Tourism Concern.

An organisation's mission is often accompanied by a series of objectives that spell out the goals that it needs to achieve to realise its mission. Objectives may be written in a closed or open form. Closed objectives describe quantifiable targets and should conform to SMART principles and thus be:

- specific;
- measurable;
- agreed with those who must attain them;
- realistic; and
- time-constrained.

On the other hand, open objectives are written in more of a qualitative style.

The mission question (what does the organisation exist for?) cannot readily be answered without consideration of the stakeholder question (who does an organisation exist for?). The term 'stakeholder' refers to a person or group of people who have an interest in the operation of a particular organisation and 'stakeholder analysis' (Mitroff, 1983; Freeman, 1984) is a useful way of analysing the importance of different stakeholders to an organisation. Stakeholder analysis starts with a mapping of a range of stakeholders who are often divided into those who are external and those who are internal to an organisation. A stakeholder map for British Airways would include:

- shareholders (may be divided into large and small);
- directors;
- workers (may be subdivided and include Trade Union groupings);
- customers;
- bankers;
- key suppliers;

- airlines in Oneworld Alliance;
- local community; and
- environmental groups.

But it is stakeholder power which will determine the influence that different groups have in an organisation's mission. The power of internal stakeholders is influenced by factors such as position in the organisation, control over resources, power of patronage, charisma and specialist knowledge. External stakeholders can wield power because of control of resources (particularly finance), their constitutional role (e.g., shareholder voting rights) and legal agreements (e.g., banks). Sautter and Leisen (1999) discuss stakeholder theory and its application as a tool for tourism development.

Strategic analysis

The next stage in the formulation of tourism corporate strategy is strategic analysis. This involves consideration of the major influences affecting the organisation's ability to fulfil its mission in terms of resources and environment. Strategic analysis reports on the current and future strengths and weaknesses and opportunities and threats (SWOT) facing the organisation.

Opportunities and threats summarise the external environmental factors that a tourism organisation faces. The key elements of the external environment may be summarised as C-PEST factors which refer to the

- competitive;
- political;
- economic;
- socio-cultural; and
- technological environments.

Strengths and weaknesses analysis summarises the state of the internal resources of an organisation.

Opportunities, threats and the external environment

The competitive environment of the tourism industry describes the extent of influence of tourism organisations or destinations upon one another, and that of suppliers and buyers. The competitive environment may be analysed in two ways. First, structural analysis examines the whole industry in which a tourism organisation operates for competitive pressures. Profit-maximising tourism organisations will seek a position within an industry where competitive threats can be minimised and competitive opportunities exploited. Porter's (1980) 'five forces' model can be used to analyse the competitive environment. The five forces proposed by Porter are:

- the threat of new entrants;
- the power of buyers;
- the power of suppliers;
- the threat of substitutes; and
- the degree of rivalry between competitors.

Secondly, competitor analysis involves a more detailed look at a tourism organisation's existing and potential competitors. It enables an organisation to formulate a strategy in the light of an assessment of its key rivals. Porter (1980) sets out a framework for competitor analysis by deploying a response profile of competitive organisations. The profile is divided into two sections. The first section asks questions about the motives of competitors and the second section asks questions about the competitors' current and future activities. The detailed questions that need to be addressed within the response profile include:

- product lines;
- prices;
- quality;
- differentiation;
- advertising;
- market segment;
- marketing practices; and
- growth and prospects.

Buhalis (2001) provides a strategic analysis of the competitiveness of tourism in Greece, identifying its unique nature, culture and heritage as strengths and the lack of differentiation of the tourism product as well as competitive disadvantages in marketing and planning as weaknesses. Dwyer, Forsyth and Prasada (2000) investigate the price competitiveness of tourism packages to Australia, basing their approach on the 'Big Mac' index used by *The Economist* magazine.

The political environment is important to tourism organisations since it is here that changes in laws, regulations and policy occur (Hall and Jenkins, 1995). It is therefore important to establish the location of political power, how political power may change in the future and the likely effects of this on policy. Dahles (2001) and Akama (2002) analyse the effects of government policy on tourism in Indonesia and Kenya, respectively. It is also important to identify the level of the political environment in which a tourism organisation is working. For example, a tour operator situated in Germany will face a political environment at local government level, at national government level and at European Union level. Additionally, it will have to operate in the different political environments of the destination countries of its tours.

Analysis of governments, oppositions and the election cycle yields information on the political environment, and government plans and party manifestos are also important sources of information. In addition, pressure group activity can be important in influencing policy in democracies, and the activities of such groups as Greenpeace and

Tourism Concern attempt to affect government policy as it relates to tourism. Political groupings, such as Al Qaeda, that exist outside the political establishment can also have significant effects on tourism. The following examples illustrate the effects of changes in the political environment on tourism organisations:

- The development of an 'open skies' policy by the European Union (EU) dating from 1987 enabled easyJet to enter a market formerly virtually closed to new airlines.
- The Gulf war, the war in former Yugoslavia and the September 11, 2001 terrorist attacks all had significant impacts in tourist movements. The latter in particular led to a significant reduction in North American tourists to Europe.

The economic environment affects tourism destinations and organisations both in terms of demand factors and, especially in the case of organisations, in terms of supply and costs as well (Tribe, 1999). The main economic variables to be analysed include:

- *Consumers' expenditure.* This is the amount of money consumers actually spend. It is mainly determined by income level, but is affected by savings, taxation and government benefit payments, consumer credit and expectations about the future. There is a direct positive relationship between growth in consumers' expenditure and growth in demand for tourism.
- *Exchange rates.* This is the value of a country's currency in terms of other currencies. A high exchange rate for the pound sterling means lower costs for tour operators buying services in foreign currency. It also encourages UK outbound tourists but discourages inbound tourists.
- *Interest rates.* This affects the cost of borrowing. High interest rates increase the costs of tourism organisations and dampen tourists' demand.
- *Taxation.* This includes taxes on income, spending and profits. Increases in the former can reduce tourism demand.
- *Inflation.* This is the change in the general level of prices and it can result in destinations becoming less competitive.

Frechtling (2001) investigates a number of ways of forecasting tourism demand and the Australia Tourism Forecasting Council (1998) analysed the effects of changes in the global economic environment on visitor arrivals to Australia with special reference to the Asian economic downturn.

Factors to analyse in the socio-cultural environment of tourism organisations include the size and structure of the population, social class, and attitudes and values. Wells and Gubar (1966) stress the importance of age in their life-cycle analysis, which can be useful in predicting tourism market trends. Poon (1993) identified a change in values between 'old tourists' and 'new tourists' and the characteristics of 'new tourists' have important implications for tourism organisations and destinations. Dredge (2001) discusses the impacts of technological, economic, social and cultural change on the development of tourism at Lake Macquarie, Australia, showing how its different roles as a region of escape for the working classes, as a lifestyle of leisure, and as a place of tourism for the gentry have evolved over the twentieth century.

The technological environment offers both opportunities and threats to tourism organisations. The opportunities resulting from technological development may be found in cheaper provision, or improvements in goods and services, better marketing and changes in distribution systems. However technology may result in an organisation's product or service becoming obsolete, or subject to new forms of competition. Buhalis (2000, 2001) offers a comprehensive analysis of the impact of information technology on tourism organisations.

Strengths, weaknesses and an organisation's resources

Analysis of its resources and products or services enables a tourism organisation to assess its strategic capability – or how well it is equipped to pursue its strategy. Resources are typically classified under four headings.

1. Physical resources, including buildings, fixtures and fittings, machinery and transport fleets.
2. Human resources, consisting mainly of skills.
3. Financial resources, demonstrated by an organisation's liquidity and its overall debt or credit situation.
4. Intangibles (Hall, 1992), including acquired knowledge and skills, patents and recipes, good will, brands and corporate image.

Performance monitoring analyses the way in which resources are being utilised and can include the following:

- analysis of efficiency;
- financial analysis;
- appraisal; and
- comparative analysis.

Efficiency measures the ratio of inputs to outputs. A specific example of this is ARGE (asset revenue generating efficiency) (Bridge and Mouthino, 2000). Broader measures of financial evaluation include share prices, earnings per share, and return on capital employed (ROCE). Appraisal is used for the evaluation of human resources and is a process where employees meet with their line managers to set targets for the future and review performance against previous targets. Comparative analysis can be made by reference to an organisation's historical record, to other organisations in an industry (best practice) or to a benchmark. For example, easyJet's load factor showed improvement in historical terms rising from 80.8% in 2000 to 83% in 2001 (easyJet, 2001).

An evaluation of an organisation's products and services is the other important part of capability analysis and methods of evaluation here include:

Figure 8.1   The Boston Consulting Group matrix

Market Share → ↓ Market Growth	High	Low
High	Star	Question Mark
Low	Cash cow	Dog

- effectiveness;
- value chain analysis;
- portfolio analysis; and
- product life-cycle analysis.

Effectiveness measures how well a product or service meets its objectives and can be measured by consumer satisfaction surveys, for example. Value chain analysis investigates whether the provision of a good or service is effective throughout its value chain (i.e., from advertising through to production and after-sales). Portfolio analysis determines whether an organisation's range of products are well balanced for future growth by use of the Boston Consulting Group (BCG) matrix (Figure 8.1). The BCG matrix assesses products in terms of their market share and market growth and from this analysis organisations should be able to plan their future portfolios – generally withdrawing products which are classified as dogs and planning for future cash cows and stars.

The four stages of the product life cycle (introduction, growth, maturity, decline) (Vernon, 1966, 1979) can be used to predict the development path of a tourism product or destination. In the case of destinations, Butler (1980) characterised the phases of destination development as exploration, involvement, development and consolidation. The latter phase might be followed by decline, stabilisation or rejuvenation. Cooper (in Witt and Mouthino, 1995) categorised various tourism destinations within Butler's model, arguing, for example, that Atlantic City in the USA had entered a rejuvenation phase.

A SWOT analysis provides a summary of the findings of strategic analysis and its elements are revisited in Figure 8.2. Narayan (2000) provides a destination SWOT analysis for Fiji.

Strategic choice

Strategic choice is concerned with the generation of strategic options, an evaluation of strategic options, and the selection of strategy. In simple terms, an organisation seeks to gain advantage over its competitors either by selling a cheaper product than the competition, or a better product than the competition, or a cheaper and better product. These are the key strategic options available. During any phase of strategic review a

Figure 8.2   SWOT matrix

Internal (Capability) Analysis	Strengths	Weaknesses
Resources	•	•
Products	•	•
External (Environment) Analysis	•	•
Competition	•	•
Political	•	•
Economic	•	•
Socio-cultural	•	•
Technological	•	•

number of strategic options will be generated from strategic analysis. The preferred option will pass the tests of suitability, feasibility and acceptability.

Michael Porter (1980) was an early analyst who identified the generic strategies (i.e., strategies that could be applied to a range of organisations and situations) of cost leadership and differentiation that could be used to gain competitive advantage over rivals. However, Olsen (1991) and Poon (1993) both argued that there were difficulties in applying Porter's analysis to tourism, with Poon suggesting that the four key strategic principles for effective tourism were putting customers first, quality leadership, product innovation and strengthening the organisation's strategic position in the value chain. Kotler (1988) and Bowman (1992) reworked Porter's typology of strategies using the dimensions of perceived quality and price. Figure 8.3 illustrates these on a matrix which incorporates Tribe's (1997) notion of zone X.

A price-based strategy seeks competitive advantage by offering the lowest prices in the industry. A key way to achieve this is to reduce costs by offering a basic, standardised, mass-produced, no-frills product with inessential aspects stripped out of the value chain. On the other hand, a differentiation strategy offers product quality and uniqueness. This is achieved through design, innovation, attention to quality and advertising. Kandampully and Duddy (2001) propose a model for superior service delivery which includes service empowerment, service guarantee and service recovery as a route to sustainable competitive advantage through differentiation.

Some organisations seek to provide high-quality products at low prices – a hybrid strategy. This is difficult to achieve because adding extra consumer value adds to costs and forces up prices. It is generally only feasible if an organisation can achieve economies of scale so that average costs fall in line with a growth in output. Each of these positions offers a strategy for gaining competitive advantage. Zone X (high prices/low quality) is generally a failure route except where an organisation is a monopoly (e.g., most train operating companies in the UK) or where consumers lack comprehensive information about a market.

Figure 8.3 Price/quality matrix

An organisation also needs to consider the directions and methods of strategic development. The main directions open to an organisation are:

- withdrawal;
- consolidation;
- market penetration;
- market development;
- product development; and
- diversification.

Organisations owning complex portfolios or with insufficient profits may follow a direction of consolidation (concentrating on best-performing products and markets) or withdrawal. For example, in 2002, Compass plc disposed of its Travelodge and Little Chef businesses to concentrate on contract food service and vending. This is sometimes referred to as 'decluttering'. Market penetration involves increasing market share, while market development seeks to bring existing products into new markets. Product development is based around innovation, improving existing products or developing new ones, while diversification involves an organisation entering into markets which are unrelated to its present portfolio. Six Continents plc is an example of an organisation which represents a diversified portfolio of hotels, pubs and restaurants.

The methods by which organisations may develop their strategy are:

- internal growth;
- mergers and take-overs;
- joint ventures and alliances; and
- franchising.

Internal growth often limits the pace and growth of an organisation but may be desirable where owners wish to retain control or avoid risk, or be unavoidable where finance is limited. Integration can occur through voluntary mergers or involuntary take-overs and can be divided into horizontal integration, vertical integration and conglomerate integration (diversification). Vertical integration is typical in the travel sector and represents ownership across different stages of production in the same industry. So the Preussag Group owns an airline (Britannia), a travel operator (Thomson) and a retail travel group (Lunn Poly). Ownership by Preussag of its own distribution channel (Lunn Poly) gives it preferential access to customers. Horizontal integration occurs at the same stage of production in the same industry. The take-over of Go airline by easyJet is an example and motives include rationalisation, economies of scale and widening the customer base. Diversification is merging with an organisation in a different industry.

Franchising offers a route to rapid market penetration, particularly of a strong, recognised brand, with limited exposure to risk or debt. About 90% of Holiday Inn hotels are owned franchises. Preble, Reichel and Hoffman (2000) explore the role of franchising in the hospitality and restaurant industries in Israel and show how independent hotels benefit from the global brand name of the franchising hotel chain and its reservations system, while the franchising hotel chain firm gains access to a new market without the risk involved in ownership. Joint ventures are popular where public sector ownership is strong. For example, in China, the hotel group Accor Asia has a joint venture agreement with the government to upgrade and manage about 100 hotels. Strategic alliances are a way of capturing the benefits of horizontal integration and globalisation while avoiding some of the financial, cultural and fit problems of a formal merger. Typically, they are networks formed for marketing benefits and are common among airlines. For example, the Oneworld Alliance allows its member airlines (e.g., British Airways and Qantas) to cross-market their products.

Strategies may be evaluated by three main techniques. First, suitability tests whether a strategy is appropriate to the situation an organisation faces, particularly with regard to its external environment and capability in terms of its own resources. Acceptability questions whether a strategy will deliver the aims and mission of an organisation, so for most private sector organisations profitability is a key test here. Finally, feasibility assesses whether a strategy is realistic in terms of the availability of funds, resources, logistics and likely competitor reaction.

Strategic implementation

The agreed organisational strategy will generally be set out in a formal document and effort then needs to be directed at strategic implementation. This is concerned with the putting into practice of an organisation's strategy. Initial consideration may need to be given to logistics and operations. Complex strategies will need a project plan which takes logistics into account and provides a logical sequence of what has to be done before each stage of the plan can be realised. It therefore takes account of time scales and the interdependency of different elements of a strategy and allows a critical path to be mapped. Operations management (Krajewski and Ritzman, 1996) entails the translating of a strategy into a series of operations and objectives with clear performance targets. This is sometimes termed 'management by objectives' (MBO). Objectives are set for key personnel to be achieved within a specific time frame.

Resource planning is a crucial part of strategic implementation. Financial resources (Atkinson et al., 1995) are paramount and planning is required to identify sources of finance and the logistics of finance (to ensure co-ordination between availability of finance and expenditure). The easyJet acquisition of Go, for example, required a rights issue of new share capital to provide the finance. A change in strategic direction will generally have implications for the acquisition and use of physical resources and in the case of a merger these may require rationalising. The easyJet/Go merger was straightforward because of the compatibility of aircraft, but required careful attention in the areas of IT systems and corporate headquarters. In terms of human resources (Baum, 1995), manpower planning will need to address the number of staff required, their skills, recruitment and redundancy, training and development, and grading and remuneration.

The relationship between organisational structure and strategy is controversial. On the one hand, it has been said that 'structure follows strategy' (Child, 1977), but Mintzberg, Quinn and Ghoshal (1998) contend that both influence each other. Structural types include functional, multidivisional, matrix structures and holding companies, and there are several issues relating to organisational design and strategy. First, how should personnel be grouped – for example, around functions (e.g., finance) or geographical markets? Secondly, organisations such as easyJet favour flat structures, whereas British Airways has a tall management structure with many layers of responsibility. Linked to this are issues of flexibility – are staff empowered to take the initiative to solve problems or must they act within a bureaucratic system? Is decision-making decentralised and near to the customer or centralised at head office? Indeed, organisational culture – the shared values and the way people do things – will be closely related to organisational structure. easyJet promotes a special 'orange culture' which is informal but 'mad about value' and 'mad about safety' (www.easyjet.com). Again, where strategy direction involves mergers, it is very important to consider the prospective 'fit' of company cultures as well as fit in terms of resources.

While market research will have contributed to strategy formulation, any change in strategic direction will have an impact on an organisation's marketing strategy. For organisations reliant on the Internet for marketing, Gretzel, Yuan YuLan and Fesenmaier (2000) found that information technology has led to a number of profound changes in the assumptions underlying communication strategies. Meethan (2002a) describes the redefining of the image of the local tourist industry in Southwest England, moving the local product away from sun-and-sand tourists towards visitors interested in culture and heritage attractions, to better respond to new types of tourist. Edgell, Ruf and Agarwal (1999) explain how strategic marketing can maintain a competitive edge for tourism organisations.

Finally, consideration has to be given to the management of change resulting from a new strategy. Tribe (1997) refers to the four Cs of change as:

- calculation;
- communication;
- culture; and
- compliance.

Calculation is the discovery and management of resisting and driving forces accompanying change. Communication is crucial in ensuring that everyone in an organisation understands the strategy of an organisation and their role in achieving it. Organisational culture may be an important factor inhibiting change as change may represent a threat to established routines. Key issues for achieving compliance with a new strategy include control of resources, building of alliances, systems of rewards and punishments, and charisma and leadership.

Conclusion

The general strategic method outlined in this chapter represents a standard cycle of strategic planning and a classical approach to strategy. However, it should be noted that the success of a strategy depends on the accuracy of much of the analysis contained in the plan. Much of the analysis involves forecasting and the future is notoriously unpredictable. Moreover, the classical approach assumes a particular rationality of those working in organisations that cannot always be relied upon. In the real world strategy is a contested concept and a messy business (see Case Study 8.1).

Case Study 8.1   easyJet plc

easyJet is a leading low-cost airline. Its principal activity is the provision of a 'low-cost–good value' airline service. It was founded in 1995 when new European Union rules allowed free competition in air transport and grew rapidly, becoming a plc in 2000. By 2001, the easyJet network consisted of 35 routes serving 17 airports in 16 cities. easyJet's mission statement is:

To provide our customers with safe, good value, point-to-point air services, to effect and to offer a consistent and reliable product and fares appealing to leisure and business markets on a range of European routes. To achieve this we will develop our people and establish lasting relationships with our suppliers.

easyJet's strategic analysis carried out in 2001 included the following findings:

- Minimal impact of the post-September 11, 2001 security regime but with some additional costs from security and insurance.
- Expected growth in the air transport market in Europe. The International Air Transport Association (IATA) estimates European scheduled passenger growth from 176 million in 1999 to 215 million in 2003 (5.1% growth per anum).
- Cranfield University estimates that low-cost airlines' share of market will grow from 4% to 12–15% by 2010.

- In the pessimistic case of slow economic growth in Europe, business travellers may seek low-cost alternatives to full-fare carriers.

easyJet's strategy is based on six key strengths that support its competitiveness:

- commitment to safety and customer service;
- simple fare structure – book early for low prices;
- low unit costs;
- strong branding;
- multi-base network – dense point-to-point services, mainly between major European airports; and
- strong corporate culture.

easyJet follows a strategy of low cost and good value. Its fares are determined by a sophisticated yield management system. They are more flexible and generally significantly lower than those of traditional airlines. It keeps costs low in the following ways:

- use of website to reduce distribution costs – about 90% seats are sold via easyJet.com. No tickets are sold through travel agents, saving in commission fees.
- maximising the utilisation of aircraft. Maximising the use of each aircraft (by time spent flying and by load factors) reduces the average cost.
- ticketless operation. This reduces the cost of issuing millions of tickets each year.
- No free on-board catering.
- Simple service model extends to no pre-assigned seats or interline connections.
- Airport use. Smaller airports such as Luton have lower handling charges and suffer less congestion and flight delays. This enables faster turnaround and extra flights.

- Standard aircraft. The use of only Boeing 737 reduces training and servicing costs.
- Paperless office. Management and administration of the company is undertaken entirely on IT systems.
- No expensive corporate HQ.
- Flat management structure.

In 2000/2001, easyJet's pre-tax profit grew to £40.1 million, on revenues of £356.9 million. This resulted from a 26.4% increase in sold seats and a total of 7.6 million passengers. It achieved aircraft utilisation of approximately 12 hours per day and load factors of 83%.

Table 8.1   easyJet revenue and profit

Year to end September	Revenue (£m)	Profit (£m)
1998	77.0	5.9
1999	139.8	1.3
2000	263.7	22.1
2001	356.9	40.1

Table 8.2   easyJet passenger statistics

Year	Total ('000)
1995	30
1996	420
1997	1,140
1998	1,880
1999	3,670
2000	5,996
2001	7,664

easyJet encourages an informal company culture and employees are encouraged to dress casually. easyJet encourages a special 'orange culture' and its values include being 'up for it', 'passionate' and 'sharp'. Most staff employed at the date of easyJet's flotation received a share incentive and share option schemes continue to be offered. Such schemes motivate employees to participate in the company's success. The company holds regular communication meetings and management briefings and publishes an employee newsletter. These channels enable the company to communicate its strategy and direction and receive feedback from employees. An executive team with extensive commercial, operational and financial experience is responsible for the overall management of the group and the company adopts a flat management structure. This eliminates unnecessary layers of management and reduces costs.

In 2002 easyJet was successful in its takeover of a competing low-cost airline, Go. This was financed through a rights issue of share capital. In the year to 31 March 2002, Go flew 4.3 million passengers, generating revenue of £233.7 million and profits before tax of £14 million. The benefits of the merger include:

- market development with the addition of routes not currently operated by easyJet;

- market penetration with the acquisition of a larger customer base;
- economies of scale, particularly in relation to the purchase of aircraft and fuel, maintenance arrangements, insurance, and marketing and advertising;
- the opportunity to achieve significant growth in a single step;
- a stronger and larger group to compete with other low-cost carriers and national flag carriers;
- ability of enlarged group to offer passengers a greater choice of destinations at competitive prices;
- similarity of Go's business model to that of easyJet;
- Go operates Boeing 737 aircraft;
- easyJet and Go have generally complementary networks;
- cultural fit with both companies, emphasising safety, high utilisation, punctuality and value for money;
- synergy benefits by the exploitation of easyJet's brand, yield management system, booking system and pricing system and Go's customer service expertise.

Source: Extracted and adapted from www.easyJet.com (2001)

Discussion questions

1. What are the key elements to a successful strategy?
2. To what extent does the easyJet case study represent a successful strategy?
3. What circumstances can cause an organisation's strategy to fail?
4. What are the different strategic challenges facing (a) a tourism destination, (b) the pressure group Tourism Concern and (c) a tour operator?

Suggested further reading

Johnson, G. and Scholes, K. (2001) *Exploring Corporate Strategy*. Hemel Hempstead: Prentice Hall.

Mintzberg, H., Quinn, J. and Ghoshal, S. (1998) *The Strategy Process*. Hemel Hempstead: Prentice Hall.

Mouthino, L. (ed.) (2000) *Strategic Management in Tourism*. Wallingford: CABI Publishing.

Tribe, J. (1997) *Corporate Strategy for Tourism*. London: Thomson Learning.

9 Managing Finance for Tourism

Tony Blackwood

Chapter objectives

The purpose of this chapter is to address some of the important issues relating to the financial management of businesses operating in the tourism industry. Having completed this chapter, the reader will be able to:

- explain the importance of financial management for businesses operating in the travel and tourism industry
- discuss the importance of long-term capital investment decisions
- explain the information requirements of decision-makers responsible for assessing potential business investment opportunities
- appreciate the implications of risk for long-term investment in the travel and tourism industry
- explain methods which may be used to assess the risk associated with investment projects and take it into account in the decision-making process
- appreciate issues influencing the sources of long-term finance which may be used to support long-term investments

Chapter contents

Introduction

This chapter considers the importance of financial management for firms operating in the travel and tourism industry. The subject area is very wide and there is a limit to the extent to which it can be addressed in a general management text such as this. Therefore, the chapter addresses it from a strategic point of view in order to give readers an appreciation of some of the fundamental issues for businesses operating in the industry. For those readers wishing to develop a deeper understanding of these issues, additional references are provided.

The objectives of businesses are initially considered before investigating two important financial management issues. The first of these considers how a business may determine which long-term business projects it should invest in. These strategic investments significantly influence all activities within a business and will therefore impact on other business disciplines, such as marketing, operational management and human resource management. Such decisions also impact on business performance and are therefore important for all business owners and managers.

As a basis for evaluation and analysis, the chapter will focus on the need to identify investments that will enhance the wealth of the owner(s) of the business. Theoretical aspects of alternative techniques and their employment in practice will be critically addressed by considering evidence from research findings. Wider issues will also be examined, emphasising the importance of risk and its strategic implications.

To be able to support these long-term investment projects financially, a business must have access to capital funds. The second main issue addressed in the chapter is therefore financing decisions. The major sources of long-term finance are considered and issues influencing the attractiveness of each from the business's point of view are highlighted.

Business objectives

The objectives of firms have been the subject of much academic study. In considering corporate firms, for example, Arnold (1998: 41) argues that 'whether we are considering a major investment programme, or trying to decide on the best kind of finance to use, the criterion of creating value for shareholders will be paramount'. However, the case for smaller firms is perhaps not so clear, with McMahon and Stanger (1995: 22) arguing that they are 'unlikely to have a single and overriding aim. ... Their intentions are apt to be numerous and complex.' This is supported by studies of small businesses operating in the tourism industry which suggest that owners of such businesses are not necessarily primarily driven by financial objectives (e.g., Blackwood and Mowl, 2000: 62). However, many academic studies have illustrated that poor financial management is a common cause of business failure (Lussier, 1985). Consequently, it is important that, in order to increase their chances of survival, prosperity and growth, all businesses consider financial management issues. The remainder of this chapter therefore addresses some of the important issues relating to sound financial management.

Financial management

The aim of commercial firms is, essentially, to raise money and invest it in attractive investment opportunities. The wealth of the business owners can be enhanced through raising appropriate finance at low cost and investing it in projects earning high returns. Consequently, the evaluation of investment opportunities, in order ascertain which are most desirable, and raising of appropriate long-term capital to support these investments are very important. We will now consider some of the significant issues relating to these activities.

Long-term Investment Decisions

Long-term investment entails the initial commitment of a capital outlay in a business project in the expectation that resulting future benefits will justify this investment. As the following extract from Airtours (now MyTravel) plc's annual report illustrates, it is therefore essential that a business identifies attractive investment opportunities in order to prosper.

> Airtours will continue to invest in new and existing markets to build sustainable passenger volumes. This will support additional investment in operating assets such as aircraft, cruise ships, hotels and vacation ownership resorts producing increased and higher quality earnings. (Crossland, 1998, Airtours Annual Report)

As this statement suggests, the investment can be in various types of activity and often entails very large sums. Such investment decisions can have a significant impact on the activities of the business for many years and can significantly affect its future performance. They can also be difficult to reverse and it is therefore imperative that the consequences of these decisions are fully contemplated before approving the investment.

Investment appraisal methods

An appraisal of a potential investment opportunity will entail estimating the likely impact of the decision on the future performance of the business. However, such forecasts are difficult in the uncertain environments in which travel and tourism businesses operate and, consequently, a business investment project entails a degree of uncertainty and risk. Therefore, risk is an inevitable and, indeed, desirable consequence of business activity. If those investing money in the business were unwilling to bear such risks, they could invest their capital in lower risk investments, such as bank deposits or government bonds. By investing in business ventures, they take greater risks but stand to reap the higher benefits.

In view of the significance of long-term investment decisions, it is important that business managers identify the range of potential long-term investment opportunities

Table 9.1 Financial analysis techniques used by large firms for the appraisal of major investments

	1975	1980	1986	1992	2000
	(%)	(%)	(%)	(%)	(%)
Payback period	73	81	92	94	66
Accounting rate of return (ARR)	51	49	56	50	55
Internal rate of return (IRR)	44	57	75	81	84
Net present value (NPV)	32	39	68	74	97
Discounted cash flow (DCF) (i.e., IRR or NPV)	58	68	84	88	100
Non-financial criteria used	7	–	–	–	39

Source: Adapted from Arnold and Hatzopoulos (2000)

available to them. Subsequently, given the risk and potential rewards, it is imperative that they fully consider the implications of each alternative before committing what may be a substantial amount of capital. This will involve forecasting the likely impact of the investment in terms of anticipated costs and benefits and attempting to quantify these in order to assess their implications for the future financial performance of the business. Numerous techniques exist which may be used to appraise investment decisions. Table 9.1 lists some of the more popular methods with the results of research studies investigating their use in practice.

A detailed analysis of the methods included in Table 9.1 is beyond the scope of this text. Readers interested in a critical examination of the alternative techniques should therefore refer to the additional texts listed at the end of this chapter. However, the table shows that the most popular are DCF (i.e., discounted cash flow) techniques. These methods reflect the fact that the wealth of the business owner(s) is influenced by not only the size of future cash flows expected as the result of the investment decision, but also their timing. In other words, investors prefer not only large cash inflows, but also desire them as early as possible due to the fact that the value of money erodes over time. That is to say, £1,000 receivable in one year's time is worth less than the same sum receivable today, as its purchasing power will be eroded. As future cash flows expected from a long-term investment project will arise in different time periods, they must be adjusted in order to compensate for this 'time value of money'. All anticipated future cash flows are converted to their value in today's terms, known as their 'present value', in order that they can be meaningfully aggregated to determine whether or not the benefits (i.e., cash inflows) exceed the costs (i.e., cash outflows).

Net present value

Case Study 9.1 illustrates the calculation of the net present value of an investment project in a hotel.

Case Study 9.1   Net present value in investment decisions – hotel vending equipment

Year	Income (£s)
1	120,000
2	140,000
3	150,000

A hotel is considering investing £100,000 in vending machines. It has forecast that the machines will have a useful life of three years and that income from the equipment will be as follows:

It is expected that the cost of the items sold will average 60% of the selling price and that the annual maintenance cost for the equipment will be £5,000. The cost of capital for the hotel is 10% per annum.

Table 9.2   Determination of expected net present value

a Year	b Initial investment (£)	c Income (£)	d Cost of items sold (£)	e Maintenance (£)	f Net cash flow (£)	g 10% discount factor	h Net present value (£)
			(c × 60%)		(b+c+d+e)		(f × g)
0	−100,000				−100,000	1.000	−100,000
1		120,000	−72,000	−5,000	43,000	0.909	39,087
2		140,000	−84,000	−5,000	51,000	0.826	42,126
3		150,000	−90,000	−5,000	55,000	0.751	41,305
							22,518

In Table 9.2, the net cash flows expected from the project in future years, which are shown in column f, have been discounted in order to account for the time value of money and reflect their value in today's terms. The result shown in column h reflects their net present value (NPV) and shows, for example, that the expected net cash flow of £55,000 in three years' time is worth only £41,305 in today's terms. The resulting figures can be compared with the expected immediate cash outlay of £100,000 (i.e., in time period 0) to determine the project's acceptability.

The cost of capital of 10% reflects the required rate of return for investing in the hotel and the resulting positive net present value for the project suggests that the proposed investment is expected to exceed this requirement. In other words, the anticipated benefits from this investment are expected to exceed the costs by £22,518 in present value terms and the wealth of the business owner(s) is expected to increase by this amount. Theoretically, any project with an anticipated NPV in excess of zero is acceptable on the grounds that it is expected to satisfy investors' required rate of return and create economic value. This approach to evaluating investment opportunities is the academically preferred method. As Table 9. 1 shows, its use appears to be increasing over time, with the most recent study showing that 97% of businesses surveyed were employing the technique.

Internal rate of return

The internal rate of return (IRR) method also uses a DCF approach, but expresses the result as a percentage return on investment rather than the absolute amount shown by the NPV method. This return can be determined using a technique known as interpolation or, alternatively, by using the IRR function on a computer spreadsheet such as Microsoft Excel. An expected return in excess of the required rate of return indicates a project which is financially viable. In the case of the hotel vending project in Case Study 9.1, an IRR of 22% can be determined using the spreadsheet function. As this exceeds the required rate of 10%, the result is further confirmation that the project is financially acceptable.

Dealing with risk

A major concern arising from the employment of these techniques is the fact that, as was explained earlier, they use *estimates* of the impact of an investment decision on the cash flows of the business. As Ross, Westerfield and Jordan (2003: 298) observe, 'we are frequently operating under considerable uncertainty about the future. We can only estimate the NPV of an investment in this case. The resulting estimate can be very "soft". Meaning that the true NPV might be very different.' Thus, the vending project will only produce the financial benefit identified if the costs incurred and benefits realised correspond with those forecast at the outset. In practice, given the uncertainty that accompanies business activity, it is highly unlikely that future outcomes will actually turn out as initially predicted. Thus, the business is taking a risk in making the investment, and while risk is an inevitable consequence of business, it is important that at the decision-making stage it is addressed in some way and its potential consequences are considered.

Assessing and managing risk is an area of growing importance for businesses in view of the fact that they operate in ever-changing and increasingly uncertain environments. Ho and Pike (1992), in a study investigating attitudes to risk analysis in large companies, found that most managers questioned were of the opinion that risk was an important issue when taking capital investment decisions and that more than half considered that a formal approach to risk analysis was important. However, they claim that managers are either incapable of using formal approaches or are unable to find an approach which is easy to use and cost-effective.

Risk is a particularly important issue for businesses operating in the travel and tourism industry due to the uncertainty arising from its high degree of sensitivity to levels of economic activity. Case Study 9.2 provides an example of this and its potential consequences.

Case Study 9.2   Risk in the travel and tourism industry

The Disney Corporation

However, the company has not been without criticism and the downturn in the international travel and tourism industry has impacted negatively on the Disney global theme parks. In August, the company advised that given the economic performance overall, earnings for the 4th quarter would be lower than expected. … There may be little doubt that Disney, like other multinationals relying on the tourist industry for segments of profit, has undergone losses due to negative economic factors....

Source: www.BusinessED.net,
16 October 2002

In view of the potential consequences of the associated risk, alternative approaches for dealing with it when appraising capital investment opportunities have evolved. Table 9.3 lists some of the more popular of these, with empirical evidence on their employment in practice. Again, a detailed critical analysis of these techniques is beyond the scope of this text and readers interested in studying these in greater depth are referred to the books listed at the end of the chapter. However, an overview of some of the more popular methods listed is given below.

Sensitivity analysis

As Table 9.3 shows, this is a very popular method in practice. It entails investigating the sensitivity of results generated to errors in forecasts used to derive those results. If we return to the hotel vending project considered earlier, we can determine the impact of an underestimation of costs as shown in Case Study 9.3.

Table 9.3   Technique(s) used by large firms when assessing the risk of a major project

	1975	1980	1986	1992	2000
	(%)	(%)	(%)	(%)	(%)
Sensitivity/scenario analysis	28	42	71	88	89
Raising the required rate of return (RRR)	37	41	61	65	50
Subjective assessment	n/a	n/a	n/a	n/a	55
Probability analysis	9	10	40	48	42
Shorten payback period	25	30	61	60	11
Beta analysis	0	0	16	20	5
Ignore risk	n/a	n/a	n/a	n/a	3
Other	2	4	n/a	n/a	5

Source: Adapted from Arnold and Hatzopoulos (2000)

Case Study 9.3   Sensitivity analysis in investment decisions

The impact of a 5% underestimation in the initial forecast of:
(a)   the vending equipment
(b)   the annual maintenance costs

(a)   The cost of the vending equipment

Table 9.4   Revised expected net present value

a Year	b initial investment (£)	c Income (£)	d Cost of items sold (£)	e Maintenance (£)	f Net cash flow (£)	g 10% discount factor	h Net present value (£)
			(c × 60%)		*(b+c+d+e)*		*(f × g)*
0	−105,000				−100,000	1.000	−105,000
1		120,000	−72,000	−5,000	43,000	0.909	39,087
2		140,000	−84,000	−5,000	51,000	0.826	42,126
3		150,000	−90,000	−5,000	55,000	0.751	41,305
							17,518

This shows that the revised NPV of £17,518 represents a reduction in value of *22%* when compared with the original anticipated NPV of £22,518.

(b)   The annual maintenance costs

Table 9.5   Revised expected net present value

a Year	b initial investment (£)	c Income (£)	d Cost of items sold (£)	e Maintenance (£)	f Net cash flow (£)	g 10% discount factor	h Net present value (£)
			(c × 60%)		*(b+c+d+e)*		*(f × g)*
0	−100,000				−100,000	1.000	−100,000
1		120,000	−72,000	−5,250	42,750	0.909	38,860
2		140,000	−84,000	−5,250	50,750	0.826	41,919
3		150,000	−90,000	−5,250	54,750	0.751	41,117
							21,896

In this case the revised NPV of £21,896 represents a reduction in value of only *2.8%* when compared with the original anticipated NPV of £22,518.

These results suggest that the financial performance of the project is more sensitive to the estimate of the initial investment than that of maintenance costs. Decision-makers should therefore be more concerned about the potential for inaccurate forecasting of the cost of the vending equipment. The technique can be applied to all variables affecting a project and highlight those to which its success is most sensitive. Before a final decision is taken to invest in the project, these 'critical success factors' can be investigated further in order to determine the likelihood of deviation from the figures estimated. If the project is subsequently approved and the investment undertaken, these factors should be closely monitored and controlled to ensure that their outcomes are not significantly different from those forecast.

Adjusting the required rate of return

This approach is based on the premise that logical investors will require a higher rate of return to compensate them for the risk associated with riskier investments. For instance, investors could invest their funds in risk-free investments such as government bonds and earn a (relatively low) return, without the risk that investing in a business entails. Therefore, in order to justify the higher risk associated with business projects, a risk premium is required, resulting in a higher required rate of return (RRR). The higher the risk associated with the proposed investment, the higher will be the investors' RRR. Thus, when appraising potential investment projects, decision-makers should set the RRR accordingly, with higher risk projects being required to demonstrate the potential to earn higher rewards to justify this higher level of risk. This approach is demonstrated in Table 9.6.

Table 9.6   Adjusting the required rate of return

	Investment opportunities		
Nature of investment	Extension of the use of existing technology	Development of the use of new technology	Expansion into a new and untested market
Risk profile	Low risk	Medium risk	High risk
Risk free rate	5%	5%	5%
Risk premium	6%	9%	15%
Required rate of return	11%	14%	20%

The results in Table 9.6 show that to justify the higher level of risk associated with the possible expansion into a new market, the investment proposal must be able to demonstrate an expected return in excess of 20%. If those responsible for taking the decision are unable to satisfy themselves that this is the case, then the proposal should be rejected on the grounds that the expected return from the project is insufficient reward to justify the risk arising for those providing the capital. Thus, rather than using a single RRR in a business, a range of target returns reflecting different levels of risk can be established.

Although this approach can be used to take into account investor attitudes towards risk, there are practical problems in its use. For example, the classification of potential investments according to risk categories will be a somewhat subjective exercise. The subsequent determination of an appropriate risk premium for a particular degree of risk is another problematic issue. An approach which addresses these problems is beta analysis using the capital asset pricing model developed by Sharpe (1964), who was awarded the Nobel Prize for Economics for his work. This can be used to help determine required rates of return for different types of business activity using information on the stock market performance of companies engaged in those types of activity.

Probability analysis

This technique can be used by assigning probabilities to various possible outcomes resulting from the investment project and using probability analysis to ascertain expected outcomes which can be used to assess the proposed investment. Again, it can be argued that the determination of a range of potential outcomes and the assignment of associated probabilities is a subjective exercise. However, in its defence, this approach at least recognises that there is a range of possible outcomes arising as a result of making the investment, with consequences for the project's success and ultimately the performance of the business.

Positive aspects of risk and uncertainty

Risk is usually considered in a negative context. However, operating in the uncertain and risky environments to which businesses in the travel and tourism industry are exposed can have its advantages. These arise due to the flexibility managers have in decision-making and the determination of business strategies. Once an investment project has been approved and the project commences, managers can affect its outcome through further initiatives provoked by new information which becomes available throughout the project's life. For example, in some cases, if actual demand proves to be higher than originally estimated, the project may be expanded to exploit this. However, if demand levels are disappointing, they are not obliged to invest further capital in expanding the project. This flexibility gives managers an option to take a particular course of action without the obligation to do so. Such choices have been dubbed 'real options' in academic circles to distinguish them from 'financial options', which grant the right (but again not the obligation) to purchase financial assets such as currencies or company shares. There is growing interest in the value of these 'real options' and the means by which this information is used when taking investment decisions.

EasyJet, for example, when announcing its aim for passenger growth of 25% per annum over a seven year period, highlighted plans to buy 120 new Airbus jets and the negotiation of an option to buy an additional 120 aircraft (*Daily Mail*, 16 October 2002). From their point of view, this expansion option has the advantage that if future market conditions are favourable, they can exercise their right to purchase the aircraft cheaply, thus making the investment a more attractive proposition. However, if this is not the case and conditions prove to be unfavourable, they are not obliged to make the purchases. Consequently, they have some protection from the volatile environment in which they operate and the option they have negotiated is therefore valuable. It provides an opportunity to exploit the benefits which can arise in favourable operating conditions, without suffering the potential adverse consequences of the uncertain environment. If operating in the risky conditions which accompany the airline business is a gamble, the negotiation of the option offers easyJet the possibility of winning, while simultaneously limiting the chance and consequences of losing. As Brealey and Myers (2003: 631) observe, when considering airlines purchasing new aircraft, 'In this industry "lead times" between an order and delivery can extend to several years. Long lead times mean that airlines which order planes today may end up not needing them. You can see why an airline might negotiate for an aircraft purchase *option*.'

Furthermore, it can be argued that the more volatile the environment in which the business operates, the more valuable the option is. This is because in conditions of increased uncertainty there is a greater range of possible outcomes. This means that, for businesses operating in these volatile conditions, the 'upside potential' is greater but the 'downside risk' is also higher, increasing the uncertainty and risk. However, as we have seen, an option offers protection from the adverse consequences while preserving the opportunity to take advantage of the high rewards accompanying favourable conditions. Consequently, it can be argued that where real options are available to a business, there is an advantage in operating in high-risk environments which are subject to great uncertainty.

As well as expansion, other options may also exist, including the opportunity to postpone a project until conditions are more favourable or, in some cases, to abandon a project which is not producing the benefits originally anticipated. Given that many businesses operating in the travel and tourism industry do operate in particularly uncertain conditions, the potential for creation of these options should be carefully considered. Where they have been identified, decision-makers should attempt to incorporate their value when appraising possible investment opportunities, in order that the potential benefits of such projects are not understated. As Dixit and Pindyck (1995: 115) observe:

> The economic environment in which most companies operate is far more volatile and unpredictable than it was 20 years ago. ... Uncertainty requires that managers become much more sophisticated in the ways they assess and account for risk. It's important for managers to get a better understanding of the options that their companies have or that they are able to create. Ultimately, options create flexibility, and, in an uncertain world, the ability to value and use flexibility is critical.

Wider issues for consideration in investment decisions

The preceding sections have focused on the expected financial implications of investment opportunities. However, in practice, there may be other factors which also merit consideration. For example, a proposal to invest in computer equipment, which will automate administrative activities, may result in staff dissatisfaction due to possible redundancy implications. In extreme cases, there may even be a threat of industrial action if the proposal is implemented. As these represent unwelcome consequences of the investment, it could be argued that their impact should be incorporated in some way into the costs associated with the project. However, such costs are difficult to quantify in practice. Consequently, decision-makers need to consider such issues alongside the financial implications of the proposal before deciding whether the project should proceed. The results of financial appraisal techniques should therefore be used to inform and guide decision-makers rather than to replace management judgement.

Financing decisions

Raising an appropriate amount of finance at the required time is essential to enable businesses to support their investment programmes. Like other business resources, finance takes different forms, each with particular characteristics, and it is important that this is taken into account. So, for example, the finance required to support long-term strategic investments should be obtained from long-term sources. The most important of these are the funds provided by the owner(s) (referred to as 'equity' in the world of corporate finance) and long-term loans secured from other parties willing to invest in the future prospects of the business. This debt may be provided by banks and other financial institutions, or by other investors buying financial instruments traded in capital markets such as the international stock exchanges.

The cost of these sources of finance reflects the rate of return required by those providing the funds. This required rate of return (RRR) is influenced by the investors' perception of risk associated with providing the finance and by the returns available to them from alternative investments. If we consider risk, then those providing debt finance to companies are legally entitled to financial reward arising from their provision of funds. However, equity providers have no such guarantees and due to this higher level of risk, require a higher rate of return on their investment. Thus, the cost of equity will exceed the cost of debt. This benefit, associated with the use of debt finance, is reinforced by the fact that it is also tax efficient. This is because interest payments servicing the debt will reduce business profits and therefore the tax payable on those profits. This principle is illustrated in Table 9.7 where a business is considering borrowing £200,000 at an interest rate of 10% per annum and the corporation tax rate is assumed to be 35%.

Table 9.7   The tax advantage of debt finance

Annual profit statement

	Without debt (£000)	With debt (£000)	Impact of debt (£000)
Income	1,000	1,000	0
Costs – interest	0	−20	−20
– other	−800	−800	0
Profit before tax	200	180	−20
Less tax @ 35%	−70	−63	7
Profit after tax	130	117	−13

$$\text{Net cost of debt} = \frac{£13,000}{£200,000} \times 100$$

$$= 6.5\% \text{ per annum}$$

Table 9.7 shows that without the debt, the business generates profit of £200,000 before tax and that the resulting tax liability reduces this by 35% to £130,000. If the loan of £200,000 were taken out, the £20,000 interest payable (i.e., £200,000 @ 10%) would reduce the pre-tax profit to £180,000. However, as a result of this reduction in taxable profit, the tax liability would be reduced from £70,000 to £63,000 a saving of £7,000. Consequently, the net cost of the debt is only £13,000, or 6.5% per annum.

The extent to which a company relies on debt finance is referred to as its financial gearing level and, as we have seen, there is an argument for increasing the level of gearing in order to take advantage of a relatively cheap source of finance. However, the extent to which borrowing should be used must be considered carefully. Debt finance places a financial burden on a business as a result of its accompanying obligation to reward providers of the funds on a regular basis, an obligation which does not apply to equity investors who have no legal right to receive a dividend. Therefore, in a period where operating results are poor, a company has the option to reduce, or even cancel, the dividend payable to shareholders in order to conserve cash. However, this flexibility is not available in the case of lenders, who have a legal right to receive their interest payments regardless of the performance of the business. Therefore over-reliance on debt can be risky for the business, especially if it is operating in an uncertain environment, such as the travel and tourism industry, where earnings may be volatile.

So while it has an advantage in terms of its cost, the impact of debt is to increase the 'financial risk' for the owners of the business. Consequently, the extent to which debt is employed should be considered carefully before a business decides on an appropriate mix of long-term finance. The theoretical arguments and practical considerations relating to the determination of an appropriate capital structure for a firm are numerous and complex and beyond the scope of this text. However, it can be argued that firms should use debt to some extent, in order to take advantage of a cheap source of finance, but that over-reliance on this source of finance should be avoided because of the level of risk that accompanies it. This latter issue may be particularly important in the travel and tourism industry, in which many businesses are subject to great uncertainty about their future levels of profitability. For example, many companies operating in the industry suffered as a result of the terrorist activities in the USA in September 2001. In a situation such as this, a business with high levels of debt would be burdened with high and unavoidable interest charges in a period in which profits were falling. This would place a strain on its liquidity position, which could ultimately result in the demise of the business due to an inability to meet its liabilities. Hotel operator Queen's Moat Houses, for example, was seen as being particularly vulnerable after the September 11 attacks because of its high debt levels (*Financial Times*, 5 October, 2001, p. 27).

Consequently, when determining the sources of long-term finance to be employed to support a business's investment projects, it is important to consider an appropriate balance between funds provided by the owners of the business and debt. As Groth and Anderson (1997) argue, when determining the capital structure of a company, using the appropriate amount of borrowing reduces a company's cost of capital, enhances returns and increases the value of the business.

Conclusion

Financial management is an issue of great importance to business managers. For the majority of businesses the overriding objective is to create wealth and even for those with other primary aims, sound financial management can have a significant impact on the chances of business survival. Financial rewards will arise where business investments earn returns in excess of the cost of the capital required to support them. Consequently, managers should seek out the most attractive investment opportunities and the most appropriate, cost-effective sources of long-term finance.

Numerous methods can be used to appraise investment opportunities. Discounted cash flow (DCF) methods, which take into account the time value of money, tend to be popular in practice. The academically preferred method is to determine the expected net present value (NPV) of the investment, which indicates the expected impact of the project on the wealth of the business's owner(s).

An important consideration when assessing potential investments is the risk arising from the need to take a decision on the basis of predicted, and therefore uncertain, outcomes. Businesses in the travel and tourism industry are often regarded as operating in particularly risky and uncertain environments because demand for their services can be highly volatile due to its sensitivity to the general level of economic activity. However, this can be advantageous for businesses which can create options that give them the opportunity, without obligation, to take particular courses of action in the future. These 'real options' permit the exploitation of favourable operating conditions without the risk associated with the unwelcome consequences accompanying adverse conditions.

When assessing the most appropriate sources of funds to be used in financing long-term business investments, the cost of each source should be considered. However, rather than regarding each source separately, the implications of the mix of finance should be considered. Although debt finance may be cheaper than equity funds provided by business owners, it is important to appreciate its impact on 'financial risk'. Due to the legal obligation to pay lenders a periodic return regardless of the performance of the business in that period, an excessive level of debt can place a great strain on the liquidity of the business. Consequently, when determining a business's long-term capital structure, the amount of debt and the associated financial risk should be considered carefully.

Discussion questions

1. Discuss the information requirements of business decision-makers responsible for capital investment decisions.
2. Explain the impact of the time value of money on expected future cash flows resulting from an investment.
3. Discuss the importance of considering risk when appraising capital investment projects within the travel and tourism industry.
4. Explain the value of 'real options' for businesses operating in the industry.
5. Explain the advantages and problems associated with increasing the amount of long-term debt finance used in a business operating in an uncertain environment.

Suggested further reading

Arnold, G. (2001) *Corporate Financial Management* (2nd edition). London: Financial Times/Prentice Hall.

Blackwood, T. (1998) *Accounting for Business* (2nd edition). Sunderland: Business Education Publishers.

Watson, D. and Head, A. (2001) *Corporate Finance: Principles and Practice* (2nd edition). London: Financial Times/Pitman Publishing.

www.real-options.com

10   The law and tourism

David Grant and Richard Sharpley

Chapter objectives

The purpose of this chapter is to introduce the complex and dynamic issue of the law as it relates to travel and tourism, focusing in particular on the management implications of the European Package Travel Directive.

Having completed this chapter, the reader will be able to:

- appreciate the diversity of the law applicable to the travel industry
- recognise the need to comply with the law and the penalties for failing to do so
- consider a variety of managerial responses to the legal regime they are subject to

Chapter contents

Introduction: the law and tourism

The supply of most, if not all, travel and tourism products and services is subject to or influenced by an ever-increasing variety of legislation. Moreover, travel and tourism businesses and organisations – and, indeed, tourists themselves – are subject to such legislation at different levels and in different jurisdictions. That is, some laws may be effective within local/regional boundaries, such as state laws in the USA, others may be national laws, while international law is becoming increasingly pervasive within travel and tourism. Thus, the law and tourism as a subject of study is enormously diverse and highly complex. It not only embraces issues varying from environmental protection, such as national park designation, to health and safety, employee rights, planning, consumer protection or licensing to name but a few, but it also involves different categories or types of law, such as contract law or company law, which vary from one legal system to another. As a result, tourism law is usually considered from the perspective of specific sectors of the industry, such as package holidays (Grant and Mason, 2003), hospitality law (Sherry, 1993; Pannett and Boella, 1999), air travel (Clarke, 2002) or travel agents (Vrancken, 2000), or within specific contexts, such as countryside law (Garner and Jones, 1997).

This complexity and diversity of tourism-related law is also reflected in the management challenges and responses within different sectors of the tourism industry, or in different organisations, with respect to legislation that affects their business. Much, of course, depends upon the nature, location and scale of the business. The owner of a small hotel, for example, may simply be obliged to comply with specific employment and health and safety legislation (although even here, a complex and long-standing body of law exists – see, for example, Sharpley and Grant, 2000; Grant and Sharpley, 2001), whereas a large, multinational organisation is not only likely to have an in-house legal department to ensure that its activities comply with domestic and international legislation, but will also need to respond to opportunities or challenges presented by the legal environment within which it operates. For example, airlines in the USA and Europe have, in general, been obliged to respond to the deregulation/liberalisation process which has resulted in an increasingly competitive operating environment (see also Chapter 3), the national carriers in Europe in particular facing the challenge presented by 'no-frills' airlines, such as easyJet. At the same time, more specific legal issues, such as the liability of airlines with respect to the incidence of deep-vein thrombosis (DVT) among long-haul passengers, also represent management challenges (although it is interesting to note that the recent differing response of the Australian and English courts to passenger group actions with respect to DVT further demonstrates the complexity of travel law at the international level, even when governed by a supposedly uniform legal regime – the Warsaw Convention). As another example, many tour operators (both large and small) have been obliged to establish customer service departments as a result of consumer protection legislation and a greater propensity to complain or claim recompense on the part of customers.

The important point is, such is the diversity and scope of the law with respect to travel and tourism that it is impossible to address all the consequential management issues – new legislation in England with respect to opening access to the countryside (HMSO, 2000) is as much an element of tourism law as are, for example, international conventions governing airline operations. Moreover, the legal environment within which the travel and tourism industry operates, both nationally and internationally, comprises laws that not only vary according to national legal systems (Boella et al., 2001) but which frequently have consequences for the industry but are not directed specifically at it. Nevertheless, one particular area of legislation, namely, the European Package Travel Directive 1990, demands attention. Not only is the Directive specifically aimed at the travel industry, but they have generated a number of management challenges within Europe with implications for the travel and tourism industry elsewhere, in particular international tourism destinations offered by European tour operators in their programmes. Moreover, as the European Union (EU) continues to expand (at the time of writing, a further ten countries are due to join in 2004), new members will be obliged to comply with the Directive as well, of course, as with other European legislation. Therefore, it is with this aspect of travel law that this chapter is concerned. Although the Directive is of general application throughout the European Union (EU) (and will have an indirect impact on suppliers outside the EU), we will illustrate its effect by examining how it has been implemented in the UK, the jurisdiction with which we are most familiar.

The Package Travel Regulations 1992: provisions and responses

For travel industry managers, the major legal challenge in recent years has been to accommodate the requirements of the Package Travel Directive 1990 (90/314/EC) which laid down a common set of rules for the sale of package holidays throughout the European Community. The avowed purpose of the Directive, apart from being a harmonisation measure, is to confer a greater degree of protection upon EC consumers of package travel.

A full consideration of the objectives and provisions of the Directive is beyond the scope of this chapter (see Grant and Mason, 2003). However, within the Directive, three broad themes can be discerned:

- protection for consumers against insolvency of tour operators;
- the creation of an 'information regime' under which consumers must be given such information prior to booking that enables them to make an informed choice; and
- the imposition of liability upon tour operators for the defaults of their suppliers, principally the airlines and hotels to which the tour operators have subcontracted the performance of most of the contract.

The Directive has been transposed into UK law by means of the Package Travel Regulations 1992 (SI No. 3288, 1992) which has created a whole range of new criminal and civil liabilities in order to implement the Directive properly. These requirements will be set out briefly below before we go on to discuss in each of the three areas the practical management responses, and the wider implications of these, made by the travel industry.

Protection against insolvency

Since the collapse of Fiesta Tours in 1964, which stranded about 5,000 tourists overseas, it has been evident that some form of protection against the financial failure of tour operators is necessary. Indeed, since the early 1960s, when tour operating emerged as a major sector of the travel industry, the collapse of tour operators has not been uncommon – spectacular failures of large operators, such as the International Leisure Group (ILG) collapse in 1992, are, however, relatively rare. In Britain, such financial protection was first provided by the Association of British Travel Agents (ABTA), which initially set up a 'common fund' based on 50% of its membership subscriptions, followed subsequently by the controversial 'Operation Stabiliser' (see Yale, 1995).[1] The Civil Aviation Authority (CAA) has also, since 1972, required anyone, other than airlines themselves, selling either air inclusive packages or air seats to apply for an Air Travel Organiser's Licence (ATOL).

However, regulations 16–21 of the Package Travel Regulations provide that a tour operator, in the event of insolvency, must be able to provide evidence of security for the refund of advance payments and also for the repatriation of consumers stranded abroad. So far as refunds are concerned, tour operators can comply in a number of ways, including bonding, by insurance or by setting up a trust fund. If a tour operator is licensed under the ATOL Regulations (SI No. 1054 1995, as amended), this is sufficient for the purposes of the Package Travel Regulations.

As mentioned above, the ATOL regulations are policed by the Civil Aviation Authority, and require that tour operators and other travel organisers must:

- undergo stringent financial health checks – an ATOL is granted for only 12 months; and
- arrange a bond with a bank or insurance company amounting, under the Regulations, to an appropriate proportion of the company's annual turnover. In practical terms, this may be anywhere between 10% and 25% of turnover.

There are no specific requirements laid down for compliance with the repatriation provisions, and failure to comply with the Regulations is a criminal offence.

There are, however, a number of points that deserve mention. Established members of ABTA with a successful track record and audited accounts find it relatively easy to comply (at a price) with the bonding requirements of the Regulations. Non-members, usually smaller operators, are often unable to find a financial institution prepared to bond them and have to resort to the trust fund option. The Regulations are not prescriptive on the rules for operating the trust fund and are plainly open to abuse. In the past there have been scandals involving operators who have become insolvent and the trust fund was found to be empty (see Sheen, 1998).

Additionally, there is large-scale non-compliance by domestic tour operators and other tourism businesses who are simply ignorant of the law. Even where there is some awareness that the Regulations might apply, there is no incentive to comply because there is little or no likelihood of the law being enforced. This is due to a combination of ignorance and lack of resources on the part of the enforcement authorities who have more pressing priorities.

Protection: the managerial response.   It is, of course, in the interests of tour operators and other air travel organisers to comply with the provisions for protecting customers against the insolvency and collapse of the business. However, compliance carries a cost. Therefore, if there exists a (legal) means of avoiding such costs, then it is likely that businesses may attempt to do so, with implications for customers and associated business.

Opportunities to avoid the cost of compliance have emerged in a number of ways, with implications, in particular, for the protection of travellers. One such opportunity is in the form of so-called 'dynamic packaging' (also referred to as 'contract-splitting' (CAA, 2002)), an activity that travel agents are increasingly participating in and which, for tour operators and for 'dot.com' organisations offering travel and related services, has been facilitated by the rapid growth in the use of the Internet. This, in turn, has to an extent been underpinned by the emergence of low-cost, no-frills airlines which, particularly in Europe, have released low-cost air travel from the control of tour operators and charter airlines.

Dynamic packaging is, essentially, the process whereby travel agents and others book the individual elements of a holiday (flight, accommodation, car hire and so on) separately with different providers, so that the traveller has separate contracts with each supplier rather than a single contract with a tour operator. This 'split-contract' method appeals to travel agents because they believe, probably erroneously, that they are not constructing or selling a package (defined as a pre-arranged combination of at least two holiday components), and therefore do not need to be bonded. Similarly, Internet companies also offer dynamic packages which are proving to be increasingly popular. For example, it was recently announced that lastminute.com's dynamic packaging offer, known as 'Breakbuilder', generated over £1 million of business in its first full month of trading. Using Breakbuilder, customers are able to self-package their holidays by booking their flights and accommodation through the Internet site at an integrated price (e-tid, 2003). Interestingly, lastminute.com are bonded for this operation, presumably because the legal advice they have received suggests that they should. This legal advice will almost certainly be based on the recent *Club Tour* case decided by the European Court of Justice in 2002, which held that a Portuguese travel agent putting separate elements of a package together at the request of a client was selling a package (for the full details see Case Study 10.1).

Case Study 10.1 *Club Tour Viagens e Turismo SA v. Alberto Carlos Lobo Goncalves Garrido* (European Court of Justice, Case 400/00, 30 April 2002)

The facts of the case were that the defendant booked a holiday through a travel agency in Portugal. The holiday consisted of accommodation at an all-inclusive resort operated by Club Med in Greece plus flights from Portugal. It was the travel agent who combined the flights with the all-inclusive resort. While on holiday, the resort became infested with thousands of wasps which prevented the defendant from enjoying his stay. Despite his complaints, neither the travel agency nor Club Med could provide suitable alternative accommodation. On his return, the defendant refused to pay for the holiday and the travel agent sued him. The domestic court in Portugal referred the case to the European Court of Justice for a ruling on two issues. The first of these was whether arrangements put together by a travel agent at the request of, and according to the specifications of, a consumer or defined group of consumers fell within the definition of a package. The second was whether the term 'pre-arranged combination' could be interpreted as meaning a package put together at the time when the contract was concluded. In a very brief judgment the European Court of Justice held that both questions should be answered in the affirmative. On the first issue the court said that there was nothing in the definition which prevented such arrangements from being a package; and on the second issue it said that, given the answer to the first question, then it necessarily followed that the arrangements were pre-arranged if they consisted of elements chosen by the consumer before the contract was concluded.

The Internet has also enabled tour operators and other travel organisations to participate in dynamic packaging. In the case of tour operators, it is likely that their dynamic packages will be included in their overall bonding. They will therefore be operating within the requirements of the Regulations. However, it is possible for other organisations, such as airlines (which do not normally require an ATOL) also to set up Internet sites which enable customers to self-package their holidays. For example, Ryanair, the Irish-based budget airline, provide links from their main website (www.ryanair.com) to a hotel booking service (ryanairhotels.com) and are probably not selling packages, but the matter is not beyond doubt.

In the event of a company going out of business, the implications of non-bonded dynamic packaging are twofold. First, tourists may well find that they are not protected and, as a result, are unable to claim compensation or, if necessary, have to cover their own repatriation costs. Secondly, principals or suppliers, particularly hotels, may find that they do not get paid by the tour organiser or are not compensated for losses incurred if the organiser goes out of business. Therefore, the required management response, particularly on the part of the appropriate authority, is to ensure that travellers are better informed about the degree of protection they enjoy and, more importantly, work towards closing the loopholes in the law.

In the UK, moves are being made in this direction. The CAA, for example, having identified over 600 companies advertising packages under split-contracts, are seeking ways of amending the ATOL regulations to cover dynamic packaging. Moreover, as Case Study 10.1 shows, the law is now recognising that travel agents also, in effect, act as tour operators.

The information regime

Regulation 5 requires tour operators to put certain information into their brochures; the failure to include information or to provide information that is inadequate, inaccurate, incomprehensible or illegible amounts to a criminal offence. Schedule 2 of the Regulations includes a long list of the essential information that is required. Two further criminal offences are created by Regulations 7 and 8 which require tour operators and/or travel agents to provide consumers with certain information before they travel, such as health and visa requirements and contact details. Complementing these provisions is a requirement in Regulation 9 to put contract terms into writing before the contract is concluded – the penalty for failure in this case is that consumers can withdraw from the contract if they so wish. Finally, Regulation 4 creates a new statutory duty under which consumers are entitled to compensation if their tour operator or travel agent supplies them with misleading information which causes loss or damage.

The information regime: the managerial response.   One of the biggest challenges currently facing tour operators is the need to reduce the number of complaints (and subsequent claims for compensation) from dissatisfied customers. In other words, people have become more experienced as consumers of tourism products and now seek a variety of benefits other than simply a low price in the holidays they purchase. In particular, non-price factors, such as the quality of services provided, have become more important. In fact, as early as the 1970s, it was predicted that price competition would become subordinate to quality competition. At the same time, tourists have become more aware of their rights as consumers and, as a result, are more ready to complain when their holiday experience does not meet expectations or, of particular relevance here, when it does not match what has been promised in the tour operator's literature, such as holiday brochures.

Given the inherent intangibility of tourism services, it is inevitable that, at times, the information provided by tour operators may be misleading, incomplete or inaccurate. Nevertheless, it is certainly within the tour operator's interest to ensure that the information it provides is as accurate as possible. A startling example of this is the case of *Mawdsley v. Cosmosair*, where a hotel description was not entirely accurate and it cost the tour operator dearly (see Case Study 10.2). Therefore, the principal management response can only be to improve the quality of the information the business provides, that is, to comply with the Regulations (see *Airtours v. Shipley* (1994) 158 J.P. 835 and *Inspirations v. Dudley MBC* (1998) 162 J.P. 800).

Case Study 10.2   Mawdsley v. Cosmosair [2002] EWCA Civ 587

Mr and Mrs Mawdsley and their two young children (aged 3½ and 6 months) booked a holiday with Cosmos at the Marmaris Palace Hotel in Turkey. The hotel was advertised as having a lift. There was a lift but it did not go to the floor on which the restaurant was situated. To get to the restaurant necessitated either going up two flights of stairs or going down two flights of stairs. One day, Mrs Mawdsley, aided by her husband, was carrying one of her children in a buggy down the stairs when she fell and hurt herself. It was held by the Court of Appeal that the brochure was misleading. To say that the hotel had a lift implied that the lift went to all floors. Furthermore, this misdescription had *caused* her accident because she would not have found herself having to carry the buggy up and down stairs if the description had been accurate – she would not have booked the holiday at all if she had known about the stairs.

However, this may not always be possible. For example, there is usually a significant lead time between the production of brochures and the actual consumption of a holiday, often between 12 and 18 months. Thus, what is promised by suppliers may not actually be provided – a common problem is where new hotel developments fall behind schedule and do not meet with the description in brochures – while specific services or facilities may also be changed or withdrawn in the period between brochure production and the purchase of the holiday. Thus, it is important that tour operator management work closely with suppliers to ensure accuracy; equally, suppliers should attempt to match as far as possible the textual and pictorial descriptions in brochures and other promotional material, otherwise they may find that the tour operators pass on the costs of compensation claims.

As noted above, operators also have a duty to provide a variety of essential information, such as health or visa requirements. This requirement is usually complied with, but the nature of the package holiday often means that customers expect a level of detail that may be considered excessive. In other words, when purchasing a package holiday, the consumer may transfer their responsibility to the tour operator who, in effect, acts *in loco parentis*. For example, some years ago, tourists who had their Caribbean holiday disrupted by a hurricane claimed that the tour operator should have warned them that a hurricane was likely to occur.

In practice, therefore, full and accurate provision of information may not always be viable and, as a result, a management strategy is to accept the inevitability of this, set up a customer service department (as many tour operators of all sizes now have) to minimise issues and/or simply accept costs and build them into the holiday price. Nevertheless, the more information that is provided, the more likely it is that customers will be satisfied and continue to use a particular company's services.

Liability for suppliers

Prior to 1990, tour operators could avoid liability to consumers injured by the negligence of their suppliers by accepting liability for their own negligence but not the negligence of their suppliers, whom they described as 'independent subcontractors'. A classic example of this is the case of *Wall v. Silverwing Surface Arrangements* (unreported, 1981, but available at http://tlc.unn.ac.uk), in which the claimant was badly injured when her hotel in Tenerife burnt down. There was clear negligence on the part of the hotelkeeper, but the tour operator escaped liability on the then grounds that they had chosen a modern hotel from a reputable hotel chain and had monitored its quality and safety. They were not personally at fault and they were not liable for the faults of the supplier.

However, in *Wong Mee Wan v. Kwan Kin Travel Services Ltd* [1996] 1 W.L.R. 38, where the claimant was killed by the negligence of a subcontractor, the court held the tour operator liable on the basis of a term in the contract that they had accepted liability for the performance of the whole contract. Taken together, these cases are authority for saying that the liabilities of a tour operator are determined by the terms of the contract – and the more the tour operator promises, the greater the liability.

Following the implementation of the Directive in 1992, tour operators and consumers were of the opinion that Regulation 15 created a form of qualified strict liability whereby tour operators were now liable for the negligence of their suppliers, unless it could be proved *by the tour operator* that neither they nor their suppliers were negligent. Some tour operators, notably Thomson, were prepared to extend that liability to defects in excursions purchased through their representatives, but not forming part of the original package. The ABTA Code of Conduct of that period also reflected the belief that tour operators were now liable for their suppliers' misconduct, requiring tour operators to accept liability for the defaults of their suppliers. Because the requirements in the Code of Conduct are mandatory for members of ABTA, this ensured a high level of protection for consumers.

However, opinion is now swinging the other way. A recent case in the Court of Appeal, *Hone v. Going Places* (see Case Study 10.3), held that Regulation 15 did *not* set out what the obligations of the tour operator were – merely that once they were established, they were to be 'properly performed'. Thus, it is possible for tour operators to define their obligations very narrowly and, by doing so, ensure a commensurately lower liability. It is noticeable that the most recent version of the ABTA Code of Conduct (February 2003), reflecting judicial opinion (and, presumably, internal pressure from members), offers far less protection to consumers than formerly.

Case Study 10.3   Hone v. Going Places [2001] EWCA Civ 947

The claimant, Mr Hone, sued Going Places, his travel agent, for injuries sustained on holiday. (It was held, both in the High Court and on appeal to the Court of Appeal, that Going Places could be sued as though they were tour operators because they had 'held themselves out' as such.) The injuries occurred when Mr Hone was evacuating the charter plane in which he was being transported home from Turkey following an emergency landing. He became stuck behind a fat lady on the emergency chute who couldn't get out of the way and was injured in the back when the next person down the chute struck him at the base of his spine with her shoes.

It was held by the Court of Appeal that there was no liability to Mr Hone under the Package Travel Regulations because although the Regulations make the tour operator responsible for the defaults of their suppliers he could not *prove* that the evacuation was conducted in a negligent fashion.

Traditionally, tour operators in the UK had also gone a stage further in endeavouring to reduce their liability by the use of exclusion clauses. Most of these attempts are now doomed to failure by a combination of the provisions of the Unfair Contract Terms Act 1977 and Regulation 15 of the Package Travel Regulations which, between them, outlaw the use of such clauses. More recently, however, the Unfair Terms in Consumer Contract Regulations 1999 have enabled the Office of Fair Trading (OFT) to attack clauses which not only exclude liability but also those which are simply unfair. In October 2002, the OFT announced that the UK's four largest tour operators had agreed to re-draft large parts of their standard terms and conditions which were unfair to consumers. Thus, on the one hand, the Regulations' provisions for liability for suppliers are not, perhaps, as rigorous as initially considered; on the other hand, other legislation, at least in Britain, increasingly prevents exclusion clauses that limit tour operators' liability.

Liability for suppliers: the managerial response.   There are a variety of ways in which tour operators can manage their liability for the negligence of their suppliers. First, and perhaps most importantly, they may focus on improving the quality of all the products and services they offer. This is, of course, a challenging task given the characteristics of the tourism/package product (see Witt and Mühlemann, 1994; Harrington and Lenehan, 1998; also Chapter 2). Not only is it made up of a number of different elements, including, of course, transport, accommodation and other core services, often owned and provided by overseas suppliers who may work according to local standards, but also other elements, such as the weather or the quality of local clubs or bars, are beyond the operator's control. Nevertheless, it is possible to improve quality (hence lessening the risk of negligence on the part of suppliers) through horizontal integration (i.e., actually buying hotels, airlines and ground handlers) or through the implementation of strict and regular inspections and quality checks. Indeed, most major tour operators regularly undertake such checks in all their contracted suppliers, with the result that some hotels, particularly those dealing with a number of different operators, are obliged to spend a significant amount of time satisfying these requirements. Similarly, many operators undertake customer satisfaction surveys, the feedback of which may affect their longer-term commitment to suppliers.

Improving quality is also important in terms of competitiveness and satisfying the demands of an increasingly quality-conscious clientele. However, in terms of supplier liability, other management responses include:

- *Promising less* – by not making extravagant promises and by not 'guaranteeing' services but making them subject only to an obligation to use reasonable endeavours to provide them.
- *Exclude liability* – although this may be problematic given the battery of legislation preventing such kinds of contractual terms from succeeding.
- *Obtaining indemnities from suppliers* – a powerful tool is to transfer the cost of claims for negligence to the suppliers (who are insured) through indemnities.
- *Insuring* – it may be possible for a tour operator to take out insurance against claims for supplier negligence.

Overall, however, the most effective means of minimising liability for supplier negligence, particularly in an increasingly competitive and value- and quality-conscious marketplace, is to focus on improving quality.

Conclusion

The legal environment within which the travel and tourism industry operates is complex and dynamic. An enormous variety of laws and conventions regulate the operations of organisations and businesses of all types and sizes and, for tourism managers, they represent a set of challenges that must be responded to or complied with. However, as this chapter has demonstrated, the European Package Travel Directive is of particular importance as it impacts not only on tour operators and other businesses within Europe, but also upon those businesses elsewhere that supply European travel companies. Thus, as the European Union continues to enlarge and as the scope of European-based tour operations continues to expand, the influence of the Directive is likely to become more widely felt.

Discussion questions

1. Do you think that consumers of travel products are overly protected by the law and that a return to principles of *caveat emptor* would be beneficial?
2. Does it concern you that in *Hone v. Going Places*, Mr Hone was badly injured while on holiday but received no compensation? (Going Places were not liable and both the tour operator and the airline were insolvent.)
3. If you were the contracts manager of a large European tour operator charged with finding basic accommodation for your customers in underdeveloped countries, what impact do you think the existence of the Package Travel Directive might have upon the decisions you make?

Suggested further reading

Clarke, M. (2002) *Contracts of Carriage by Air*. London: Lloyd's of London Press.
Cordato, J. (1990) *Australian Travel and Tourism Law*. Sydney: Butterworths.
Dickerson, T. (1981–2002) *Travel Law*. New York: Law Journals Seminar Press.
Saggerson, A. (2000) *Travel Law and Litigation*. Welwyn Garden City: CLT Professional Publishing.
Vrancken, P. (ed.) (2002) *Tourism and the Law in South Africa*. Port Elizabeth: Butterworths.

Note

[1]Stabiliser, which required ABTA tour operator members only to sell via ABTA travel agencies and required ABTA agencies only to sell ABTA tour operators' products, came under scrutiny as a restrictive practice and was challenged by the Office of Fair Trading. In *Re Association of British Travel Agents Ltd's Agreement* [1984] ICR 12, however, a case before the Restrictive Trade Practices Court, it survived because ABTA demonstrated that without it, consumers would be deprived of benefits which they would not otherwise obtain in a free market – principally the protection offered by ABTA members against insolvency.

Subsequently ABTA dispensed with Stabiliser because the Directive made it largely redundant in consumer protection terms, and therefore almost certainly illegal.

PART 3: MANAGING TOURISM IN ITS ENVIRONMENT

11   Managing urban tourism

Richard Sharpley and Lesley Roberts

Chapter objectives

The purpose of this chapter is to explore the means of effectively managing and marketing urban tourism in order to optimise its long-term contribution to wider development objectives. Having completed this chapter, the reader will be able to:

- identify key issues in the management of urban tourism
- appreciate the need for a systematic and holistic framework for managing tourism in urban spaces
- recognise and consider the challenges of promoting urban tourism in an increasingly homogeneous place market.

Chapter contents

Introduction: urban tourism within tourism studies

Towns and cities have, throughout history, been a focus of tourist activity, providing accommodation, entertainment and other facilities for visitors (Page and Hall, 2003: 1).

For example, the early development of spa tourism in the sixteenth century and the emergence of resort-based seaside tourism in the eighteenth century were both related to urban locations, while the structure of the Grand Tour was determined to a great extent by the culturally significant cities of Europe (Towner, 1996). However, it is only more recently that the importance of urban tourism has come to be realised. Not only has tourism become, according to Law (2002: 1), a 'significant component of the economy of most large cities' but also it is now widely perceived as an effective vehicle of urban development and regeneration. Since Baltimore famously revitalised its inner-harbour area in the 1970s through the development of business and leisure facilities (see Shaw and Williams, 2002: 257–60), innumerable other towns and cities have also adopted tourism development as an integral element of their socio-economic development policies (Swarbrooke, 2000).

Not surprisingly, perhaps, this increased interest in and dependence upon tourism in the urban context has been reflected in greater attention being placed upon it in the tourism literature. As Page (2000: 197) observes, 'the 1980s saw the emergence of new and popular research areas in tourism, and urban tourism was no exception to this'. Following Ashworth's (1989) ground-breaking study lamenting the then lack of research into urban tourism, a variety of both general and issue-specific textbooks and papers have been published, significantly adding to the corpus of knowledge with respect to the nature, development and inherent processes of urban tourism (e.g., Ashworth and Tunbridge, 1990; Law, 1993, 1996; Gold and Ward, 1994; Page, 1995; Mazanec, 1997; Tyler et al., 1998; Judd and Fainstein, 1999; Page and Hall, 2003). However, despite this increased attention within the literature, it has been suggested that 'urban tourism research has ... suffered from a range of seemingly novice tourism researchers attempting to write on the area which appears simple, uncomplicated and well-suited to descriptive case studies' (Page, 2000: 198). Certainly, much of the literature focuses upon destination-specific cases of tourism-related urban development and there is, therefore, some validity in the argument that insufficient 'theoretical and conceptual development has taken place ... to justify the delineation of urban tourism as a sub-field of tourism studies' (Page, 2000: 198).

As discussed shortly, urban tourism is a varied, complex and dynamic phenomenon that, perhaps, defies specific definition and analysis, hence the preference of some, such as Law (2002), to refer more specifically to 'city tourism'. Nevertheless, there is no doubt that, globally, tourism has become increasingly prevalent, albeit in a variety of forms or guises (such as heritage tourism, cultural tourism or special event tourism), in urban spaces. Many cities in Europe attract significant numbers of domestic and international visitors (see Wöber (2000) for a discussion of standardising city tourism statistics), while 'mega-events', such as the Olympic Games, are increasingly seen as providing an effective boost to tourism in both the short and longer term. For example, visitor numbers to Barcelona almost doubled during the 1990s following the 1992 Summer Olympics (Smith and Jenner, 1999), while, since hosting the World Student Games, Sheffield generated some £30 million between 1991 and 1999 from hosting subsequent sporting events (Gratton and Dobson, 1999).

There is also no doubt that, given the increasingly widespread incidence of urban tourism – particularly as a perceived contributor to urban regeneration programmes – there are two broad challenges facing the management of urban tourism destinations. First, 'the interrelationship of tourism with urban regeneration is … a common phenomenon' (Page and Hall, 2003: 324) yet, given the enormous diversity of both urban contexts and potential forms of tourism, the nature of this interrelationship is almost infinitely variable and, frequently, regeneration objectives are not met (Swarbrooke, 2000). There is, then, a need to develop a framework for urban tourism management that embraces this diversity at the same time as optimising the developmental benefits of tourism in the longer term.

Secondly, the relationship between the demand for and supply of urban tourism has, arguably, undergone a subtle shift in recent years. Whereas towns and cities were once able to sell their distinctive tourism products to specific markets through effective 'place-marketing' (see Kotler et al., 1993), many destinations have now lost their distinctiveness in what has become a crowded 'place market'. That is, in addition to the now almost universality of the tourist-town/city, a variety of factors, such as transformations in leisure time and practices, the growth in short city-break package holidays, increasing use of the Internet and developments in transport, particularly the advent of low-cost, no-frills flights throughout Europe, mean that urban tourists are able to pick and choose between destinations which offer the most appropriate and accessible 'bundle' of experiences. In a sense, urban tourism destinations have become interchangeable and therefore need to implement appropriate strategies to respond to the dynamic environment within which they operate.

The purpose of this chapter is to address these two broad management challenges. First, however, it is important to review briefly the dominant themes/issues in the study of urban tourism as a background to the subsequent discussion.

Urban tourism: key themes and issues

Typically, the academic study of urban tourism embraces a number of core themes. These include:

- *The demand for urban tourism* – identifying the 'urban tourist'; motivational factors; measuring demand; trends/patterns in demand; tourist-consumer behaviour; modelling/forecasting demand, etc.
- *The supply of urban tourism* – primary elements, including 'activity' and 'leisure' settings; secondary elements, such as accommodation and restaurants; and additional elements, including information services, car parking and so on (see Jansen-Verbeke, 1986), for more detail.
- *Marketing urban tourism* – selling the city; re-branding and re-imaging the city.
- *Policy, planning and management issues* – tourism and regeneration; organisational structures and relationships (partnerships, networks, collaboration); tourism policies (attractions, events, regional focus), etc.
- *The impacts of urban tourism* – economic benefits/costs; socio-cultural development; sustainable regeneration, etc.

This list is by no means exhaustive. Nevertheless, it serves to illustrate the variety of topics that are not only embraced by the concept of urban tourism, but which also, perhaps, demand a case-study approach as each destination is likely to adopt a unique combination of planning, management, marketing and product development policies according to local needs.

However, there are a number of broader issues that are relevant to all urban tourism destinations and which point towards the two principal management challenges referred to above.

Is there an 'urban tourism'?

Although it is clearly evident that many towns and cities are important tourism destinations in their own right, the existence of an identifiable and definable phenomenon (i.e., 'urban tourism'), under which all tourism supply and demand in urban areas can be categorised, remains debatable. At the same time and, perhaps, of greater importance, is there an 'urban tourist', or are towns and cities simply convenient locations in which tourists can enjoy a variety of different experiences? As Ashworth (1992: 3) argues, 'the physical existence of tourism in cities does not in itself create an urban tourism that has any significance beyond the self-evident combination of a particular activity at a particular place'.

At a basic level, urban tourism is a complex, or even chaotic (Law, 1996), concept because of the diversity of contexts in which it occurs. As Shaw and Williams (2002: 244) suggest, urban areas are heterogeneous, 'distinguished as they are by size, location, function and age' and, as a result, attempts have been made to categorise urban tourism destinations. Judd and Fainstein (1999), for example, refer to *resort cities* (built with tourism as the primary function), the *tourist-historic city* (where historic cores have become the object of tourist consumption) and *converted cities* (where a change of function has occurred). Blank (1996) classifies American cities according to perceived tourist experiences (high-amenity sites, speciality tourism cities and hinterland metropolitan areas), whereas Page (1995) more simply lists different types of urban destination.

Further to this, Shaw and Williams (2002) also observe that urban areas are complex, multifunctional places within which tourism's role may be difficult to delineate, while attractions and facilities are not usually specifically produced for, or consumed by, tourists. Thus, the same urban area may be used by residents and visitors alike for a variety of purposes (shopping, entertainment, sport, culture, education, etc.), raising questions about the motivation and behaviour of visitors. Moreover, towns and cities may also operate as part of national or international tourism networks, they may be tourism 'gateways' or they may act as the focus for regional tourism, all of which highlight the complexity and fuzziness of the concept of urban tourism. Nevertheless, a unifying factor is that in an urban context, the nature and function of tourism will, to an extent, be shaped by the city, while the nature and function of the city will, to an extent, be shaped by tourism (Ashworth, 1992; Tyler, 2000).

Figure 11.1   Tourism strategies for urban regeneration

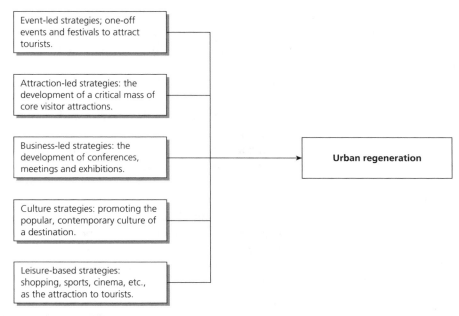

Source: Adapted from Swarbrooke (2000)

Tourism and urban regeneration

A principal purpose of developing urban tourism (and, indeed, all other forms of tourism) is socio-economic development of the destination/region. In the urban context, this is frequently referred to as regeneration (Page and Hall, 2003: 319–37), reflecting the more recent focus upon the use of tourism as a means of restructuring inner-city or docklands areas in order to encourage wider inward investment, to stimulate economic growth, to underpin physical redevelopment and to contribute to more general place-marketing and re-imaging. A variety of strategies are typically employed, usually in combination (Figure 11.1).

However, all urban tourism development focuses upon the socio-cultural and economic well-being and development of local communities. Whether the promotion of a city's historical attractions, the redevelopment of a waterfront, or the staging of a mega-event such as the Olympic Games, the overall purpose is to provide income and employment opportunities, to provide facilities and services for local people and to underpin the improvement of the physical environment. Frequently, however, the longer-term benefits of urban tourism development are not realised. In the UK during the 1980s, for example, garden festivals were held in five urban centres yet few benefits flowed to local communities from the substantial public investment. Similarly, the city of Glasgow, epitomised as an excellent example of successful tourism-based urban regeneration, has struggled both to maintain its earlier momentum and to achieve wider development potential (see Case Study 11.1).

Therefore, within this universal objective, a number of sub-issues become pertinent:

- *Urban tourism and social exclusion*. New tourism-related developments in towns and cities are frequently socially-exclusive and bring least benefit to those who need it most. Tourist areas become gentrified, providing a 'fantasy city' (Hannigan, 1998) for those who can afford it.
- *Contestation of space*. Related to the point above and more generally, there is often a diversity of views over how urban space should be developed and used, particularly between those who wish to institute change, such as developers and politicians, and those who seek to limit change (often, local communities).
- *Resource allocation*. It is sometimes argued that the resources allocated to tourist development, particularly the public funding of flagship attractions designed to act as a catalyst for further investment and development (e.g., the infamous Millennium Dome in London), would be better earmarked for other, more socially worthwhile causes.
- *Community involvement*. As Swarbrooke (2000: 274) observes, 'rarely have concerted efforts been made to involve citizens in key decisions' with respect to urban tourism developments. As a result, mistakes can be made, resentment may evolve and the very people that such developments were designed to help may, in the longer term, become further alienated from the society in which they live.
- *Political environment*. The broader political environment, manifested in, for example, the establishment of regional or national agencies committed to implementing national development policy or schemes, such as the European Capital of Culture, may drive urban tourism development towards externally imposed, rather than locally decided, objectives.

Case Study 11.1 Tourism and urban regeneration in Glasgow

Once the second city of the British Empire, Glasgow, in the west of Scotland, thrived on traditional heavy engineering industries and shipbuilding. The steady and widespread industrial decline witnessed across Western Europe in the twentieth century accelerated after the Second World War and in Glasgow manufacturing jobs in the city fell from 265,000 to 32,000 between 1951 and 1977 (Law, 2002: 151). There was an associated fall in population as regional policy initiatives failed to redress the problems of unemployment, poverty, poor housing and urban decay. Additionally, Glasgow was unattractive to potential investors because of its enduring notoriety for industrial militancy, making it difficult to shake off its erstwhile reputation as 'Red Clydeside'. So severe were Glasgow's industrial decline and its associated social and economic problems that by the mid-1970s, the city had become recognised as the most depressed locality in Britain (MacLeod, 2002).

It might have seemed impossible to many observers that within 15 years a depressed city with no evident tourist icons and attractions could achieve European City of Culture status, yet Glasgow did in 1990. Such a considerable achievement positioned Glasgow as a tourist destination, arguably for the first time, and reflected a number of bold and enterprising initiatives by the City Council and the Scottish Development Agency. Styling itself as 'Europe's first post-industrial city' (TTI, 2000: 39), new galleries and museums such as the Burrell Collection and the Transport Museum were added to Glasgow's cultural resources. The newly-built Scottish Exhibition and Conference Centre aimed to attract an expanding business tourism market, while retail spaces grew with the development of shopping centres to service both residents and a growing leisure tourism sector. The staging of music festivals and events, and the hosting of a National Garden Festival in 1988 contributed to Glasgow's growing cultural and organisational capital as a visitor destination.

The year-long City of Culture event built on all of these achievements with strong events programmes of international standing. As a result, 1990 saw the number of visitors from outside Glasgow grow by 72% in one year, and the Year of Culture was estimated to have earned a net income for the City of somewhere between £10 and £14 million, and generated around 5,500 jobs for the year (Law, 2002: 153). Within Britain, the publicity given to the city by virtue of its cultural status improved perceptions of it as a rapidly changing place and somewhere worth visiting.

After the 1990 event, Glasgow continued to strengthen its position as a visitor destination by opening more exhibition and arts centres and museums, and by further improving shopping and leisure facilities. It has since been a British City of Sport (1995), host to a National Festival of Visual Arts (1996), and Britain's City of Architecture (1999). Between 1989 and 1998, domestic tourism in Glasgow increased by over 75% with a concomitant growth in visitor expenditure of 50%. International visiting also grew by 25% in volume and over 70%

in expenditure (TTI, 2000: 40). Focusing on visitor data and image enhancement, few would take issue with the widely acclaimed success of Glasgow's cultural renaissance. On closer inspection, however, a number of issues have been identified that require further scrutiny.

Despite the continued momentum with regard to the increased supply of cultural and tourism resources, demand has not responded similarly. Greater competition from other European cities also in pursuit of fickle tourist spend has resulted in falling visitor numbers over recent years. Across Europe, cities, particularly those without indigenous attractions of international significance, are likely to face difficulties in the competitive environment (Gospodini, 2001). It seems, therefore, that even in the short to medium term, tourism development in many urban zones may be difficult to sustain.

Furthermore, and perhaps more significant in the longer term, development processes themselves have been criticised for their haste and superficiality, and for their potential in inequitable social engineering. There was criticism that the city's cultural status was largely built on renaissance in the 'high arts' that did little to celebrate Glasgow's industrial heritage (MacLeod, 2002) (this, despite events outside the usual arenas for cultural events, such as 'The Ship', rooted in Glasgow's shipbuilding past and staged in a Govan shipyard). Law (2002: 154) describes the city's transformation as a 'make-over' that has 'sanitized the City and, in the process, obscured many of its real problems'. MacLeod (2002) explains how the City Council's plans failed to achieve their potential for social and economic restructuring, embracing instead the concept of place-marketing (aided in the process by the skills of marketing gurus, Saatchi and Saatchi) which has led to a gentrification process typified by café culture, the fostering of high arts and cultures, and a general consumerist appeal. Such outcomes hide a number of what MacLeod terms 'geographies of exclusion'. For example, despite the economic success of the new tourism, one-third of Glasgow's residents are still in receipt of state benefits of some kind; rather than lessening, poverty is becoming entrenched by above-average levels of long-term unemployment and a jobs gap where new service sector jobs fail to compensate for those lost in manufacturing industries; parts of Glasgow have some of the world's poorest health records and a mortality rate 2.3 times higher than the UK national average; and, crucially, many of the city's newly-created civic spaces are actively designed to exclude marginalised groups whose presence spoils their aesthetic value and is held to harm the tourism product and discourage visitors (see MacLeod, 2002).

Two caveats apply to the above brief analysis. First, Glasgow's social and economic problems, although more severe in some respects, are shared by a number of other European cities and for similar reasons. Secondly, the issue of social inclusion is a ubiquitous one, recognised as a key element of both national and local government policies. Indeed, urban leisure and recreation may have an important role to play in this regard. A potential contribution by museums to social inclusion strategies is recognised, and research is presently underway into the means by which museums in Glasgow can promote social inclusion and encourage underrepresented groups to participate in the city's cultural renaissance. The Greater Pollok Kist initiative provides a free service that aims to give access for local people to cultural resources and enables them to create their own exhibitions and stage their own events. The People's Palace Museum reserves space for the presentation of such exhibitions and displays.

Nevertheless, the broader social and economic evidence suggests that analysis of tourism in Glasgow reveals development processes that have, as yet, failed to find ways of integrating tourism development objectives within wider development concerns and of achieving a more equitable distribution of wealth arising from the increasingly important visitor economy.

The dynamic city

The context within which urban tourism occurs is dynamic in structure, function and culture; that is, towns and cities undergo a constant process of economic, social and cultural change, often in response to wider national and global influences. Most evident of these transformations is the decline of manufacturing in many modern, Western cities, the growth of high-technology industries and the service economy, and associated changes in the structure of the urban workforce (see Law, 2002: 27–48 for more detail). At the same time, the mobility of both capital and labour means that cities now compete on an international stage to attract new investment, while the phenomenon of cultural globalisation has served to diminish the distinctiveness of many urban centres. Also deserving mention is the advent of the alleged 'postmodern' city (see Page and Hall, 2003: 31–9), representing a new, somewhat nebulous cultural context of play, spectacle, pastiche and consumerism. The development and management of urban tourism, although frequently a response to such change, must also evidently be able to embrace this dynamic nature of the urban context.

A framework for managing urban tourism

From the above discussion, two points are evident. First, urban tourism is a complex concept, manifest in practice in an enormous diversity of development perspectives, city attractions, tourist behaviour, and so on. Secondly, irrespective of this diversity, a number of issues, in particular with respect to effective and appropriate tourism development, are common to most, if not all, urban tourism contexts. Therefore, there is, perhaps, the need for a framework which is not only able to demonstrate the multitude of factors, influences and processes which may affect the development of urban tourism in different contexts, but which also provides a logical and systematic process to be followed in managing urban tourism development. One such framework is proposed in Figure 11.2.

In this model, the starting point is not tourism, but the broader, dynamic urban context to which tourism development may, potentially, make a contribution (one implication being that, as result of this initial process, tourism may not in fact be selected as an appropriate development strategy under certain circumstances). Here, the political environment, which includes both local and national government structures and prevailing policies, as well as the economic and socio-cultural environment must be taken into account in order to identify not only appropriate management structures and roles in developing urban tourism, but also the multitude of political economic and social forces that represent either opportunities or barriers. Thus, the need for viewing tourism not in isolation but as a part of an holistic approach to economic and social policy-making (Swarbrooke, 2000) might be satisfied.

Of equal importance is the need to avoid either social exclusion (i.e., where sections of the local community are excluded from the very developments intended for their benefit) or the lack of local community involvement in decision-making. Community involvement in tourism has long been advocated (Murphy, 1985, 1988; Haywood, 1988). Equally, the potential for involving local community members in tourism planning remains the subject of intense debate (Taylor, 1995). Nevertheless, it is both logical and sensible that the views of the local community should be sought on the use of 'their' urban space, what sorts of tourism development should be created that best meet local social and economic needs, and how financial resources should be allocated (i.e., to which projects and/or on what basis – public finance, private/public finance partnerships, etc.).

Once these initial steps have been taken, attention can be paid to preparing a tourism development strategy that embraces the supply of attractions and facilities, associated infrastructural developments and appropriate marketing campaigns, as well as visitor management strategies designed to optimise the visitor experience while minimising the negative consequences for local communities. The success of these should then be monitored, with particular emphasis placed upon resident attitudes towards the interrelationship between tourism development and the changes in the form and function of their city.

Of course, this framework focuses upon the individual urban context for tourism development. However, as observed previously, most, if not all, urban tourism destinations compete in what has evolved into a crowded, international place-market.

Figure 11.2   A framework for managing urban tourism

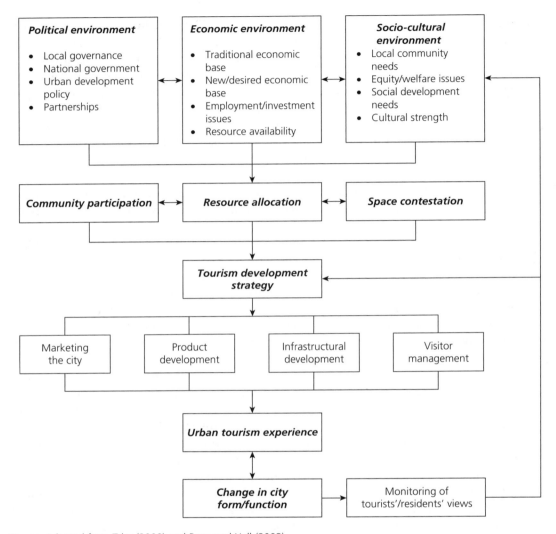

Source: Adapted from Tyler (2000) and Page and Hall (2003)

In turning to questions of marketing in this context, the final part of the chapter examines the potential relationships between local development issues and the global processes of marketing and place promotion.

Marketing urban tourism: place versus territory

If tourism development has a role to play in urban renaissance and such a contribution is to be optimised, then a key element in any development strategy must be marketing.

Place promotion is now a well-known feature of contemporary urban life (Kearns and Philo, 1993: 18) and of city marketing campaigns. Ashworth and Voogd (1988) define it as the process of identifying a place as a 'place product' and developing and promoting it to meet the needs of identified users. Paris is thus known for its reputation as the romantic capital of Europe (rather than for the ingenuity of French engineering that has provided us with one of the most enduring tourist icons of our time), Milan for its fashion focus, and Prague as the Bohemian capital of gothic architecture. As a result of marketing processes, place images have become closely associated with each city in the creation of perceptual global place maps. But the placement of cities within global maps is neither a new nor a fixed phenomenon. In 1900, the world's great cities were almost all in Europe and North America. Since then, however, growth of cities such as London, Paris and New York has been far outstripped by those in Asia, for example, which have grown more than a hundred-fold in the last century (Spearritt, 2002). Tokyo, Seoul and Bejing, among others, are all now important world cities competing for global industry, business, residents – and tourists. Fortunes change, however. That which attracts capital (of different kinds) alters over time. For some industries, skilled and experienced (and cheap) labour draws them to a place. For others, environmental resources provide raw materials that decide the attractiveness of a location. Too little is understood of the complex motivations of tourists to be able to summarise a destination's appeal similarly, but it is generally accepted that a city's image, and the resulting perceptions of it, influence visitor preferences for it (Holcomb, 1993: 133; Bramwell and Rawding, 1996; Bramwell, 1998; Law, 2002: 82).

However, it seems that while cities work to identify those distinguishing features that provide them with unique tourist resources (Barcelona's Gaudi architecture, for example, and L'Hermitage in St Petersburg), they simultaneously create an urban homogeneity that works to blur distinctions and to render cities almost indistinguishable in potential visitors' perceptual maps. This paradox results from three processes.

First, in a process referred to as 'serial reproduction' (Harvey, 1989), the formula for successful urban development in one location is transposed to others in similar format. In the UK this has been witnessed in docklands developments in a number of ports, such as London, Cardiff, Edinburgh and Liverpool. Many tourism developments are similar in structure and character across the world (Law, 2002: 196). As a result, areas of cities, often disused and in decay, are transformed into places with few distinguishing features, and a geography of nowhere rather than a sense of somewhere emerges. The characterless glass towers, homogeneous walkways, themed shopping malls, and generally monotonous urban landscapes of the international postmodern city are surely the antithesis of distinctiveness marketing.

Secondly, research has shown that, even where cities are distinctly different, the effort and resources put into image creation, reflecting historic cores or vibrant urban environments as somewhere exciting to be, demonstrate striking similarities across campaigns that render diverse places indistinguishable in their images (Holcomb, 1994). Thus even those cities that can boast unique attractions may be rendered homogeneous by the very marketing processes that set out to identify and promote their distinctions.

Lastly, perhaps in recognition of the futility of trying to distinguish increasingly homogeneous products, international marketing alliances have emerged. One such alliance, European Cities Tourism, acts to strengthen city tourism through communication and the sharing of expertise. In such a way, rather than competing for shares of an existing market, cities work together to increase the size of the overall market. One such example of shared practice is the City Card, purchase of which combines reductions for entry to attractions with easy access to local transport and discounts for shops and local tours to improve access to the city for visitors. Once a unique characteristic of a visit to Helsinki, as many as 35 European cities now offer City Cards and they have become both standard practice and a standardising characteristic of the urban tourism experience.

How emerging destinations are to achieve a position in this over-crowded and complex place-market understandably taxes the intellect and ingenuity of some of the world's most inventive marketers. Faced with a wide variety of competing destinations, tourists will first eliminate a number of options on the grounds of cost, for example. Then, within a reduced choice set, the tourist is likely to choose a destination with a favourable image (Gartner, 1989). As discussed, destinations respond by adopting place-marketing strategies to improve their competitive position. But cities have 'organic' images resulting from histories, geographies and other non-tourism information sources (Gunn, 1972). Potential visitors, therefore, may have incomplete organic images of a place that are outside the control of destinations. Such was the case with many cities of the former socialist states of Central and Eastern Europe (CEE), even those sharing boundaries with Western Europe. The example of Prague (Case Study 11.2) offers some interesting insights into the problems of positioning a 'new' destination for which potential visitors have established organic images, and within a highly competitive market.

Case study 11.2 Marketing Prague as a tourism destination

Within Central and Eastern Europe, tourism has significance within political, economic and social restructuring processes. Many of the region's post-socialist countries have attempted to re-position themselves in an effort to shake off images of their communist past. But the (re-) imaging of the region faces a number of challenges. First, the need to promote 'Europeanness' is vital in the drive to European Union accession. Importantly, too, destinations must project safe and friendly environments for visitors. Additionally, the changing nature of global tourism requires that emerging destinations

clearly identify target markets and develop products to meet their specific demands (Hall, 1999). Nevertheless, the opening and restructuring of borders revealed to many of the world's tourism-generating countries new and exciting destinations largely untouched by the induced images of place-marketers.

Key development issues in the Czech Republic in the 1990s placed demands on Prague to become a capital city and a major service centre, and the city has turned to tourism as one means of achieving both. Over 100 million visitors arrive in the country each year, and 36% of them go to Prague, a capital city with a striking skyline of baroque spires and a compact centre displaying some of the most beautiful gothic architecture in the world. Cultural tourism might therefore have been an obvious niche for marketers to exploit (if such a niche can be said to exist). However, despite relying on its culture as an integral part of the city's organic image, Prague developers have not promoted it as a distinctive tourism product – although efforts were directed at the protection and restoration of buildings in recognition of their potential as major tourist attractions and the city's historical background has been an important feature in development processes (Metaxas, 2002: 19). Rather than develop place-marketing strategies based on cultural packages, managers have used strategic planning to consolidate the city's cultural identity with a resulting appeal to a number of potential target markets (Simpson and Chapman, 1999). One such target has been the growing business tourism market, and Prague is positioning itself as a destination for conferences and business meetings. The Prague Congress Centre, now furnished with state-of-the-art communications technologies, audio-visual equipment and data links, is complemented by a growing number of four-star hotels, many of which have benefited from investments equivalent to millions of Euros, upgrading accommodation to provide facilities for business travellers. Facilities such as wireless Internet access and video-conferencing facilities are widely available across the city, and the Hilton Hotel has a conference centre that seats 1,350 delegates.

Prague's success in its marketing efforts is evidenced by the profile of some of the events held there in 2002: the IMF/World Bank annual meeting was based in the Congress Centre in September, and the NATO summit was held in Prague only two months later. As security issues have become paramount, this relatively safe place has developed extensive security procedures that can now be offered to all conference delegates. Security experts maintain a presence and conduct hotel staff training from which all visitors can benefit.

It will take time for induced city images to overcome the hesitancies caused by organic images of the city, and it may be some time yet before Prague can completely shake off its image as an Eastern Bloc city that is infrastructurally and technologically inadequate (Andress, 2002). Nevertheless, the two high-profile events of 2002 have gone some way to dismissing doubts about the city's business facilities and to reinforce its new position as a business tourism destination.

Perhaps an answer, in part at least, to the complexities of marketing cities in the longer term lies within the semantics of the urban development literature. The term 'place' is notably different from that of 'territory', which includes issues primarily of ownership but also of use, character and jurisdiction – the very features that create a sense or spirit of place. Sense of place can emanate from a number of different characteristics of a location – architectural or planning style, land- or skyscape, land use and people-oriented communities and their resulting customs and practices. Indeed, it frequently results from a combination of these cultural attributes and is often an intangible amalgam of them. Nevertheless, it is a sense of place which marketers seek when they embark on the place promotion process. Illustrating the commodification of local cultures, visitors are invited by media advertisements to 'come and meet the locals of Poitiers' and to 'live out stories, legends and traditions' in Spain's historic cities. As the term 'commodification' suggests, the extent to which social inclusion plays a part in such development processes is questionable, but in this highly competitive marketplace it is likely to prove critical to the creation of a sense of *territory* that is both representative and credible and can form the basis of a tourism environment that is attractive and welcoming to visitors in the longer term. A city's individuality, through its sense of *territory* (its 'somewhere-*ness*') rather than *place* (or 'anywhere*ness*') therefore becomes an integrated concept.

Conclusion

Tourism development is a means to an end rather than an end in itself and, as a result, tourism development is also a question of integration, requiring an embedding within wider social and political agendas. And so it may be that the two management challenges identified earlier in this chapter are, likewise, linked. For if one possible contribution to the problems faced by urban location marketers is the inclusion of a wider range of stakehold-ers in the identification and creation of a *territory* for tourism development, this approach may simultaneously contribute to a greater achievement of regeneration objectives through increased participation and ownership, and a reduction in the spatial inequalities that result from the exclusive developments of dominant actors, as highlighted in Case Study 11.1.

As suggested by Travel and Tourism Intelligence (TTI, 2000: 59), Glasgow's sense of place might be insufficient to maintain the city's position in the 'destination stakes', but it possesses a strong territorial identity that might benefit the city's tourism development in the future. Through their planning approach, Prague developers have attempted to build their tourism product within an historical territorial identity. In both cases, the benefits of recognising the importance of such a concept may be harnessed through an application of the authors' suggested framework for the management of urban tourism in the twenty-first century.

Discussion questions

1. To what extent does tourism represent a universal panacea to the challenges of urban regeneration?
2. Is it possible to identify/measure 'urban tourism' as a specific sector of tourism?
3. Does urban tourism development inevitably encourage social exclusion?
4. In a homogeneous 'place market', what are the challenges of place-marketing?

Suggested further reading

Law, C. (2002) *Urban Tourism: The Visitor Economy and the Growth of Large Cities* (2nd edition). London: Continuum.

Page, S. and Hall, C.M. (2003) *Managing Urban Tourism*. Harlow: Pearson Education.

Shaw, G. and Williams, A. (2002) *Critical Issues in Tourism: A Geographical Perspective* (2nd edition). Oxford: Blackwell, Chapter 10.

12 Managing the countryside for tourism: a governance perspective

Richard Sharpley

Chapter objectives

The purpose of this chapter is to explore the concept of governance, combining local inputs and initiatives with national policy, as an effective framework for the management of sustainable rural tourism. Having completed this chapter, the reader will be able to:

- appreciate the challenges inherent in the management of rural tourism
- apply the concept of governance to the management of rural tourism
- consider the relative importance of local control and national policy in optimising rural tourism's contribution to rural development

Chapter contents

Introduction: rural tourism

The countryside has long been a tourism destination. From the late 1700s, tourists who had traditionally visited the cultural centres of Europe were influenced by a 'belief in the restorative effects of happily constituted scenes and an increasingly romantic orientation to aesthetic sightseeing' (Adler, 1989) to visit rural areas. As a result, the countryside and mountains throughout Europe became the object of the tourist 'gaze'

(Urry, 1990), with Switzerland, in particular, becoming a popular destination. Similarly, the English Lake District, revered by the poets and artists of the Romantic Movement, attracted increasing numbers of visitors from the start of the nineteenth century, as did the Scottish Highlands (Butler, 1985). Indeed, rapid technological advances in transport, the emergence of a fledgling tourism industry and a desire to escape the burgeoning urban centres collectively fuelled the growth in rural tourism throughout the nineteenth century.

It was also during the nineteenth century that attempts were first made to manage the countryside for tourism. In England, for example, organisations such as the Commons, Open Spaces and Footpaths Preservation Society, founded in 1865, sought to maintain public access to the countryside in the face of creeping urbanisation and industrialisation, while a more formal approach was manifested in the development of national parks. The first, Yellowstone, was designated in 1872 and, by the end of the century, national parks had been established in a number of countries, including the USA, Canada and Australia (Europe's first park, in Sweden, was not created until 1909) (Hoggart et al., 1995). Interestingly, the initial purpose of national parks was the promotion of recreation and associated commercial opportunities. In Australia, for example, the national parks around Sydney were created not for conservation purposes, but because the land was considered unsuitable for either housing or agriculture (Pigram, 1983). Similarly, Yellowstone originally boasted a large number of businesses providing for the needs of visitors and it was not until after the US National Parks Service was set up in 1916 that the basic (conservation) function of national parks was implemented (Albright and Cahn, 1985).

During this period and, indeed, up to the 1940s, tourism in the countryside remained a relatively small-scale, passive activity. However, since the end of the Second World War, both the nature and scale of rural tourism and the socio-economic structure of the countryside that plays host to tourists have undergone a fundamental transformation. Not only has rural tourism become a significant tourism activity in many countries, for example, almost a quarter of Europeans choose the countryside as their holiday destination (EuroBarometer, 1998), but also the range of activities that may be classified under the heading of rural tourism has expanded enormously (see Roberts and Hall, 2001: 2). As a result, ever-increasing pressure has been placed upon the natural and human resources in rural areas. At the same time, rural economies and societies in most industrialised nations have undergone a process of restructuring, manifested in the fragmentation of rural systems in general and the declining role of the agrarian economy in particular (Jenkins et al., 1998). Thus, while the urban–rural fringe has, for the most part, become 'gentrified' countryside for an urban population seeking a 'rural' lifestyle, peripheral rural areas have, in contrast, suffered a collapse in agricultural incomes and employment, and a subsequent out-migration and loss of services. Nevertheless, it is no coincidence that, generally, the peripheral countryside is also the most attractive to tourists. As a consequence, tourism has become increasingly viewed as a panacea to the socio-economic challenges facing peripheral rural areas (Cavaco, 1995; Hoggart et al., 1995; Williams and Shaw, 1998a).

Collectively, these factors have significantly increased the complexity of managing the countryside in general, and its role as a resource for tourism in particular. Not only must access to and within the countryside be provided for tourists with an increasing variety of demands, but such demands must be catered for in a manner which is environmentally appropriate, which does not preclude other legitimate demands on the rural resource, which optimises tourists' experiences and which contributes positively to the socio-economic regeneration of the destination area. In short, managing the countryside for tourism should, ideally, be in accordance with what has been referred to as the sustainability 'imperative' (Hall, 2000).

However, sustainable tourism development remains a contested concept (Wall, 1997; Butler, 1998; Sharpley, 2000), and thus its potential contribution to the effective management of tourism remains in doubt. As Butler (1998: 31) observes in the context of Scotland, 'no example of the successful application of sustainable development of tourism has been found', while the impact of the outbreak of foot and mouth disease in the UK in 2001 (see Case Study 12.2 below) was stark evidence of the inherent unsustainability of the rural tourism sector (Sharpley and Craven, 2001). In particular, there is what many commentators refer to as a 'policy implementation gap' (Pigram, 1993; Butler and Hall, 1998) between the recognised challenges of managing the countryside for tourism and the implementation of appropriate policies and management processes.

The purpose of this chapter, therefore, is to explore ways in which this 'implementation gap' may be addressed. More specifically, it considers the notion of governance as an effective framework for managing the complex relationship between tourism and the countryside. First, however, it is necessary to review briefly the challenges of managing rural tourism and some contemporary management responses in order to contextualise a broader governance perspective.

Tourism in the countryside: challenges

Despite its virtual ubiquity in industrialised countries, rural tourism remains variously defined and takes a multitude of different forms in different countries and regions. This is due, in part, to the lack of a universally accepted definition of 'rural' – concepts of 'rural', 'rurality' and, hence, the characteristics of rural tourism in different countries are culturally, economically, politically and geographically determined. In Germany, for example, rural tourism is primarily associated with farm tourism (Opperman, 1996), while in Australia it is synonymous, perhaps, with the adventurous 'Outback' experience (Sofield and Getz, 1997). At the same time, the importance of rural tourism as a social activity, as an element of overall tourism activity and as a developmental/regeneration vehicle varies enormously from one country to another, as do consequential policies for rural tourism (Page and Getz, 1997). In short, there is no single 'rural tourism', while different countryside destinations face different management problems and issues.

Nevertheless, a number of challenges common to all countryside destinations may be identified, as follows (see also Roberts and Hall, 2001: 71–2):

- *Rurality*. Rural tourism is, typically, underpinned by 'rurality'. Tourists seek rural (non-urban, traditional, natural) experiences, the countryside, however defined, representing a touristic 'refuge from modernity'(Short, 1991: 34). Rural tourism developments and management should therefore seek to maintain and enhance the experience of rurality.
- *Regeneration/development*. Tourism must be planned and managed to meet the ultimate objective of revitalising the countryside through employment and income generation, attracting investment, service provision, realising linkage opportunities in the local economy, and so on. Thus, tourism must be developed according to local socio-economic development needs and opportunities.
- *Integration*. Rural tourism should be integrated with broader rural development strategies at both the local and national level, as well as with regional and national tourism policies.
- *Balance*. There is a requirement to balance tourism with other demands on the rural resource base, while the potentially conflicting needs of local communities, landowners, visitors and the 'national interest' must all be optimised.
- *Environmental sustainability*. The countryside is both finite and fragile. The centrality of the environment (physical and cultural) to the rural tourism experience demands appropriate monitoring, protection and conservation, and tourism development policies are necessary to maintain the integrity and attraction of the rural environment.
- *Realism*. Different forms of tourism (e.g., inland resorts) may be more developmentally appropriate to local or regional needs than other 'traditional' types of tourism. Equally, 'new' rural tourism activities must also be catered for. Therefore, rural tourism policy must embrace the notion of a dynamic countryside responding to wider socio-cultural change, rather than be constrained by a conservative countryside 'aesthetic' (Harrison, 1991).
- *Business development*. Rural tourism businesses themselves face a variety of challenges, including poor returns on investment (Fleischer and Felenstein, 2000), insufficient skills or resources for marketing (Embacher, 1994), a lack of training and the inability to adapt to a service culture (Hjalager, 1996), seasonality and a lack of collaboration with other small tourism businesses in the locality (Gannon, 1994).

This list is by no means exhaustive; nor do all countryside destinations face all, or even some of these problems. Indeed, for some popular rural areas, the dominant issue may be an excessive dependency on tourism and, hence, the need to develop a more balanced, diverse and, implicitly, sustainable economy. Nevertheless, as the following section discusses, there are different ways in which attempts are made to address collectively these challenges.

Tourism in the countryside: management responses

As suggested above, the management of the countryside for tourism should, ideally, be guided by the sustainability 'imperative'; that is, rural tourism should be developed and managed in such a way that it contributes to the longer term, sustainable development of the destination area or region. The extent to which this is achievable remains, as also previously argued, the subject of an intense debate that is beyond the scope of this chapter (see Chapter 18). Nevertheless, since the early 1990s, sustainable tourism development has become almost universally accepted as a desirable and politically appropriate approach to, and goal of, tourism development in general, and rural tourism in particular (Countryside Commission, 1995; Tribe et al., 2000: 22–36).

In the context of managing the countryside, there are three broad perspectives on how this sustainability imperative is, or should be, manifested in practice: (1) managing the rural tourism environment; (2) managing the tourism business; and (3) tourism as an element of overall rural development policy.

Managing the rural tourism environment

Given the difficulties inherent in the practical application of sustainable rural tourism development, the principal focus of plans and policies for managing the countryside as a resource for tourism has, not surprisingly, been upon the relationship between tourism and the physical/social environment upon which it depends. Stated more simply, the primary objective of many 'sustainable' rural tourism policies has been to minimise the negative consequences of tourism development and activity through appropriate resource planning and management – in short, sustainable tourism is equated with sustainable resource use. As a result, much of the literature is concerned with appropriate site management or visitor management techniques, embodied in approaches such as 'Environmental Management Systems' (Tribe et al., 2000; also, Broadhurst, 2001), while in practice, attention has been focused mainly on small-scale, local tourism development projects or environmental improvement schemes within defined areas. Thus, although both economically and environmentally justifiable, this perspective treats rural tourism largely 'in isolation from the other factors which constitute the social, environmental and economic fabric of rural regions' (Butler and Hall, 1998: 254).

Managing the tourism business

The challenges facing tourism businesses in rural areas have long been recognised (Wilson et al., 2001). For some years, private/public sector partnerships were a favoured method of supporting and managing the development of local tourism businesses and addressing the problems faced by small, new businesses in a highly competitive market. More recently, however, attention has been increasingly focused on the contribution of clusters/networks as a means of generating regional competitiveness and positive economies for rural tourism businesses. A cluster is, simply, a collection of businesses or industries within a particular region that are interconnected by their products, their markets and other businesses or organisations, such as suppliers, with which they interact (Porter, 1998).

The benefits of clusters include increased competitiveness, economies of scale and a focus on co-operation and innovation. Such clusters/networks can therefore make a significant contribution to the management of the tourism business in rural areas. Indeed, wine tourism has been cited as an example of the successful development of clusters (Hall, 2001), while other manifestations of networks have also been found to be a component of regional tourism-related economic development (Meyer-Cech, 2001).

Tourism as an element of overall rural development policy

Tourism is widely considered an effective panacea to many of the socio-economic problems facing peripheral rural areas. Therefore, policies for the support of rural tourism development are evident at both the national and regional level. Within the European Union (EU), for example, rural tourism initiatives receive support from a variety of structural funding sources, the most proactive project being the LEADER programme (Roberts and Hall, 2001). At the national level, a notable example of rural tourism policy is that of Finland (Nylander, 2001), while in the USA, some 30 states have developed tourism policies specifically targeted at rural areas (Luloff et al., 1994). Nevertheless, as Getz and Page (1997) observe, national rural tourism policies are the exception rather than the rule.

Of these three approaches to managing the countryside for tourism, site-based environmental management is undoubtedly the most widespread. It is also an essential prerequisite to the effective management of sustainable rural tourism development, yet equally essential are policies for both sustaining a viable tourism business sector and for promoting tourism as an element of broader rural development. In short, for the realisation of a positive, symbiotic relationship between tourism and the countryside – that is, for the contribution of tourism to the development/regeneration of rural areas to be optimised – all three management perspectives should be embraced. However, for the most part, a gap exists between local environmental management initiatives and broader national rural development policy, a gap which, as this chapter now goes on to suggest, may be bridged by the adoption of a governance approach to countryside management.

The governance of the countryside

Reflecting the fragmentation of socio-economic structures within the countryside and the increasingly diverse array of demands, including tourism, placed on the rural resource base, the manner in which the countryside is governed has undergone a significant transformation in recent years. In particular, a preoccupation with agricultural interests and concerns at both the local and national level has been superseded by a more diverse, multidimensional approach to the governing of rural areas, an approach which attempts to manage the complex political, economic and social conflicts that characterise the contemporary countryside. In short, rural government has now 'splintered into a multitude of political processes' (Marsden and Murdoch, 1998: 1).

This transformation of rural political structures reflects a broader shift in state structures and political processes, based upon a search for 'an efficient and effective blend of governmental and non-governmental forces' (Goodwin, 1998: 5). In other words, in many countries traditional 'government' is being replaced with 'governance', a process whereby the more formal, centralised institutional structure and location of authoritative management and decision-making is being replaced by a wider, more decentralised 'distribution of power both internal and external to the state' (Stoker, 1997: 10). In particular, governance is concerned with a plurality of governmental and non-governmental institutions and organisations working together to address particular social and economic issues and challenges and is, perhaps, most clearly evident in the changing emphasis of the state intervention versus free market debate. Thus, the neo-liberal, free market approach of the 1980s and early 1990s, itself a radical departure from the preceding focus on 'old style' state intervention, is being replaced with what is referred to in Britain as the 'third way' – an attempt to achieve the effective integration of state-sponsored redistribution with a market-led economy.

The concept of governance, therefore, may be summarised as follows (see Goodwin, 1998).

- It refers to a complex set of institutions and actors that are drawn from but also beyond government.
- It identifies the blurring of boundaries and responsibilities for tackling social and economic issues;
- It identifies the power dependence in the relationship between institutions involved in collective action.
- It is about autonomous self-governing networks of actors.
- It recognises the capacity to get things done which does not rest on the power of government to command or use its authority.

The extent to which governance, as opposed to government, is an effective decision-making and management process at the national level remains to be seen. Nevertheless, it does provide a valid theoretical basis for analysing and mapping the complex institutional structure and the interrelationships between the enormous range of public, private and voluntary organisations involved in the governance of the countryside in general, and of the rural tourism sector in particular. At the same time, it also provides a practical framework for developing an approach to managing the countryside for tourism that blends the three perspectives on rural management outlined above. Indeed, a type of governance has long been in evidence in the context of managing rural tourism, albeit at the local level, in the form of partnerships. As Wilson et al. (2001) observe, co-operation between tourism entrepreneurs themselves and between the business sector and local government (and, ideally between the tourism industry and the local community) is an essential ingredient of successful rural tourism development and such public–private partnerships have become increasingly widespread.

However, governance, as a means of effectively managing the tourism–countryside relationship, is more complex than establishing co-operative partnerships. That is, it provides a framework for determining and implementing courses of action that maintain and optimise tourism's contribution to rural development as a whole. Therefore, it is essential to question the roles, interests and rationales of relevant organisations, businesses and agencies in order to understand how such courses of action are decided upon, or how various influences within a sphere of governance may facilitate or militate against the achievement of specific objectives. In other words, all actors within a particular governance context will embrace differing ideologies and purposes with respect to the development or exploitation of the rural resource base. Therefore, as Goodwin (1998: 10) proposes, 'the task is to … interrogate the reasons both for their emergence and for their outputs. What exactly do they do, and why?' As the next section demonstrates, such an enquiry reveals that sustainable countryside management for tourism depends upon not only the effective mediation of competing ideologies, but also appropriate policies and support at the national level.

Rural governance and tourism: competing ideologies

The modern countryside has become an arena in which a multitude of tensions and competing demands are played out, frequently reflecting wider social and economic differences and conflicts (Clark et al., 1994). Issues such as access, equal opportunities for participation in rural recreation, the gentrification of rural areas and competing perspectives on development, land use and, more generally, what the countryside 'is', are all high on the rural political agenda, while, at a more micro level, appropriate recreational use of the countryside remains the subject of intense debate. However, despite the enormous variety of organisations and agencies involved in the planning, management and exploitation of the countryside, it is possible, according to Stone (2000), to categorise their activities, purpose and direction under the heading of one of two underlying ideological perspectives.

On the one hand, a dominant ideology followed by many organisations in the public sector, as well as landowners and, arguably, the middle classes, is the so-called 'countryside aesthetic' (Harrison, 1991), an ideology driven by the desire to maintain a picturesque rural idyll, a green and pleasant land which, in the tourism context, supports 'appropriate' quiet or solitary recreational pursuits. To this group can be added all the organisations concerned with the protection or preservation of the countryside, its environment, wildlife and culture, to collectively form what can be termed the conservation ideology. This is driven principally by environmental concerns that focus not only on conserving or protecting the natural rural environment, but also on maintaining an implicitly pre-industrial landscape to be enjoyed by (predominantly) urban visitors. One recent example of this ideology in practice was the decision to ban motorised water sports on Lake Windermere in the English Lake District (see Case Study 12.1).

Case Study 12.1   The Windermere speed limit

The Lake District, in the Northwest of England, was designated a national park in 1951. Covering an area of some 2,280 sq. km, it has long been a magnet for tourists drawn by the unique landscape that first attracted the writers and artists of the Romantic Movement in the early 1800s. Nowadays, an estimated 20 million people live within a three-hour drive of the Lake District. It has therefore become increasingly popular as a destination for those wishing to participate in a variety of land- and water-based activities. However, few of the lakes may actually be used for watersports and, since 1981, when a speed limit of 10mph was imposed on Ullswater, only Lake Windermere has been open for motorised activities such as water-skiing and jet-skiing.

In 1991, the then Lake District Special Planning Board (now the Lake District National Park Authority, LDNPA) decided to apply for a 10mph byelaw for Windermere, arguing that water-skiing and other forms of fast power boating were noisy, incompatible with government policies for national parks, and conflicted with other quieter and more appropriate uses of the lake. There followed a protracted public enquiry which eventually found in favour of the byelaw. However, the outcome was rejected by the then Environment Secretary on the basis of the loss of facilities for power boaters and the potential loss of local income and employment. Nevertheless, an appeal by the LDNPA led to a judicial review and, in 2000, subsequent confirmation that the 10mph byelaw will become effective from March 2005, effectively banning most motorised water sports from the lake. This final decision was based on the belief that not only was there no reason to expect the Lake District to accommodate every kind of recreational activity, but also that the perceived desire of the majority to enjoy the environment in peace should prevail.

On the other hand, innumerable organisations and businesses are, of course, concerned with the commercial exploitation of the rural resource. They adopt a rational (as opposed to an idyllic) approach to the countryside, viewing it as a resource from which a profit can be earned. In the tourism context, this group of actors includes not only the rural tourism 'industry', that is, all those businesses that directly and indirectly depend upon the rural resource, but also certain public sector agencies, such as tourist boards, whose prime objective is the profitable development of tourism. Together, these organisations and businesses are influenced by a dominant 'commercial' ideology which, in comparison to the conservation ideology, is driven principally by economic concerns. Thus, the maintenance of a static, culturally defined 'rurality' is subordinated to the dynamic exploitation of the countryside that responds to new and emerging social demands.

Inevitably, distinctions between these two competing ideologies are not always clear, particularly in the rural tourism context. For example, the success of any rural tourism enterprise depends upon the maintenance of a healthy, attractive and culturally 'traditional' rural environment. Hence the commercial logic of striving to achieve environmentally

Figure 12.1 A model of sustainable rural tourism governance

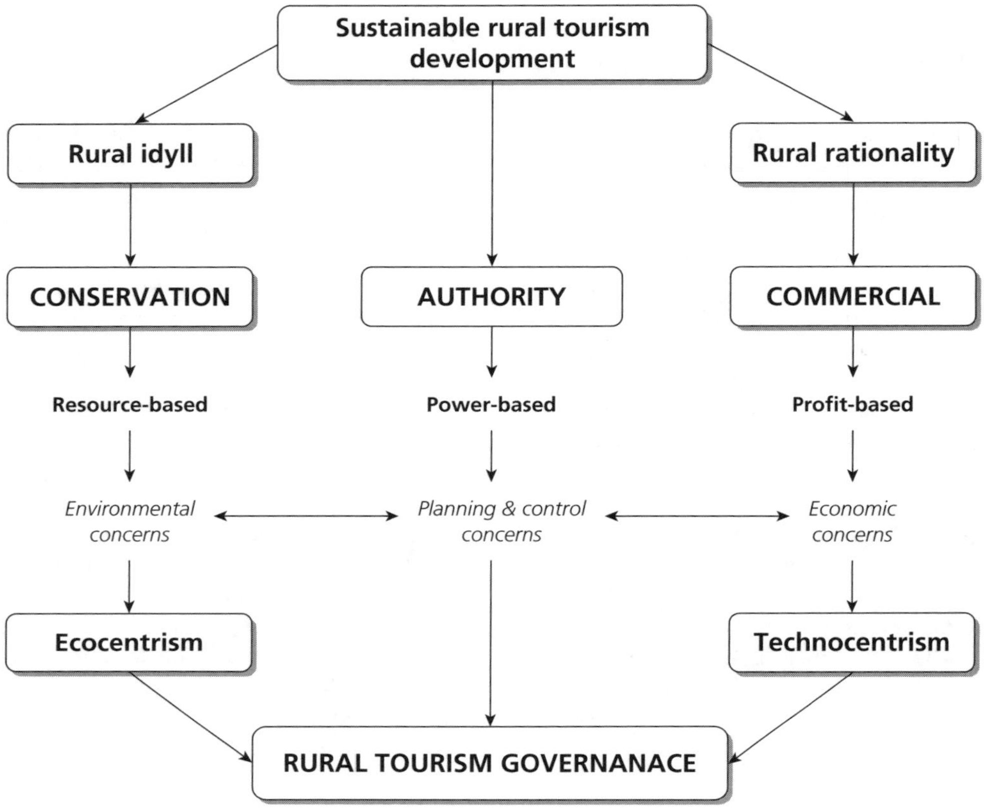

Source: Stone (2000)

sustainable resource exploitation (as distinct from sustainable development). Nevertheless, the concept of two competing ideologies provides a useful framework for developing a model of the governance of sustainable rural tourism, as shown in Figure 12.1. As this chapter now proposes, this model provides the basis for the effective management of the countryside for tourism.

The rural governance model: management implications

The model of rural tourism governance outlined in Figure 12.1 proposes that the successful management of the countryside must, at one level, seek to recognise, satisfy and balance the opposing needs of the conservation and commercial groups of actors within broader tourism and rural developmental objectives. This may be achieved through either a partnership of relevant stakeholders or, in the case of specific areas, such as national parks, through an institution invested with appropriate powers and authority.

To an extent, of course, this reflects the partnership approach that has already been widely accepted as a means of managing and planning rural tourism development. However, a number of points deserve mention. First, most contemporary partnerships tend to be based upon members from both the public and private sectors with a vested, implicitly business, interest in tourism development, with the result that an essentially tourism-centric perspective is frequently adopted. Establishing such a partnership on ideological grounds, however, is likely to embrace a wider and more representative group of stakeholders, while placing the management and decision-making process in a broader, rural development framework.

Secondly, while the achievement of a balance between the competing needs and ideologies of stakeholders may, in practice, be possible, it is only likely to occur at the very local level (i.e., within the context of specific projects or developments involving relatively few participants). Such is the potential number and diversity of stakeholders at a broader context, whether local or regional, that consensus is unlikely to be achieved. This, perhaps, explains the fact that, in reality, sustainable rural tourism is manifested in small-scale projects.

Thirdly, and perhaps most importantly, although governance implies operations beyond the control of formal structures of government, it is nevertheless impossible to divorce the rural governance process from the influence of central government and national policy-making. For example, public sector agencies, though not directly controlled by government, remain dependent upon the public purse for funding and their activities are often constrained by national policy; in the case of tourism, the responsibilities of the national or regional tourist boards and the extent to which they can support tourism are significantly restrained by their defined roles and their levels of funding. At the same time, through its various policies with respect to, for example, employment and taxation, central government establishes the broader parameters within which any sector, including tourism, must operate. Moreover, in the context of the countryside in particular, such is the degree of interdependence between different rural activities and sectors, such as agriculture, forestry and, of course, tourism, that policies related to one sector will inevitably impact on another (see Case Study 12.2).

Case Study 12.2   The impact of the 2001 foot and mouth outbreak on rural tourism

On 21 February 2001, the first case of foot and mouth disease (FMD) was confirmed, heralding the first major outbreak of the disease in Britain since 1967. By January 2002, when the country was finally declared 'disease free', over 8 million animals has been slaughtered and the cost of the outbreak, in terms of compensation to farmers and 'clear-up' costs, was approaching £2 billion. However, the tourism industry in Britain was facing an estimated total loss of £5 billion for 2001, not directly because of the outbreak but as a result of government policies designed to control it.

Owing to the highly contagious nature of the disease, an immediate ban was placed on the movement of all animals. At the same time, most footpaths and other rights of way in the countryside were closed, as were many rural attractions, country parks, forests and other destinations. In effect, the government's immediate response was to place the entire British countryside under quarantine. More significantly, the government also pursued a policy of culling not only infected herds, but also 'contiguous' herds – those on neighbouring farms and within a 3 km radius of confirmed cases – driven by a political (though economically unjustifiable) desire to retain the country's 'disease free status' and, hence, its ability to export livestock. As a result, a huge backlog of carcasses awaiting disposal rapidly built up. The subsequent policy of burning slaughtered animals on huge pyres (images of which were transmitted globally by the international media) acted as a further deterrent. Indeed, one survey found that 46% of people in Britain were put off visiting the countryside because of the sight of

the destruction and disposal of animals. At the same time, the widespread cull simply 'emptied the countryside', further diminishing its attraction to visitors.

The consequence of these policies was a significant loss of business for most rural tourism enterprises, particularly in the worst affected areas of the countryside. Associated businesses, such as outdoor leisurewear retailers, also suffered a severe downturn, with inevitable job losses across the entire rural tourism and leisure sector. Thus, the attempts to control the outbreak of FMD, determined primarily by agricultural policy and influenced by a powerful agricultural lobby, had a far greater social and economic impact upon the rural tourism sector. Indeed, policies designed to protect a livestock export business worth some £320 million annually placed the future prosperity of rural tourism in Britain – generating an annual £12 billion – in jeopardy.

Source: Sharpley and Craven (2001)

Therefore, as Figure 12.1 shows, appropriate central government policy and guidance is also an essential ingredient of effective countryside management for tourism. Not only does this provide the policy framework for planning and management decisions at the local level, but it also places the management of a multitude of local rural tourism destinations, projects and developments within a broader regional or national rural development context. In other words, while the management of rural tourism attractions and destinations at the local level (i.e., the site management and business management perspectives referred to above) can be largely devolved to local partnerships and business clusters, albeit according to national planning guidelines, managing tourism development as a vehicle of rural socio-economic regeneration must remain the responsibility of central government.

Conclusion

Rural tourism is but one element of an integrated, interdependent set of socio-economic structures within the contemporary countryside. Its success depends upon the health and attraction of the countryside, while it supports a diverse array of commercial interests. Moreover, in many rural areas, tourism has become the dominant, though often unrecognised, economic sector. Therefore, not only should tourism policy be synonymous with rural policy at the national level, but also the effective management of the countryside for tourism is dependent on the marriage, through a governance process, of broader rural (tourism) policy with site- or destination-level business and environmental management.

Discussion questions

1. Should rural tourism development be an element of national *rural* policy or national *tourism* policy?
2. What are the benefits of a governance approach to the local management of rural tourism?
3. How realistic is the achievement of a 'middle way' between competing ideologies in the context of rural tourism management?

Suggested further reading

Broadhurst, R. (2001) *Managing Environments for Leisure and Recreation*. London: Routledge.

Butler, R., Hall, C.M. and Jenkins, J. (eds) *Tourism and Recreation in Rural Areas*. Chichester: John Wiley & Sons.

Roberts, L. and Hall, D. (2001) *Rural Tourism and Recreation: Principles to Practice*. Wallingford: CABI Publishing.

Sharpley, R. and Sharpley, J. (1997) *Rural Tourism: An Introduction*. London: International Thomson Business Press.

13   Managing tourism for development

David J. Telfer

Chapter objectives

The purpose of this chapter is to explore management approaches leading to the optimisation of the developmental contribution of tourism. Having completed this chapter, the reader will be able to:

- appreciate the changing nature of development in the context of tourism
- understand the role of the destination environment, government regulatory frameworks and industry management decisions in optimising development in a destination
- appreciate the competing ideologies and forces at work in a tourism destination

Chapter contents

Introduction

The tourism industry is often cited as an attractive agent of development or redevelopment, generating employment and foreign exchange in a destination. However, the degree to which tourism has the potential to contribute to the broader socio-economic development of a destination is, to a large extent, conditional on the nature of the environment that exists in the destination and the management decisions taken by the industry and local government. External linkages beyond the destination, such as globalisation, also affect potential development. At the same time, tourism development itself can bring change, complexity, uncertainty and conflict, creating opportunities and

Figure 13.1 Managing tourism for development – a chapter framework

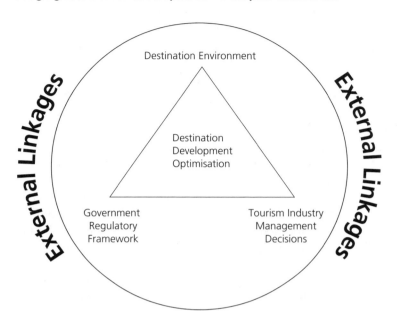

problems for analysts, planners, managers, decision-makers and members of the public (Mitchell, 1997). As Mitchell (1997) suggests, the challenge is to recognise the importance of these forces and to function in their presence, as well as knowing how to manage them so that they become agents for positive change. This chapter will explore management approaches to optimise tourism's development potential so that tourism is a positive force for change in a variety of tourism settings.

The structure of this chapter will follow the elements in Figure 13.1. The three end-points in the triangle represent three broad categories which demand consideration when exploring the extent to which the tourism industry can contribute to the broader socio-economic development of destination areas. First, however, the chapter examines the nature of development and the potential tourism can bring to optimise development in the destination, focusing in particular on how sustainable development may be used as one framework to help guide management decisions to maximise development. It then considers the three categories shown in Figure 13.1, highlighting the importance of planning and management in order to strike a balance between developing a profitable tourism industry yet protecting the local environment and community.

The nature of tourism in development

If tourism is to contribute to optimal development in a destination, it is necessary to understand the nature of development and what role, if any, tourism can play in promoting development. Development is a highly contested notion which has changed in scope over time (Telfer, 2002a). Initial definitions of development centred only on economic growth, a concept easily identifiable with tourism development. Indeed, those in favour of using tourism as an agent of development often note increases in employment or foreign exchange. Much more difficult, however, is to link tourism to the expanded notions of development as the term has come to include human better-ment and the expansion of choice, incorporating social, moral, ethical and environmental considerations (Ingham, 1993). A further indication of the increasing complexity sur-rounding the term is Sen's (1999) call for expanding freedoms for development in terms of economic opportunities, political freedoms, social facilities, transparency guarantees and protective security. The question is, then, how can tourism contribute to these expanded notions of development?

Importantly, not only has the definition of development changed, but how it is mea-sured has also changed (Hashimoto, 2002). For example, the widely-cited United Nations Human Development Index (HDI) calculates longevity (life expectancy at birth), knowledge (adult literacy and mean years of schooling) and income (real income per capita). Hashimoto (2002) argues that many indices for measuring development are, however, based on Western concepts and are not truly cultural-bias free. In an attempt to summarise the debate, Basu (2001) suggests that the development debate appears to be coasting towards a consensus. Developing nations must not focus their energies on the growth rates of their GDP, NNP or GNP, but should instead focus on achieving 'human development' or 'comprehensive development'. However, one of the main dif-ficulties for those studying development is that, while these new broad goals of devel-opment are attractive and receive wide support, few know what they mean (Basu, 2001).

One perspective attempting to incorporate many of the broader notions of develop-ment is 'sustainable development', often defined as meeting the needs of the present generation without compromising the needs of future generations (WCED, 1987). In an analysis of the literature, Sharpley (2002) identifies a number of fundamental principles, including a holistic approach integrating development and environmental issues within a global social, economic and ecological context; equity; and a focus on the long-term capacity for continuance of the global ecosystem. Development objects of sustain-able development include the improvement of the quality of life for all; education, life expectancy, opportunities to fulfil potential; satisfaction of basic needs; self-reliance; political freedoms and local decision-making; and endogenous development.

The broad concepts of sustainable development have been incorporated into sus-tainable tourism. One of the first public strategies on tourism and sustainability developed out of the Globe '90 conference in Canada. This discussed the future relationship between tourism and the environment (Fennell, 1999) and, since then, a plethora of publications on how to move towards sustainable tourism development, such as the World Tourism Organisation's *Sustainable Tourism Development: A Guide for Local Planners* (1993), has been produced. However, in their examination of the relationship between tourism and sustainability, Mowforth and Munt (1998: 105) argue that there is 'no absolutely true nature of sustainability … it is not definable except in terms of the context, control and position of those who are defining it'. They suggest an approach more frequently taken is to determine if tourist activities satisfy a number of criteria of sustainability, including environmental sustainability, social sustainability, cultural sustainability, economic sustainability, an educational component and, finally, local participation. Telfer (2002a), for example, developed a set of considerations for 'Appropriate and Sustainable Tourism' under two main categories, namely (a) the scale and control of development and (b) local community and environmental linkages. Similarly, Weaver and Opperman (2000) presented a list of potential sustainable tourism indicators (environmental, economic, social, cultural and management) as a step towards more sustainable tourism. They do, however, acknowledge that there are uncertainties and complexities associated with sustainable tourism indicators, many of them being difficult to measure.

It must be noted that sustainable development, and hence sustainable tourism development, is highly criticised. In fact, Sharpley (2002) argues that sustainability may even be a barrier to development, while it has also been criticised as being West-centric and therefore culturally biased. Swarbrooke (1999) points out that a still generally held view is that some forms of tourism are more sustainable than other forms – it is suggested, for example, that large-scale coastal mass tourism is not sustainable while smaller-scale tourism developments like ecotourism are sustainable. However, Swarbrooke (1999) argues that this is a very simplistic view based primarily on subjective judgements, and instead suggests that all forms of tourism need to be looked upon and that perhaps they all can be more sustainable.

The above analysis of development focuses largely on theoretical aspects and, thus, the extent to which development theories are put into practice needs to be explored. As Hettne (1995) suggests, development theory can be divided into development ideology (the ends) and development strategy (the means). What is important to consider is what is the overall objective of development and how that will be achieved. Issues such as the type and scale of tourism to be introduced into a specific destination and who controls it will, to a great extent, determine how much the destination will actually benefit. Is a government trying to promote national-level development or is it targeting local or region development in an attempt to counter regional imbalances within a country? Decisions may be made which see concentrated coastal mass tourism development as preferable to small-scale remote ecotourism in promoting overall development for some destinations.

In examining tourism planning, Burns (1999) developed a continuum from 'Tourism First' to 'Development First'. The 'Tourism First' perspective, which is the dominant model for aid-assisted planning at a national level for non-industrialised countries, has developing the industry as the focus of planning. It is argued that this supply-led approach to tourism development is epitomised by the World Bank and its executing agents (consultant planners). Of primary concern is the identification of sites suitable for the development of resorts, hotels and other tourist attractions (Burns, 1999). Arguments supporting this approach emphasise gross national receipts in a nation's tourism account and applying a Keynesian multiplier. The focus is therefore on developing tourism with national or regional development following as a result. Conversely, the 'Development First' perspective focuses on national developmental needs; it is concerned with using tourism as a tool for national development. This perspective takes a multidisciplinary approach, emphasising a symbiotic relationship between tourism and its environment, and focuses on the net benefits of tourism versus a range of costs such as social, cultural and environmental (Burns, 1999).

The 'Development First' approach is closely linked to the discussion in this chapter, which, following the three categories shown in Figure 13.1, now addresses the question: how can management decisions be made to increase the possibility that the tourism industry will contribute positively to the overall development of the destination? Many of the management recommendations will link to the broad concepts of sustainable tourism development although, given the difficulties present in measuring sustainability, especially with some of the more complicated indicators, it may be more prudent to assess if a destination *appears* to be sustainable or unsustainable (Weaver and Opperman, 2000). Thus, if there is an attempt to identify, measure and monitor indicators and to take remedial action if necessary, then there will be an increased likelihood that a destination will be more sustainable. In other words, the likelihood of one industry, such as tourism, contributing to all of the areas of development is remote. However, tourism developed under the guidelines of sustainability may be able to meet some of the new broader notions of development so that the destination will also benefit.

Nature of the destination

The nature of the destination environment will influence the extent to which tourism can be managed effectively to promote development. Scale is an important consideration as the term 'destination' is applied at a wide variety of scales, from an entire country to an individual attraction (Davidson and Maitland, 1997). Scale is also related to the size of the area which ideally is supposed to benefit from tourism. Whether the destination be rural, urban, mountain, coastal, island, or wilderness, and where it is located along a continuum from a developed region/country to a developing region/country, also presents different potentials to contribute to the overall development of the destination. Are adequate supplies and human resources available in the area or do they have to be imported? An abundant good supply of these resources locally will improve the potential that the tourism industry can have a positive impact on development. Management decisions which source food and construction materials locally will increase the local multiplier effect. Human resources covers a range of issues, from the availability of skilled workers to be employed in a variety of positions in the formal tourism sector to those workers who occupy positions in the informal sector, such as guides. In terms of the political environment, it is important that more than just the local elite benefit from tourism and that there is the potential for many to participate in tourism. Human resources in the destination can also include the attitudes of the host population towards tourism development and to what extent they are able to participate in the development process. A community supportive of tourism may be more willing to accept the industry and the changes that occur as a result. The presence of tourism in a community can bring a variety of social impacts, including migration, language change and the demonstration effect (Hashimoto, 2002). How these impacts are handled both by the local community and the government will, in part, determine whether tourism is a positive or negative force for development.

The conditions in the destination will also have an impact on the types of tourist who will want to travel to the destination and, thereby, will potentially have an impact on the amount of money brought into a location. The extent to which tourists are able to spend money locally that remains in the destination and surrounding area will be a function of the level of tourism services and infrastructure and who controls the system. One common factor that faces many destinations is seasonality. Management strategies to extend the season, such as diversifying the product along with marketing campaigns, have been used, although it is important to note that, owing to the uniqueness of many destinations, tourism management strategies that work in one tourism destination may not work in the next.

In order to structure the discussion on the nature of the destination, Butler's (1980) tourism area life cycle (TALC) can be used to illustrate that managers need to consider where their product is located on a product life cycle. Of course, not all destinations go through every stage of the TALC. The shape of the TALC will vary from destination to destination and will be dependent upon the rate of development, access, government policy, market trends and competing destinations (Cooper et al., 1998). In each of these stages, the local community, government and the industry will be making decisions which affect the nature of development, and who has the ultimate control in these decisions will determine how development proceeds. It is now considered how the principles of sustainable development can be integrated at the destination level in the different stages of the model, as suggested by Cooper et al., 1998. It is argued that, if the general principles of sustainable development are followed, there is a greater chance that steps can be made towards a more holistic state of development.

In the exploration stage, there are small numbers of adventurous or explorer-type tourists who shun institutionalised travel. Natural attractions, scale and the culture of the resort area are the main draw, but tourist numbers are constrained by the lack of access and facilities. To this point, the attraction for the most part remains unchanged and contact with the local people will be high. In the involvement stage, communities need to decide if they want to encourage tourism or not. Local residents may begin to provide facilities for visitors, increasing visitor numbers and impacts. A tourist season and a market area begin to emerge, placing pressures on the public sector to provide infrastructure. In order to ensure that development objectives of the destination are met, it is important to establish organisation and decision-making processes for tourism. Cooper et al. (1998) suggest that there should be local community involvement to ensure that capacity limits are followed and sustainable principles are introduced.

Large numbers are attracted at peak times in the development stage, which may exceed the size of the local population. The organisation and control of the industry may change as companies from outside the area move in and take over providing services. These outside companies may have different agendas from the local community in terms of sustainable development. If local decision-making structures are weak, problems may occur and regional or national planing may be necessary to solve problems (Cooper et al., 1998). If the decision has been made to pursue tourism, then not only must the problems which arise be sorted out, but governments may have to take action in terms of marketing to international tourism-generating areas as visitors are more dependent on package tours. The nature of the resort area will change and, if allowed to continue in an unplanned manner, over-development and deterioration may result (Cooper et al., 1998).

As development proceeds, the resort may pass into the consolidation stage where the destination is fully part of the tourism industry with an identifiable recreation business district. As at all stages, questions related to development need to be asked here, such as who is actually benefiting from tourism development? Are the overriding development goals for the destination being met and who is responsible for making these decisions? In the stagnation stage, peak numbers are reached, the destination is no longer fashionable and, thus, major promotional and development efforts may be required to maintain numbers. What is important at this stage is that there are often economic, social and environmental problems with the resort. If this proceeds, then overall development objectives for the destination on a number of different fronts may no longer be attainable and steps must be taken to solve the problems. What needs to be asked is, if there is a threshold in terms of overall development, is there a stage at which it is better for the destination to get out of the tourism industry altogether, or is it impossible to stop tourism development once it has started? In the decline stage of the TALC, visitor numbers are lost to the newer, more fashionable resorts. From a development perspective, the destination needs to consider taking steps to put the industry back on track if it still intends to pursue tourism as a development option. New markets must be found and possibly the resort needs to be repositioned (Cooper et al., 1998).

The final stage of the TALC is the rejuvenation stage, where steps are taken to attract more visitors. It is suggested that casino development is often a common response and, as illustrated in Case Study 13.1, Niagara Falls, Ontario has been very successful at reviving its tourism industry through the introduction of a new casino. According to Cooper et al. (1998), rejuvenation strategies can be difficult to implement as managers are dealing with the built fabric of the destination rather than a product. They also argue that this is where the TALC breaks down as, at this stage, the industry is so very tightly woven in the fabric of society.

The tourism area life cycle is useful in that it can indicate the level to which local people participate in the industry in the destination. Local entrepreneurs can respond to the presence of tourists and offer services from acting as guides to providing accommodation. It is suggested that, over time, outside operators can control developments. How well tourism is integrated into the destination will determine who actually benefits. However, the tourism area life cycle has been criticised particularly for the fact that not all destinations go through all of the stages. A remote undeveloped area may be targeted as a growth pole and in a very short time, a resort complex can be built by-passing the local community. In this case, a destination may jump some of the initial stages and the local community may have little choice as to the direction of tourism development. Multinational companies, local elites or the government may control the tourism industry. The contradiction in development is apparent as this form of rapid development may raise more tax dollars for the government to put into other development projects than a form of tourism development which is slow in pace and involves the local community, such as in Case Study 13.2 in Bangunkerto, Indonesia.

Case Study 13.1   Casino Niagara

After a period of decline, Niagara Falls, Ontario, Canada is currently in an economic revitalisation phase and the heart of the expansion lies in the $800 million Niagara Falls Casino/Gateway Project. After setting up a temporary casino, construction is now underway on a permanent multimillion-dollar casino complex. The sign in front of the complex reads 'Bringing Jobs and Tourism to Niagara'. The new casino complex will have 3,000 slot machines and 150 table games, a 368-room Hyatt hotel, extensive meeting and exhibition space, retail space, restaurants and entertainment venues. It is estimated that construction of the casino will generate $100–125 million in construction contracts for mechanical, electrical and concrete work resulting in an immediate ripple effect on the Niagara region. There will be 6,000 construction jobs, and the permanent casino complex will create 800–1,000 new direct jobs and employ approximately 5,000 people. The casino is part of the Gateway Project, which includes several off-site attractions such as River Country (theme park), a 12,000-seat amphitheatre and a people mover system (expansion of the transit system) (City of Niagara Falls, 2001). The City of Niagara Falls is also set to benefit directly from hosting the new casino. In an agreement signed with the Province of Ontario, the city will receive a revenue stream of $2.6 million annually for ten years, $3 million for the following ten years, and payments of $3 million (CPI adjusted) in perpetuity after that. The provincial government also includes a financial contribution towards off-site infrastructure and the purchase of the CN/CP rail line, which runs through the Tourist Core. The agreement will also bring financial benefits through building permit fees, development charges, infrastructure contributions and annual property taxes estimated at over $10 million. The Province also benefits through the income it receives from the Ontario Lottery and Gaming Corporation (City of Niagara Falls, 2000).

Case Study 13.2   Community tourism development in Bangunkerto, Indonesia

Bangunkerto is located in the highly productive agricultural lands of central Java to the north of Yogyakarta. The community has established a 27 hectare agritourism site with a plantation centre for tourists. With assistance from the Provincial Agricultural Department in the form of 4,000 plants, they have switched production to the more profitable salak crop (small fruit of hard white flesh with a distinctive scaly brown skin). The purpose of the project is to expose tourists to the natural environment but also to stimulate awareness and demand for salak. The objectives of the project include: increasing agricultural production, increasing farmers' income, developing the area in an environmentally sound manner, generating a promotional medium for agricultural production, expanding the market, increasing foreign exchange and promoting human development. One of the key elements of the project is community involvement. All aspects of the attraction are controlled at the local level, which has helped to strengthen local identity. The site was built by local residents on community land and area youth are employed as guides and perform traditional dances. Local officials want to maintain control over the site, not wanting to sell out to a private company. Across the road from the site, locals have responded to the developments by setting up a small market to sell salak to tourists. In the area around the site are over 2,000 households. The leader of the project committee was in the process of trying to promote the crop in Indonesia and abroad.

The crop has been exported to Hong Kong and there are hopes of exporting it to Singapore and Australia. The Agricultural Department at the local university (Gadjah Mada) is also involved, offering training programmes on topics including production, marketing, management and project evaluation. While the site itself has not generated a large number of jobs, the switch to salak has generated some additional income, although small farm size is a barrier. The project has introduced a new tourism product in the community, which has become a source of pride for the community. The agritourism project is controlled at the community level and is helping to build a strong community culture (Telfer, 2000).

Government regulatory framework for development optimisation

Government involvement is evident in varying degrees in both of the case studies presented. Hall (1994) outlines seven roles of government in tourism: co-ordination, planning, legislation and regulation, entrepreneurship, providing stimulation, social tourism and interest protection. Governments can operate to attract specific tourist attractions or hotels or they can enter the competition to host a large-scale international event such as the Olympics. Management and policy decisions taken by different levels of government will influence the type of tourism developed in a destination. The Canadian Tourism Commission provides funds to small and medium-sized businesses to help establish Product Clubs and the European Union provides Structural Funds which help generate regional development through tourism (Telfer, 2002b). Policy can be as broad as a national tourism development plan or it can be as specific as a zoning by-law, either permitting or prohibiting tourism development. It is important, however, to place this discussion within the context of the development philosophy of the government and the political climate of the times. Referring back to Burns's (1999) framework, governments could elect to pursue a 'Tourism First' policy or a 'Development First' policy. Countries such as Mexico and Indonesia have, for example, created tourism development zones that act as growth poles generating further development.

Governments can influence development through fiscal and investment policies, including investment in general and tourism-specific infrastructure, investment incentives and influencing exchange rates (Elliot, 1997; Opperman and Chon, 1997). Blair (1995) also points out a number of government subsidies offered to attract businesses, including tax abatement, infrastructure and site assistance, low interest loans, labour force training, regulatory relief, sale-lease back and technical assistance. In addition to providing subsidies, a government can take a position of requiring that local products be used in the industry (import substitution) or require the industry to hire locals. For example, the five star hotel Aquila Prambanan in the city of Yogyakarta, Indonesia, was required to hire 22% of their staff from the area of Sleman immediately surrounding the hotel (Telfer, 1996). In examining multinational tourism companies, Witt, Brooke and Buckley (1992) note that the most important influence will be the government of the home (or parent) country. The objectives of the company will be constrained by

> necessity to conform to laws, directives, statutory requirements, exhortations and ad hoc mechanisms of the country. Complicity in matters of taxation, anti-trust (anti-monopoly or cartel) legislation, accounting practices, trade regulations, product liability and the myriad of other public policies of government is a crucial element of careful strategy formulation. (Witt et al., 1992: 182)

Referring back to Figure 13.1, a government may take advantage of external linkages to other levels of government (regional, state/provincial, national or international) and to the industry to co-operate in developing marketing and development strategies. Governments also have the ability to facilitate cluster development. Porter defines clusters as 'geographic concentrations of interconnected companies, specialised suppliers, service providers, firms in related industries, and associated institutions (for example, universities, standards agencies and trade associations) in particular fields that compete but also co-operate' (Porter, 1998: 197). Clusters are becoming increasingly important as regions and governments are becoming more competitive in the tourism market and this increasing competition is most easily identifiable in the competition of hosting special events. As noted by Telfer (2002b), the Niagara Economic and Tourism Development Corporation (NETCOR) in the Niagara Region of Ontario, Canada, is attempting to attract investors to the Niagara Region.

In establishing a regulatory framework that is built around sustainability, Williams and Shaw (1998b) argue that a holistic approach is needed in which the actions and interests of all major stakeholders are combined and which also includes appropriate levels of the state. The Finnish government funded a programme though the Finnish Tourism Board for eco-audits that focused on tourism operations. As a result of this process, the ten companies involved reduced their disposable products, produced less waste and decreased consumption of raw materials, water and electricity (Parviainen et al., 1995; also cited in Holden, 2000). While the state can take on a variety of roles in attempting to achieve sustainable tourism development there are, however, constraints. As Williams and Shaw (1998b: 58) point out, 'while the state may indicate goals and can invest in public transport and other means to facilitate particular tourism programmes, ultimately the implementation of sustainability programmes depends on private capital, which may have diverse and conflicting goals'. The next section focuses on the actions of private industry which may have the potential to enhance overall development under a framework of sustainability.

Industry management decisions for development optimisation

The final element of Figure 13.1 is 'tourism industry management decisions'. The question is, how can management decisions taken by the industry help promote overall development? It has already been noted that there are competing interests within the tourism industry and decisions taken by one firm may be at odds with a government's overall development scheme.

In examining management decisions taken in tourism, it is necessary to place the discussion within the political economy of tourism. As highlighted in Figure 13.1, there are external linkages which cross state boundaries, especially in the case of multinational corporations. Bianchi (2002) argues that there has been increasing dominance of transnational tourism corporations and growing structural power of market forces at a global and regional level. Decisions may be taken for profit maximisation of the entire global company rather than for the benefit of the local destination.

In keeping with the theme of sustainability, Wight (1998) has argued that responsible environmental practices have recently moved to the forefront of many industry agendas, embracing environmental, social and economic values. Swarbrooke (1999) also indicates that there has been increased public and political pressure for companies to behave more ethically in relation to a range of issues, including environmental impacts, relations with local communities, investment policies and relations with investors, corruption, compliance or otherwise with government legislation, relations with suppliers and marketing intermediaries, promotion techniques, such as honest advertising, pricing policies, product safety and human resources, such as equal opportunities and pay. Swarbrooke (1999) argues that many of these elements are part of sustainable tourism. Similarly, Pride et al. (1999) indicate that, in many organisations, business people have taken steps to encourage socially responsible and ethical decisions and actions; however, they point out that some have not, viewing these business practices as a poor investment.

While many firms are attempting to behave in a more sustainable manner, criticisms have been raised that some firms have adopted so-called sustainability practices only to retain or increase their market share and their profitability. It has been suggested that some firms only selectively pursue measures that contribute to profitability, such as recycling and resource use reduction, while avoiding more complex issues, such as social equity. Others argue that the industry cannot be trusted to regulate itself in a meaningful way and following codes of conduct or certification schemes will not necessarily lead to sustainability (Weaver and Opperman, 2000). While these criticisms have been raised, Weaver and Opperman (2000) have proposed a long set of candidate sustainable indicators under the headings of management, cultural, environmental, economic and social. They argue that, even though there are complexities and uncertainties with these indicators, without attempts to identify, measure and take remedial action, there is an increased likelihood that tourism development will be unsustainable.

Management decisions on a variety of issues, such as strengthening backward economic linkages to reduce leakage, enhancing collaboration and partnerships (Bramwell and Lane, 2000), use of the informal sector and generating a destination competitive enough to attract the correct market (Malecki, 1997), all have implications for the effectiveness of tourism in broader socio-economic development goals. Management decisions can be taken on the sustainable indicators, outlined by Weaver and Opperman (2000) above, to maximise the positive impacts and minimise the negative impacts of tourism in development. A few of these indicators are presented here in order to structure the discussion.

In terms of economics, indicators include revenues and multipliers from tourism, tourism-related employment, backward linkages to other sectors, percentage of all tourism-related imports, level of profit repatriation, position in the product life cycle and overall economic impact. If management decisions are taken so that local resources are used in the industry and the money generated stays in the local economy, there will be a stronger chance that overall development will proceed in the destination. One of these indicators relates to hiring local people. The Hilton Batang Ai Longhouse Resort in Malaysia was committed to hiring local people – however, most of the positions required English language proficiency. The hotel found hiring indigenous peoples with minimal language and formal education a challenge, and therefore the resort developed a language training programme which focused on basic hotel vocabulary and more specialised communication that was specific to employee duties (Williams and Watts, 2002).

In terms of management, some of the potential sustainability indicators presented by Weaver and Opperman (2000) include recycling and fuel efficiency, Environmental Impact Assessment (EIA) procedures for tourism, existence of a tourism-related master plan, codes of ethics and good practice, and the existence of tourism education and awareness programmes. These indicators are also closely linked with their environmental indicators, which include environmental carrying capacity, effect on natural environment, resource consumption, levels of traffic, the nature of tourism development, and seasonality. How the industry decides to operate with respect to the natural environment will go a long way in determining how the destination will benefit over the long term. For example, the environmental policy of the Thomson Travel Group, one of Europe's largest travel groups, covers both technical and social aspects of their operation, with particular emphasis placed on ensuring the operations of Britannia Airways meet all codes in terms of fuel and noise emissions (Holden, 2000). In terms of social elements, Fritidsresor (a Swedish-based tour company owned by Thomson) state they will terminate a contract with a hotel found to be connected to child prostitution (Holden, 2000). Holden (2000) also outlines the efforts of Grecotels, the largest hotel company in Greece. This company has a number of initiatives, including funding an agricultural production programme on Crete, promoting Greek products in hotels and shops, using local building materials, conveying results of their environmental programmes to other hoteliers, tourism associations, tourism students and policy-makers, and they also sponsor archaeological sites on Crete.

One of the more well-known international efforts in terms of environmental management systems is Green Globe, launched by the World Travel and Tourism Council (WTTC) in 1994. In 1999, Green Globe 21 Certification was established independent of the WTTC and is concerned with verifying environmental standards of tourism companies and destinations (Holden, 2000). Elsewhere in their report for WWF (UK) on Tourism Certification Programmes, Synergy (2000) identified a number of related management strategies, which include Benchmarking, Certification Programmes, Environmental Auditing, Environmental Impact Assessments, Environmental Management Systems, ISO 14001, Life Cycle Assessment, Sigma, Social Auditing and Strategic Environmental Assessment.

Finally, Weaver and Opperman (2000) propose a potential set of both social and cultural sustainability indicators which include the adoption of local architectural styles, the extent of cultural commoditisation, resident reactions to tourism, in-migration associated with tourism, local patronage of tourist attractions and facilities, tourism-related crime, distribution of jobs by wage level and equity, and social carrying capacity. While they point out that firms may avoid more complex issues, such as social equity, in their sustainability programmes, there may be a number of management decisions that can be taken to reduce negative impacts and promote overall development. Efforts to build strong links to the local community, including hiring local residents in a variety of positions, involving local community groups in the planning process, using local supplies, ensuring locals benefit from tourism infrastructure, permitting locals to use tourist facilities, sponsoring local community initiatives, adapting to local building styles and developing tourism awareness programmes are a few of the potential options to ensure that the local community benefits. There are, however, difficulties inherent in the involvement of locals. As Hashimoto (2002) points out, social changes may result, particularly in developing countries, from the presence of tourism changes. Such changes can include gender empowerment and changes in family structure and traditional values which collectively may cause conflicts within the host community that outweigh the benefits of tourism development.

Conclusion

This chapter has explored how the destination, industry and government can all have an impact on the extent to which tourism promotes broader socio-economic goals of the destination. It is worth restating that no one industry, such as tourism, can or should have the responsibility for overall development and that it can only play a smaller role in a larger development scheme. Tourism is also an industry motivated by profit and, frequently, it may make more business sense to take actions which may help the industry but which do not contribute much to the overall development of the destination. The tourism industry is one often controlled beyond the borders of the destination (Bianchi, 2002) and, hence, management decisions made abroad may not necessarily coincide with destination development objectives. As Mitchell (1997) indicates, individuals are connected willingly or unwillingly to a larger global system that has implications for their lifestyles and livelihood. The tourism industry may not be able to contribute much to overall destination development beyond the economics of the industry.

There are, however, a number of recommendations in terms of decisions that can be made by the industry or government to increase the possibility that the tourism industry can increase the overall development of the destination. To what extent these recommendations can realistically be implemented depends on the interactions of the elements illustrated in Figure 13.1. Is there the willingness for the industry, local government and those in the local community to work together for broader goals than just those of self-interest and profit? Should we expect the tourism industry to operate in a different manner from any other industry as it seeks to maintain its long-term viability and competitiveness? The nature of development has changed drastically to become more holistic, but how can the tourism industry help meet these broad development goals? The complexities and contradictions present in development make targets difficult to hit. For example, it could be argued that a firm acting in a very unsustainable manner may be generating employment for a large number of people. The question is then, how long can they keep their overall operation running if parts of it are not sustainable? If it is a foreign tour company, they may in fact eventually choose to shut their operation down and open up in a new country with the same operating procedures. As illustrated by the two case studies in this chapter, tourism takes on many different forms in destinations and may develop very differently over time. It has, however, been argued here that under the framework of sustainability and through strong collaboration with members of the government, industry and the local population in the destination that strategies can be developed which will maximise the overall development benefits to the destination.

Discussion questions

1. What responsibility does the tourism industry have to ensure its operations promote broader socio-economic development in destination areas?
2. Should governments in destination areas regulate the tourism industry in order to achieve their socio-economic development goals?
3. How should development be measured in tourism destination areas?
4. Do Tourism Certification Programmes work?
5. Can sustainable tourism indicators provide tourism managers an adequate framework to ensure their operations are contributing to overall development in the destination?

Suggested further reading

Sharpley, R. and Telfer, D.J. (eds) (2002) *Tourism and Development: Concepts and Issues.* Clevedon: Channel View Publications.
Swarbrooke, J. (1999) *Sustainable Tourism Management.* Wallingford: CABI Publishing.

14 Site and Visitor Management at Natural Attractions

Chris Ryan

Chapter objectives

The purpose of this chapter is to describe operational considerations that face site managers when seeking to both protect natural environments and create satisfactory visitor experiences. Having completed this chapter, the reader will be able to:

- consider the context within which operational site management is located
- describe different techniques that managers can use
- stress the importance of proper care in the implementation of these policies

Chapter contents

Introduction

This chapter describes operational site management within natural areas by concentrating on visitor flow controls. It commences with a general description of issues before proceeding to a more detailed consideration of the role of brochures, visitor information centres, footpaths, signposting and zoning. It finishes with a brief discussion of the need to establish operational management within a broader plan that recognises recreational and environmental needs.

The management task

Visitors to natural attractions may be motivated by any number of reasons, reasons which determine different modes of behaviour. For example, some visitors may simply wish to relax within family groups, and thus meander, watch children play and not necessarily walk great distances. Other people may be motivated by specific wishes to observe particular fauna and flora, while yet others may use the natural setting as simply a backdrop within which to undertake some sporting or adventure pursuit. Whatever motive might dominate, the visitor will generally seek satisfaction. As a result, site and attraction management poses many problems due to the potential for any one area to be effectively a multiple product. Any one site might therefore be viewed as a collection of physical attributes of terrain, scenery and topography, complete with man-made assets such as heritage, accommodation and visitor centres. Such sites are also repositories of psychological benefits and appraisals on the part of those people who visit and use a site. Therefore, in addition to the operational management tasks of developing and maintaining natural and built fabric, site managers must also consider issues such as psychological crowding, the nature of the visitor experience and the sources of satisfaction associated with different needs and behaviours. For example, some visitors will seek a sense of isolation and emotional identification with natural places, and will not appreciate the cries of adventure seekers, or the chatter of family groups. Indeed, past studies have shown that it takes very small numbers of visitors to detract from the enjoyment of other types of visitor. In a study of those angling for trout in Central Otago in New Zealand, Walrond (2000, 2001) found that for many the presence of a single angler was sufficient to cause annoyance. One issue for site management is to ensure that users with conflicting needs are kept separate as far as is possible.

To these concerns can be added those of wanting to sustain the quality of the natural, social and historical environment. Site managers, especially those in park regimes, are often charged with the primary care of not only existing flora and fauna, but also perhaps the removal of exotics and pests. For example, in Australia, Canada, New Zealand and the USA, park authorities are often engaged in the reintroduction of native species that have become extinct in a given region, the removal of introduced species not originally native to the area, and the restoration of original natural environments as far as is possible.

It can be seen from this general introduction that site management of natural places involves at least three considerations:

1. The nature of the terrain and the maintenance of physical infrastructure.
2. The needs of visitors.
3. The needs for environmental conservation and restoration.

These are not separate dimensions, but rather represent three closely linked and interacting regimes. Conservation might be the primary concern, as illustrated by the 1987 New Zealand Conservation Act, but conservation requires sustaining the natural environment, its restoration and the promotion of 'acceptable' utilisation rates. Additionally, given the experience of the 1980s and 1990s, when park authority budgets became subject to political demands for more revenue generation, partly based on ideologies of 'user pays principles', the need to attract visitors who spend money at such sites became an increasing concern, as described by Sickle and Eagles (1998) and Eagles (2001, 2002) in their analyses of the Canadian experience. To the above three needs, therefore, might be added a fourth, namely the sustainability of the operational viability of the conservation agency.

This had the effect of many park authorities seeking to enhance service provision through the introduction of new interpretative services, which, in turn, has impacted upon the way in which park rangers have fulfilled their duties, with more time now being spent in meeting visitor demand for conducted tours and talks. Some of these activities are well established, such as the wolf howl night walks conducted by park rangers at Saskatchewan's Prince Albert National Park, while others are comparatively new. One such Australian example is that of Tindinbilla Park in the Australian Capital Territory. Since the mid-1990s a range of new services have been provided, including the building of a new educational centre, an extension of ranger guided tours and the involvement of Aboriginal people in story-telling 'events'. Such activities take managers into a marketing as well as conservation ethic and, in consequence, the story of a site becomes an important part of any location's marketing and planning.

From a tourism marketing perspective, the place is the product, in so far as a place is a collection of physical assets, but story-telling is about the involvement of emotions. For those visitors to parks who wish to engage with the place, the provision of such services involves the cognitive as well as the emotional – these visitors are information gatherers and from this act of information gathering emerges a process of evaluation that often engages an emotive response. Consequently, site management involves a reiterative process between the attributes of the place, the different potentialities it possesses for affective as well as cognitive experiences, and the way that the place is presented to the public and the stories told in the marketing literature. If there is no congruence between these dimensions, possible outcomes can include disappointed visitors, diminishing revenue, and threatened landscapes and heritage sites due to reduced expenditure on conservation and a subsequent deterioration of the place, experience and organisation. One implication of this scenario is that site managers can use 'de-marketing' as a means of conservation where opportunities exist. One such example is Steel Rigg on Hadrian's Wall in the UK. Christopher Young, Director for Hadrian's Wall, noted that while English Heritage sought 'to improve the visitor's visual, cultural and educational experience of the World Heritage Site' and attempted to improve access to and within Hadrian's Wall World Heritage Site, nevertheless the area between Steel Rigg and Housesteads 'has been a problem for over twenty years' (Young, nd: 8). He noted significant erosion effects and possibilities of friction between visitors and land managers. He also highlighted a growing need to engage in policies that recognised limitations to carrying capacities and acceptable change. Consequently, in 2002, English Heritage began to drop Steel Rigg car park from its maps with the result that visitor numbers declined by approximately one-third.

The remainder of this chapter will identify a number of operational methods by which site management can enhance visitor satisfaction while protecting natural environments. The list does not pretend to be exhaustive, but its purpose is simply to indicate the means that site managers can adopt to reconcile the variables of visitor satisfaction, environment protection and enhancement, and the protection agency's organisational viability. It should be noted that this last dimension is often overlooked in writings about tourism and environmental planning, as it is often assumed that, as government agencies, funding will generally be present. Sickle and Eagles (1998) have illustrated that this is not always the case. It must also be recognised that operational viability is about more than simply finance. It includes sustaining the numbers and skills of employees, particularly park rangers. Rangers perform a variety of tasks that involve care for the natural and built environment, the interpretation of sites, communication with different kinds of visitor, enforcement of regulations and the running of visitor and educational centres. Operational viability thus includes issues concerning the morale and retention of skilled staff, that is the need to sustain an important human resource.

Operational techniques

Marketing materials

Marketing materials in terms of brochures, maps and booklets are important in shaping visitor expectations. Information can be presented in a 'dry' manner, dominated by a text written in the third person and primarily concerned with the presentation of 'facts' about the history and culture associated with a place. Or the same information can be presented in glossy brochures with photographic and pictorial illustrations and interpretations of data in terms of visitors' experience. For example, compare 'Housesteads was an important location on Hadrian's Wall because of its ability to control large areas of land' to 'Experience the outposts of the Roman Empire. Stand where Roman soldiers looked out on the landscapes of Northern England …'. The first text is impersonal, the second promises to place you, the visitor, in the sandals of a soldier from the past, seeing what he saw. It is also evident that the second is designed to attract visitors, while the former text makes little concession to the casual visitor. Consequently, the tone, text and presentation of promotional material is not neutral, but is vital in either attracting or inhibiting visitors. Words are symbols and signs of expected experiences as well as being interpretations of place, culture and terrain.

Promotional materials are therefore important in bringing messages to the notice of the public: they are not simply an advertising medium, but are part of the product design itself. By creating expectation about experience, in an industry whose main product is experience of place and the subsequent evaluations of that experience, promotional materials become a tool that site managers can use to promote those messages that they feel are pertinent to the objectives of their site plans.

Information and visitor centres

Information centres have an important role to play for a number of reasons. First, they are sources of information about a place and the natural and cultural environment of that place. Secondly, they are places of visitation in their own right, and through careful design and investment can become proxies for the place, detaining visitors for significant periods of time. Thirdly, they may be sites of revenue generation. Fourthly, they are places of refreshment and convenience through the provision of restaurants, cafés, toilets and car parking. Finally, information centres fulfil the role of gatekeeper to the attributes of a place. Site managers are continuously engaged in acts of selection, identifying those aspects of the place they want to bring to the attention of visitors, and interpreting those places for visitors. Often information centres engage in visual presentation, again involving many acts of selection – which places to photograph, the angles from which they are photographed, the seasons represented, the sequencing of items, etc. – and the very act of selection bestows a legitimacy on what is shown, and an implied diminution of importance about that which is not shown. From a conservation perspective, this directing of the visitors' attention, and the potential visitor behaviour that may result, is very important. It may make visitors aware of the specific importance of a site, but can redirect their travel patterns away from the locations of greatest fragility and vulnerability to human disturbance. The very act of detaining a visitor at a centre may lessen the possible impacts of large numbers of visitors at a specific site. Given that many visits to National Parks are day trips, the combination of a well-established information centre with trails that are easily accessed from the car park, plus catering and toilet facilities at the centre, may well mean that a high proportion of day visitors access only a small part of the total area of the park. Consequently, visitors may acquire high levels of satisfaction but with little intrusion upon the very nature that attracted them in the first place.

A number of different techniques exist to detain visitors. One of the more successful is that of audio-visual presentations. For example, in 2002, Mount Zion National Park in the USA established the Human History Museum in the Park's former Visitor Centre. Part of the story-telling includes a 22-minute audio-visual presentation that commences every half hour. For the day-tripper to the park, parking the car, visiting the museum, seeing the audio-visual presentation, looking at the other exhibits, visiting the shop and buying refreshments can easily take up about two hours of the total time spent at the park. Given that the park attracts over 2 million visitors a year, this ability to concentrate visitors into an area that is capable of sustaining high numbers is important. Additionally, the park has specifically built trails that emanate from the visitor centres that are not only accessible to those in wheelchairs, but also to the less energetic. These are supplemented by ranger guided tours both during the day and at night. The park also makes available shuttle bus tours and provides a range of walks, many of which are of less than two hours duration. These techniques of holding visitors at sites, conducting visitors, providing ease of access to certain locations and providing maps for defined walks are copied by many park authorities around the world. The advantages of such schemes include:

- creating accessibility to natural areas for the less mobile (whether through physical handicaps or advancing age);
- providing information to enable people to better understand the locations;
- creating safe environments where people are less exposed to risk;
- creating high levels of satisfaction by allowing people to engage with the site through presentations by, and contact with, rangers and by not exposing them to conditions with which they cannot cope;
- generating revenue through sales of food stuffs, souvenirs, tours and perhaps franchised operations;
- preventing people from wandering into areas where threatened species might be at risk; and
- concentrating people into areas that can be easily patrolled by rangers, thereby helping to ensure visitor safety.

Footpaths

Associated with visitor centres are footpaths and trails. These, too, are important parts in the mix of operational flows of visitors and enhancement of visitor satisfaction. They can take several forms, ranging from concrete or tarmac paths that permit ease of movement for those in wheelchairs to the rugged trails used by four-wheel-drive enthusiasts. They all possess a common feature in that they direct flows of visitors, acting as conduits by which sites of interest are connected. The construction of footpaths has attracted considerable attention in both the academic and site management literature. First, there is the issue of path widening and erosion as tracks become subject to heavy usage, especially during periods of poor weather, that makes paths boggy. Left alone, overused paths become not only less attractive to users, but also begin to have severe micro-environmental impacts as they adversely affect flora distribution through ground hardening, reduced seed distribution, directing water flows, sediment distribution, etc. Footpaths on slopes are particularly sensitive to water flow problems, and path hardening combined with significant slopes can produce very obvious water channelling. Secondly, there is the issue of what materials should be used in constructing footpaths. Thirdly, issues of access to and exit from footpaths have to be considered. Fourthly, there is the direction and planning of footpaths in terms of where they actually go. Fifthly, there is an issue of what types of signage should be used along the footpaths, and what other facilities might have to be provided. Finally, any footpath development is usually required to be considerate of, and consistent with, the nature of the terrain that it traverses.

Footpath designs are normally dictated by the expected amount of usage and the desire to be harmonious with surrounding nature. As a simple generalisation, the greater the amount of foot traffic a path has to sustain, the harder the construction materials that have to be used. However, hard materials may not always be consistent with the normal aesthetics of the countryside. For example, the heavy usage of the Pennine Way in the UK, and the fact that the route can be surrounded by mists in the uplands, might lead one to conclude that a tarmac path would have several advantages. On the other hand, there are aesthetic reasons why a long, black-surfaced path stretching into the distance would not be acceptable, representing, as it would, a distinct human intrusion on what many would perceive as a natural setting to be enjoyed as an escape from built-up environments. Problems of footpath erosion are endemic on long-distance trails like the Pennine Way. Indeed, the web page of the UK Ramblers' Association (fact sheet 14, accessed September 2002) includes the story:

> 'The day we nearly lost Gordon remains firmly etched on [my] memory,' wrote Stan Abbott in the RA's magazine in 1989. He was referring to a walk in the Three Peaks area of North Yorkshire along a path so eroded that one of his companions sank deep into the 'murky quagmire' of exposed peat.

The fact sheet notes that 'Not long after, the Yorkshire Dales National Park Authority embarked on the Three Peaks Project, a counter-erosion scheme that variously included laying duckboards across the mud, replacing the peat with hardcore, and laying geotextile fabrics across the damaged surface.'

Such an example is illustrative of similar problems around the world, but site managers now have recourse to a wide range of technologies. Board walks are a favourite method, as wood is a natural material that is generally acceptable. Examples that the author has come across include board walks around magnetic termite mounds in Litchfield Park in the Northern Territory of Australia that are constructed so as to protect the base of the mounds from footsteps, and, at Fogg Dam, also in the Northern Territory, where board walks safely take visitors through freshwater mangrove swamps, keeping them above water-logged areas where snakes or crocodiles might reside. Other techniques use wood bark, which is able to absorb walkers trampling effects without changing drainage patterns. One aspect about the use of wood products that site managers have to consider is whether natural or treated wood materials can be used. While, for example, treated wood products are longer lasting and less susceptible to degradation from excessive moisture, and thus might well be safer when used in platform construction, there might be a danger of chemical leakage into natural waters.

Among the other forms of footpath construction are 'gabions', which are rock-filled wire cages that can be laid as a base on which soils and grass can be laid to reserve a natural looking surface, and the use of 'hydraseeding', as practised along the Cleveland Way on the North York Moors. This involves power-spraying a slurry of grass seed, slow-release fertiliser, bitumen and organic material like peat and wood pulp, in an effort to re-establish a protective grass covering on vulnerable slopes and alongside the main track. In addition, geotextile matting has been used to hold the soil in place until the grass seed has germinated, at which point the matting slowly rots away. Some examples of footpath protection are shown in Case Study 14.1.

Case Study 14.1   Footpath protection at Housesteads Fort and Museum, Hadrian's Wall, UK

Housesteads Fort and Museum on Hadrian's Wall in Northumberland is owned by the National Trust and maintained and managed by English Heritage. Hadrian's Wall was built in 122AD on the orders of the Roman Emperor Hadrian to protect the northern borders of Roman Britain against incursions from Scotland. Being one of the first significant sites of the Wall on driving west from Newcastle Housestead's Fort is very popular with tourists. It is also one of the few sites where it is possible to stand on the walls looking northward across a precipitous drop. Access to the Wall and the public rights of way is from car parks operated by Northumberland National Park Authority at Housesteads and Cawfields. At the car park at Housesteads can be found an information centre with souvenir sales and a tea shop. Visitors climb from the car park along an ungrassed track to the ticket office, which is about 60 metres from the actual entrance to the fort. Figures 14.1 and 14.2 show different footpath protection measures to deal with the high flow of visitors. The path from the ticket office to the entrance gate is a grass track, but the roots of the grass are protected by being inserted within a grid comprising hexagonal plastic 'walls'. This means that the path retains a grassy appearance even though in practice most of the public are walking on the ridges of the grid. Figure 14.1 shows the actual path from the gate into the fort. It will be seen that English Heritage has had to lay matting down to protect the soil from erosion effects. Elsewhere within the site, the settlement foundations are protected by a walkway that permits visitors to walk over the area but not on the walls themselves (Figure 14.2).

Figure 14.1   Entrance gate to Housesteads Fort, Hadrian's Wall (September 2002)

Figure 14.2   Steps over the settlement foundations (September 2002)

Footpath design may also have to consider a range of other issues. The national parks of the UK, for example, differ from many of the other parks to be found in the English-speaking world because of the high level of private ownership. Indeed, over 90% of any National Park in the UK may be in private ownership, and public access may be limited in spite of other landowners, including bodies like the National Trust. Consequently, paths may have to be bounded by fencing in different locations, and the park authorities will have to negotiate carefully with landowners not only about maintaining public rights of way, but also about issues such as fencing. For example, who is to pay for its construction and maintenance? Where possible hedgerows are often preferred to fencing, but landowners may still have to take responsibility for their trimming.

In other parts of the world different considerations might prevail. In northern Canada, summer paths can become winter ski trails and the park authorities can choose to designate some as groomed trails while others are left as powdered snow. Safety considerations might require the erection of huts as refuges for skiers. The opposite consideration is found in central Australia where the intense heat means park authorities can close trails, or where huts are built to provide shade and water. In New Zealand, the Department of Conservation has been re-examining its huts policy and attempting to discern whether the presence of a hut encourages tramping in high country while perhaps resources might be better used in improvements to the front country (i.e., those areas of wilderness that are easily accessible to visitors and therefore have high usage rates).

Signposting

Routes, trails and paths are designed to take people safely through the countryside and, in doing so, direct them to sites of specific interest. Signposts may be simply directional or they may contain information. What is evident is that signposting has a role to play in enhancing visitor satisfaction. They perform a reassurance function by confirming directions, informing visitors of key sites, and providing data about those sites.

One issue that has been the subject of various reports about national parks in the UK has been patterns of usage. A number of reports have observed that a large proportion of car-borne arrivals walk comparatively short distances from the car park and when walking their dogs, and a debate has arisen over whether this is appropriate (e.g., see DEFRA, 1999). On the one hand, it means comparatively little intrusion on natural areas but, on the other hand, it raises the issue as to the degree of knowledge and appreciation of the countryside people can acquire. As a general principle, UK park authorities deem it important that visitors acquire an appreciation of the countryside so as to better support conservation policies. It is suggested that one reason why people are reluctant to leave their cars is because they are uncertain of what there is to see, how long it might take to reach a given site, and whether the walk was suitable for various family members – all factors that might cause physical or psychological discomfort for family members. Providing such practical information can overcome these issues. For example, the provision of informational and directional signs at car parks encourages people to walk further than they would normally do in the absence of such signage. As a result, it is becoming commonplace for signposts to give more information, such as:

- the length and average duration of a walk to a specific site;
- the nature of the terrain and what type of walking gear might be required;
- some information about the site itself.

Equally, the opposite principle exists. Park authorities might deliberately adopt a policy of non-information in order to help protect a given area within a park because it is considered fragile and vulnerable to human intrusion. This is not always an easy decision. For example, in Scotland debates continue about the nesting sites of Osprey. In 1998 the Raptor Conservation website (www.raptor.uk.com) reported that egg collectors robbed six nests of eggs in spite of efforts to keep the sites secret. On the other hand, nesting sites at locations like the RSPB osprey site at Loch Garten are very public, even to the extent of having web cams directly on the nest. In this case the very public 24-hour surveillance helps protects the osprey.

There are many aspects to consider in signpost design. Among these is the structure of the signpost – to what extent is it exposed to weathering and bright sunlight? While metal or plastic signposts may be longer-lasting, the context of the signpost has a bearing on the material to be used so that it is consistent with its surroundings. The base area of signage also has to be considered when informational signs are being constructed. By their very purpose, people will be detained in front of signs, and therefore it is usual to harden the surface in front of such signs. Again, there are issues of appropriate materials. Generally, the supporting posts of the signs will be sunk in concrete to secure the signs, even if the concrete is then overlaid with another surface thought to be more appropriate for the landscape. The message content and the length of the text have also to be considered. Evidence from museum and other studies indicates that few visitors retain all of the information that is provided unless a notice is short (Moscardo, 1991, 1999). Figure 14.3 provides an example of informational signage at Hadrian's Wall that is short but, because of the need to present the information in different languages and to retain a balance between text and informational images, results in a large sign.

In outside locations much depends on the sort of information that is to be displayed. In many instances maps are provided, and these can be detailed or holistic in nature. In some cases, at parks and other venues, information signs are clustered together within a covered area to become not simply a source of information but a minor attraction in their own right. In the Northern Territory of Australia this technique is used not only in national parks but also along the Stuart Highway from Alice Springs to Darwin, with the purpose of not only providing information but to encourage motorists to take breaks from driving along the 1,300 kilometre route in order to avoid over-tiredness.

The location of the signpost must also be considered. Signposts, by their nature, attract attention, and site managers and planners can deliberately use this to draw people to one spot and away from other locations. For example, the perimeter zones around woodlands are important areas of transition between wooded and grassed areas. Within approximately one metre of the wood might be found insects and plants that are specific to such zones. Among such species in the UK are various primroses, small orchids and docks. Consequently, when people leave a wooded area and are

Figure 14.3 Detailed signage at Housesteads Fort, Hadrian's Wall (September 2002)

exposed to more open vistas, there is the potential for them to delay within this zone, with possible trampling effects occurring at points of exit from the copses and woods. The strategic placement of an informational signpost can therefore draw people to the sign and away from this vulnerable area. If vistas are part of the experience, seating can be placed by these signs to avoid further damage in the transitional zone that might occur through people picnicking in such spots.

Zoning

Zoning is common policy at national, regional and park locations, and many park regimes adopt zoning policies. While there may be national differences, the general principles are the same in most cases. From a conservationist perspective, zoning is a means of identifying areas that range from those with specific environmental fragilities, where human intrusion is restricted solely to scientific work, to those used for popular recreational purposes. From this perspective there is a need to establish ecological indicators that measure the health of the natural environment and the species that they support. Such indicators might be said to be two-fold. First, there are general indicators common to most sites. These would include measures of water and air quality and generalised counts of bio-diversity. Secondly, there are criteria specific to the nature of the site. For example, in Pukaskwa National Park in Canada, Parks Canada are establishing monitoring indicators that relate to woodland caribou, artic-alpine flora, jack pine forest and the Pukaskwa Pit structures that are remnants of ancient human habitation of the area.

An example of zoning is shown in Table 14.1 which is derived from the zoning measures used by the Great Barrier Reef Marine Park Authority in Australia. The Park is regulated under the Great Barrier Reef Marine Park Act of 1975 with five principal objectives:

1. The conservation of the Great Barrier Reef.
2. The regulation of the use of the Marine Park so as to protect the Great Barrier Reef while allowing reasonable use of the Great Barrier Reef Region.
3. The regulation of activities that exploit the resources of the Great Barrier Reef Region so as to minimise the effect of those activities on the Great Barrier Reef.
4. The reservation of some areas of the Great Barrier Reef for its appreciation and enjoyment by the public.
5. The preservation of some areas of the Great Barrier Reef in its natural state, undisturbed by man except for the purposes of scientific research. (Section. 32(7) of the Great Barrier Reef Marine Park Act)

In marine areas that involve sea mammal observation, diving operators will also be subject to regulations relating to behaviours at approved sites. For example, whale watching operators will not be permitted to approach within given distances and may not be permitted to use engines under certain conditions.

An aspect of zoning regulations is that park authorities and site managers will be involved in sets of responsibilities and rights. From Table 14.1 and the above, it can be seen that there are activities that people can engage in as of right, and there are activities that are subject to permission, while, finally, there are certain behaviours and activities that are prohibited. Given this, it is not surprising that some of these are contestable issues, and before any operational techniques come into play managers may well be involved in protracted negotiations with differing stakeholders.

Zoning may well require not only environmental indicators, but also careful assessments of what some have termed 'the recreational opportunity spectrum' (Daniels and Krannich, 1990). Located around the dimensions of access, remoteness, naturalness, level of site development, visitor management methods, social encounter indices and visitor impact on environments, differing recreational opportunities are identified that range from mass usage, including possibly large-scale entertainments, at one extreme to solitary pursuits at the other. Associated with each of the spectrums are the levels of site development that may be permitted.

Table 14.1   Zones under the Great Barrier Marine Park Act, 1975

General Use Zones
Provides areas of Marine Parks for a diverse range of recreational and commercial activities, consistent with the Region's long-term conservation.

General Use 'A' Zone
The least restrictive of zones, this provides for all reasonable uses, including shipping and trawling. Prohibited activities are mining, oil drilling, commercial spearfishing and spearfishing with underwater breathing apparatus.

General Use 'B' Zone
Provides for reasonable use, including most commercial and recreational activities. Trawling and general shipping are prohibited as well as those activities not allowed in General Use 'A' Zone.

Buffer Zone
Provides protected areas of Marine Parks and allows opportunities for their appreciation and enjoyment. Buffer Zones allow mackerel trolling in areas adjacent to reefs zoned as National Park.

Marine National Park Buffer Zone
Normally 500 metres wide, this zone provides for trolling for pelagic species around reefs which have been given a level of protection which prohibits all fishing. Trolling for pelagic species is unlikely to significantly affect the 'resident' marine life for which protection is needed.

National Park Zone
Provides protected areas of Marine Parks of high conservation value – a 'look but don't take' area.

Marine National Park 'A' Zone
Provides for appreciation and recreational use, including limited line fishing. Fishing is restricted to one line with one hook per person. (When trolling for pelagic species more than one line may be used.) Spearfishing and collecting are prohibited, as well as those activities not allowed in General Use 'B' Zone.

Marine National Park 'B' Zone
Provides for appreciation and enjoyment of areas in their relatively undisturbed state. It is a 'look but don't take' zone. Fishing and all other activities which remove natural resources are prohibited.

Habitat Protection Zone
Provides areas of Marine Parks free from the effects of trawling, while allowing for a diverse range of recreational and commercial activities.

Estuarine Conservation Zone
Provides for estuarine areas free from loss of vegetation and disturbance and from changes to the natural tidal flushing regime, while maintaining opportunities for commercial and recreational activities.

Scientific Research Zone
Set aside exclusively for scientific research. Entry and use for other reasons is prohibited.

Preservation Zone
Provides for the preservation of the area in an undisturbed state. All entry is prohibited, except in an emergency, with the exception of permitted scientific research which cannot be conducted elsewhere.

Conclusion

While this chapter has concentrated on operational issues pertaining to site development, it is obvious that such techniques need to be developed within an overall strategic plan. Indeed, the operational and strategic become intermeshed when considering zoning and permitted recreational activities. Where a site is located on the continuum between prohibited and mass recreational usage depends on what is valued as requiring protection and what is thought pertinent for human leisure. In practice, this relationship is far from easy to determine, and an examination of the literature relating to natural area management indicates that planning processes are often contentious and occur over sustained periods. Additionally, such procedures may be subject to legislative procedures that control developments through assessments of possible impacts on the natural environment. Many countries today have environmental policies that require proposals to be subject to review, that invite public submissions and that allow a process of negotiation between stakeholders. In some senses the operational techniques highlighted above represent the easiest stages in the management of natural attractions, and can only take place once decisions have been made about the acceptable purpose of a site in terms of its protection and recreational roles. Nevertheless, these operational considerations are important as they are the means by which management gives voice to the actualisation of policy decisions. It is these techniques that both protect environments and ensure visitor satisfaction, and a failure to implement these techniques properly can negate the hopes of the policy-makers. These are not therefore matters of secondary importance. Indeed, their importance can be assessed by what happens in the case of failure. For example, the failure to build proper viewing platforms has led to the loss of life, as happened tragically at Cave Creek. On 28 April 1995, a viewing platform constructed at Cave Creek in Paparoa National Park, South Island, New Zealand, collapsed while being used by 18 people. It fell over 30 metres, resulting in the death of 13 students and one Department of Conservation field officer. In other instances around the world, visitors to natural areas have become lost and died as a result. Information provision, guidance, signposting and track design are therefore matters not only of site protection and appreciation, but also perhaps, in extreme cases, of the preservation of life itself. In short, operational concerns are of prime importance, even if they are sometimes seen as being less 'glamorous' when compared to issues of policy and the development of strategic directions.

Discussion Questions

1. To what extent can higher prices be used to deter visitor numbers in fragile locations?
2. In what ways can information signs be used in directing visitor flows?
3. To what extent can limiting car parking spaces at a site be used as a management tool?

Suggested Further Reading

Liddle, L. (1997) *Recreation Ecology*. London: Chapman and Hall.

Newsome, D., Moore, S.A. and Dowling, R. (2002) *Natural Area Tourism: Ecology, Impacts and Management*. Clevedon: Channel View Publications.

Ryan, C. (2003) *Recreational Tourism: Demand and Impacts*. Clevedon: Channel View Publications.

Shackley, M. (ed.) (1998) *Visitor Management Case Studies from World Heritage Sites*. Oxford: Butterworth Heinemann.

PART 4: CONTEMPORARY ISSUES IN TOURISM MANAGEMENT

15 The role of government in the management of tourism: the public sector and tourism policies

C. Michael Hall

Chapter objectives

The purpose of this chapter is to examine the role of government in the management of tourism with respect to the different functions of the state as well as particular management issues, such as co-ordination and the nature of state intervention. Having completed this chapter, the reader will be able to:

- appreciate the role of government in tourism
- identify linkages between different levels of the state
- appreciate the relevant legislative/regulatory environment
- recognise the changing dimensions of central government involvement in tourism

Chapter contents

Introduction

The term 'public sector' is the name usually given to the public bureaucracies or agencies that enact and implement the decisions of politicians and parliament. Other terms with which it is usually associated include those of public service, public administration, government and the state. However, in many people's minds, it is almost impossible to divorce the activities of elected public officials from those of the agencies which undertake the work of government. Indeed, former notions of a value-free, rational, Weberian model of a hierarchical, rule-dominated public administration have all but disappeared. Instead, public administration is now recognised as a patchwork quilt of complex relationships and numerous decision points, on which politics is brought to bear (Self, 1977). Nevertheless, notions of the public interest remain important and a task to which the public sector, along with politicians, are meant to aspire. Indeed, many statements by politicians often refer to the public interest when they are trying to make it clear that they are not acting in self-interest.

The allocation of formal powers and resources to public agencies and officials is regulated by a complex system of institutions, laws, regulations and conventions. The scope of such public agencies has expanded, along with a proliferation of government tasks, the emergence of new issues for government to deal with, the allocation of discretionary powers to administrative agencies, and the greater use of professional and specialised staffs. Tourism is one such area in which the scope of public sector involvement has grown.

Public policy is the focal point of government activity. Public policy-making, including tourism policy-making, is first and foremost a political activity. Public policy is influenced by the economic, social and cultural characteristics of society as well as the formal structures of government and other features of the political system. Policy is therefore a consequence of the political environment, values and ideologies, the distribution of power, institutional frameworks and of decision-making processes (Hogwood and Gunn, 1984; Hall and Jenkins, 1995). Nevertheless, although there are differences in tourism policies between jurisdictions, some overall trends and similarities can be recognised. International tourism policies among the developed nations can be divided into four distinct phases (Table 15.1). Of particular importance has been the increased direct involvement of government in regional development, environmental regulation and the marketing of tourism, although more recently there has been reduced direct government involvement in the supply of tourism infrastructure and a greater emphasis on the development of public–private partnerships and industry self-regulation (Airey, 1983; Hall, 1994, 2000).

There is an almost universal acceptance by governments around the world, regardless of ideology, that tourism is a good thing, with most tourism policies being designed to expand the tourist industry. Although tourism is often regarded as a private sector activity, 'government agencies at every level from the international down to small towns have adopted a progressively more active role in the use of tourism as a development tool … government agencies currently promote tourism as a panacea for underemployment in economically depressed areas' (Smith, 1989: x–xi). Governments

Table 15.1   International tourism policies, 1945–present

Phase	Characteristics
1945–1955	The dismantling and streamlining of police, customs, currency, and health regulations following the Second World War.
1955–1970	Greater government involvement in tourism marketing in order to increase tourism earning potential.
1970–1985	Government involvement in the supply of tourism infrastructure and in the use of tourism as a tool of regional development.
1985–present	Continued use of tourism as a tool for regional development, increased focus on environmental issues, reduced direct government involvement in the supply of tourism infrastructure, greater emphasis on the development of public–private partnerships and industry self-regulation.
Late 1990s–	In addition to the characteristics for the period from 1985 to the present, there is now an emerging stage of international tourism policy marked by international regulation and agreement with respect to matters such as the environment, trade in goods and services, investment and movement of people.

Sources: OECD (1974), Hall (1994, 2000) and Hall and Jenkins (1995)

shape the economic climate for industry, help provide the infrastructure and educational requirements for tourism, establish the regulatory environment in which business operates and take an active role in promotion and marketing. Indeed, as Wanhill noted:

> Every government must have a policy for tourism both at national and local level. To adopt a *laissez-faire* philosophy and stand on the sidelines is to court confrontation between hosts and guests leading to poor attitudes, bad manners and an anti-tourism lobby. Only the most determined tourists will visit those places where they are overtly made to feel unwelcome and where they perceive difficulties with regard to their personal safety. (Wanhill, 1987: 54).

Nevertheless, there is increasing scepticism and uneasiness about the effectiveness of government and the intended consequences and impacts of much government policy, including policy relating to tourism. For example, Richter observed that 'critics of current tourism policies are becoming aware and are more than a little cynical about the excesses and "mistakes" occasioned by national tourism development schemes' (Richter, 1989: 21). However, with very few exceptions, there is little questioning of the role that government authorities and corporations undertake with respect to tourism, their policies, or their relationship with industry except to the uncritical extent that what they do 'must be good for tourism'. Few question, as Jenkins (2001: 215) has done in the Australian context, 'Do the interests of these corporations reflect the interests of Australia? Do they act in the Australian public's interest?'

Government therefore plays a critical role in tourism which cannot be ignored. Government provides the overall regulatory framework within which the tourism industry operates as well as directly intervening in many aspects of the tourism system. This chapter therefore examines the role of government in tourism with respect to the different functions of the state as well as particular management issues, such as co-ordination and the nature of state intervention.

The role of government in tourism

The state can be conceptualised as a relatively permanent set of *political institutions* operating in relation to civil society (Nordlinger, 1981). Therefore, the term 'state' encompasses the whole apparatus whereby a government exercises its power. It includes elected politicians, the various arms of the public sector, unelected public/civil servants, and the plethora of rules, regulations, laws, conventions and policies which surround government and private action. The main institutions of the state include: the elected legislatures, government departments and authorities, the judiciary, enforcement agencies, other levels of government, government–business enterprises and corporations, regulatory authorities, and a range of para-state organisations, such as labour organisations (Hall and Jenkins, 1995) (Figure 15.1).

The functions of the state will affect tourism to different degrees. However, the extent to which individual functions are related to particular tourism policies, decisions and developments will depend on the specific objectives of institutions, interest groups and significant individuals relative to the policy process as well as the nature of the specific jurisdiction within which policy is being developed (Hall, 1994). The state therefore performs many functions:

- as developer and producer;
- as protector and upholder;
- as regulator;
- as arbitrator and distributor; and
- as organiser (Davis et al., 1993).

Each of these functions affects various aspects of tourism, including development, marketing, policy, promotion, planning and regulation. Two important themes in tourism research which implicitly address the issue of the regulatory role of the state in tourism are those of the appropriate role of public sector tourism agencies and the search for sustainability at different policy and planning scales (macro, meso and micro) (Hall and Jenkins, 1995). However, the state often fails to act in a co-ordinated way, with some decisions and actions being confusing to many observers. For example, while one arm of government may be actively promoting environmental conservation in a given location, another may be encouraging large-scale tourism development in order to attract employment and investment. Furthermore, there are limits to effective state intervention in economy and society, particularly as the effects of globalisation are felt by individual cities and regions at the sub-national level, also referred to as the 'local state'. Different policies in different policy arenas are often in conflict, and different levels of

Figure 15.1   Schematic structure of institutions of the state with reference to tourism

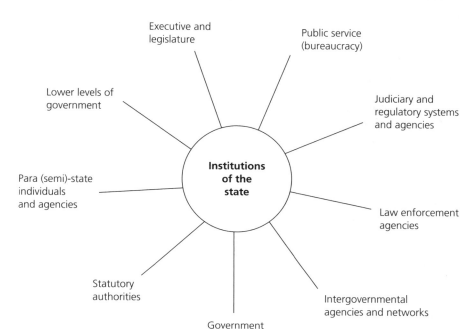

- *Executive and legislature*: e.g., systems of government, heads of state, government and opposition, minister responsible for tourism.
- *Public service (bureaucracy)*: e.g., government agencies and departments (and their staff), Departments of Tourism, national tourism promotion organisations, tourism bureaucrats.
- *Judiciary and regulatory systems and agencies*: courts of law.
- *Law enforcement agencies*: armed forces, police, customs.
- *Intergovernmental agencies and networks*: committees, councils, conferences, networks and partnerships (formal and informal), ministerial committees on tourism.
- *Government enterprises*: trading banks, essential services (e.g., communications and transport), economic development agencies, statutory travel and tourism promotion organisations.
- *Statutory authorities*: central banks, educational institutions (schools and higher education), regional development authorities.
- *Para (semi)–state individuals and agencies*: media, interest groups, trade unions, peak industry bodies, chambers of commerce, regional tourism industry associations.
- *Lower levels of government*: state/provincial and local/regional governments.

Source: After Hall and Jenkins (1995: 20)

state action, particularly in a federal system, may have conflicting goals, objectives, outcomes and impacts (Jenkins and Hall, 1997), therefore raising substantial questions about the possibility of co-ordinating an industry as diffuse through the modern economy as tourism and which is characterised by a series of domestic and international economic and political relationships (Figure 15.2).

Figure 15.2 Intrastate and extrastate relationships of different levels of public governance

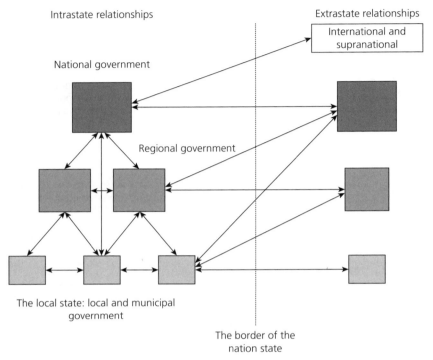

Vertical and horizontal linkages between different levels of the state
occur both domestically (intrastate) and internationally (extrastate)

The functions of the state affect tourism to different degrees. Government helps shape the economic framework for the tourism industry by influencing exchange rates, interest rates and investor confidence. It helps provide the infrastructure and educational requirements for tourism, establishes the regulatory environment in which business operates, and takes an active role in promotion and marketing. In addition, tourism may be politically appealing to government because it can potentially give the appearance of producing results from policy initiatives in a short period of time in terms of visitor numbers and/or employment generation (Hall, 1998; Hall and Kearsley, 2001). Hall (1994, 2000) listed seven functions of government in relation to tourism: co-ordination, planning, legislation and regulation, entrepreneur, stimulation, a social tourism role, and a broader role of interest protection.

Co-ordination

Co-ordination refers to formal institutionalised relationships among existing networks of organisations, interests and/or individuals. Because of the diffuse nature of tourism within the economy and within the government system, co-ordination for tourism tends to occur both horizontally, for example, between different government agencies which may have responsibilities for various tourism-related activities at the same level of governance (i.e., national parks, tourism promotion, transport), and vertically, for example, between different levels of government (local, regional, national) within an administrative and policy system.

Of all the roles of government, probably the most important is that of co-ordination. This is because the successful implementation of all the other roles will, to a large extent, be dependent on the ability of government to co-ordinate and balance its various roles in the tourism development process. The need for a co-ordinated tourism strategy has become one of the great truisms of tourism marketing, policy and planning. For example, Harris, Kerr, Forster and Company argued in their 1966 report on Australia's tourism industry that tourism 'should be regarded as an industry requiring co-ordination, planning and research and a high level of co-operative action by State and Commonwealth Governments and private enterprise organizations directly engaged in the travel industry' (1966: 65). Some 35 years later the same issues were still being identified (Testoni, 2001) and Australia was embarking on yet another national tourism planning exercise in which co-ordination would again be a central theme (see Department of Industry, Tourism and Resources at: http://www.industry.gov.au).

'"Co-ordination" usually refers to the problem of relating units or decisions so that they fit in with one another, are not at cross-purposes and operate in ways that are reasonably consistent and coherent' (Spann, 1979: 411). Co-ordination occurs both horizontally and vertically within an administrative and policy system. In federal systems, such as those of Australia, Canada, Germany, India and the USA, co-ordination is made all the more complicated because of the existence of strong political powers at both the national and state levels (Richter, 1989; Hall, 1998). Two different types of co-ordination are covered under Spann's definition: administrative co-ordination and policy co-ordination. The need for administrative co-ordination can be said to occur when there has been agreement on aims, objectives and policies between the parties that have to be co-ordinated, but the mechanism for co-ordination is undecided or there are inconsistencies in implementation. The necessity of policy co-ordination arises when there is conflict over the objectives of the policy that has to be co-ordinated and implemented. Undoubtedly, the two types of co-ordination may sometimes be hard to distinguish, as co-ordination will nearly always mean that one policy or decision will be dominant over others.

Co-ordination is a political activity and it is because of this that co-ordination can prove extremely difficult, especially when, as in the tourism industry, there are a large number of parties involved in the decision-making process. As Edgell observed, 'there is no other industry in the economy that is linked to so many diverse and different kinds of products and services as is the tourism industry' (Edgell, 1990: 7). However, it must be noted that perhaps the need for co-ordination only becomes paramount when it is not occurring. Most co-ordination occurs in a very loose fashion that does not require formal arrangement (Hall, 2000). In addition, a good case could be argued that a situation of conflict can also be productive in the formulation of new ideas or strategies for dealing with problems. Furthermore, the need for co-ordination will be issue-specific. Nevertheless, the continued calls for a co-ordinated strategy for tourism development would tend to indicate that there are differences over the direction of tourism that may require both administrative and policy measures. However, Hall (1999) has also urged caution with respect to repeated calls for co-ordination or collaboration, particularly between government and industry. At what point does tourism industry membership of government advisory committees or of a national, regional or local tourism agency represent a 'closing up' of the policy process to other interest groups rather than an exercise in consultation, co-ordination, partnership or collaboration? As Deutsch (1970: 56) recognised: 'this co-operation between groups and bureaucrats can sometimes be a good thing. But it may sometimes be a very bad thing. These groups, used to each other's needs, may become increasingly preoccupied with each other, insensitive to the needs of outsiders, and impervious to new recruitment and to new ideas.' The relationship between the tourism industry and government tourism agencies clearly raises questions about the extent to which established policy processes lead to outcomes which are in the 'public interest' rather than meeting just narrow sectoral interests (Hall, 1999).

Arguably, the likelihood of the establishment of a policy network between tourism public sector agencies and the tourism industry increases when elected politicians do not rate tourism high on the policy agenda and instead focus on more prominent issues such as crime, employment, national security or the environment. Where this occurs, policy decisions and developments are arguably often more likely to be left to policy networks, as has been argued to be the case in Australia (Hall, 1999; Jenkins, 2001) and New Zealand (Hall and Kearsley, 2001) (see Case Study 15.1).

Case Study 15.1 Tourism as an election issue in New Zealand

For example, in a survey of candidates at the 1999 New Zealand general election by Padgett and Hall (2001), tourism was generally considered by candidates to be a very important election issue. However, in the context of all issues, it ranked poorly. When asked directly about tourism's election issue significance, candidates rated it as only somewhat important. This was also the attitude taken on the relevance of different parties' tourism policies to the industry. Many candidates had no knowledge of other parties' tourism policies. Results suggest that, because candidate knowledge of tourism policies was low, it would be unlikely that issues could be

successfully debated, thus leaving tourism out of the election campaign. Indeed, a content analysis of the major newspapers during the election campaign revealed that tourism rarely featured as an election issue (only four election-related articles concerning tourism were identified in the major New Zealand daily newspapers during the election period). Tourism did not have the same political appeal as economic policies, governance and constitution issues, and taxation. It therefore attracted insignificant media attention compared to its economic significance.

Candidates were predominantly professional males over the age of 35. The majority had experience in public policy-making. Most, however, had not had any contact with the tourism industry over the past

12 months. Candidates predicted that tourism contributed significantly to New Zealand's economy and that it would be the basis of the economy in the future. However, candidates were divided over the exact nature of government involvement. The New Zealand tourism industry was considered to be environmentally and ecologically sustainable. However, candidates believed that there needed to be a sustainable tourism development strategy and there were high levels of support for government intervention in the protection of the tourism product. Marketing and promotion, another method of government intervention in the tourism industry, were also advocated, yet support for funding was weak.

Planning

Planning is the process of preparing a set of decisions for action in the future, directed at achieving goals by preferable means (Dror, 1973). Public planning for tourism occurs in a number of forms (e.g., development, infrastructure, land and resource use, promotion and marketing), institutions (e.g., different government organisations) and scales (e.g., national, regional, local and sectoral) (Hall, 1994).

Legislation and regulation

Government has a range of legislative and regulative powers which directly and indirectly impinge on tourism. These powers will range from Acts which may specifically mention tourism activities, such as the enabling act of a national tourism organisation such as Tourism Canada or the Australian Tourist Commission, to Acts which impinge upon tourism indirectly, for example, licensing laws, conservation acts, labour and employment law, health and safety regulations. The level and area of government regulation of tourism tends to be a major issue for the various components of the tourism industry, particularly as regulation may impose costs on industry or on visitors which industry perceive as threatening their profitability or viability.

Government as entrepreneur

Historically, government has played a substantial entrepreneurial function in tourism. Governments not only provide basic infrastructure, such as roads and sewage, but may also own and operate tourist ventures, including hotels and travel companies, and transport networks such as national airline and rail systems. According to Pearce (1992: 11), 'because of the scale of development and the element of the common good, provision of infrastructure is a widely accepted task of public authorities and one which can greatly facilitate tourist development and selectively direct it to particular areas'.

However, the entrepreneurial role of government in tourism, in which private costs are transformed into public costs, is changing in a climate in which less government intervention is being sought (Hall, 1999). For example, many national governments have sold off national airlines to private investors, including Qantas (Australia), British Airways (United Kingdom) and Air New Zealand, which was sold off to private interests in 1989. Following financial difficulties in late 2001 and early 2002 the New Zealand national government has again taken a major shareholding in the company, although this is meant to be only a temporary injection of capital until other private investment can be found. Nevertheless, in some jurisdictions government still maintains a major shareholding in transport infrastructure. For example, SAS (Scandinavian Air Systems) still has major shareholdings by the Danish, Norwegian and Swedish governments.

Stimulation

Similar to the entrepreneurial role is the action that government can take to stimulate tourism development. According to Mill and Morrison (1985), governments can stimulate tourism in three ways:

- financial incentives such as low-interest loans or a depreciation allowance on tourism infrastructure, such as accommodation, attractions or tourism transport;
- through sponsoring public research on tourism. In the case of Australia, for example, the federal government established a non-statutory intergovernmental agency, the Bureau of Tourism Research (BTR), in late 1987 (Hall, 1998); and
- marketing and promotion, generally aimed at generating tourism demand, although it can also take the form of investment promotion aimed at encouraging capital investment in tourism attractions and facilities. However, such is the size of the role that government plays in promotion that it is usually recognised as a separate function.

Promotion

One of the main activities of government in tourism is the promotion of tourism through tourism marketing and promotion campaigns which may be geared to stimulate either international or domestic tourism demand and, in some cases, may also be used to attract investment. However, given calls for smaller government in Western society in recent years, there have been increasing demands from government and economic rationalists for greater industry self-sufficiency in tourism marketing and promotion (see Case Study 15.2). As Hughes (1984: 14) noted: 'The advocates of a free enterprise economy would look to consumer freedom of choice and not to governments to promote firms; the consumer ought to be sovereign in decisions relating to the allocation of the nation's resources'.

Case Study 15.2   Why should government fund tourism promotion?

According to Pearce (1992: 8): 'General destination promotion tends to benefit all sectors of the tourist industry in the place concerned; it becomes a "public good" ... The question of "freeloaders" thus arises, for they too will benefit along with those who may have contributed directly to the promotional campaign.' The freeloader problem can therefore be regarded as rational business behaviour in the absence of some form of government intervention in tourism promotion (Hall, 2000). As Access Economics (1997: 29) described the situation in the Australian context: 'There will be a strong incentive for individual producers of tourism/travel services to minimise their contribution to cooperative marketing, or even not to contribute at all, and other private sector producers have no power to coerce such producers and the beneficiaries of tourism activity, anyway.' However, this argument could still be put with regards to any producer sector. For example, as there is increased international pressure for 'free trade' and a reduction in government subsidies in producer areas, so a number of areas of agricultural production are now receiving less government support. Indeed, there are a number of policy alternatives open to government for the funding of tourism promotion (Hall, 2000), including:

- forcing businesses to pay a funding levy;
- 'user pays'/co-operative funding systems;
- levies on foreign exchange earnings;
- making government funding conditional on industry funding;
- levies on tourism investment;
- funding from a passenger movement charge;
- a bed tax;

- funding out of the Goods and Services Tax (GST), possibly in relation to the amount of GST collected from international visitors; and
- funding out of consolidated revenue (the present situation).

In the Australian context, Access Economics (1997) concluded that the most appropriate form of government intervention is the appropriation of funds from consolidated revenue funds through standard budgetary processes. Several reasons for this conclusion were put forward:

- the inability to capture the benefits of generic marketing activity is severe in the light of the fragmented nature of the tourism industry;
- levies, user pays charges and business tax arrangements, including bed taxes, will institutionalise the 'freerider' or 'freeloader' problem; and
- the benefits of successful generic promotion as a travel destination are dispersed across the community.

One of the more unusual features of tourism promotion by government tourism organisations is that they have only limited control over the product they are marketing, with very few actually owning the goods, facilities and services that make up the tourism product (Pearce, 1992). This lack of control is perhaps testimony to the power of the public good argument used by industry to justify continued maintenance of government funding for destination promotion. Another response which would be more in keeping with the monetarist policies of successive governments in the 1990s, and which would fulfil the often-reported desire of industry in other areas of government intervention in the market to ensure a 'level playing field' would be no funding at all. However, this is usually opposed by the tourism industry because, clearly, it is not in their interest to reject this particular form of state intervention and the continued funding of national and regional promotion may indicate the political power of the tourism lobby to influence government tourism policies (Hall and Jenkins, 1995; Jenkins, 2001).

Social tourism

Social tourism involves the extension of the benefits of holidays to economically marginal groups, such as the unemployed, single-parent families, pensioners and the handicapped. According to Haulot (1981: 212), 'Social tourism ... finds justification in that its individual and collective objectives are consistent with the view that all measures taken by modern society should ensure more justice, more dignity and improved enjoyment of life for all citizens'. However, the growth of a conservative ideology in Western society which seeks to reduce the extent of government intervention in economic and private life and focus more on individual as opposed to the public interest has meant a substantial decline in support for social tourism in recent years (Hall, 2000), although some elements are still retained within Europe.

Government as public interest protector

Although not necessarily tourism-specific, government has a role to protect the wider public interest rather than to be meeting the needs of narrow sectoral interests, such as that of a specific industry such as tourism. Much public planning has traditionally been undertaken in order to balance competing interests. Indeed, the defence of local and minority interests, such as specific ethnic, cultural or religious groups, has traditionally occupied much government activity. Therefore, tourism policy needs to be considered as being potentially subsumed beneath a broader range of government economic, social, welfare and environmental policies in order to meet the wider national or public interest.

These various functions of government in relation to tourism will vary both between and often within countries. For example, different levels of government will typically have different goals, institutional structures and values with respect to tourism, depending on where they lie within the tourism system and the political communities to which they answer. It should also be noted that these various functions may even be in conflict in some situations and that these functions may not always be undertaken by a specifically named government tourism organisation. Indeed, many national and regional tourism organisations in the developed world, including Australia, Austria, Canada, Germany and New Zealand, have been refocused to concentrate on promotion and marketing activities and to develop stronger public–private partnerships (Hall, 2000).

The changing dimensions of central government involvement in tourism

The actions of government with respect to tourism are forged and shaped within a complex arrangement of political and public institutions, and with varying influence from interests in the private sector (Hall and Jenkins, 1998). However, as noted above, the nation state should not be seen as a unitary structure, particularly given the importance of regional and local government in tourism development and promotion. The sources of power in tourism policy, planning and promotion affect the location, structure and behaviour of public agencies responsible for tourism policy formulation and implementation. The diversity, complexity and changing nature of the tourist industry, and changing ideas about the appropriate role of the state in tourism, result in ongoing shifts in tourism policy and administration at all levels of government. For example, in Australia in 1974, tourism at the federal level was part of the Department of Tourism and Recreation; in 1985, tourism was in the Department of Sport, Recreation and Tourism; in the late 1980s, tourism became part of the Department of the Arts, Sport, the Environment, Tourism and Territories; and in 1991 tourism finally became a separate Federal Government department. In 1996, with the Liberal-National Party coalition coming to power for the first time in 13 years, the Department of Tourism was abolished and amalgamated with the Industry and Science portfolio as an Office of National Tourism (Jenkins and Hall, 1997). However, even though the same political parties were still in office by 2002, the situation had changed again with tourism being a specific section within a Department of Industry, Tourism and Resources (Hall, 2002). As Mercer (1979: 107) observed:

> The setting up of entirely new government departments, advisory bodies or sections within the existing administration is a well-established strategy on the part of governments for demonstrating loudly and clearly that 'something positive is being done' with respect to a given problem. Moreover, because public service bureaucracies are inherently conservative in terms of their approach to problem delineation and favoured mode of functioning … administrative restructuring, together with the associated legislation, is almost always a significant indicator of public pressure for action and change.

The Australian experience has been closely replicated in other jurisdictions, including Canada, New Zealand and the USA. Indeed, changes in the place of tourism in the machinery of government and in structure, aims and objectives of such organisations is a familiar occurrence at all levels of government. Throughout the world, governments have struggled to resolve their roles in tourism planning, development, marketing and promotion, and in dealing with the claims of the tourist industry on a range of public policy issues (Jenkins, 2001). This situation is reflected in the way in which governments frequently alter public sector arrangements for tourism planning, development, marketing and promotion. Such a situation has been well described by Hogwood and Peters (1985; also in Lane, 1993: 4):

> Public ends are ambiguous and shifting, the means are unreliable and controversial; decision rules may vary from one situation to another. Instead of rational processes for the making and

implementation of public policies we may expect to find irrational events in the public sector: solutions looking for problems, participants searching for choice opportunities and outcomes which seek some relation to organizational [and more generally political] goals.

As a result of shifts in ideologies and policies throughout the Western world, tourism planning and development functions have tended to be abolished at the central level and are increasingly held at the regional or local level. Reasons for such a shift, however, probably lie not so much with the recognition of the economic, environmental and political significance of tourism, but with broader changes in ideology and philosophy about the appropriate size and role of the state in the wider political environment within which tourism operates. Tourism is not immune from such changes in political philosophy. Indeed, in seeking to understand the changing nature of the management of tourism, as well as changes in the role of government and the associated policies, institutions and interventions in tourism, it becomes important not so much to look inside tourism for explanations but outside.

Conclusion

The role of government in tourism therefore covers a variety of areas. This chapter has provided an overview of these while also considering the changing dimensions of central government involvement in tourism.

Discussion questions

1. How has the role of government changed with respect to tourism in the past 50 years?
2. Why is co-ordination such a key issue with respect to the management of tourism?
3. What are the positives and negatives with respect to government involving themselves in tourism promotion?
4. What is the appropriate level of intervention by government in the tourism industry?
5. How does the role of local and national government differ in respect of tourism? Discuss in relation to where you live.

Suggested further reading

Bramwell, B. and Lane, B. (eds) (2000) *Tourism Collaboration and Partnerships: Politics, Practice and Sustainability*. Clevedon: Channel View Publications.
Elliot, J. (1997) *Tourism: Politics and Public Sector Management*. London: Routledge.
Hall, C.M. (1994) *Tourism and Politics: Policy, Power and Place*. Chichester: John Wiley & Sons.

Hall, C.M. (2000) *Tourism Planning*. Harlow: Prentice Hall.

Hall, C.M. and Jenkins, J. (1995) *Tourism and Public Policy*. London: Routledge.

Jenkins, J. (2001) Statutory authorities in whose interests? The case of Tourism New South Wales, the bed tax, and 'the Games'. *Pacific Tourism Review*, 4(4): 201–18.

Jenkins, J. and Schaap, R. (2003) *Political Economy of Tourism*. Clevedon: Channel View Publications.

16 Information and communications technologies for tourism

Dimitrios Buhalis

Chapter objectives

The purpose of this chapter is to examine the use of information and communication technologies (ICTs) in tourism, concentrating on their use in the private sector. The chapter elaborates on how ICTs can support the profitability and competitiveness of organisations. Having completed this chapter, the reader will be able to:

- recognise how ICTs support business functions as well as their role in operating the industry as a whole
- identify the impacts of ICTs on the marketing mix
- recognise the application of ICTs to airlines, the hospitality industry, tour operators, travel agencies and destinations

Chapter contents

Introduction: eTourism – demand and technology-driven revolution

Information and communications technologies (ICTs) provide a powerful tool that can bring great advantages in promoting and strengthening the tourism industry's strategy and operations (Buhalis, 1998, 2002; Sheldon, 1997; Werthner and Klein, 1999). Several ICT applications facilitate the management and marketing of tourism organisations. These systems use databases as well as software for inventory control and for strategic and tactical administration. The Internet gives organisations a window to the world and allows them to demonstrate their competencies widely. Increasingly, Intranets and Extranets provide user-friendly access to employees of organisations, as well as their authorised partners, so that staff can use company data in order to perform their tasks. Knowledge management systems enable organisations to collect information about their functions and to build knowledge on approaches to resolving problems and other emerging issues.

The Internet revolutionises flexibility in both consumer choice and service delivery processes. Customers have become much more sophisticated and discerning. This is because they have experienced high levels of service and also because the standard of living has grown considerably. As a result, tourists have become more demanding, requesting high-quality products and value for their money and, perhaps more importantly, value for time. This reflects people's shortage of time, something that is particularly evident in Western societies. Having been exposed to several tourism products and destinations, experienced, sophisticated, demanding travellers rely heavily on electronic media to obtain information about destinations, as well as to be able to communicate their needs and wishes to suppliers rapidly.

The use of ICTs in the tourism industry is therefore driven by the development of both the size and complexity of tourism demand. Every tourist is different, carrying a unique blend of experiences, motivations and desires. Tourists from the major generating regions of the world have become frequent travellers, are linguistically and technologically skilled, and can function in multicultural and demanding environments overseas. The rapid growth of both the volume and the quality requirements of contemporary travellers require powerful ICTs for the administration of the expanding traffic. Quantitative growth and qualitative trends of tourism demand therefore force industry members to adopt ICTs and to expand the volume and sophistication of their products. Hence, on the one hand, ICTs facilitate the expansion of the industry and the enlargement of the market and, on the other, the growing volume of demand requires advanced ICTs for the management of tourism organisations.

In addition to tourism demand propelling the penetration of ICTs in tourism, the supply side has also grown gradually to realise the transformation of the industry as a result of the emerging tools. This chapter concentrates on the use of ICTs in private sector enterprises and elaborates on how ICTs can support the profitability and competitiveness of organisations. Few other industries require as much information and collaboration between actors for delivering their products as the tourism industry, and hence the emerging ICTs tools provide a comprehensive infostructure for the development and fulfilment of tourism (WTO, 1988, 2001a; O'Connor, 1999; Buhalis, 2002).

eTourism and the tourism industry – strategic and tactical functions

The tourism industry has traditionally been using ICTs in a number of key strategic and operational functions, as summarised in Table 16.1. However, it is increasingly recognised

Table 16.1 Key tourism strategic and operational functions empowered by ICTs

Key strategic functions	Key operational functions
• Enhance organisational efficiency and effectiveness • Improve quality of services • Undertake strategic research for new markets and products • Follow up competition • Penetrate existing and new markets and expand market share • Diversify to new products and services or new markets • Formulate new combinations of tourist products • Differentiate and personalise products and add value at all stages • Reduce cost and achieve cost competitive advantage by creating value for money • Achieve time competitive advantage by maximising efficiency for consumers and creating value for time • Re-engineer business processes and rationalise operations • Constantly reinvent new and innovative business practices • Outperform competition in the long run • Develop partnerships and explore virtual corporations	• Information distribution and reservation process • International tourism management and marketing • Facilitation of producer, intermediary and consumer interaction • Production and delivery of tourism products • Organisation, management and control of tourism enterprises • Front office: reservations, check-in, billing, communicating • Back office: accounting, payroll, procurement, administration • Customer entertainment and service • Communicate with consumers and partners • React to unexpected events and adopt flexibility and reflective procedures • Dynamic yield management and adjust price and capacity • Monitor performance and build in feedback mechanisms • Control and administration

Source: Buhalis (2002)

that the use of ICTs in tourism is pervasive, as information is critical for both day-to-day operations and the strategic management of tourism organisations. ICTs therefore support all business functions and are critical for operating the industry as a whole.

In particular, the World Wide Web (WWW) enables the interaction and networking of computer users, using the Internet to facilitate instant access and the distribution of tourism information (WTO, 1995; Smith and Jenner, 1998). Networking provided the infrastructure for both intra- and interorganisational co-operation. As a result, the development of the Internet, as well as Intranets and Extranets in the 1990s, has revolutionised the use of ICTs in the tourism industry and has enhanced tourism distribution to a global electronic marketplace. The vast majority of tourism providers have developed Internet interfaces to communicate directly and efficiently with their clientele and partners. Combining loyalty clubs, guest histories and other information held in operation databases gives airlines and hotel chains powerful information, which enables them to interact with their existing and prospective clientele through sophisticated Customer Relationship Management (CRM) systems. This has only been achieved through using ICTs effectively for co-ordinating and maximising the efficiency of tourism organisations. ICTs are therefore centrally placed as one of the most critical factors for both the operational and strategic management of the tourism industry.

ICTs have undoubtedly become one of the most important elements of the tourism industry as in few other economic activities are the generation, gathering, processing, application and communication of information as important for day-to-day operations.

The rapid development of both tourism supply and demand makes ICTs an imperative partner of the industry, especially for the marketing, distribution, promotion and co-ordination of the industry. The re-engineering of these processes is particularly evident in the distribution of tourism products, where a paradigm shift is conspicuously experienced, altering best practices and introducing new players (Poon, 1993; Sheldon, 1993, 1997; Buhalis, 1998). Business process re-engineering is a systematic approach that critically evaluates and radically redesigns all key processes in order to improve organisational performance (Hammer and Champy, 1993). As information is the life-blood of the travel industry, effective use of technology is fundamental: 'a whole system of ICTs is being rapidly diffused throughout the tourism industry and no player will escape its impacts' (Poon, 1993; 173).

eTourism impacts on the marketing mix

ICTs have gradually propelled the redesign of the *marketing mix of tourism enterprises* by providing new tools. ICTs provide unique opportunities for innovative organisations to redesign tourism *products* to address individual needs and to satisfy consumer wants. Organisations can not only have a better understanding of their consumer by mining their data warehouses, but they can also pilot new products effectively by using different communication strategies. ICTs have also become part of the core product, especially for business travellers who now expect certain facilities to be available during their trip.

The Internet, and the World Wide Web in particular, has revolutionised the *promotion and communication* functions of tourism. They empower personal marketing campaigns and one-to-one marketing. Instead of addressing broad audiences through mass media, such as television and radio, tourism organisations are developing personal relationships with their customers, so as to understand their needs and make sure that they address them through personal communications. The new methods offer a much more cost-effective approach, while at the same time they can improve customer satisfaction by offering tailor-made packages of suitable products. In addition, the *place-distribution* functions have changed dramatically as ICTs have re-engineered the entire channel of tourism. Principals can reduce their commission costs as well as improve their relationship marketing. As a result, a widespread disintermediation (or the removal of middlemen from the value system or the supply chain) has been experienced in the tourism distribution channel, as consumers increasingly work out their own itineraries. However, new tools have enabled a wide range of new players, such as Expedia or eBookers, to emerge and gain a significant market share, propelling a reintermediation in the distribution channel (Buhalis and Licata, 2002). Reintermediation is the process of using the Internet to reassemble buyers, sellers and other partners in a traditional supply chain in new ways. It implies both new intermediaries that were not there before and existing intermediaries that use new ways to intermediate the supply chain.

Tourism organisations need to react to demand variations in order to maximise their profitability. By providing critical tools, ICTs allow tourism organisations to forecast and alter pricing almost instantly. *Pricing* therefore becomes a much more dynamic function, with better-informed managers and developed yield management systems which ensure that organisations maximise their profitability by optimising their prices and occupancy levels (Ingold et al., 2000). Auctions and the new practice of customers suggesting the prices that they would be willing to pay in order to purchase the product (e.g., Priceline.com) will enable tourism enterprises to reduce their distressed capacity (or unsold tourism product) as well as to save commissions to intermediaries. Market intelligence also enables organisations to identify the pricing strategies of competing organisations and respond with more flexible and dynamic fares.

The rapid increase in the reliability, speed and capacity of ICTs, in combination with the reduction of their cost, has forced tourism organisations to adapt and use these new tools. Innovative tourism organisations take advantage of the new tools to enhance their value added and to gain competitive advantage. Location becomes much less significant in transactions and therefore global competition intensifies. ICTs have also reduced the cost of operations by decreasing the number of people required for back-office jobs. Some of these resources can be re-directed to consumer care and contact. However, a large proportion of tourism organisations has been observing these trends passively and have failed to address the requirements of the marketplace. These organisations increasingly lose market share and eventually will be forced out of the market as they will be unable to compete with the value added and interaction benefits offered in the new global market. The following sections synthesise the developments in ICTs' utilisation for strategic and tactical management during the last decade for key tourism sectors and also illustrate some indications for the future directions of the industry.

eAirlines

Airlines have been investing heavily on ICTs since the early stages of their development. They realised the need for efficient, quick, inexpensive and accurate handling of their inventory and communication with travel agencies and other distributors. Originally, in the 1950s, reservations were made on manual display boards where passengers were listed. Travel agencies had to locate the best routes and fares for their customers in a manual and then telephone for availability, reservation and confirmation before issuing a ticket manually. In 1962, American Airlines introduced its SABRE Computerised Reservations System (CRS) (Boberg and Collison, 1985; Feldman, 1987; Hopper, 1990). The growth of air traffic as well as the US air transportation deregulation in the 1970s enabled airlines to change their routes and fares as frequently as desired. This generated a great demand for flexibility as well as internal and external communications. As a result, it stimulated the widespread use of CRS, which expanded rapidly to gigantic computerised networks. CRSs allowed airlines to compete fiercely by adapting their schedules and fares to demand. The sophistication of CRSs expanded in order to distribute up-to-date information to all potential customers worldwide and to support the operation and administration of airlines. It also resulted in the development of CRSs in marketing and distribution systems, as they contributed significantly to the competitiveness of vendor/host airlines (Wardell, 1987; Copeland and McKenney, 1988; Copeland, 1991; Truitt et al., 1991).

Global Distribution Systems (GDSs) emerged in the mid-1980s, offering a wide range of tourism products and providing the backbone mechanism for communication between principals and travel agencies. The development of CRSs to GDSs, with the integration of comprehensive tourism services, provided a range of value added services. GDSs effectively became travel supermarkets, offering information and reservation capabilities for the entire range of travel products, including accommodation, car rentals, schedules for non-air transportation, etc. GDSs are at the heart of scheduled airline operational and strategic agendas as they control and distribute the vast majority of the airline seats. Four major GDSs, namely SABRE, Worldspan, Amadeus and Galileo, currently compete fiercely for recruiting travel agencies and for penetration of the marketplace (Kärcher, 1996). GDSs emerge as the main technology suppliers for a wide range of tourism organisations, reinventing yet again their strategic objectives and aiming at developing solutions that will enable them to provide the infostructure for distributing products through the Internet.

On the operational side, ICTs are critical for managing the inventory of carriers because they assist in their reservations management and ticketing. Increasingly, eTicketing instigates paperless transactions, while offering significant savings. Tactical pricing, yield management and special offers and promotions are all facilitated by constantly assessing demand and supply and by taking both proactive and reactive measures. There are several operational management requirements, including check-in procedures, allocation of seats, generating a number of reports and orders, such as flight paths, weather forecasts, load and balance calculations, manifests for airports, in-flight catering orders and crew rotas. ICTs also facilitate eProcurement and management of suppliers and partners on a regular basis, maximising efficiency. In addition, as airlines have bases and distributors globally, and particularly at the destinations they serve, they need efficient co-ordination and communication with stations, branches, distributors and customers globally. Interaction with travel agencies and other distributors can determine levels of sales, while efficient invoicing and revenue collection will be critical for both cash flow and profitability. Finally, airlines have been investing into CRM programmes in order to manage their loyalty clubs.

The development of the World Wide Web has assisted airlines in the launch of another communication and purchasing channel that has reduced the power and costs of conventional intermediaries. By 1998 most airlines already offered websites, which not only informed consumers but also supported itinerary building, fare construction and reservations. So far, however, it is reported that there are still far too many 'lookers' but few 'bookers' on the Internet. Airlines' Internet sites attract consumers directly and assist by by-passing travel agencies and their commissions. In 2001 online bookings contributed less than 5% of the total bookings globally. However, innovative carriers take advantage and sell a great percentage of their seats online. British Airways' Internet site (www.britishairways.com) achieves 1.5 million visits per month, while the average growth of online bookings is 11% per month. The figures quoted for American carriers are significantly greater, as a result of the penetration of the Internet. EasyJet was advertised as the Web's favourite airline and achieved more than 90% of its bookings online by 2002. As a result of the airlines' use of the Internet and their ability to communicate directly with consumers, several structural changes in the industry emerged. Airlines, initially in the USA and increasingly globally, reduced their commission rates significantly and introduced 'commission capping'.

ICTs are also instrumental for the globalisation of the airlines industry. The global alliances, such as the Oneworld, Qualiflyer, Star Alliance and others, are only possible because of the co-ordination that can be achieved through harmonised ICT systems or through effective interfaces. In effect, consumers receive a seamless service, collect frequent flyer miles and enjoy privileges from different carriers in all continents simply because ICTs provide the infostructure for close collaboration. Hence, ICTs will not only formulate all elements of the marketing mix of airlines in the future, but they will also determine their strategic directions, partnerships and ownership. The launch of Internet portals such as Orbitz and Opodo by competing airlines demonstrates clearly that airlines appreciate the need to co-operate with competitors (co-opete). They develop links through alliances, industrial bodies such as The International Air Transport Association (IATA), to develop common platforms for eCommerce, eProcurement and for facilitating all their strategic and operational functions.

eHospitality

The lodging industry is the most under-automated segment of the international travel industry. *Property Management Systems* (PMSs) were introduced to facilitate the front-office, sales, planning and operation functions. This was achieved by administering a database with all reservations, rates, occupancy and cancellations, thus managing the hotel inventory. Most reservations are still rooted directly to hotel properties or through Central Reservation Offices (CRO), often by subsidised toll free telephones, while the percentage of bookings emerging from GDSs and the Internet is still fairly limited. Expensive technology and large amounts of time are top on the list of challenges holding up the process. This is partly due to the difficulty the industry experiences in rationally describing, standardising and managing the hospitality product electronically and in communicating the entire range of information required for consumers to make a transaction online. Nevertheless, in the last decade hotels also capitalised on the newly available ICTs tools. Hospitality organisations increasingly use computerised systems to improve their inventory management, communicate with their clientele and maximise their profitability. The Internet has allowed them to increase their interaction with consumers and reduce some of their operational costs. Larger hotels have introduced systems to manage their inventory (Peacock, 1995; O'Connor and Horan, 1999; O'Connor and Frew, 2000).

ICTs have penetrated hospitality management at a fast pace, integrating the hotel operation, reshaping the marketing function, improving total efficiency, providing tools for marketing research and partnership building, and enhancing customer services, while also providing strategic opportunities. In addition, consumers increasingly expect ICT facilities in their rooms; Internet access via the television set and data ports have become standard for higher hotel categories. The Internet has improved the hotel representation and reservation processes dramatically. A wide range of distribution and reservation mechanisms is offered online, providing reliable and adequate service as well as instant confirmations to both consumers and the travel trade. Hotels are able to develop their own presence and to collaborate with distributors to present multimedia information on their properties, facilities and services. They can also provide online reservations and interaction with consumers and partners. Booking through the Web is particularly convenient for customers who frequent the hotel as that provides an efficient and effective communication mechanism. The greater the capacity, number of departments, transactions, arrivals, departures and reservations, the greater the need for technologies to facilitate these processes. Equally, the greater the number of properties in a hotel chain/company, the more sophisticated the technology needs to be to manage and control all the remote properties (Buhalis and Main, 1998; Buhalis, 1999; Sigala, 2002).

Hotel chains use systems to link all their properties, and these systems help to co-ordinate their activities and maximise their collective performance. Understandably, hotel chains, particularly multinational ones, gain more benefits from PMSs, as they introduce a unified system for planning, budgeting and control of all their properties. PMSs integrate back-office operations and improve general administration, as well as specific functions such as accounting, marketing research and planning, yield management, payroll, personnel management and purchasing at individual properties.

Hotel CRSs were developed in the 1990s to connect hotels electronically with GDSs (Emmer et al., 1993). They allowed availability and room rates to be displayed globally. Being able to confirm reservations online and within a few seconds was critical for the integration of hotels in the GDSs. In addition, it offered the opportunity to introduce more personalised service and relationship marketing as agents had access to guest histories and could recover information for individual customers and agencies. Further integration between PMSs and hotel CRSs can improve efficiency, facilitate control, reduce personnel and minimise the response time to both customers and management requests.

eTour operators

Tour operators need constantly to interact with all their partners, including accommodation and transportation principals, travel agencies and consumers. Co-ordinating the movement of large numbers of travellers, often in many different countries and continents simultaneously, represents a major operational management challenge and ICTs are critical for their operations. ICTs are also critical for the distribution of tour operators' packages. Traditionally, tour operators distribute their products by displaying brochures of their packages in travel agencies. A pre-printed form is normally provided to be completed by travel agencies, in order to request a holiday from a tour operator (Wanhill, 1998). Hitherto, travel agencies search tour operators' databases and make bookings through *videotext systems*.

The domination of the videotext systems in the UK leisure travel means that many tour operators still support low technology viewdata traffic. Despite attempts by key network providers to upgrade videotext to computer systems, communicating through their Internet Protocol (IP) by developing their web-style travel trade portals (e.g. Telewest's is Endeavour and X-TANT's is Traveleye), a large percentage of retail travel agencies and tour operators has failed to upgrade their systems. These portals can combine a real-time booking capability with the 'added value' of useful information, while migrating to IP solutions will enable the systems to increase speed and make far more efficient use of the networks. However, the initial investment has been acting as a major deterrent for many organisations. Tour operators have also feared that if they upgrade their systems they will be unable to communicate with travel agencies who will not have IP technology, and thus, they will be jeopardising bookings (Kärcher, 1997; Inkpen, 1998).

The introduction of the Internet, Intranets and Extranets as strategic tools has a number of benefits for tour operators. The co-ordination and exchange of timely information is important because it allows tour operators to co-ordinate activities, to resolve potential problems and to ensure that customer requirements are communicated to all principals delivering the tourism product. Strategically, ICTs also play a critical role for tour operators. Vertically integrated travel organisations, which own both travel agency and tour operator businesses, often use information from retailers, or *market intelligence*, as a base for strategic decisions, such as mergers and acquisitions or hostile take-overs of retail units. In addition, being able to *interact closely with consumers*, tour operators have the opportunity to understand the needs of their clients better, to alter elements of the marketing mix according to the market conditions and to improve the level of flexibility they offer. Kuoni, for example, allows consumers to alter their tourism package online and to build their own itinerary by making it possible to extend the trip, change accommodation, meal plans and add value-added services such as car rentals, scuba diving lessons, etc. By enabling consumers to search by the brochure reference, Kuoni also strengthens its offline and online marketing drive. Consumers are often willing to pay premiums for customised products and a greater degree of flexibility, and tour operators who facilitate this process will gain considerable benefits.

Tour operators are threatened with disintermediation, as the Internet enables consumers and travel agencies to build their own personalised packages and to purchase them online. However, it is quite evident that tour operators will need to shift their focus from the information provision and the reservation mechanism to a more strategic role of adding value to the product and the process. Tour operators will therefore need to re-assess their core values and identify specific market segments that they can satisfy in the future.

eTravel agencies

Retail travel agencies are essentially intermediaries who serve as sales outlets for tourism principals and wholesalers. As such, they do not own the services and cannot stock travel products. Instead, they only stock travel information in the form of brochures, leaflets and data, and the personal expertise of travel consultants. Consequently, agencies carry limited financial risk, as they do not purchase tourism products in advance. They only reserve, confirm, purchase and issue travel documents (i.e., tickets and vouchers), upon request from customers. ICTs provide a wide range of *tools for travel agencies*, by providing the mechanism for information exchange and tourism product distribution. ICTs have enabled agencies to build complicated travel itineraries in minutes, while they provide up-to-date schedules, prices and availability data. The proliferation of CRSs and GDSs also provides an effective reservation mechanism which supports travel agencies in getting information, making reservations and issuing travel documents for the entire range of tourism products efficiently and at a fraction of the time required if these processes were completed manually. Travel agencies therefore use ICTs to access tourism suppliers' databases, to verify availability and rates, and to confirm reservations (Sheldon, 1997; Inkpen, 1998).

ICTs have introduced major improvements in the internal organisation of travel agencies. By integrating their back-office (e.g., accounting, commission monitoring, personnel) and front-office (e.g., customers' history, itinerary development, ticketing and communication with suppliers) functions, travel agencies have achieved significant synergies, efficiencies and cost savings. Multiple travel agencies in particular experience more benefits by facilitating branch control by their headquarters. As transactions made in branches can automatically be reported back to the head office, tighter financial control can be achieved. In addition, transactions provide invaluable marketing research data, which can almost instantly report market movements and aid tactical decisions. At the individual level, CRM systems support agencies in tracking the activity of their clients and allow them to provide a customised service. This can strengthen their efficiency, control and competitiveness. Storing information in data warehouses can also help them to develop proactive marketing tools in order to target individual customers with specialised products, thereby increasing the value-added services offered to each customer, and also to defend themselves against disintermediation.

However, ICTs and the Internet introduce some key challenges. Availability of information through a wide range of media, as well as price and product transparency through the Internet, means that agencies need to work harder to earn the respect of their clients. As consumers become more experienced, they require more specialised information and demand that their travel agency provides that information. The level of Internet usage in travel agencies is still minimal. Moreover, traditional travel agencies need to compete with several ICT-based newcomers, such as Expedia, Travelocity and lastminute.com, which allow consumers to have access to information and make online bookings (Buhalis, 1998; Wardell, 1998). Choosing the right technological platform and suppliers and integrating Internet provision with legacy systems (the established hardware and software applications in the company) can also be tricky for uninitiated travel agencies. It is evident, however, that only a few innovative agencies have developed platforms for communication with suppliers and customers. Most agencies continue to jeopardise their competitiveness by ignoring many of these developments and by failing to prepare for the new industrial challenges.

eDestinations

In several cases, Destination Management Systems (DMSs) have been used to integrate the entire tourism supply at the destination. Their contribution to strategic management and marketing is demonstrated by their ability to integrate all stakeholders at destinations and to reach a global market at a fairly affordable cost. DMSs have gradually emerged for all destinations around the world, offering online information and in some cases facilitating reservations. Increasingly, Destination Marketing Organisations provide innovative information that allows people to plan their itineraries and develop their individualised packages online or purchase commercial packages from tour operators. A number of DMSs are also moving to fully functional websites that can support the entire range of customer purchasing requirements. Tiscover in Austria and Gulliver in Ireland have been leading these developments, and gradually other destinations, including The Netherlands and Jersey, are following their example. Australia.com offers a number of pre-set itineraries for its main tourist regions, while Singapore offers a comprehensive tour planner based on the dates of the tour and the key interests of the holidaymaker. Often micro-sites are developed for specific events or for special-interest tourism. Australia managed all the information about the 2000 Olympic Games online, taking the opportunity to involve prospective tourists with the Australian brand and product. DMSs usually include a product database, a customer database and a mechanism to connect the two. More advanced systems tend to include a number of the additional services and features (Sheldon, 1993; Buhalis, 1997; Pollock, 1998; WTO, 2001a):

- Information search by category, geography or keyword
- Itinerary planning for customers
- Reservations
- Customer/contact database management
- Customer relationship management functions
- Market research and analysis
- Image library and PR material for the press
- Publishing in electronic and traditional forms
- Event planning and management
- Marketing optimisation and yield management
- Data editing and management
- Financial management
- Management information systems and performance evaluation
- Economic impact analysis
- Access to third-party sources, such as weather, transport timetables and travel planning, theatre and event ticket reservations

The DMS concept can be taken a step forward to formulate a more comprehensive and substantial system, which can revolutionise all aspects of destination management as well as integrate all tourism actors at the local level. Destination Integrated Computerised Information Reservation Management Systems (DICIRMSs) address the entire range of needs and services required by both tourism enterprises and consumers for specific destinations. In its conception a DICIRMS is an advanced DMS, digitising the entire tourism industry and integrating all aspects of its value chain. DICIRMSs provide the infostructure for communications and business processes between all stakeholders, including consumers, principals, distributors and Destination Marketing Organisations. Although a variety of the elements proposed for these systems already exists in some DMSs, there is currently no operational DMS offering such a comprehensive and integrated service to its users (Buhalis, 1997).

DICIRMSs should be accessible to all prospective visitors, business partners and travel intermediaries on all technological platforms. At the destination area, local and wide area networks can facilitate interconnectivity among all tourism suppliers. Intelligent self-service kiosks with interactive multimedia capabilities can also assist visitors who arrive at destinations to identify and purchase suitable tourism products. In addition, links to Internet portals, CRSs, GDSs and videotext networks can support the distribution network of the system (Buhalis, 1993, 1994, 1997).

The low cost involved in distributing information through the Web, in combination with its pace of development and usage by consumers, demonstrates that this medium will be pivotal in developing and distributing DICIRMSs. The global acceptance of both the interface and programming language in the Internet, with its open, interconnected operational environment, also provides a certain degree of homogeneity and compatibility between DICIRMSs representing different regions, enabling users to browse through similar types of information for alternative destinations. This, in fact, is one of the prerequisites expressed by the travel trade in utilising DICIRMSs. These systems therefore emerge as essential tools for both tourism demand and supply, as they establish a flexible and profitable communication bridge and a strategic management tool. They effectively provide the infostructure at the destination level and can network the entire range of principals and operators on a neural network.

Case Study 16.1   lastminute.com

Lastminute.com seeks to differentiate itself by generating some of the lowest prices for many travel and entertainment deals, and by packaging and delivering products and services, such as restaurant reservations, entertainment tickets and gifts, in convenient, novel and distinctive ways. It positions its business as a lifestyle portal offering a wide range of products and services to impulse purchasers. The site aims to inspire its customers to try something different. Although tourism products dominate the site, several additional products are available, including meals delivered at home, gifts such as electronics and underwear, and insurance. Lastminute.com was founded by Brent Hoberman and Martha Lane Fox in 1998. Their website was launched in the UK in October 1998. Using the Internet it matches suppliers' distressed capacity with consumer last-minute demand at short notice.

Lastminute.com works with a range of suppliers in the travel, entertainment and gift industries and is dedicated to bringing its customers attractive products and services.

Lastminute.com has relationships with over 9,300 suppliers, including international scheduled airlines, hotels, package tour operators, theatre, sports and entertainment promoters, restaurants, speciality service providers, gift suppliers and car hire, both in the UK and internationally. Supplier relationships include Lufthansa, Air France, Alitalia, British Midland, United Airlines, Virgin Atlantic Airways, Starwood Hotels and Resorts Worldwide, The Savoy Group, Sol Melia, Kempinski Hotels, English National Ballet, The Royal Albert Hall and Conran Restaurants.

In September 2001 the company had a total of over 4.2 million registered subscribers in Europe. Lastminute.com aims to be the global marketplace for all last-minute services and transactions. Following the success of the UK site, localised versions of the website have since been launched in France, Germany, Sweden, Italy, Spain, The Netherlands, Australia, New Zealand and South Africa. This growing multinational presence will enable the company to develop and further strengthen the last-minute.com brand. The company believes that, since 1998, it has developed a distinctive brand, which communicates spontaneity and a sense of adventure, attracting a loyal community of registered subscribers that use the lastminute.com website and have submitted their email addresses and other data to receive lastminute.com's weekly email. (For more information, see www.lastminute.com.)

Conclusion

ICTs empower tourism marketing and management as they provide cost-effective tools for organisations and destinations to target appropriate market segments and to develop strategic tools. They also support the interaction between tourism enterprises and consumers and, as a result, they re-engineer the entire process of developing, managing and marketing tourism products and destinations. ICTs can introduce great benefits to the efficiency, differentiation, cost reduction and response time of tourism organisations. Consequently, ICTs stimulate radical changes in the operation, distribution and structure of the tourism industry. The proliferation of technology throughout the tourism distribution channels essentially means that both consumers and professionals use the newly available tools in order to retrieve information, identify suitable products and perform reservations. Thus, the visibility of tourism principals in the marketplace will be a function of the technologies and networks that are utilised to interact with their individual and institutional customers. This will, therefore, determine their ability to distribute their product efficiently and to communicate interactively with their clientele. Should tourism principals neglect the significance of ICTs in their distribution function, they will effectively jeopardise their competitiveness and become marginalised. Hence, tourism enterprises need to understand, incorporate and utilise ICTs in order to be able to serve their target markets, improve their efficiency, maximise profitability, enhance services and maintain long-term prosperity for both themselves and destinations. ICTs have a great influence on the strategic management of contemporary organisations, as a paradigm shift is experienced, transforming the 'best' business practices.

However, it should be recognised that ICTs are not a panacea; they require a restructuring of several management practices to ensure that organisations achieve their strategic objectives. Therefore, a thorough and realistic audit of the ICT capabilities and requirements as well as a cost and benefit analysis are needed by all tourism organisations. This will help them to appreciate their position and to design the most appropriate action to enhance their competitiveness. Certain prerequisites are necessary for achieving success. Long-term planning and strategy and top management commitment will be needed to ensure that ICTs become part of the strategic planning and management of tourism enterprises. This will enable organisations to capitalise on the ICTs-generated paradigm shift in the tourism industry, which transforms the best business practices and redefines the role and the competitiveness of all tourism enterprises and destinations.

Discussion questions

1. Explain why technologies revolutionise the tourism industry.
2. What is eTourism and what are the critical implications for the tourism organisation of the future?
3. Why do hotel systems need to be integrated?
4. What are the key strategic ICT functions for airlines and hotels?
5. Explain why ICTs are critical for the operational management of each tourism sector.
6. What ICT requirements and challenges emerge as a result of alliances and partnerships?
7. What are the tourism demand and supply factors that propel Destination Management Systems?
8. Why do tourism organisations require multi-channel strategies?
9. How can DMSs support the online and offline branding of destinations?

Suggested further reading

Buhalis, D. (2002) *eTourism*. London: Pearson Education.

Inkpen, G. (1998) *Information Technology for Travel and Tourism* (2nd edition). London: Addison-Wesley Longman.

Kärcher, K. (1997) *Reinventing Package Holiday Business*. Berlin: DeutscherUniversitätsVerlag.

Marcussen C. (1999) *Internet Distribution of European Travel and Tourism Services*. Denmark: Research Centre of Bornholm.

O'Connor, P. (1999) *Electronic Information Distribution in Tourism and Hospitality*. Wallingford: CABI Publishing.

O'Connor, P. (1995) *Using Computers in Hospitality*. London: Cassell.

Poon, A. (1993) *Tourism, Technology and Competitive Strategies*. Wallingford: CABI Publishing.

Sheldon, P. (1997) *Information Technologies for Tourism*. Wallingford: CABI Publishing.

Werthner, H. and Klein, S. (1999) *Information Technology and Tourism: A Challenging Relationship*. New York: Springer.

WTO (2001) *eBusiness for Tourism: Practical Guidelines for Destinations and Businesses*. Madrid: World Tourism Organisation.

17 Destination marketing and technology: the case of web-based data mining

Chris Ryan

Chapter objectives

The purpose of this chapter is to describe trends in destination marketing in the early twenty-first century. Having completed this chapter, the reader will be able to:

- describe the implications of web-based marketing and information technology like cell phones as a means of relationship marketing in tourism
- indicate how data mining techniques might help better target potential visitors to destinations
- indicate the limitations under which regional tourism organisations operate when engaging in information technology-based marketing

Chapter contents

Introduction: destination marketing
Use of websites in destination marketing
Identifying visitors
Forms of web-based data mining
Conclusion
Case study 17.1   The Purenz.com website
Discussion questions
Suggested further reading

Introduction: destination marketing

That destination marketing has exercised the minds of both practioners and academics is evident from the published academic literature and consultancy reports that litter the desks of national, regional and local tourist organisations. In 2002, Pike was able to review 142 academic papers that had been published about destination image during the period 1973 to 2000 (Pike, 2002a). The reasons for the popularity of the topic are not difficult to fathom. Simply put, destinations require tourists so that their commercial attractions and accommodation suppliers are financially viable, thereby delivering the employment and income impacts promised by tourism destination marketing organisations, which, not uncommonly, are financed by governmental bodies as well as commercial operators.

From a conceptual perspective, the perhaps simplistic AIDA marketing model also explains the popularity of the subject. The AIDA model argues that consumer purchases are the outcome of a sequential process of gaining *attention*, creating *interest* and the *desire* to buy, and taking the final *action* of making the commercial transactions. While noting that the operationalisation of destination image may be overly dependent on attribute lists (e.g., is a destination safe? Does it contain aesthetically pleasing beaches? etc.), Pike (2002a: 542) comments that, thus far, 'there is not yet an accepted theory to replace the multi-attribute models'. Two other equally clear conclusions also emerge. First, perceptions of place may be favourable or unfavourable (with the unfavourable also including simple ignorance of a destination), and secondly, any destination lacking a favourable image will find it difficult to compete in what is an extremely competitive marketplace. In his own research and modelling of the decision-making process with reference to short break holidays, Pike (2002b) reinforces the notion of ToMA, 'Top of the Mind Awareness'. Arguably, this can be differentiated from the 'evoked set' of Howard and Sheth (1969) by reason of it being the unsolicited sub-set of an actual set of impressions that lead to predisposition to action. ToMA is also contextualised within an experiential and actionable context specific to a current state of being induced by sets of consciousness inherent in holiday destination selection.

Drawing on the same research project, Pike and Ryan (2003) note the importance of positioning theory, arguing that in an increasingly competitive tourism industry, a key challenge for destination marketers is to succinctly position their multi-attributed product range in a manner that cuts through a dynamic and heterogeneous marketplace. The explosion in destination choice and destination publicity material has only served to increase confusion among potential travellers (Gunn, 1988). Positioning theory is based on three propositions (Ries and Trout, 1986). First, we live in a society bombarded with information on a daily basis. Secondly, the human mind has developed a defence system against the clutter. Thirdly, the only way to cut through the clutter is through simplified and focused messages:

> Marketing battles are not fought in the customer's office or in the supermarkets or the drugstores of America. Those are only distribution points for the merchandise whose brand selection is decided elsewhere. Marketing battles are fought in a mean and ugly place. A place that's dark and damp with much unexplored territory and deep pitfalls to trap the unwary. Marketing battles are fought inside the mind. (Ries and Trout, 1986: 169)

Image is the key construct in destination positioning. Kotler, Haider and Rein (1993: 141) highlighted the way in which minds simplify the process of destination image formation: 'Images represent a simplification of a large number of associations and pieces of information connected with the place. They are the product of the mind trying to process and essentialize huge amounts of data about a place.' In the three decades since the first destination image studies appeared (see Anderssen and Colberg, 1973; Matejka, 1973; Mayo, 1973), the topic has become one of the most prevalent in the tourism literature. Chon's (1990) review of 23 frequently cited destination image studies, found the most popular themes were the role and influence of destination image in traveller buyer behaviour and satisfaction. It has been suggested that images held by potential travellers are so important in the destination selection process that they can affect the very viability of the destination (Hunt, 1975). Many tourism products are intangible and can often only compete via images. A major objective of any destination positioning strategy will be to reinforce positive images already held by the target markets, correct negative images or create a new image.

Use of websites in destination marketing

To this perpetual marketing dilemma of attracting and holding the attention of potential tourists, can be added the technologies of the twenty-first century. It is a commonplace that tourism, as an experiential service, cannot be sampled prior to the act of purchase and consumption. While caveats exist to this statement, for example, in the case of repeat visitation to a specific place, or in the repetition of a given type of holiday activity (e.g., an adventure holiday based on a specific activity), nevertheless every touristic experience arguably retains the potential for difference when compared to past actions. Indeed, Dann (2000a, 2000b, 2001) has argued that the quintessential appeal of holidaying behaviour lies precisely in the comparison arising from difference, that is the differences between holiday and non-holiday life, and between one holiday and another. Learning is based upon evaluations of difference, and thus every search for knowledge about a destination and the attractions and activities it offers is accompanied by the removal of uncertainty of what might be. To reduce uncertainty about whether a destination is suitable, tourists use search rules and modes of information acquisition to ensure, as best they can, that their purchases are not going to be wasted monies.

After a decade of development, websites have now become an increasingly common method of information search. They also offer many advantages to destination marketing organisations with restricted budgets, as noted by Ryan (2000). These advantages include cost-effective advertising at a time when more traditional advertising media are becoming increasingly fractured as a result of the growing number of television channels (because of cable and satellite TV) and competing magazines and papers (reflecting ever more specialised leisure interests). The World Wide Web now permits a one-to-one communication with self-selecting tourists who have decided to 'hit' the website. In addition, the website offers the potential for direct purchase action. Unlike conventional television and magazine advertising, the purchaser does not have to make a telephone call, cut out a coupon or see a travel agent. The linkage between seeing and buying, at least in theory, has become shorter than was previously the case.

Thus, for many tourism marketing organisations, the website has become an important component within their promotional mix. Doolin, Burgess and Cooper (2002: 557) note 'commercial web site development typically begins simply and evolves over time with the addition of more functionality and complexity'. The same may be said of the academic literature in the field of websites and their application to tourism. Initial literature tended to be descriptive and based upon two broad sets of considerations:

- What were the components of attractive web site design?
- What were the characteristics of users of such websites?

Website attractiveness considered not only the aesthetics of web pages, but also the factors that encouraged 'hits' and transactions (see Rachman and Richins, 1997). Burgess and Cooper (2000) advanced the debate with reference to the eMICA model, arguing that web-based business models entail three stages: web-based *promotion*, *provision* of information and transaction *processing*. Doolin, Burgess and Cooper (2002) applied this model to New Zealand websites. They concluded that, at the time of the research, in 2001, most New Zealand Regional Tourism Organisation (RTO) tourism websites had reached stage two, with the main differences between sites being explained by the level of interactivity with the client through the use of hyperlinks, customer support, chat rooms and newsletters. Other, more complex models, are reported by Sheldon, Wöber and Fesenmaier (2001) and Wöber, Frew and Hitz (2002).

Identifying visitors

By 2002 new opportunities for web-based destination marketing began to present themselves as a result of improvements in both software and hardware. From the perspective of software development, significant advances were made, and continue to be made, in the field of web-based data mining techniques, while the advent of new Internet access services in cellular telephones have also presented opportunities to destination marketers. In some ways, web-based data mining techniques simply represent an extension of database marketing. In the retail industry, organisations learnt long ago that till receipts represented a wealth of data about customers and purchasing habits, if it were possible to access them. The advent of more powerful computing technologies made that possible and from the 1980s onwards retailers began to take advantage through the establishment of various credit card and loyalty schemes. For example, an analysis of till receipts can indicate any temporal patterns in the purchase of various products. Regional analyses are also possible. While such analyses are also achievable through stock control recording, the capture of customer identifiers offers real marketing knowledge about consumers. Frequent shoppers and their purchasing habits become readily identifiable, and with this knowledge comes the creation of various promotional packages designed to appeal to the shopper.

Relationship marketing became the catchword of the late 1980s and early 1990s. Shoppers were made aware of new products, were offered privileged shopping hours and much else. In the tourism industry, the loyalty schemes offered by airlines, car rental and accommodation suppliers worked on the same principle. By the end of the twentieth century networks of such suppliers, as well as banking and insurance interests among others, had been established.

Destination marketing organisations, however, face major difficulties in seeking to replicate such promotional practices. Among the reasons that inhibit the development of any form of relational marketing are, first, that tourists are not, in many instances, the contractual customers of the destination marketing organisation. Even where tourist information centres (often part of a destination marketing organisation's operations) make bookings for activities, attractions and accommodation, they do so as an agency on behalf of a principal. In short, the tourist is the client of the hotel or attraction operator, not that of the destination marketing organisation. Secondly, for many visitors, particularly international tourists, the likelihood of frequent repeat travel to a given destination is comparatively low. This is especially true in the case of long-haul destinations from the originating country (e.g., from the UK to either New Zealand or Australia). Consequently, any attempt to establish a longer-term relationship with the visitor is invariably unproductive, especially if such relationships are dependent upon relatively expensive modes of communication such as brochures and postage. Thirdly, even if a destination marketing organisation seeks such relationships, for the most part such investments are impossible because many of the marketing organisations operate with constrained financial resources.

Forms of web-based data mining

The advent of the Web, as noted above, means that relationship marketing is not only possible but potentially profitable. First, the initial costs of establishing a website can be budgeted, and are not open-ended. Secondly, any requests for information from potential customers, via email, allow a cost-effective relationship marketing to occur. Thirdly, the Web offers a means by which destination marketing organisations can take advantage of what has consistently been shown to be one of the major components in any tourism marketing, namely the word-of-mouth syndrome.

There are three forms of web-based data mining. These are:

- *Web usage.* This looks at the sequential patterns of pages and URLs that users log on to.
- *Web structure mining.* This refers to the structure of pages. It looks at the usage patterns of menus within a page and patterns of usage across the items contained in a page or series of pages.
- *Web content mining.* This is akin to the establishment of relational databases, where linkages between user types, user patterns and web pages, and information sought (e.g., country where the enquiry originates, data sought, time spent on a page) are being established.

As described with reference to retailing, tour operators and airlines, a key determinant of usefulness to a destination is the acquisition of not only usage patterns but also user identification. In other areas of commerce, such data mining techniques have permitted commercial organisations to put together packages designed to appeal to the purchaser when he/she accesses that operation's web page. Perhaps one of the better-known examples is that of Amazon.com. There, a registered user will be greeted by name, and the web page will display offers constructed for that user based on the user's past searches of the various catalogues maintained by Amazon.com.

However, at the beginning of the twenty-first century, a number of factors still exist to inhibit the use of such techniques by destination marketing organisations. Although, over time, they will become less important, Olmeda and Sheldon (2001) note the following inhibiting factors:

- The current techniques are hungry for computing power because of a need to monitor and make sense of literally millions of website hits. Increasing the computer power raises the costs.
- Complex algorithms, requiring skilled technicians, are required to solve computing problems.
- As techniques and systems become more successful, the costs of support systems, such as off-the-shelf data mining packages, increase.
- Issues of privacy can occur.
- Any messages sent by the destination marketing organisation may be treated as spam.
- High volumes of email may be required to secure 'hits'.

The main inhibitors to the widespread use of data mining techniques, however, may not be technical in nature, but organisational, legal and behavioural. First, it has been suggested by many writers in the field that tourism organisations are slow in responding to email enquiries (Alford, 1998; Morrison et al., 2002). Secondly, Olemeda and Sheldon (2001) discuss problems with privacy legislation, citing the Swedish case where, in 1994 and 1995, SABRE was not permitted to export data from Sweden to its US parent company. European legislation permits the exchange of information about persons within the European Union between those member states which are signatories to a series of rights whereby individuals have access to their records. However, Article 25, 'on the protection of individuals with regard to the processing of personal data and on the free movement of such data', prohibits the transfer of information to those countries where the same rights do not exist. Given that the USA does not extend the same legislative protection as the EU, the situation arises whereby, in a world of global business and purchasing patterns, a significant gap in business practice between two of the leading trade blocs exists, a gap which inhibits information exchanges of this nature. While ethical issues are obviously present, the practical outcome is that internationally linked tourism businesses cannot exchange data. From the point of view of a destination promotion and marketing organisation, this may not be a major restraint where (a) the enquirer has freely given personal information and (b) where records are not transferred across national boundaries, but the delegation of a task to a website developer or Internet Protocol server might create some problems where the second condition does not apply.

With reference to behavourial issues, most writers have concentrated on the question of the way tourists use websites. However, as Sigala (2002: 213) notes, in web-based marketing it is a battle for 'trust, hearts and mind, not simply for attention and eye-balls'. One issue that has yet to receive much attention from academic commentators in the tourism field is how visitors respond to messages from a RTO or other destination marketing company, when, arguably, many email users already complain of a growing frequency of unsolicited emails, commonly known as 'spam'. Many users of the Internet have become used to spam and have developed their own means of dealing with it. If users recognise the address of the sender, they are more likely to open the email message, particularly if it originates from a point from which they have already sought information. If they do not recognise the sender, they invariably delete the emails unread. This can work against destination marketing companies where they have obtained a name and address from a secondary source. In such circumstances deleted messages are a wasted effort and not a cost-effective marketing tool.

Yet, the 'rules' of Internet use may be about to be rewritten yet again. The growing use of the cellular telephone for text messaging and access to the Internet, wherever one is, opens many more avenues for destination marketing companies. For example, Vodafone's sim$_2$ card permits the user to access geographical data about the location of restaurants and other leisure places. Cellular telephones can act as cameras by adding pictures to emails. In short, the mobile phone has joined the laptop in becoming part of a communication-information-leisure technology with international reach. The potential for tourism purposes is evident. For example, when visitors to a given location make enquiries of a destination marketing organisation, they can leave a mobile phone number to which the marketing organisation can text messages providing information about a range of services, from accommodation, activities and places to eat to ferry time tables, prices and much else. While many marketing organisations may consider using employees to respond specifically to email enquiries, a more profitable way forward may be to utilise the software associated with data mining, such as the ability to generate appropriate messages that are based on the profiling of enquiry types and search patterns (as provided by the Amazon.com example).

The growing use of the mobile telephone is ushering in an era of m(obile)-commerce, albeit with possibly more restraint than the promotional promises that accompanied the introduction of e-commerce and the trading in dot.com shares. M-commerce represents a dynamic pre-trip and in-trip means of communication by destination marketing organisations, as is indicated in Figure 17.1.

Figure 17.1 also reveals a constraint upon the use of the cellular telephone, namely that it is but one means of communication among many. However, the World Tourism Organisation Business Council (2001) identifies one group of users for whom m-commerce might possess real advantages, and that is the 'last-minute and busy traveller'. The Council notes:

> Customerisation is increasingly becoming an opportunity with last-minute travellers. Although [various applications like CRS] ... will become dominant for planned guests arrivals and for those willing to lend their loyalty to small hotels, the growth of busy travellers and the

Figure 17.1   Type of Tourism Information Media

	Static	Dynamic
Pre-trip	Brochures Guidebooks CD-ROM	Phone, fax, email, Travel agent access to GDS Internet
In-trip	Kiosks Guidebooks TV Channels in hotels	Phone, fax, email Destination Information Systems Internet

Source: Sheldon (1997: 9)

premium opportunities they offer should not be overlooked. According to a recent study by Cap Gemini America Ernst and Young, it is projected the number of US Internet users using cell phones for wireless data applications will increase from 3% in 2001 to 78% by the end of 2002.

Interestingly enough, the needs of last minute travellers will be even easier to satisfy than in the past, thanks to customerisation features. However, one key dimension to satisfy this segment must be considered: mobile commerce or M-Commerce, which is the facility offered to busy travellers to access reservation systems through their mobile units (e.g. cellulars, PDSs, etc.) (World Tourism Organisation Business Council, 2001: 143).

Conclusion

To conclude this chapter, three further observations can be made, the last of which relates to the introduction. First, if destination marketing organisations are fully to exploit data mining from a growing number of users who will increasingly be freed from the need to access a computer, some fundamental truths still apply. The destination marketing organisation needs to be able to offer a full service to any user, and its web pages need to act as a portal for those operators, attractions and accommodation providers that exist within its region. The traditional need for relationships with key tourism industry stakeholders remains and the strength of those relationships will often depend upon personal relationships. But before one becomes too excited by the technological opportunities opening up, one has to be realistic. Many marketing organisations have scarce resources. They are also driven by a range of competing motives. Ryan (2002) describes the political framework within which destination marketing organisations operate (Figure 17.2). In short, in spite of calls for strategic and rational planning regimes, the nature of both the funding and the stakeholders often means that destination marketing organisations are flexible and inconsistent in marketing. In part, this also reflects the nature of the product – few destinations remain static as to their attractions. Hotels, attractions, restaurants and other facilities represent a changing portfolio of activities, and resorts can reinvent themselves in surprisingly short periods of time.

Figure 17.2 Dimensions of political perspectives

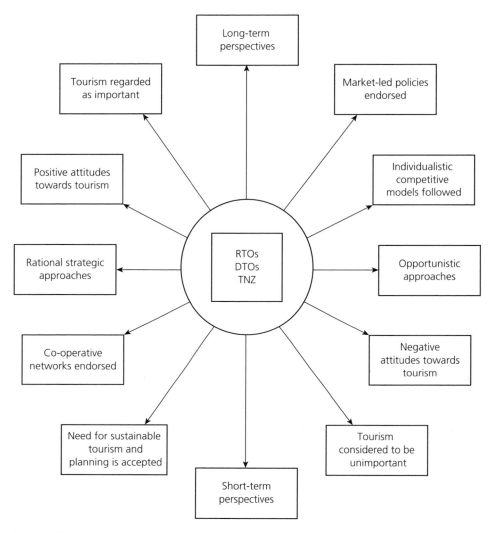

Source: Ryan (2002)

Secondly, image and technology are related in the sense that a destination marketing organisation that fully utilises current technologies is creating an image of being contemporary, efficient and dynamic. It is up with the times, even if promising quiet escapes. Research undertaken by A.C. Nielsen for Tourism New Zealand in 2002, based on 3,000 interviews with tourists, indicated that a destination product consisted of three components. These were the iconic attractions (i.e., the trigger for Pike's ToMA (Pike, 2002b)), the core product (i.e., the commissionable products sold through the channels of distribution) and the activities (i.e., the experiential aspects of tourism). The utilisation of techniques like web data mining also permits a destination marketing organisation to develop products for the tour operators and travel agents, by better understanding the nature of packaging that might appeal to some aspects of the market. This can be reinforced by statistical analyses of tourist flows.

Finally, one can return to the concept of 'Top of the Mind Awareness'. From the late 1970s there have been a number of studies that have reconfirmed the findings that destination choice is made from a small set of alternatives. Woodside and Sherrell (1977) found it to be 5.7, Thompson and Cooper (1979) 6.2, Bronner and de Hoog (1985) 4 plus or minus two destinations in an evoked set, and Ryan (1994) 3.1. Hence, to be competitive, destinations must use whatever means possible, first, to be within the considered set and, second, to take advantage of that positioning to convert interest to purchase.

It is suggested here that while web-based data mining might not succeed in the first of these two tasks, it certainly helps in achieving the second goal by aiding customerisation. It further helps a destination by supporting those who enquire as a result of word-of-mouth recommendation. Many studies reconfirm the importance of word-of-mouth recommendation (e.g., for restaurants, Su WenYu and Bowen, 2000; for senior citizens, Prideaux, Wei and Ruys, 2001; for bed and breakfast and small hotel accommodation, Lubetkin, 1999; and for hotels, Callan, 1998, to mention but a few recent examples). For instance, visitors to a region that has been recommended to them will be able to telephone a destination marketing organisation or access their web page and immediately receive first general, but increasingly customerised data that fits their interests. Using profiling methods based upon others who indicate similar search patterns, the web data mining destination marketing organisation will be able to continually confirm ToMA by producing information that matches enquirers' needs, and be physically accessible through the cellular telephone.

As tourism destination marketing organisations move into an age where a convergence of communication media, entertainment and tourism combine into a seamless flow of experiences, where the means of deriving information can be games playing or part of the visitor experience, those destination marketing organisations that are best able to identify the patterns of use that visitors make of computer/cellular phone/ PDA-based searches will be those best able to provide the individualisation that tourists seek. It is suggested that, at least for the current state of technologies, web-based data mining offers one way forward.

Case Study 17.1   The Purenz.com website

Tourism New Zealand is the National Tourism Organisation (NTO) for New Zealand and under the 1991 New Zealand Tourism Board Act that established its immediate predecessor, the New Zealand Tourism Board, has the specific function of marketing and promoting New Zealand overseas, with the objective of attracting 'high yield' visitors to the country. However, in world terms, New Zealand is a small country, possessing a population of a little over 4 million people. With such a restricted economic base the budget permitted to Tourism New Zealand is also small, approximately £40 million in 2002.

As a result, in 1999 the then board began to consider costs-effective marketing methods. It decided to develop a web-based campaign around a theme of 'Pure 100% New Zealand' that in turn was based upon images of a fresh, green New Zealand with its spectacular scenery.

Over the intervening years the web page has evolved and has become a key element of any advertising the NTO has conducted. For example, it has taken advantage of the success of the three *Lord of the Rings* films, using images from the films (with the agreement of the film company) accompanied with the byline 'Country in a best supporting film role', a campaign that has also been carried over into print-based advertising media. As a result, in January 2002, in association with the first film in the *Lord of the Rings* trilogy, a total of 85,292 hits were recorded. In April 2002, Tourism New Zealand sought to support the Discovery Channel's broadcast of the Eco-Challenge event, in which competitors race across the Southern Alps in New Zealand's South Island, thereby creating more positive images of the landscape. In that period 78,377 hits were recorded (see Figure 17.3). The NTO also uses the website to support specific overseas promotions, and an example of this was in May 2002 when 89,694 hits were recorded for a marketing initiative in Taiwan. Altogether, the year July 2001 to June 2002 indicated a 29% growth rate in website usage. The troughs in usage were around September 11, 2001, and in the pre-Christmas period of 2001, when hits fell to 51,798 and about 60,000, respectively.

Figure 17.3   An example of Tourism New Zealand's purenz.com web page, showing links to *Lord of the Rings* and the Discovery Channel

The website acts as a portal that catalogues attractions and activities in New Zealand so that visitors can directly access and communicate with individual operators and providers of accommodation. The site is available in an increasing number of languages, although the pages of individual operators may only be in English.

The website is carefully monitored by Tourism New Zealand, and in 2002 was used to identify actual and potential visitors to New Zealand as a means of constructing a sample for research into visitor attitudes and behaviours to the country (Nielsen, 2002). Research conducted by the board revealed that 94% of website users rated it as 'good' or 'very good'. In addition to recording the number of hits, Tourism New Zealand also measure the actual number of pages being accessed, and the average number of pages per user now exceeds 17. In June 2002 over 1,148,500 pages were accessed.

While the proportion of bookings being made via the website differs from operator to operator, in 2002 over a quarter of all bookings were made on the Internet. This represented a significant increase from data obtained in 1998, and indeed even in 2000 the comparative figure was about 14%.

In 2003 the board purchased rights to the dot.com name 'New Zealand.com' in what was a controversial move because of the price paid (NZ$1 million). This was done with a view that this would become the base page of the board, but at the time of writing (2003) it is a testimony to the brand strength of the purenz.com name that the original site still carries most of the traffic.

There is little doubt that web page usage is an important means of destination marketing for Tourism New Zealand, and a key feature is that every effort is made to link the site with existing promotions and known television coverage of events in New Zealand. The link with the Discovery Channel has also been important as research showed that the socio-demographic nature of the channel's viewers matched that of the desired visitor profile to New Zealand. Tourism New Zealand also use the website in marketing promotions undertaken in association with a visiting media programme so that journalists and television crews can be informed of attractions and operations that exist within the country. By using such methods, Tourism New Zealand has been very effective in making the most of a limited promotional budget.

Discussion questions

1. For attractions and destinations operating in an increasingly competitive marketplace what are the advantages and disadvantages of Web-based marketing?
2. Is the proliferation of Web-based marketing likely to dilute the impact or contribution to 'Top of Mind Awareness' of any particular Web-based campaign?
3. To what extent can the behaviour of consumers be considered the most significant of the three inhibitors to the use of data mining techniques cited in this chapter?

Suggested further reading

Morgan, N., Pritchard, A. and Pride, R. (eds) (2004) *Destination Branding: Creating the Unique Destination Proposition* (2nd edition). Oxford: Butterworth Heinemann.

Sheldon, P.J., Wöber, K.W. and Fesenmaier, D.R. (eds) (2001) *Information and Communication Technologies in Tourism 2001*: *Proceedings of the International Conference in Montreal, Canada*, 2001. Vienna: Springer.

Wöber, K., Frew, A.J. and Hitz, M. (eds) (2002) *Information and Communication Technologies in Tourism 2002*: *Proceedings of the International Conference in Innsbruck, Austria, 2002.* Vienna: Springer.

18 Tourism and the environment

Richard Sharpley

Chapter objectives

This chapter explores the tourism–environment relationship, focusing in particular on a systems approach to environmental management which permits more appropriate, destination-specific policies for managing tourism's environmental impacts. Having completed this chapter, the reader will be able to:

- understand the multidimensional and variable nature of the tourism environment
- appreciate the need for a destination-specific focus in environmental management policies
- recognise the inherent weaknesses of the sustainable tourism development paradigm
- appraise the benefits of a systems approach to tourism environmental management

Chapter contents

Introduction: tourism and the environment

'Of all the political, economic and social revolutions of the last century, none has so fundamentally changed human values and behaviour as the environmental revolution' (McCormick, 1995: xi). More specifically, concern over the relationship between humanity and the environment has, since the late 1960s, remained high on the international political agenda (Lowe and Rüdig, 1986; Macnaghten and Urry, 1998), attention long being paid not only to the exploitation and degradation of the global ecosystem but also to the socio-cultural, political and economic systems underpinning excessive or inappropriate resource use. Consequently, competing perspectives on the means of achieving a more sustainable future for the planet and its inhabitants have fuelled what has now become a weary intellectual debate (Southgate and Sharpley, 2002: 231).

Not surprisingly, perhaps, this emergence of environmentalism in general has been reflected in ever-increasing criticism of the environmental consequences of the development of tourism in particular. As Cater (1995: 21) observes, 'no other economic activity ... transects so many sectors, levels and interests as tourism' and, therefore, it was inevitable that it would become the focus of environmental concern. Nevertheless, the initial emergence of international mass tourism attracted relatively little environmental criticism, 'the image of tourism being predominantly one of an "environmentally friendly" activity, the "smokeless industry"' (Holden, 2000: 65). Indeed, during the 1960s, tourism development was largely seen as having few, if any, deleterious impacts upon the natural environment (Dowling, 1992) and opposition to the expansion of international tourism was rare (see Mishan, 1969). Throughout the 1970s, however, as international tourism grew rapidly, the socio-environmental costs of tourism development became more widely recognised (Young, 1973; Turner and Ash, 1975; Smith, 1977; de Kadt, 1979). Furthermore, by the early 1980s, an OECD report based upon a three-year study concluded that further uncontrolled expansion of tourism would seriously damage the global environment (OECD, 1981).

As a result, the 1980s witnessed the first attempts to manage the relationship between tourism and the environment more effectively. Demonstrating ecocentric idealism rather than a more pragmatic understanding of tourism's 'fundamental truths' (McKercher, 1993), it was believed that, with appropriate planning and management, not only could tourism be developed in harmony with the environment, but also it could be a mutually supportive, 'symbiotic' process (Budowski, 1976). Alternatives (to mass) tourism (mass tourism being considered from an apocalyptic perspective as 'a spectre haunting our planet' (Croall, 1995: 1)) and community-based tourism development (Murphy, 1985) emerged as dominant approaches to managing tourism, yet these largely overlooked the exogenous factors that influence both the production and consumption of tourism. Thus, the acceptance that some degree of tourism-related environmental impact is inevitable led to a more realistic management approach focused upon developing tourism within the capacity of the environment to sustain such development at the same time as optimising the benefits to tourists, the tourism industry, the environment and local communities. In short, by the early 1990s, 'sustainable tourism development' had emerged as a new approach to managing tourism.

Since then, sustainable tourism development has 'achieved virtual global endorsement as the new [tourism] industry paradigm' (Godfrey, 1996: 60). At the international, national, local and industrial sectoral levels, a plethora of policy documents, planning guidelines, statements of 'good practice', case studies, codes of conduct for tourists and other publications have been produced, all broadly concerned with the issue of sustainable tourism development. Similarly, throughout the 1990s, it became one of the most popular subjects of academic research, spawning innumerable articles, books, conferences and even a dedicated academic journal.

Despite this degree of attention and support, however, sustainable tourism development remains the subject of intense debate, a lack of consensus existing over both definitions and its viability in practice (Butler, 1998; Weaver, 2000; Sharpley, 2002). For example, although sustainable tourism development should, in theory, represent the contribution of tourism to sustainable development (Cronin, 1990), some commentators observe that, in reality, it has evolved as little more than 'an exercise in sustainable resource management' (Pigram, 1990). Nevertheless, and irrespective of this debate, sustainable tourism development represents the prevailing approach to managing the tourism–environment relationship, a set of principles that have been almost universally adopted for minimising tourism's environmental impacts.

It is, however, an approach that is overly prescriptive and managerialist, displaying a highly Western-centric perspective on both development and environmentalism – criticisms that are frequently directed towards the broader concept of sustainable development itself (Reid, 1995). Thus, it also fails to address a number of fundamental questions with respect to managing the tourism environment, including:

- Whose environment is the tourism environment?
- How much environmental damage is acceptable?
- By what or whose yardstick is 'acceptable' damage measurable?
- Should individual liberty to exploit the environment (for tourism) be subordinated to collective environmental interest?

The purpose of this chapter, therefore, is to highlight the inherent weaknesses of sustainable tourism development in the specific context of environmental management before exploring the means of managing the relationship between tourism and the environment more effectively. The first task, however, is to consider what actually constitutes the 'tourism environment'.

What is the tourism environment?

Tourism is an environmentally dependent activity (Mowl, 2002: 219). That is, the environment is a fundamental element of the tourism product – tourists seek out attractive, different or distinctive environments which may support specific touristic activities and, thus, the maintenance of a healthy, attractive environment is essential to the longer-term success of tourism.

Frequently, the environment is thought of simply in terms of the physical attributes of the destination. Indeed, many texts refer to physical/environmental impacts of tourism as distinct from social and cultural consequences (e.g., Mathieson and Wall, 1982). However, the attraction of any destination may reside in factors beyond its physical (natural or built) attributes, with tourists seeking opportunities to learn about or experience new societies or cultures. Thus, the tourism environment 'can be viewed as possessing social, cultural, economic and political dimensions, besides a physical one'

(Holden, 2000: 24; see also Hunter and Green, 1995). In this sense, the tourism environment may be defined as:

> that vast array of factors which represent external (dis)-economies of a tourism resort: natural ... anthropological, economic, social, cultural, historical, architectural and infrastructural factors which represent a habitat onto which tourism activities are grafted and which is thereby exploited and changed by the exercise of tourism business. (EC, 1993: 4)

However, while this definition embraces the *parameters* of the tourism environment, from a management point of view it is also important to consider the varying *perceptions* of it. In other words, although the factors included in the above definition are descriptive and tangible, the ways in which they are perceived or valued by different groups may vary significantly. In particular, there is likely to be a distinction between the ways in which local communities and tourists perceive or value the destination environment; while tourists may value highly a pristine or undeveloped environment, locals may simply view it as a legitimate resource for exploitation. In Cyprus, for example, most of the coast has been developed, or earmarked for development for tourism, the process being driven by both the entrepreneurial spirit of the Cypriots and the socio-cultural importance attached to property ownership and development on the island (Sharpley, 2001a).

This points to the fundamental dilemma of tourism development. Whereas tourism is principally a vehicle of socio-economic development and modernisation for local communities, the touristic attraction of destinations frequently lies in their lack of development, their traditional, 'authentic' character, their 'otherness' (Urry, 1990). Thus, destinations may be required to remain traditional or undeveloped in order to continue to attract tourists (Silver, 1993). Conversely, local communities may value particular elements of their environment to the extent that they seek to protect them, despite their attraction to tourists. As outlined in Case Study 18.1, this is certainly the case in the Himalayan kingdom of Bhutan.

Case Study 18.1   Tourism development in Bhutan

The Himalayan kingdom of Bhutan remained relatively isolated from the rest of the world up until the 1960s. Indeed, it was not until the mid-1970s that small numbers of tourists began to visit the country although, at that time, both gaining the necessary visas and actually travelling to Bhutan (there was no airport, so access was by road from India) was a complex and lengthy process. As a result, very 'few hardy adventurers chose to visit the kingdom' (Brunet et al., 2001: 252) and it was not until the opening of the airport in 1983, and the subsequent extending of the runway in 1990, that greater numbers (in Bhutanese terms) began to arrive.

Given its mountainous terrain, Bhutan has few natural resources upon which to build its economy – although agriculture and forestry account for around 40% of GDP, for example, just 7% of its land is suitable for cultivation. However, the country possesses a rich and diverse natural and cultural heritage. It is home to a number of rare Himalayan species, it boasts spectacular scenery, and its vibrant culture is manifested in its distinctive architecture and its religious festivals, the latter having long been an attraction to overseas visitors. Therefore, it is justifiable to claim that Bhutan is, potentially, 'one of the most sought-after tourism destinations in the world' (Brunet et al., 2001: 252).

Nevertheless, despite its potential attraction to visitors (and the opportunity to achieve rapid economic growth through tourism), tourism development in Bhutan has focused upon a policy of high-yield but low impact tourism. In other words, it has long been recognised that, in order to preserve its culture for the benefit of visitors and local communities alike, the scale and nature of tourism in Bhutan must be tightly controlled. For the most part, this

has been achieved by strictly regulating the numbers of tourists travelling to the country and setting a minimum daily price. Thus, initially, just 200 tourists a year (at a cost of US$130 per tourist per day) were permitted entry, although, by 1999, 6,000 arrivals were permitted. That year, the daily cost of US$200 per tourist (the government takes a US$65 'slice', the remainder going to local registered tour operators who provide services to tourists in Bhutan) generated some US$14 million in gross expenditure. The activities of tourists within the country are also carefully controlled to minimise negative socio-cultural impacts. As a result, the yield from tourism is maximised while there is minimum impact, thereby protecting the Bhutanese culture both for and from tourism (see Brunet et al., 2001 for more detail).

However, there not only exists a distinction between locals' and tourists' perceptions of environment. As Holden (2000) summarises, tourists do not represent an homogeneous group of consumers; they are likely to perceive and interact with the destination environment in a multitude of different ways, depending upon their attitudes, motivations and expectations. In other words, 'the attitudes of the tourist to the environment will be reflected in their behaviour' (Holden, 2000: 48) which, in turn, will determine the degree of impact upon the environment. Thus, at one extreme, tourists may have a complete disregard for the environment, placing the satisfaction of personal needs above environmental concerns; at the other extreme, they may feel a strong attachment to the destination environment and will attempt to integrate themselves into it. This suggests that tourists' experience of the environment can be placed upon a continuum of perception/behaviour (Figure 18.1).

Implicitly, any one tourism environment may be perceived, and consumed, in different ways by different tourists. At the same time, these perceptions may be at odds with those of the local community whose well-being, prosperity and socio-economic development may be dependent upon the way in which 'their' environment is managed. Therefore, it is logical to suggest that any environmental management system in tourism, while taking into account the needs of potential tourists, should also give primacy to the perceptions, knowledge and developmental needs of the local community.

However, as discussed shortly, the 'blueprint' of sustainable tourism development does not always allow for this. It is, essentially, a meta-policy, a 'one-size-fits-all'

Figure 18.1 Tourist experience of destination environments

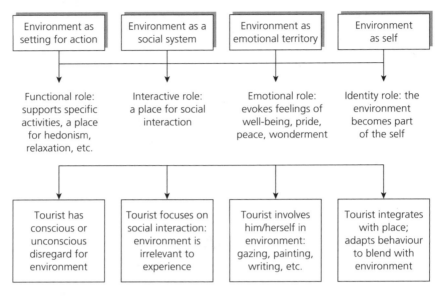

Source: After Holden (2000: 49–50)

approach to managing the tourism environment founded upon Western-influenced, overly simplistic notions of resource use and carrying capacities, top-down planning systems and a belief in the 'moralisation' of tourism consumption (see Butcher, 2003). Indeed, the long-evident politicisation of the environmental movement is reflected in sustainable tourism policies that implicitly focus as much on social equity as on environmental concerns (Southgate and Sharpley, 2002). In short, the sustainable tourism development blueprint is simply not adaptable to the enormous diversity of contexts that comprise global tourism activity.

It is also important to note that sustainable tourism development is proposed as a solution to what are considered universal environmental conflicts – destination environments do not, of course, suffer from all types of impact, but the nature and implications of such impacts are seen as being consistent. However, as the following section now suggests, tourism–environment conflicts are, in effect, unique to each destination.

Tourism and environment conflicts: the context

Not only have the environmental consequences of tourism development – both negative and positive – been long recognised and discussed, but also they have been variously addressed in the literature (e.g., Mathieson and Wall, 1982; Lea, 1988; Pearce, 1989; Hunter and Green, 1995; Mieczkowski, 1995). Typically, however, the environment is implicitly defined as the physical, as opposed to socio-cultural, resource base.

The focus is principally upon negative impacts, or the environmental costs, of tourism development in the destination area and the analysis is usually structured around particular impacts, such as pollution or erosion, or around the constituent elements of the natural environment – land, water, air, flora and fauna – as well as the man-made environment.

While such a perspective is both logical and objective, it does have a number of weaknesses. In particular, it implies a causal relationship between certain forms of tourism development and their inevitable environmental consequences, and that, importantly, such consequences are considered undesirable or 'bad' and should therefore be minimised or avoided. Moreover, as most research into tourism's impacts is reactive, no baseline for measuring or monitoring change (against local community perceptions of acceptable 'damage') is provided (Holden, 2000: 69). In other words, it facilitates neither a recognition of local attitudes to environmental values and change, nor a flexible approach to managing the environment. In addition, as noted earlier, not only does the tourism environment possess socio-cultural, political and economic dimensions in addition to its physical elements, but also the analysis of tourism's impacts should not be divorced from these dimensions. Also, while the development of tourism undoubtedly has consequences for destination environments, impacts may be exacerbated or even caused not by tourism or tourists but by other economic or human activity. Finally, while all societies, cultures and economies are dynamic, the environmental values embodied in (sustainable) tourism planning and policies are, however, static. For example, the development of the English countryside for tourism remains guided by an 'aesthetic' (Harrison, 1991) that seeks to maintain a pre-industrial, Wordsworthian image of rurality (Clark et al., 1994). Similarly, policies to protect tourism destinations in less developed countries principally seek to prevent the contamination by Western-style modernisation of both the physical and socio-cultural environment.

In short, much of the research into the environmental consequences of tourism development is not located within the particular socio-cultural, political and economic contexts of individual destinations or, indeed, of tourist-generating and transit regions (see Pearce, 1989: 190–2). As a result, the approaches to the management of the tourism environment as defined in this chapter also tend to be generic and uncontextualised. Therefore, as a prerequisite to developing more effective means of managing the tourism–environment relationship, it is important to establish first a framework for studying the environmental consequences of tourism development.

One such framework is shown in Figure 18.2. Here, following a model proposed by the OECD (1981), the focus is not upon the environmental resources but upon the tourism-related activities that put stress on the environment. The environmental consequences of such stress are referred to as primary responses, while secondary responses are the management measures undertaken to limit or control environmental stress. Importantly, however, local factors, such as developmental needs, stage of tourism development, economic structures, environmental values and so on, provide the dynamic context within which the stress–response model is located and, in a continual process, feed into responses to the consequences of tourism development.

Figure 18.2   A model for the study of the tourism–environment relationship

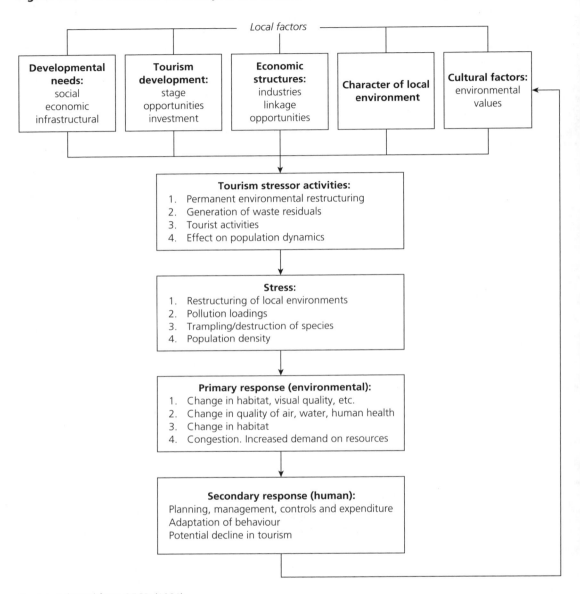

Source: Adapted from OECD (1981)

This desire to embrace the needs and values of local communities in tourism planning and management in general has long been recognised (Murphy, 1985). It is also implicit within the concept of sustainable tourism development, one of the principles of which is the encouragement of community involvement in the planning, development and control of tourism (see Table 18.1 below). However, as this chapter now argues, environmental management schemes in general, and policies for sustainable tourism development in particular, do not offer a realistic basis for operationalising such community input into the management process and, hence, do not represent the most effective means of achieving forms of environmental management appropriate to particular tourism destinations.

Managing the tourism–environment relationship

It is not possible within the context of this chapter to review fully the enormous variety of prevailing tourism environmental management strategies, whether at a broad policy level or with respect to specific sites and locations. Nevertheless, there exist three principal approaches to managing the environment for tourism.

1.   Managing physical resources

It is not, perhaps, surprising that, given the traditional definition of environment as either natural or built physical resources, much emphasis is placed on methods of protecting or conserving the physical tourism resource base. These are widely discussed in the literature (e.g., Broadhurst, 2001; Newsome et al., 2002) and may be typically categorised as follows:

■ *Land designation*. The most common strategy for protecting areas of ecological, scientific, historical, scenic or, in the present context, tourism/recreational importance is designation, whereby identified areas are designated according to necessary degrees of protection. The best-known form of designation, representing 57% of the world's protected areas (Newsome et al., 2002: 191), is national park status, which seeks to protect nationally important areas for ecological, educational and recreational purposes. Often, however, the local interest (and, indeed, knowledge and experience of land management) is subordinated to the national conservation/tourism development interest. In much of the developing world, for example, national park designation has significantly disadvantaged local communities (Murphree and Hulme, 1998).

■ *Spatial planning strategies*. A variety of methods are employed to encourage tourism development in some areas while relieving pressure on sensitive or already degraded sites. The most popular of these is zoning, which attempts to prescribe varying levels of public use and conservation in different parts or zones of a larger area, such as a national park. It may also be utilised to separate incompatible tourism uses both spatially and temporally.

■ *Site management techniques*. At the local, site level, various techniques are employed to either protect sensitive areas or to facilitate the regeneration or restoration of damaged sites. Such techniques may include, for example, the appropriate location and signing of roads and trails, the careful positioning of visitor facilities and the enormous diversity of methods employed, from 'site-hardening' measures to the temporary denial of access, to protect or restore particular resources, such as coastal areas, mountain trails, and so on.

2. Managing visitors

By definition, the impacts of tourism are directly related to the behaviour or activities of tourists themselves. Moreover, as observed earlier, differing attitudes and perceptions towards the environment on the part of tourists are likely to be influential in determining the degree of impact experienced by any one tourism destination. It is not surprising, therefore, that effective visitor management is widely considered an integral element of environmental management (Jim, 1989).

The purpose of visitor management is to match the nature, scale, timing and distribution of tourism activity to the environment within which it occurs – that is, to ensure that the capacity of the environment to absorb tourists is not exceeded – as well as attempting to encourage 'appropriate' behaviour on the part of individual tourists. In a broad sense, calls for tourists to adopt 'good' behaviour (e.g., Wood and House, 1991) are a form of visitor management, but the wide range of more specific techniques employed to manage visitor behaviour vary from soft, low-regulatory methods designed to inform or educate, such as information centres, interpretation and codes of conduct (Mason and Mowforth, 1995), through to high-regulatory methods designed to limit access. In many instances, such techniques are successful; reducing the number of car-park spaces has, for example, been found to be an effective means of limiting tourist numbers at particular natural area sites (Sharpley, 1996). However, visitor management more generally tends to be a reactive 'solution' to a problem rather than an element of a wider, proactive environmental management process.

3. Sustainable tourism development

The two approaches to managing the tourism environment described above focus specifically on two separate elements of the tourism–environment relationship, namely, the physical environment and visitor behaviour. Conversely, sustainable tourism development attempts to address collectively the needs of all the players in the tourism destination – the local community, the physical environment, the cultural environment, the tourism industry and tourists themselves – in an approach that is 'intended to reduce tensions and friction created by the complex interactions' (Bramwell and Lane, 1993: 2) between them. In other words, sustainable tourism development seeks to optimise the benefits of tourism to tourists (their experiences), the industry (profits) and local people (their socio-economic development) while minimising the impacts of tourism development on the environment.

Typically, the aims and objectives of sustainable tourism development are embodied in varying sets of principles (see Table 18.1 for a summary of key elements). However, despite the widespread acceptance of such principles and, indeed, the significant

Table 18.1   Principles of sustainable tourism development: a summary

- The conservation and sustainable use of natural, social and cultural resources is crucial. Therefore, tourism should be planned and managed within environmental limits and with due regard for the long-term appropriate use of natural and human resources.
- Tourism planning, development and operation should be integrated into national and local sustainable development strategies. In particular, consideration should be given to different types of tourism development and the ways in which they link with existing land and resource uses and socio-cultural factors.
- Tourism should support a wide range of local economic activities, taking environmental costs and benefits into account, but it should not be permitted to become an activity which dominates the economic base of an area.
- Local communities should be encouraged and expected to participate in the planning, development and control of tourism with the support of government and the industry. Particular attention should be paid to involving indigenous people, women and minority groups to ensure the equitable distribution of the benefits of tourism.
- All organisations and individuals should respect the culture, the economy, the way of life, the environment and political structures in the destination area.
- All stakeholders within tourism should be educated about the need to develop more sustainable forms of tourism. This includes staff training and raising awareness, through education and marketing tourism responsibly, of sustainability issues among host communities and tourists themselves.
- Research should be undertaken throughout all stages of tourism development and operation to monitor impacts, to solve problems and to allow local people and others to respond to changes and to take advantage of opportunities.
- All agencies, organisations, businesses and individuals should co-operate and work together to avoid potential conflict and to optimise the benefits to all involved in the development and management of tourism.

Source: ETB (1991), Eber (1992), EC (1993), WTO (1993), WTO/WTTC (1996)

degree of attention paid to the subject, sustainable tourism development remains the subject of intense debate. This is, in part, due to the fact that sustainable development is itself a contested concept, replete with ambiguity and contradiction (Redclift, 1987). For example, the widely cited World Commission on Environment and Development (the Brundtland Report) seeks to conserve the global resource base while suggesting a growth in the world economy by a factor of five to ten (with inevitable resource implications) is necessary to alleviate poverty (WCED, 1987: 50).

At the same time, however, it is increasingly recognised that there is a lack of 'fit' between tourism as a specific developmental activity and the broader requirements of sustainable development. In particular, the diverse and fragmented character of a profit-oriented tourism production system and its inherent power relationships, plus the meaning of tourism as a widespread form of consumption, together militate against the achievement of 'true' sustainable tourism development (see Butler, 1998; Sharpley, 2000, 2002 for more detail). As a result, not only does the debate remain entrenched in definitional issues (Garrod and Fyall, 1998) but also, in practice, sustainable tourism policies focus principally on local, small-scale projects with broader development challenges being subordinated to environmental management issues.

It is this latter point that is of most relevance to this chapter. That is, even as an approach to managing the tourism environment, sustainable tourism development is not adaptable to the diverse economic, ecological and socio-cultural characteristics of different destinations. Rather, it represents a universal management policy based upon rigid planning controls and managerial tools designed to ensure that environmental limits or 'carrying capacities' – according to a Western, positivist perspective on environmental management – are respected (Southgate and Sharpley, 2002). Thus, it does not allow for:

- local attitudes towards resource exploitation and development;
- varying perceptions of the so-called 'limits of acceptable change' (Wight, 1998);
- local economic and social development needs;
- the right of local communities to manage their environment; and
- the value of local experience and knowledge in environmental management.

This is not to say that regional or national planning and management frameworks, such as planning laws or land designation policies, are not necessary – it has long been recognised that allowing individual needs to dominate the collective good can be destructive (Hardin, 1968). However, as this chapter now suggests, a systems approach that not only recognises the unique and dynamic characteristics of destinations but also effectively embraces local governance may represent a more appropriate means of managing the tourism environment.

Managing the tourism environment: a systems approach

In contrast to the specific, reactive responses referred to above, a systems approach to managing the tourism environment offers a logical 'approach by which … wider environmental issues and specific local responses can be incorporated into the long-term strategies and day-to-day operations' of the tourism destination (Tribe et al., 2000: 71). In other words, it is a management approach that seeks to link all the relevant elements or stakeholders in the destination in a methodical and continual process of planning, implementation and review.

Environmental management systems (EMS) were first developed and implemented as a means of identifying and minimising the environmental risks posed by an organisation's activities and operations. Essentially, they seek to merge environmental management into an organisation's overall management framework. In 1996, the International Standards Organisation published ISO 14001 as an international standard for guiding and measuring environmental performance. This proposes that any organisation should establish an environmental policy, identify the environmental consequences of its past and present activities and implement its policy on a continual basis, supported by ongoing review and, where necessary, corrective action. It therefore provides a useful framework for a more general systems approach to managing the tourism environment (see Figure 18.3). Implicit within this model are two key principles that are necessary for the achievement of a more appropriate, destination-specific approach to managing the tourism environment:

1. *Local environmental governance.* Although community involvement in tourism planning and management has long been advocated, effective and appropriate environmental management is, arguably, dependent on more than simply shifting the responsibility from state to community within policy frameworks determined at the national level. In other words, local communities should be viewed not, as is often the case, as disadvantageous to environmental management and conservation, but as architects of

Figure 18.3   A tourism environment management system

Source: Adapted from Tribe et al. (2000: 81)

their own development. In particular, local communities' cultural attitudes towards the environment with respect to the relationship between conservation and development, indigenous environmental knowledge and the ability or right of local people to embrace the free market as contributor to environmental protection and management (see Mihalič, 2002) should all be recognised and harnessed. In so doing, environmental management may not be in accordance with more conventional Western concepts of conservation, carrying capacities and acceptable damage, but it is more likely to meet the local community's longer-term social and economic needs.

2.   *Ecological dynamism.* Related to the issue of local governance in environmental management is the concept of ecological dynamism. That is, it has become increasingly accepted that environments are unique and inherently dynamic rather than moving towards an equilibrium or desired end-state as defined by notions of carrying capacities. At the same time, the recognition that all 'natural' environments have, to a greater or lesser extent, long been shaped by human activity has called into question the viability or, indeed, morality of management policies that, in effect, seek to put a halt to further human influence on specific environments. Thus, environmental management should respect such ecological dynamism (of which local communities are a part), utilising techniques such as Limits to Acceptable Change, a planning procedure 'designed to identify preferred resource and social environmental conditions in a given recreation area and to guide development techniques to achieve and protect these conditions' (Wight, 1998: 82).

If these two principles are applied to the above model, it becomes evident that, as a prerequisite to the creation of an environmental policy, stage one of the management process involves the identification of local environmental attitudes and knowledge and the formulation of appropriate governance structures to ensure that subsequent policies and actions embrace and utilise such attitudes and knowledge. Stage two provides the socio-economic framework (which itself may determine, for example, the nature or scale of tourism development) within which a local environmental policy is formulated, possibly according to agreed limits of acceptable change (stage 3). The review of the destination's environmental status (stage 4) provides the baseline for predicting and assessing the consequences of tourism development, while the fifth stage covers the development and implementation of the environmental management programme. Finally, the review feeds back into the process to ensure that environmental management procedures are supporting the achievement of longer-term development objectives.

Implications of a systems approach to tourism environmental management

The development of tourism, in particular international mass tourism, has long been blamed for the environmental degradation or destruction of destination areas. Such blame is not always justifiable yet, as sustainable development has become the globally dominant approach to managing the development–environment relationship in general, so too has sustainable tourism become the guiding principle for managing the tourism–environment relationship in particular. However, as this chapter has argued, a universal 'meta-policy', such as sustainable tourism development, is not adaptable to the innumerable environmental contexts within which tourism occurs and, as a result, inappropriate policies are imposed upon destinations.

Conversely, a systems approach to managing tourism destinations, as suggested here, firmly places environmental management policies within the local context. That is, it allows for environmental management policies and techniques to reflect local conditions and needs and, importantly, changes in those conditions and needs. Thus, rather than imposing artificial ceilings on development or resource use, a systems approach enables local communities to maintain control over 'their' environment and to exploit it as they see fit. Moreover, where that environment has a value (i.e., as a resource for tourism), management policies are likely to encourage protection or conservation of the resource within locally determined parameters so as to maintain its attraction to tourists.

The main implication, therefore, is that the nature, scale and rate of tourism development in any destination is more likely to meet local needs if management policies are not constrained by universal and arbitrarily formulated environmental policies and development limits. In other words, although the implementation of rigid sustainable tourism policies may minimise environmental degradation, local communities may not be receiving optimal benefits from tourism and, more importantly, may be willing to exploit their resources further to do so. For example, the Central Region Project, a local, sustainable tourism project in Ghana, was a winner of the British Airways' 'Tourism for Tomorrow' awards in 1998, yet a major challenge remains the need to increase and spread the benefits of tourism beyond the vicinity of the project (Ampadu-Agyei, 1999). Conversely, as Case Study 18.2 demonstrates, what many would claim to be excessive and unsustainable resource exploitation through tourism in Cyprus has underpinned rapid and successful social and economic development on the island.

Case Study 18.2   Cyprus: tourism, development and the environment

Since 1974, when the northern third of the island came under Turkish occupation, the Republic of Cyprus has developed into a major Mediterranean tourism destination. In 1975, international arrivals amounted to just 47,000 but between 1976 and 1989 the annual number of tourists increased by 700%. During the 1980s in particular, arrivals grew at an average annual rate of 16% and, despite a slowdown and more erratic figures in recent years, over 2.6 million arrivals were recorded in 2000. Earnings from tourism in Cyprus have increased correspondingly; in 2000, tourism receipts totalled CY£1,194 million (approximately US$1.8 billion).

To a great extent, this dramatic growth of tourism in Cyprus is evidence of its increasing popularity as a mass, summer-sun destination. Although relatively expensive (holidays in Cyprus cost on average about 15% more than comparable holidays in other Mediterranean destinations), the most popular time to visit the island remains the summer season. In fact, 40% of all tourists visit between July and September. Not surprisingly, therefore, the growth in tourism has been fuelled by the no less rapid growth in coastal resort development on the island. In 1975, for example, there were fewer than 4,000 available bedspaces, the majority of which were located in the mountain resorts. Currently there is a total of about 86,000 bedspaces in four major coastal resort areas, the development of which has attracted widespread criticism for being unsustainable. In particular, attention is focused on what is widely considered to be excessive and concentrated development, demands on natural resources, especially water, and pollution (Apostolides, 1996).

However, two points demand emphasis. First, in terms of socio-economic development, tourism contributes 20% of the island's GDP (or 31% if indirect economic activity is included) and covers 54% of the cost of imports, while one-quarter of the working population are employed directly or indirectly in tourism. Perhaps more importantly, with a per capita income of over US$13,000, Greek Cypriots enjoy the third highest standard of living of all Mediterranean countries after France and Italy. Therefore, although the rapid emergence of tourism in Cyprus conforms to what some would describe as unsustainable mass tourism development, the Cypriots have, by and large, benefited greatly both socially and economically. Secondly, despite the criticism of tourism's environmental impacts, large numbers of tourists continue to visit the island, the implication being that they, as well as Cypriots themselves, place their respective benefits from tourism above environmental concerns.

Conclusion

The development of tourism has inevitable and, in many cases, unavoidable environmental consequences which, if uncontrolled, may destroy a destination's attraction to tourists. However, the imposition of universal, blueprint approaches to environmental management does not allow for the multitude of contexts within which tourism development occurs. In contrast, a systems approach, as described here, not only embraces local needs and environmental attitudes and knowledge, but also, in the longer term, may encourage more appropriate and sustainable resource use.

Discussion questions

1. How appropriate is the concept of carrying capacity to the environmental management of tourist destinations?
2. Can traditional, mass tourism development be environmentally sustainable?
3. To what extent should tourist destinations be permitted to exploit their environment as they see fit?

Suggested further reading

Hall, C.M. and Lew, A. (eds) (1998) *Sustainable Tourism: A Geographical Perspective*. Harlow: Longman.

Holden, A. (2002) *Environment and Tourism*. London: Routledge.

Hunter, C. and Green, H. (1995) *Tourism and the Environment: A Sustainable Relationship?* London: Routledge.

Mieczkowski, Z. (1995) *Environmental Issues of Tourism and Recreation*. Lanham, MD: University Press of America.

Southgate, C. and Sharpley, R. (2002) Tourism, development and the environment. In R. Sharpley and D. Telfer (eds), *Tourism and Development: Concepts and Issues*. Clevedon: Channel View Publications, pp. 231–62.

19 International tourism: the management of crisis

Richard Sharpley

Chapter objectives

The purpose of this chapter is to consider the causes and nature of crises in tourism and to suggest a potential framework for the management of crisis at the level of tourism destinations. Having completed this chapter, the reader will be able to:

- understand the relationship between disaster, crisis and tourism
- appreciate the diversity of forces and influences that lead to crisis in tourism
- explore the potential for developing effective crisis management plans in tourism destinations

Chapter contents

Introduction: crisis and international tourism

International tourism has, over the last half century, emerged as one of the world's largest and fastest-growing economic sectors. Consequentially, it has also become one of the most widely adopted development strategies at the national and regional levels, representing an effective and, for many countries, the only realistic means of achieving social and economic development. At the same time, however, it would appear to the casual observer that tourism – and tourists – has become increasingly subjected to risks, crises and disasters that threaten the tourism industry itself and its contribution to destination development. Indeed, over the last decade, international tourism has suffered a variety of environmental, political and economic disasters that have not only had a significant impact on tourism both nationally and globally, but which also have occurred with, apparently, ever-increasing frequency. For example, the latter half of the 1990s witnessed a spate of terrorism-related incidents, such as the Luxor massacre in 1997 and, in 1999, the abduction and subsequent murder of tourists in the Yemen and the murder of British and American tourists in Uganda, while, in 1997, Southeast Asia experienced a major tourism downturn as a result of the regional economic crisis and the environmental pollution from forest fires in Indonesia (Henderson, 2002). More recently, of course, the events of '9/11' in New York, the nightclub bombing in Bali in October 2002 and the outbreak of Severe Acute Respiratory Syndrome (SARS) (see Case Studies 19.1 and 19.2 below) not only resulted in significant (but relatively temporary) reductions in tourist flows either globally or regionally, but also contributed to the perception that international tourism faces an increasingly constant array of disasters and crises.

A number of points, however, must immediately be made. First, it has long been recognised that tourism is highly susceptible and responsive to external forces or shocks, as well as actual or perceived destinational factors or 'barriers', such as inferior health and sanitary conditions, poor food, overcrowding or personal risks to tourists (see Ascher, 1984). In other words, the history of modern international tourism is replete with examples of economic crises (the oil price rises in the 1970s and global economic recession in the early 1980s), environmental disasters (Chernobyl in 1986), health scares (the Indian plague scare of 1994, see Grabowski and Chatterjee, 1997), political upheaval (military coups in Fiji in 1987; Tiananmen Square, Beijing, in 1989), terrorist activity (Egypt in the mid 1990s, see Wahab, 1996, and, more generally, Ryan, 1991), and warfare (the Gulf wars of 1991 and 2003), all of which have influenced the direction and scale of tourist flows. Indeed, as Faulkner (2001: 142) observes, 'tourism destinations in every corner of the globe face the virtual certainty of experiencing a disaster of one form or another at some point in their history'.

Secondly, although much of the tourism literature (and, indeed, this chapter) is concerned with the nature and influence of such crises and disasters in the context of tourist flows to destinations, it must also be recognised that individual organisations or particular sectors of the travel and tourism industry also suffer from disasters or crises which require immediate and appropriate management responses. These may, in a sense, be self-induced, as in the case of airline crashes that result from mechanical failure or human error (see Henderson, 2003), or they may result from external and unexpected sources, such as terrorist attacks. However, they may also be crises which are caused or exacerbated by other factors (e.g., the impact of SARS on international travel in 2003 served to highlight the longer-term inherent economic fragility of many international airlines), or they may be intimately linked to a wider disaster, the hijacking of the aircraft which were subsequently flown into the twin towers of the World Trade Center being an obvious example. Thus, a complex cause–effect relationship may exist between diverse elements of the tourism system, with a major disaster potentially embracing a number of 'sub-disasters' which also demand a management response.

Thirdly, most disasters and crises within international tourism have relatively short-term economic impacts which also tend to be locally or regionally defined. In other words, over the last 50 years, international tourism has been adversely affected by an enormous diversity of problems yet, at the global level, it has demonstrated 'an extraordinary resistance and an ability unmatched by any other industry to survive' (WTO, 2001b: 7). Indeed, 2001 was only the second year since 1950 that global international tourist arrivals experienced negative growth as a result of an economic slowdown in Western countries in general and the events of '9/11' in particular – previously, global recession had resulted in a minor contraction in worldwide arrivals in 1982. Even in 2001, global arrivals decreased by just 0.6% over the previous year and, as the WTO (2002a: 9) points out, the results for that year would have followed the growth trend of the previous decade had it not been for the 'magnitude of the increase in tourist arrivals in 2000, which was much larger than the figures obtained during the preceding years'. By 2002, international tourist arrivals had substantially recovered; almost 715 million arrivals were recorded, representing a 3.1% increase over 2001. Importantly, however, at the regional, national or destinational level, the economic consequences of tourism disasters or crises may be significant. In the UK, for example, the combined impact of the foot and mouth disease outbreak and the events of '9/11' resulted in a decline of 9.5% in international tourist arrivals, while the arguably excessive international response to the *coup d'état* in The Gambia in 1994 brought about a virtual collapse of the local tourism industry for the 1994/95 season (Sharpley et al., 1996). More recently, and as considered in this chapter's case studies, both the Bali bombing and the SARS outbreak had a considerable impact on tourist arrivals, with consequential economic problems for the countries concerned.

Finally, it is evident that not only are crises and disasters in tourism frequent and numerous, but also they are infinitely variable in nature, intensity, duration, impact and recovery time. Thus, whereas some events, such as hurricanes in the Caribbean, may have short-term effects on tourist flows and costs associated with repair and rebuilding, some destinations, such as Israel, Peru and Northern Ireland, have experienced long-term crises in their tourism sectors (Sönmez et al., 1999). Sri Lanka, for example, built a successful tourism industry from the mid-1960s, with international arrivals growing from around 19,000 in 1966 to over 407,000 by 1982 (Crick, 1992). Since then, however, terrorist activity has, until recently, resulted in a 'roller-coaster' record for tourist arrivals and receipts, with periods of relative calm interspersed with specific events that have impacted on tourism and the island's image as a destination. Most recently, an attack on Columbo Airport in 2001 destroyed four aircraft belonging to the national carrier and seven soldiers lost their lives. Although no tourists were injured (as has been the case throughout this long crisis), the loss of seat capacity and subsequent holiday cancellations resulted in significant economic losses for the island's tourism industry. The current peace initiative, however, suggests that the 20-year crisis may finally be resolved to the socio-economic benefit of Sri Lanka in general, and the tourism industry in particular.

Collectively, these points suggest that tourist destinations should have in place crisis management strategies in order to respond to potential disasters. In other words, given the virtual inevitability of some form of crisis that may have significant social and economic consequences locally, regionally or even globally, it would be logical to assume that tourist destinations have appropriate mechanisms in place to 'deal with emergencies and crises, both prior to their occurrence ... and to manage those that will inevitably happen' (Santana, 2001: 237). However, it has been suggested that few destinations actually have properly developed crisis management plans (Sönmez et al., 1999; Faulkner, 2001; Henderson, 2002) and, as a result, the industry remains only 'reactive to divergent situations' (Santana, 2001: 236).

The purpose of this chapter, therefore, is to consider a potential framework within which crisis management strategies may be developed. First, however, it is useful to review briefly the meaning of 'crisis' in international tourism for, if effective frameworks are to be established for the management of crises in tourism, it is essential to understand the nature of such crises.

From disaster and crisis to tourism in crisis

As already observed, it has long been recognised that international tourism, though globally a resilient and, to date, continuously growing economic sector, is nevertheless a fragile activity; that is, it is highly vulnerable to external forces or shocks that, either temporarily or permanently, disrupt, decrease or divert tourist flows. Within the tourism literature, a significant degree of attention has been paid to these external forces which, for the purposes of simplicity here, may be categorised under five headings.

1.   Political factors

A number of authors have explored the relationship between tourism and its political environment (e.g., Richter, 1980, 1992; Richter and Waugh, 1983, 1986; Hall, 1994; Hall and O'Sullivan, 1996, Sönmez, 1998). Many studies focus upon the effects of political instability or turmoil at the destination, such as *coups d'état* (The Gambia, Fiji), although the activities of particular regimes may also directly or indirectly impact upon tourist flows. For example, the UK-based pressure group Tourism Concern has for a number of years been running a campaign to dissuade tourists from visiting Burma in response to the military government's alleged use of forced labour to build tourist facilities. At the same time, it is also recognised that tourism may be used by destinations to seek political legitimacy in the international community, although any negative effect on tourist flows may be less marked. Wars may also be included under the heading of political factors and many examples exist of the impacts of both civil (Yugoslavia in the early 1990s) and international (the Gulf wars) conflicts on tourist flows (see Mihalič, 1996).

2.   Terrorism

Strictly a subset of the political factors referred to above, terrorism represents a significant barrier to tourist flows. Generally, destinations where terrorist activity is ongoing have, over time, experienced an overall reduction in arrivals – the activities of the Sendero Luminoso (Shining Path) terrorist group in Peru, for example, resulted in a steep fall in international arrivals in the late 1980s and early 1990s, while Northern Ireland's tourism industry suffered almost two decades of decline during the 1970s and 1980s (O'Neill and Fitz, 1996; Wall, 1996). More specifically, however, tourists are often the deliberate target of terrorist activity; as Sönmez (1998) considers, terrorists are able to achieve a variety of symbolic objectives through purposeful attacks against tourists, the murder by Palestinian terrorists of the only Jewish-American on board the hijacked cruise ship *Achille Lauro* in 1985 being a tragic example.

3.   Personal safety

A variety of factors, actual or perceived, may lead tourists to fear for their personal safety and hence, discourage international travel. Of these, the most common deterrents are, arguably, health concerns and the risk of crime. Although a relatively extensive literature exists on the relationship between health and tourism (e.g., Clift and Grabowski, 1997), little attention has been paid to the impact of health scares on tourist flows, one notable exception being Grabowski and Chatterjee's (1997) study of the Indian plague scare. Nevertheless, a number of examples exist of where health concerns have impacted upon travel, including widespread food poisoning in the Dominican Republic in the early 1990s and, most recently, the SARS outbreak (see Case Study 19.1 below). Conversely, the impact of crime on tourism is well documented (generally, Pizam and Mansfeld, 1996), the attacks on unwary tourists in Florida, again in the early 1990s, being one particular example (Hollinger and Schiebler, 1995).

Case Study 19.1   The impact of SARS on international tourism

In late February 2003, the first cases of Severe Acute Respiratory Syndrome (SARS) were reported. A pneumonia-type disease thought to have originated in southern China, SARS was carried by international travellers and spread rapidly, initially around the Southeast Asian region but also globally. By July, when the outbreak was officially declared over by the World Health Organisation, a total of almost 8,500 people in 30 countries around the world had been infected and over 800 victims had died. The majority of sufferers were from China and other nearby countries – indeed, with the exception of Canada and the city of Toronto in particular, most countries reported low rates of infection and even lower death rates.

Inevitably, television images of people in places such as Hong Kong wearing face masks, reports of the rapid growth in the number of cases and dramatic newspaper headlines (in the UK, for example, tabloid newspapers referred to SARS as the 'Killer Bug' although no one in the UK died from the disease) had a major impact on tourist flows, particularly to Southeast Asia. In many countries in the region, international arrivals were reported to have fallen by as much as 80%, while Hong Kong was particularly badly affected. During March, for example, hotel occupancy fell to an average of 20% with five-star hotels reporting single-figure occupancy levels, over 40% of all flights into Hong Kong had been cancelled, and both inbound and outbound travel had fallen by some 80%. According to the World Travel and Tourism Council (2003), as a result of SARS, the Hong Kong tourism industry lost 41% of its GDP in 2003, with over 40,000 jobs being lost, with similarly severe figures in China, Singapore and Vietnam. Many international airlines (already suffering from the effects of '9/11') also suffered – Air Canada, for example, reported a loss of $400 million attributable to SARS in its second quarter results.

According to one commentator (McKercher, 2003), the impact on tourism in Hong Kong and elsewhere was due more to 'SIP' (SARS-induced panic), or the hysteria surrounding the spread of the disease. He points out that, after two months, just 0.02% of the local population had been affected, with most cases limited to health care workers and neighbourhoods in Hong Kong rarely visited by tourists. In other words, the reaction of tourists was completely out of proportion to the actual (rather than perceived) threat, although factors such as the unwillingness of insurance companies to offer travel cover to tourists travelling to the region inevitably contributed to the decline in arrivals. Interestingly, this 'panic' surrounding the SARS outbreak continues to afflict the financial sector: the reporting of just one new case of the disease in Singapore in September 2003, two months after the 'all clear', immediately led to a fall in the value of a number of international airlines' shares.

4. Economic factors

Less commonly, perhaps, than other externalities, economic factors may lead to crises in tourism. It has long been recognised that tourist flows are highly price elastic, that is, tourism is very susceptible to changes in the relative cost of holidays and travel, particularly where substitute destinations exist. At the same time, however, national, regional or even global economic problems have impacted upon international tourism – reference has already been made to the global economic recession in the early 1980s and the subsequent negative growth in worldwide arrivals figures in 1982, while the Asian economic crisis of 1997 had a significant impact on tourism in many countries in that region (Prideaux, 1999).

5. Environmental/natural disasters

Finally, environmental or natural disasters may have a significant impact on tourism. Some of these may be expected and inevitable, such as hurricanes in the Caribbean, and plans usually exist to reduce the risks to tourists and to rebuild swiftly tourism facilities and infrastructure. Other natural disasters, including flooding, earthquakes, hurricanes or volcano eruptions, may be less predictable or unexpected yet, nevertheless, there remains the need to protect tourists and to regenerate the tourism sector (Faulkner and Vikulov, 2001; Huang and Min, 2002). At the other extreme, environmental disasters, such as Chernobyl in 1986 or the all-too-frequent pollution of beaches by oil slicks, cannot be expected and disaster management will, by necessity, be reactive.

What is a tourism crisis?

Given this enormous diversity of potentially catastrophic events or forces that may impact on tourism, the question is then: what actually constitutes a tourism crisis? In other words, many of the externalities categorised above are disasters or crises in their own right (and in some cases may have little or no impact on tourism); therefore, how are they translated into tourism crises?

As a starting point, Faulkner (2001), drawing on the work of Selbst (1978), usefully distinguishes between disasters and crises (see also Booth, 1993: 85–6). He argues that, for an organisation (or a group of organisations in the case of a tourist destination), a crisis may be defined as an event or occurrence that is in some way attributable to the organisation itself, that is, a crisis is internally induced or self-inflicted, often as a result of poor management practices or structures or a failure to adapt to change. Implicitly, therefore, crises could be avoided or partially managed. Conversely, disasters are external, often catastrophic, events that are unpredictable, unexpected and relatively uncontrollable. However, this distinction is not always clear; for example, an air crash is usually referred to as a disaster but is, according to Faulkner's definition, a crisis, and it may certainly evolve into one for the airline concerned. Similarly, an earthquake or a hurricane may be a natural disaster; its impact on tourism, however, may result in a crisis.

Two points must be stressed, therefore, in understanding the nature of a tourism crisis. First and, to an extent, irrespective of the causal agent, a tourism crisis is a situation which can, according to Sönmez et al.:

> …threaten the normal operation and conduct of tourism-related businesses; damage a tourist destination's overall reputation for safety, attractiveness and comfort by negatively affecting visitors' perceptions of that destination; and, in turn, cause a downturn in the local travel and tourism economy … by the reduction in tourist arrivals and expenditure. (Sönmez et al., 1999: 13–14)

To put it more succinctly, a tourism crisis is, in the context of this chapter, a situation in which a destination suffers a sudden and significant decline in its tourist arrivals.

Normally, this decline in arrivals is, in turn, a function of tourists' reactions to actual or perceived threats to their personal security, health or, more simply, enjoyment of their holiday. That is, given the intangible nature of tourist experiences and the dominant motivational factors of escape/avoidance, the tourist decision-making process is heavily influenced by images of a destination, which themselves may be influenced by a variety of factors, such as prior knowledge of the destination, travel experience, cultural influences (e.g., nationality), and so on (Money and Crotts, 2003). As a result, tourists frequently adapt their travel/holiday plans in response to perceived threats, selecting destinations or types of holiday that may be closer to home, cheaper or involve less risk (Sönmez and Graefe, 1998a, 1998b; Coshall, 2003). Hence, while global tourism arrivals figures have, over the last half-century, demonstrated almost constant growth, there have been significant interruptions at the national or regional levels.

Secondly, given the complexity of the tourism system, disasters or crises in one arena (either internal or external to the tourism system) may be transferred or amplified through inappropriate management responses or the failure of management systems into potentially major tourism crises. Faulkner (2001) supports this argument by making reference to chaos theory in general and the so-called 'butterfly effect' in particular. This holds that, in a technology-dominated world, a small or insignificant action or event in one part of the global system may lead to a disproportionate outcome elsewhere. In the context of tourism, one example is the manner in which images and reports of the UK's foot and mouth disease outbreak in 2001 were transmitted around the world, resulting in a major fall in international tourist arrivals who would not have travelled to affected areas anyway (see Chapter 12).

In addition to these points, it is also important to note that the potential for, if not the incidence of, tourism crises is on the increase. Certainly, the continued growth in the volume of global tourism activity combined with both the spread of the 'pleasure periphery' to embrace more distant and exotic destinations and the increasing popularity of activity/adventure forms of tourism has led to increasing numbers of tourists being exposed to a widening array of potential risks. At the same time, however, it has been suggested that the process of globalisation, particularly in the post-Cold War era, is providing a climate for increased political and economic instability with associated risks for international tourism (Santana, 2001). For example, the Cold War contributed, paradoxically, to global security; more recently, terrorist groups have been able to proliferate (hence, incidents such as the Bali bombing – see Case Study 19.2) there has been a dramatic increase in the availability of conventional weapons, a greater disparity has emerged between many countries of the developed and developing worlds and international security mechanisms are proving to be inefficient. As a result, there is greater potential for tourists to be caught up in terrorist or criminal activities or to be affected by local or regional unrest.

Case Study 19.2   The Bali bombing: impacts and responses

The island of Bali is one of the most visited destinations in Indonesia and one of the more popular tourist destinations in the region. In 2001, for example, around 5.2 million international arrivals were recorded in Indonesia as a whole and, of these, 1.4 million arrived directly in Bali. Of the other 3.8 million arrivals elsewhere in Indonesia, 2.3 million also visited Bali (WTO, 2002a: 33). Thus, there can be no doubting the popularity of the island or the importance of tourism to its economy; over 50% of its income and 40% of direct employment is dependent on tourism.

On the night of 12 October 2002, Bali's tourism industry was devastated by a terrorist bomb attack on the Sari nightclub in Kuta, one of the island's most popular resorts. The blast left over 200 people, mostly overseas tourists, dead, it injured 325 others and destroyed almost 450 buildings, ripping the heart out of the centre of the resort. Within three days, almost

19,000 tourists had left the island and, within a fortnight, arrivals had dropped by 80%. Hotel occupancy dropped to about 18% and many overseas tour operators removed Bali from their operations. In short, following the bomb attack, the island's tourism industry and economy as a whole faced a crisis that many feared would take many years to recover from. In January 2003, for example, there were just 60,000 tourists on the island compared with 110,000 in January 2002 and commentators expect it to take up to two years for tourism to recover.

In response to the crisis, the Indonesian government promised US$54 million for the reconstruction of the devastated area, while the World Bank announced US$30 million in aid. It also suggested that product re-development should focus upon higher quality, the crisis being used as an opportunity for the resort of Kuta to move more upmarket. At the same time, it was proposed that marketing should address safety concerns and, among other things, make use of price-based promotions to generate arrivals in the short term (a strategy that had proved successful in Sri Lanka). The Bali Tourist Board also considered it wise to focus on the domestic and regional markets to boost arrivals in the short term. In support of this, the Indonesian government instructed all state companies (and encouraged private ones) to hold corporate functions on the island, while efforts would be made to boost international tourism from within the region. At the time of writing, it is too soon to judge the success of these policies, although the speed with which some of those responsible for the bombing were arrested and tried will have contributed to tourists' confidence to visit the island again.

Collectively, these points suggest that there is an evident need for tourism destinations to have in place plans for the effective management of crises, not only to ensure, where relevant, the safety and security of tourists, but also, given the ever-increasing dependence placed on tourism as a means of achieving socio-economic development, to aid the rapid recovery of the tourism sector. Inevitably, the diversity and, frequently, unpredictability of potential crises mean that not every eventuality can be planned for. Nevertheless, as the following section demonstrates, a general framework for managing tourism crises can be proposed to address the fundamental challenges of a crisis in tourism.

Towards a framework for tourism crisis management

Thus far, this chapter has argued that, given the likelihood of a crisis of some kind at some stage in the history of a tourism destination, it is essential that a crisis management policy or framework is in place. The purpose of such a framework should be not only to address the immediate challenges, such as ensuring the safety of both visitors and the local community, but also to meet the longer-term requirement of maintaining or rebuilding the tourism industry. In particular, and in recognition of tourists' typical response to crisis situations, the emphasis of both immediate and longer-term planning should be on encouraging tourists, through appropriate means, to visit the destination – a lack of confidence on the part of tourists and a 'tarnished image can threaten tourism sustainability which, in turn can jeopardise the area's long-term economic viability' (Sönmez et al., 1999: 13).

From the above discussion, of course, it is also evident that there is no universal formula to be applied to the management of crises in tourism destinations. For example, where a natural disaster is the underlying cause of the crisis, the emphasis is inevitably on rebuilding the tourism infrastructure; conversely, where a reputation for crime is the principal issue, the implementation of an effective (and well-publicised) policing strategy is likely to make an important contribution to rebuilding tourists' confidence.

Nevertheless, a number of attempts have been made in the literature to develop frameworks for crisis management, the most comprehensive being that proposed by Faulkner (2001) (see also Sönmez et al., 1999; Henderson, 2002; and, more generally, Glaesser, 2003). Typically, these draw on the theory of crisis management as it relates to the business organisation, providing a useful conceptual basis for exploring crisis management in tourism. In particular, it provides a chronological framework for understanding the crisis process, from the 'pre-event' (the period before any crisis is predicted or recognised) through to the longer-term post-crisis phase, which may represent a return to the pre-crisis state of normality/routine or an ongoing process of recovery and improvement. This crisis-stage approach will be adopted here but, first, it is important to introduce a number of principles which, it is suggested, should guide the development of any tourism crisis management strategy.

Principles of tourism crisis management

Given the diverse, fragmented yet interdependent nature of the tourism industry, as well as the fragility of tourist flows with respect to actual or perceived threats or crises, four principles should underpin tourism crisis management.

1. *Co-ordination*. The tourism industry or production system comprises a complex array of public and private sector organisations, both at the destination and in tourist-generating countries. Therefore, a co-ordinated approach which embraces, for example, local businesses, overseas tour operators, the appropriate national tourism organisation and even government agencies (e.g., those which provide travel advisories in tourism-generating countries) is an evident necessity. Links with other organisations, such as local emergency services, should also be established. This, in turn, implies that an appropriate crisis management team with identified roles and activities is established, supported, perhaps, by a crisis management 'guidebook' (Sönmez et al., 1999).
2. *Collaboration*. In addition to co-ordination of the diverse elements of the tourism system, all organisations involved in disaster or crisis management should be prepared to collaborate. As Faulkner (2001) observes, competition or rivalries between different agencies may appear during times of crisis and, therefore, any crisis management strategy should attempt to eliminate any such conflict.

3. *Communication.* The management of crisis situations is frequently hindered by a lack of communication, while crises may be exacerbated by either a lack of information or incorrect information. Thus, ongoing communication between all parties is essential both during the development of a crisis management strategy and during any crisis. It is not surprising, therefore, that most crisis management strategies call for the establishment of a communication centre (see WTO, 2002a: 77).

4. *Commitment.* As Faulkner (2001) argues, all parties involved in the development of a crisis management plan must be committed to it, particularly in terms of levels of preparedness. In other words, all organisations should reject the idea that crises happen to someone else and be committed to acting as necessary (e.g., by providing ongoing training to staff). In short, all parties should accept that a crisis will, at some time, occur.

As will now be seen, these principles and implied actions are of greatest relevance at the pre-event phase of a crisis. In other words, not only is it essential for destinations to develop a crisis management strategy, but also such a strategy is more likely to be successful if these principles are followed.

Managing a tourism crisis: a framework

Based upon models in the literature, Table 19.1 proposes a simplified framework for the management of a tourism crisis. Within this framework there are five periods, two of which, in the tourism context, are the most significant – the pre-event (planning) stage and the containment or 'damage limitation' stage (Henderson, 2002). This is not to suggest that the other phases are unimportant; emergency procedures must be put in place, particularly in the case where a destination has suffered a natural/environmental disaster, and longer-term post-event recovery strategies are vital to restore consumer confidence, rebuild infrastructure as necessary, and so on. Similarly, where a crisis can be predicted, appropriate action may protect tourists from exposure to risk. However, it can be argued that, in the context of this chapter, the most important elements of the framework are planning for a crisis and, in particular, containing or limiting damage to the tourism industry during the crisis – there are many examples where mis-information or the dramatisation of events by the media have exacerbated a crisis and therefore made recovery more difficult.

1. *Pre-event phase.* Anticipating and planning for a crisis is as important, if not more so, than taking actions during the crisis itself. Therefore, 'an action plan must be prepared ready for immediate implementation' should a crisis occur (WTO, 2002a: 77). The purpose of such a plan is, in effect, to provide a map to guide the destination's tourism industry back to recovery. Based on potential crisis scenarios dependent upon a destination's political, economic and geographic characteristics, the plan should establish a crisis management team with clear lines of communication and authority, along with a set of actions to be taken by all relevant individuals and organisations. It should be reviewed regularly, and the collaboration and commitment of all stakeholders should be sought.

Table 19.1 A tourism crisis management framework

Phase	Requirements
Pre-event (planning)	• Development of a crisis management plan (to be reviewed regularly) • Establish crisis management team/team leader • Set up communication channels with appropriate agencies, organisations • Identification/anticipation of potential crises • Production/distribution of crisis management guidebook
Crisis detection	• Mobilise protection/evacuation plans (e.g., when a hurricane is forecast) • Issue warnings to tourists/tour companies etc. not to travel to the destination • Activate crisis management team
Emergency	• Establish a communication centre • Activate rescue/evacuation procedures • Provide emergency accommodation/food, etc. • Ensure provision of health/medical services

Containment	• Damage audit/initial repair
	• Communication strategy:
	  – accurate/authoritative/regular press statements
	  – objective analysis of situation
	  – transparency/full disclosure
	  – emphasise positive points
	  – background information: crisis in a national/regional context
	  – liaise with embassies, etc. to ensure appropriate travel advisories

Post-event (recovery)	• Investment in new facilities/infrastructure where relevant
	• Rebuild image of and confidence in destination:
	  – appropriate marketing strategy
	  – investment in targeted promotion
	  – media information to stress safety of destination

Source: Adapted from Faulkner (2001), Henderson (2002) and WTO (2002a)

2. *Containment phase.* Experience has shown that the greatest damage to a tourism destination can be caused not by an event or disaster itself but by the manner in which a crisis is managed, particularly in the context of communication and information provision. Reference has already been made to the 2003 SARS outbreak (Case Study 19.1 above) which, through dramatic media reporting, resulted in the 'SARS-induced panic' that brought crisis to the Southeast Asian tourism industry. It has also been observed that, in 1985, 162 Americans were killed or injured by terrorist activities overseas but, as a result, 2 million Americans changed their travel plans in the following year (Edgell, 1990). Therefore, in order to lessen its potential impact on tourists' confidence and their image of the destination, it is essential that during a crisis and in its immediate aftermath, there is a timely and continual flow of objective, full, clear and accurate information that promotes positive points but also provides a complete picture. The role of the media is crucial in this process. As Faulker (2001: 142) describes, the 'impacts of tourism disasters on the market are often out of proportion with their actual disruptive effects because of exaggeration by the media', and therefore a communication centre should be set up to meet the information needs of the media and other parties.

Conclusion

The framework proposed here is not necessarily appropriate to all crisis situations in tourism; as Sönmez et al. (1999: 17) observe, 'each crisis situation is unique and difficult to resolve with simple formulas'. However, an important step in managing crisis in tourism is accepting the inevitability of crises and, hence, the necessity to plan for them. This will require increasing levels of co-ordination among public and private sector tourism organisations, governments, security agencies, emergency services and the media but, as both tourism and the incidence of disasters and crises continue to increase, so too will the need for effective crisis management.

Discussion questions

1. To what extent do you agree with the statement that a tourism crisis is a destination image crisis?
2. How inevitable is it that, as an increasing volume of international tourists travel ever more widely around the world, tourism crises will become increasingly common?
3. Given the diversity and, frequently, unpredictability of major tourism crises, is it possible for destinations to establish effective crisis management strategies?

Suggested further reading

Faulkner, B. (2001) Towards a framework for tourism disaster management. *Tourism Management*, 22(2): 135–47.

Glaesser, D. (2003) *Crisis Management in the Tourism Industry*. Oxford: Butterworth Heinemann.

Pizam, A. and Mansfeld, Y. (eds) (1996) *Tourism, Crime and International Security Issues*. Chichester: John Wiley & Sons.

WTO (2002) *Special Report Number 21–2002: Climbing Towards Recovery?* Madrid: World Tourism Organisation.

20 Ethics in Tourism Management

Harold Goodwin and Lesley Pender

Chapter objectives

The purposes of this chapter are to familiarise the reader with the ways in which ethical issues arise and to examine strategies for their management. Having completed this chapter, the reader will be able to:

- recognise the complexity surrounding debates about ethics
- appreciate reasons for the production of responsible tourism policies
- recognise the need for a clear management framework for ethical issues
- identify means by which management can incorporate ethical dimensions into their business

Chapter contents

Introduction

There have always been impacts in relation to tourism and many of these have already been discussed elsewhere in this book. Since the 1980s there have been a variety of approaches for dealing with these impacts, from the concept of sustainability to the appropriate management of ethical considerations. The management of tourism businesses leads inevitably to ethical considerations and this chapter aims to familiarise the reader with both the ways in which such issues arise and strategies for their management. As Lord Marshall said at the British Airways Tourism for Tomorrow Awards in 1994, tourism and the travel industry are 'essentially the renting out for short-term lets, of other people's environments, whether that is a coastline, a city, a mountain range or a rainforest. These "products" must be kept fresh and unsullied not just for the next day, but for every tomorrow' (Goodwin, 2002: 17). It is the latter part of this quote that is most often used to emphasise the environmental case for sustainable tourism. However, the environmental impacts of tourism are only one of the components of sustainability. The social and economic impacts of tourism that were introduced in Chapter 18 are also important but often neglected.

Ethics is both a field of philosophical enquiry and part of our daily lives, part of the way business is done. Ethics refers to the codes by which human conduct is guided; for example, it is about the way business is done, the way we treat each other and the way we travel. The ethics of tourism management is therefore concerned with the ways in which tourism is managed. This is not an abstract philosophical issue. Rather, it is about how the business of the travel and tourism industry is conducted. There is no one professional code of conduct which can be applied to the industry as a whole. Nor is there ever likely to be one in such an international and culturally diverse industry. The diversity of the Earth's places and people (and their ethics) is the raw material of the industry and it is this very diversity that precludes any one ethical code from predominating. However, different sets of guidelines aimed at different parts of the tourism industry do exist and some are provided later in this chapter.

Clearly, there is a legislative framework within which business is conducted. At least in principle, those legally constituted sets of rules, enforceable by the state, apply to everyone engaged in tourism. The relevant legal codes range from company to consumer law, through more specific measures like the EU Package Travel Directive (discussed in Chapter 10) to the regulations that govern tourism in national parks. The ethical basis of legal and regulatory codes is debated in the legal and philosophical literature but need not concern us here. For the purpose of this chapter, compliance with the law and the regulations of national parks, places of worship, hotels etc. will be assumed.

While there is a large philosophical literature on ethics (e.g., Cooper, 1997), much of this is concerned with the meaning and justification of statements about whether acts are right or wrong, the moral character of those actions and whether or not moral utterances are statements of fact. The focus here, however, is merely on the ways in which the business of tourism is conducted. The chapter outlines some of the ethical issues that arise in the management of tourism and considers some of the management responses to have emerged. Ethical responses generally derive either from a particular value set held by an individual, or group, or from a response to a particular issue. Tour operators like Tribes Travel and Discovery Initiatives have adopted clear commitments to conservation and benefiting local communities in the destinations to which they operate (www.responsibletravel.com). Similarly, tour operators offering pilgrimages for particular religious groups reflect the ethics of their user group or target market.

The problem of implementation

Despite the fact that most people would claim to be concerned by ethical issues, these are seen to exist at a national or even an international level rather than at an individual level, and so it is not always an easy task to persuade individuals to accept ethical responsibility. While much work has been done to bring attention to ethics in tourism management, this has primarily been based on the development of codes of conduct. This approach clearly relies on the co-operation of industry yet research has shown that there is an unwillingness on the part of the industry to comply with such codes (Forsyth, 1995).

It could be argued that there is a need for a clearer management framework in relation to ethics. A true management approach would be to encourage the development of global standards and movement beyond voluntary codes. Although there are strong arguments for more ethical approaches in business generally, and in tourism businesses more specifically, a major problem is the proliferation of small-scale businesses with low levels of profit and associated issues.

What about the ethical approach itself? There is currently evidence of a backlash against ethical approaches. Authors such as Butcher (2003) are questioning whether ethical considerations are in fact taking the fun out of tourism. How ethical is it, for example, to restrict the movements of a tourist who has paid a high price for, say, a safari in Kenya. There are inevitable costs to tourism that surely have to be expected, and in many cases accepted, in exchange for the tourist dollar.

Conflicts surrounding ethics

Debates about ethical tourism assume compliance with the legal and regulatory framework and focus instead on additional codes and principles of behaviour, generally at individual, company or trade association levels. It is important to recognise that debates about ethics are often complex and that the language used in moral and ethical debate can be confusing. For example, it is relatively common for people to accuse others of unethical behaviour or business practices. Generally this means that the ethical principle upon which the business practice is based is being challenged. It is not that the practice is itself unethical – the unethical practice may well be based on an ethical principle. Rather it is the principle itself that is being challenged. Case Study 20.1 helps to illustrate this point.

Case Study 20.1 Tourism Concern and Myanmar

Tourism Concern has been campaigning against travel to Myanmar (Burma) because of the policies and practices of the regime in Myanmar. Tourism Concern believes that tour operators should not provide holidays to the country and they have campaigned against Lonely Planet for refusing to withdraw its guide to Burma.

Patricia Barnett, Director of Tourism Concern, argues that:

> Whether we like it or not there are often ethical decisions to be made when we think about going travelling. They may not be comfortable but by turning a blind eye we can enable human rights abuses to be perpetuated. Whether we intend to go to Burma or not, we can all play a part in supporting those who campaign for justice in that country, by rejecting Lonely Planet's promotion of tourism to Burma through boycotting their books. (Tourism Concern Press Release, June 2002)

Lonely Planet is not unaware of the ethical issues, arguing that 'the question of whether informed tourism helps or hinders the restoration of democracy and human rights in Myanmar is the subject of ongoing debate both in and out of the country. This edition includes practical spending advice to directly benefit the Burmese people' (http://press.lonelyplanet.com/press/pr-srila.htm).

This is a clash between two different ethics of travel. Tourism Concern argues that it is unethical to promote tourism to a repressive regime. Lonely Planet takes the position that it is at least arguable that travel to Myanmar can contribute to the restoration of democracy. This argument need not be resolved here; it is presented purely to illustrate a clash between two different ethical frameworks. It is possible to hold both ethical standpoints and to argue that individuals may wish to travel to Myanmar to encourage and support change, but that it would be unethical to encourage others to go without that explicit purpose. Thus it would be possible to argue that it is acceptable to travel as an individual to Myanmar in order to contribute to change but not to organise beach holidays to Burma, contributing to the national exchequer of an oppressive regime. Both arguments are ethical, but people will have different views about which is the superior ethical position. As Richard Harries, the Bishop of Oxford, argues, 'it is not so much a choice between good and bad as a choice between various "goods" or various "bads". We cannot hope to escape these real dilemmas ... the fact is that we must live in the real world' (quoted in Sparkes, 1995: 1).

Ethical and responsible business

The issues around ethical and responsible business are not unique to tourism. Traidcraft was established in 1979 and has grown into the largest Fair Trade company in the UK. Oxfam and Café Direct subsequently joined Traidcraft and in 1984 Friends Provident launched the first ethical unit trust. Ethical investment is defined as an 'investment philosophy that combines ethical or environmental goals with financial ones' (Sparkes, 1995: 4). The range of products now sold on Fair Trade terms includes investments, food, clothing, furniture, carpets and toys. Datamonitor reported in October 2002 that the sector had grown 40% in the previous 12 months and opined that 'paradoxically, the Fair Trade phenomenon surfs a wave of egocentrism. What has catapulted Fair Trade products into the mainstream are not the altruistic principles of those with whom the idea originated but the more widespread desire among consumers to make themselves feel good' (Datamonitor, www.datamonitor.com, 18 October 2002).

Consumers and investors engage in ethical or responsible behaviour when they choose to have nothing to do with a particular product (not buying cosmetics tested on animals or investing in the arms industry) or choose to make investments or purchase products which have positive social, economic or environmental impacts. Ethical business is about the avoidance of ethically tainted consumption (employment or investment) and/or the conscious exercise of choice. Ami Domini, a pioneer of responsible investment, wrote in 1984:

> The positive approach complements the avoidance approach. Those adopting it seek investments in companies that enhance the quality of life. These companies produce goods or services of high quality and have good relations with their employees and the communities in which they operate. (Sparkes, 1995: 6)

It is this kind of thinking which informs responsible business, in tourism as in other sectors.

Most major companies now have Corporate Social Responsibility (CSR) policies. Following the Rio Earth Summit in 1992, the primary emphasis was on environmental responsibility, reducing negative impacts and where possible enhancing the positive impacts of business activity on the environment. As the debate about sustainable development moved on, companies became increasingly concerned with the social and economic agenda.

The membership of the UK Ethical Trading Initiative (www.ethicaltrade.org) reflects this. It includes multinational and transnational companies which are committed to business ethics and corporate responsibility. Its particular emphasis is on the promotion of worker rights and human rights in general:

> In employment, ethical business includes working towards the ending of child labour, forced labour and sweatshops, looking at health and safety, labour conditions and labour rights. Ethical sourcing establishes a company's responsibility for labour and human rights practices in its supply chain. In doing so, it aims to ensure the rights and improve the conditions of workers through good supply chain management. Specifically, it refers to a company taking responsibility to work with its suppliers to implement internationally accepted labour standards in the workplace. (www.ethicaltrade.org)

The World Travel and Tourism Council (WTTC), composed of the leaders of the world's largest 100 travel and tourism businesses have also endorsed corporate social responsibility. In Corporate Social Leadership in Travel and Tourism the WTTC recognises that there is 'growing concern about poverty and the widening gap between rich and poor' and that in 'the private sector, while profit is the foundation on which business is constructed, many companies are now seeking ways to create value for society while creating value for their business' (WTTC, 2002a: 1). CSR means more than the making of charitable donations 'detached from a company's core business'. Rather it

> means adopting open and transparent business practices that are based on ethical values. It means responsibly managing all aspects of operations for their impact not just on shareholders, but also on employees, communities and the environment. Ultimately, CSR is about delivering sustainable value to society at large, as well as to shareholders, for the long-term benefit of both. (WTTC 2002a: 2)

Corporate philanthropy is making way for corporate social responsibility. The emphasis is now on changing the way in which businesses do business in order to increase the positive impacts and minimise the negative ones. It is increasingly recognised that the stakeholders include employees, governments and local communities as well as shareholders, investors and consumers. Increasing numbers of companies in the global economy are adopting 'triple bottom line reporting' where social and environmental results are reported alongside the financial. Case Study 20.2 profiles one company's responsible business ethos.

Case Study 20.2   Radisson Hotels and Resorts

Radisson Hotels and Resorts is one example of a WTTC member company, which has adopted the ethos of responsible business. As Kurt Ritter, President and CEO, argues, Radisson Hotels and Resorts 'recognises that we are entangled in a complex web of co-dependence where we cannot thrive without the help of the community and the surrounding environment' and commits Radisson to 'do all it can to balance economic development with environmental and social responsibility' (Radisson Hotels and Resorts, 2002: 2).

Following the Rio Earth Summit, the primary focus was on the environmental issues and the International Hotels Environment Initiative (IHEI) demonstrated what large hotels could do to reduce their negative environmental impacts. By the time of the Johannesburg World Summit on Sustainable Development in 2002, ten years on from Rio, considerably more emphasis was being placed on the social and economic dimensions of development. Poverty has moved up the international and business agenda. The Commission on Sustainable Development meeting in New York in April 1999 was the first time tourism was specifically addressed. There was a marked refocusing on social and economic issues, a movement beyond the relatively narrow green agenda. An ethical approach required that poverty reduction

be given a higher priority. The World Tourism Organisation launched a report on Tourism and Poverty Alleviation in Johannesburg.

Radisson Hotels and Resorts, members of the IHEI, have broadened their agenda. Within their Responsible Business programme they aim to improve their environmental performance and their relationships with their suppliers and the communities in which their hotels are located.

For us Responsible Business is Local Business

Responsible Business

- Taking responsibility for the health and safety of employees and customers.
- Respecting social and ethical issues in the company, as well as in the community.
- Reducing our negative impact on the environment.

Headlines

- Being a local hero: 'We participate in the community by sponsoring local projects and charities and by supporting UNESCO's restoration of World Heritage sites'.
- Trying to be less thirsty: 'During the past three years we achieved a 25 percent reduction in water consumption per guest night, across all our hotels, without affecting guest comfort'.
- Your key to a responsible hotel: 'For us responsible business is local business, therefore each Radisson SAS hotel has a Responsible Business action plan'.

Some of the key results reported in 2002 included:

- Job satisfaction at 79.2%.
- Overall customer satisfaction index at 86.2, top brand ranking in the Nordic countries.

- 7 years of consecutive economic growth and revenues up 5.3%.
- 76% of hotels have one or more community projects each year.
- 25% of electricity is purchased from renewable energy sources.
- reduced waste by 9% since 2000. (Radisson Hotels and Resorts, 2002)

A plethora of codes

As Fennell (1999), D'Amore (1993) and Payne and Dimanche (1996) have pointed out, there has been relatively little academic work on tourism ethics to date. Much of the work in this field has been done by NGOs, companies and trade associations. Fennell points out that a recurrent theme in the academic literature has been the advocacy of codes of conduct and ethics for the tourism industry and for tourists (Fennell, 1999: 255–7). Indeed, a plethora of codes exists. These are not universally accepted as offering appropriate solutions; Wheeller has pointedly asked 'Who really believes these codes are effective?' (Wheeller, 1994: 651). Codes of conduct, behaviour and practice can, however, usefully suggest to tourism enterprises, tourists and local communities ways in which they can minimise negative impacts and maximise positive ones. They can be a prompt to action – without a management framework within which they are monitored and promoted they are unlikely to have significant effect. Many codes are aspirational in tone and seek to secure change by inspiring action. Tearfund published ten suggestions for companies wanting to move towards responsible tourism as a guide and a prompt to action (see Box 20.1).

Box 20.1 Ten Actions a Tour Operator Can Take

Not everything can be done at once, but all operators can start to look at their own operations and determine what they can do. Here is a suggested checklist towards becoming a responsible tourism company.

1. Establish a clear policy for responsible tourism and ensure that it covers operations both in the UK and in overseas destinations, right through the supply chain. Ensure that any charitable giving is integrated into the business process and is focused on improving the situation in the destinations.

2. Appoint a responsible tourism staff member who will oversee the development and integration of these issues throughout the organisation. Ensure that there is also support for this at board level.

3. Commit funds to becoming a more responsible operator in the areas of charitable giving, developing local business partnerships, training and giving advice to clients.
4. Write down best practice and seek to learn from it, publicise it to clients and share it with others.
5. Produce and disseminate a code for tourists to help them travel in a more informed and responsible way. Include advice on how they can support local charities.
6. Take time to research destinations and speak to local development and environment groups and tourism associations, not just to the hotels. Find out which local businesses you can use, and with whom you may be able to develop a partnership. This will enable you to provide better quality holidays.
7. Work throughout your supply chain to develop and implement policies that will use local labour, local foods and local crafts. Make your policies available to your suppliers.
8. Build on health and safety guidelines for hotels to include social and environmental issues such as labour standards, minimum wage levels and good recycling and waste disposal systems.
9. Set clear targets for year-on-year improvement in terms of building partnerships, using local suppliers and improving social and environmental conditions in hotels. Evaluate your activities regularly so that you can learn from them.
10. Use your annual report to publicise what you have been doing to promote responsible tourism and to gain support among your key stakeholders.

Source: Tearfund (2001)

As Fennell and Malloy concluded, few industry associations or political jurisdictions employ any ethical codes or standards in the evaluation of tourism businesses:

> The field is wide open with respect to how ethics may aid in determining what is to be viewed as acceptable and unacceptable behaviour by tourists and those working in the field. Codes of ethics, organizational behaviour, ethical scales … are some of the forces needed to help shape a new frontier of tourism research and scholarship. (Fennell and Malloy, 1999: 941)

WTO Global Code of Ethics

The World Tourism Organisation (WTO) committed to a Global Code of Ethics for Tourism in 1999. The code provides a framework designed to 'promote responsible, sustainable and universally accessible tourism' (WTO, 1999b: 2). Recognising that all the stakeholders in tourism – government (at all levels), enterprises, business associations, workers, NGOs, host communities, the media and the tourists themselves – have 'different albeit interdependent responsibilities in the individual and societal development of tourism', the code commits to WTO members to 'promote an equitable, responsible and sustainable world tourism order' (ibid.: 3). The WTO Global Code recognises the 'diversity of religious, philosophical and moral beliefs [which] are both the foundation

Figure 20.1 Global Code of Ethics, sustainable tourism and responsible tourism

and the consequence of responsible tourism' (ibid.: 4). The Global Code of Ethics provides the framework within which stakeholders take responsibility for achieving sustainable tourism. Achieving ethical and responsible tourism requires action by all the stakeholders in the industry: it requires the implementation of policy by tour operators and travel agents in the originating markets, by the transport companies (coaching, ships, trains and aircraft which move travellers to the destinations), and in the destinations by tourism businesses, attractions and local communities (Figure 20.1).

Codes for travellers

One area where there has been a great deal of activity is in drawing up codes of behaviour for tourists. There are a plethora of codes for tourists produced by NGOs and operators. The International Bicycle Fund (Box 20.2) offers both an exhortation to travel responsibly and a set of suggestions about how to get more out of a holiday. Tearfund also promotes a code for tourists, which enjoins them to make the most of their holidays (see Box 20.3).

Box 20.2   International Bicycle Fund Code of Responsible Travel

Introduction

Tourism can promote national and international understanding and economic development, and it can destroy cultures and environments. The challenge is to create an activity that benefits both the host and guest and hurts neither, that respects and protects the natural and human environment, and that leaves decision making about development to the indigenous people who are most directly affected.

Bicycle tourism tends to be a positive form, hence IBF's interest in tourism and sponsorship of some travel programmes. To help make travel a culturally, economically, and environmentally sensitive activity, we have developed the 'Code of Responsible Travel'. Please share it with friends who travel.

Travel to Meet not Conquer

Understand your reasons for travelling. Pick destinations that you care about. Travel to meet the world and for the experience that brings, not to 'conquer it'. Travel in a spirit of humility and with a genuine desire to meet and share with local people, and appreciate their dignity. Rather than counting rolls of film shot, calculating miles travelled, blasting through villages to reach mountains, racing along the coast to 'discover' a beach paradise, rushing to collect entries in your passport or accumulating other items of travel materialism, take the time to discover the enrichment that comes from seeing another way of life in its fullness. Be sensitive that what enriches you may rob or violate others. Select activities that celebrate and preserve the diversity of the world. Reflect daily on your experiences: seek to deepen your understanding.

Be Culturally Sensitive

Be aware of the feelings, values, customs and beliefs of other people, thus preventing what might be offensive behaviour. Remember this especially concerning dress, photography and religion. Realise that people in the area you visit often have time concepts and thought patterns different from your own. Not inferior, just different. Don't wear sacred items or buy unique artifacts central to the culture. Don't patronise tourism projects or activities that undermine the local culture or value system. Remember that you may be one of thousands of visitors. Do not expect special privileges. Make no promises to local people unless you are certain you can fulfil them.

Understand Cultures in their Own Context

Don't just compare the superficial aspects of places you've been. Ask how the community is getting along within itself. How are the people interacting with their family and friends and their environment? Learn to observe, think, speak and write in a language that is non-ethnocentric, non-racist, non-pejorative and non-sensationalising. Cultivate the habit of listening and observing, rather than merely hearing and seeing. Make a habit of asking questions instead of knowing all of the answers.

Don't Create Barriers

Travel in a manner that doesn't create barriers between you and the place you came to experience. Take advantage of opportunities to walk, bicycle and use other available forms of non-motorised transport. Consider using these as your primary means of travel. Only bring necessary technological gadgetry. Don't let gadgets get between you and the natural ways of your destination. Be especially wary of video and camera equipment (especially Polaroid), and electronic equipment that produces noise.

Be Environmentally Friendly

Use energy, water and other resources efficiently, and consistent with their availability and wise practice in the locale. Use reusable materials when possible. Participate in local recycling programmes. Use the lowest impact, practicable, transportation option. Don't participate in activities that cause the destruction of the environment. Don't harass or collect ecologically crucial life-forms or materials from the water, land or sky.

Be Economically Beneficial

Spend money so that it stays in the community's economy: use services and stay in lodgings that are owned by a member of the community, and that use and serve locally produced goods. If food and beverages are sufficiently available, purchase your needs from locally produced items. If food is scarce don't compete! Travel someplace else or be self-sufficient in your dietary needs. When buying, remember that the bargains you obtain are only possible because of low wages paid to the producer. Don't patronise tourist enterprises that undermine the society or ecology. Recognise that in most areas, spending on motorised transportation only minimally benefits the local economy because the equipment and energy is imported. Be satisfied with the comforts that the local economy can provide. If you need all the comfort of home, why travel? Critique tourism 'development projects' to see if they siphon money away from other basic development needs, and/or to offshore corporations or the absentee elite.

Source: International Bicycle Fund
(www.ibike.org/index.html)

Box 20.3   Make the Most of Your Holidays

1. **Find out about your destination** – take some time before you go to read about the cultural, social and political background of the place and people you are visiting.
2. **Go equipped with basic words and phrases in the local language** – this may open up opportunities for you to meet people who live there.
3. **Buy locally made goods and use locally provided services wherever possible** – your support is often vital to local people.
4. **Pay a fair price for the goods or services you buy** – if you haggle for the lowest price your bargain may be at someone else's expense.
5. **Be sensitive to the local culture** – dress and act in a way that respects local beliefs and customs, particularly at religious sites.
6. **Ask permission before taking photographs of individuals or of people's homes** – and remember that you may be expected to pay for the privilege.
7. **Avoid conspicuous displays of wealth** – this can accentuate the gap between rich and poor and distance you from the cultures you came to experience.
8. **Make no promises to local people that you can't keep** – be realistic about what you will do when you return home.
9. **Minimize your environmental impact** – keep to footpaths and marked routes, don't remove any of the natural habitat and reduce the packaging you bring.
10. **Slow down to enjoy the differences** – you'll be back with the familiar soon enough. ... And ensure that others can too.

Source: www.tearfund.org

Responsible travel

Responsible travel takes a variety of forms. It is characterised by travel and tourism which:

- minimises negative economic, environmental and social impacts;
- generates greater economic benefits for local people and enhances the well-being of host communities, improves working conditions and access to the industry;
- involves local people in decisions that affect their lives and life chances;
- makes positive contributions to the conservation of natural and cultural heritage, to the maintenance of the world's diversity;
- provides more enjoyable experiences for tourists through more meaningful connections with local people, and a greater understanding of local cultural, social and environmental issues;
- provides access for physically challenged people; and
- is culturally sensitive, engenders respect between tourists and hosts, and builds local pride and confidence. (Cape Town Declaration, www.theresponsibletourismpartnership.com)

The first of a series of conferences on Responsible Tourism in Destinations took place in Cape Town in August 2002. The conference addressed the ways in which stakeholders can work together to take responsibility for achieving the aspirations of the Global Code of Ethics and the principles of sustainable tourism.

In his seminal work on the holidaymakers, Krippendorf (1987) argued with passion the case for responsible tourism. He called for the 'birth of a new travel culture' (Krippendorf, 1987: 74), a culture which brings self-fulfilment for tourists: 'new forms of tourism, which will bring the greatest possible benefit to all the participants – travellers, the host population and the tourist business – without causing intolerable ecological and social damage' (ibid.: 106). He envisaged this being achieved by 'rebellious tourists and rebellious locals', and made the important point that 'every individual tourist builds up or destroys human values while travelling' (ibid.: 107, 109). We all have responsibility. He cautioned that 'guidelines for improving the quality of travel must not degenerate into rules for regimentation and manipulation. They must make the experience of freedom possible' (ibid.: 109–10). 'Orders and prohibitions will not do the job – because it is not a bad conscience that we need to make progress, but positive experience, not the feeling of compulsion, but that of responsibility' (ibid.: 109).

This was the ethos of Voluntary Service Overseas (VSO) WorldWise Campaign. It advocated holidays which offer tourists real choice, real variety and real contact with local people *and* real benefits to local communities. They told holidaymakers: 'Your choice of holiday and the way that you visit can make a difference.'

Market trends

There is mounting evidence that consumer preferences are shifting. In November 1999, Tearfund commissioned a survey of consumer attitudes towards ethical issues in

Table 20.1   Choice criteria in holiday bookings

For the last overseas holiday that you booked (whether via a tour company or independently), how important were the following criteria in determining your choice?

	Importance rating (%)				Index
	High	**Mid**	**Low**	**None**	
Affordable cost	82	12	3	3	3.7
Good weather	78	14	5	3	3.7
Guaranteed a good hotel with facilities	71	15	8	4	3.5
Good information is available on the social, economic and political situation of the country and local area to be visited	42	30	23	3	3.1
There is a significant opportunity for interaction with the local people	37	37	23	3	3.1
Trip has been specifically designed to cause as little damage as possible to the environment	32	34	27	5	2.9
Company has ethical policies	27	34	30	7	2.8
Used the company before	26	30	38	5	2.8

Source: Tearfund (2000a)

tourism among a nationally and regionally representative sample of adults (15+). 27% of the respondents had never been on an overseas holiday. The results in Table 20.1 are computed having excluded those who had never been abroad on holiday. The fourth most important criterion in determining holiday choice (after price, weather and accommodation) was good information on the social, economic and political situation of the destination. Having a significant opportunity for interaction with local people, the trip having been specifically designed to minimise its environmental impact and the company having ethical polices were all more important than having used the company before. This was a major surprise to UK operators.

Tour operators and travel agents value their long-term relationships with customers and the fact that this criterion was the least important to this representative group of the British travelling public caused concern. It was also important in building interest in the concepts of ethical and responsible tourism among tour operators. 45% of respondents said that they would be more likely to book a holiday with a company 'if they had a written code to guarantee good working conditions, protect the environment and support local charities in the tourist destination' (Tearfund, 2000a: 3). Tearfund asked the same question again in 2001. Over the two years the percentage that would be willing to pay more for an ethical holiday increased by 7% from 45% to 52% (Tearfund, 2000a, 2002) (Table 20.2).

Tour operators

Tearfund (2001: 20) surveyed UK tour operators with responsible tourism policies and asked them why they had produced a policy. The two main reasons for developing

Table 20.2   Likelihood of booking

Would you be more likely to book a holiday with a company if they had a written code to guarantee good working conditions, protect the environment and support local charities in the tourist destinations?

	1999	2001
Yes	45%	52%
Would make no difference	42%	33%
Don't Know	13%	15%

Source: Tearfund (2002)

policies that were cited were (1) that policies were seen as integral to the principles of the company and (2) they were a mechanism for educating tourists.

The Association of Independent Tour Operators (AITO), which has 150 independent medium-sized companies as members, is committed to an association-wide responsible tourism policy (Box 20.4). It requires members to produce policies and has also launched a responsible tourism award scheme.

Box 20.4   AITO responsible tourism policy

Responsible Tourism Guidelines

As members of AITO we recognise that in carrying out our work as Tour Operators we have a responsibility to respect other people's places and ways of life. We acknowledge that wherever a Tour Operator does business or sends clients it has a potential to do both good and harm, and we are aware that all too often in the past the harm has outweighed the good.

All tourism potentially has an **environmental, social and economic** impact on the destination involved. We accept, therefore, that we as Tour Operators should aim to be responsible in all our dealings on each of these three levels. To help us to do so we have proposed a set of guidelines intended to help companies, customers

and local suppliers recognise their common responsibilities to:

- **protect the environment** – its flora, fauna and landscapes
- **respect local cultures** – traditions, religions and built heritage
- **benefit local communities** – both economically and socially
- **conserve natural resources** – from office to destination
- **minimise pollution** – through noise, waste disposal and congestion.

We are an association of individual, independent companies, each with our own distinctive style and field of operation. As such, we each have our own ways of fulfilling the details of these responsibilities by:

- **establishing** our own policies and involving our staff

- **informing** our clients about Responsible Tourism and, where appropriate,
- **encouraging** them to participate
- **working** with our suppliers and partners to achieve responsible goals and practices

- **publicising** good practice to encourage and spread Responsible Tourism.

Source: www.aito.co.uk/v2home/
responsibletourism.html

There are over 100 tour operators and tourism properties on www.responsibletravel.com, each of which has a responsible tourism policy and explains the responsible tourism aspects of each trip promoted on the site.

There are now a wealth of initiatives in responsible tourism, including the Tour Operators Initiative, The Travel Foundation in the UK and the Fair Trade in Tourism movement. In South Africa, the Fair Trade in Tourism is designed to open access for structurally disadvantaged tourism enterprises by promoting six principles: fair share; democracy; respect for human rights; culture and environment; reliability; and transparency and sustainability. There are expectations and obligations on both sides – for the consumers and the producers of goods and services. Multi-stakeholder partnerships are nearly always necessary for the successful delivery and consumption of Responsible Tourism, that is partnerships between destinations (local communities and government), the tourism industry (in originating markets and destinations) and the tourists (travellers and holidaymakers).

Responsible tourism in destinations

While tour operators in the originating markets can raise the issue and begin to change the way they do business, ultimately it is in the destination that responsible tourism is created and delivered. The increasing demand for responsible tourism in the originating markets leads operators to expect and demand more of their suppliers.

The 1996 White Paper on the Development and Promotion of Tourism in South Africa committed South Africa to the principle of responsible tourism. The principles were elaborated in the responsible tourism guidelines published by the Department of Environmental Affairs and Tourism (DEAT) in 2002:

> Responsible tourism is about enabling local communities to enjoy a better quality of life, through increased socio-economic benefits and an improved environment. It is also about providing better holiday experiences for guests and good business opportunities for tourism enterprises. (DEAT, 2002: 2)

The guidelines offered enterprises and trade associations 104 suggestions about what they might do to exercise responsibility and ensure that tourism becomes more economically, socially and environmentally responsible. The responsible tourism guidelines identify specific ways in which these commitments can be realised. Each enterprise and association is expected to develop its own agenda for action, prioritising those issues where the particular business or group of businesses can make a significant impact by improving its product, the destination, or the livelihoods and quality of life of local people. The guidelines can be readily adapted for use in other destinations (DEAT, 2002).

In The Gambia, the UK Department for International Development funded work with the Association of Small-Scale Enterprises in Tourism (ASSET) to improve the access of small entrepreneurs – fruit sellers, juice pressers, craft workers and stall holders – to official guides within the formal sector operators and hotels. By working through multi-stakeholder processes, it was possible to increase market access and earnings to poor producers and to create better experiences for tourists by reducing hassle and increasing the quality and diversity of the products (NRI, 2002; Bah and Goodwin, 2003; www.propoortourism.org.uk)

Conclusion

Responsible and ethical tourism is a business and consumer response to some of the major economic, social and environmental issues which affect our world. It is about travelling in a better way and about taking responsibility for the impacts that our actions have socially and economically on others and on their social, cultural and natural environment. Responsible business practices in travel and tourism reflect the diversity of the industry and the commitment of staff and management to improving the ways that businesses operate in order to maximise positive impacts and reduce negative ones. The commitment to responsible business may add to brand value, increase customer loyalty, aid staff retention and assist in maintaining motivation. It will also add to costs, particularly as travel and tourism businesses move beyond the cost savings associated with not providing clean towels every day, for example.

Responsible business is about doing more than the minimum required by legislation and regulation. There is a role for regulation in ensuring that over time all businesses do more. Businesses and communities (and their environments) share a common interest in regulating the 'freeloaders' who undercut more responsible businesses. The relationship between responsible business and regulation is a key area for debate, a debate that will continue as rising expectations ratchet up responsible business practice and regulation is used to ensure that rogues do not undercut responsible businesses. The level playing field which businesses seek often requires a regulatory framework.

Any company's commitment to responsible and ethical practices can and should be challenged and positive contributions should be recognised. Overall, there is a need for more to be done. While tourism businesses can contribute to achieving the triple bottom line of economic, social and environmental sustainability, it is important to recognise that the primary purpose of business is to deliver products to consumers at prices they are willing to pay and to still make a profit. Without profits, businesses are not sustainable. Responsible and ethical business practices can go some way to making the world a better place, yet it is not the core business of organisations. For that, human societies have developed other forms of collective action through government and political parties. Ethical considerations need to be part of a broader curriculum.

Discussion questions

1. What is the appropriate balance between market pressures for responsible business and regulation to enforce minimum standards and level the playing field?
2. What arguments are there for legislating for ethical business practice in tourism?
3. How realistic is it to impose ethical responsibility on tourists themselves?

Suggestions for further reading

Bah, A. and Goodwin, H. (2003) *Improving Access for the Informal Sector to Tourism in The Gambia*. London: Pro-Poor Tourism. Available from www.propoortourism.org.uk.

Department of Environmental Affairs and Tourism (2002) *Guidelines for Responsible Tourism*. Pretoria: DEAT. Available from www.icrtourism.org.

Fennell, D.A. and Malloy, D.C. (1999) Measuring the ethical nature of tour operations. *Annals of Tourism Research*, 26(4): 928–43.

Goodwin, H. and Francis, J. (2003) Ethical and responsible tourism: consumer trends in the UK. *Journal of Vacation Marketing*, 9 (3): 271–84. Available from www.haroldgoodwin. info/resources/goodwin.pdf.

Jenkins, T., Birkett, D., Goodwin, H., Goldstein, P., Butcher, J. and Leech, K. (2002) *Ethical Tourism: Who Benefits?* London: Hodder and Stoughton/Institute of Ideas.

Krippendorf, J. (1987) *The Holiday Makers: Understanding the Impact of Leisure and Travel*. Oxford: Butterworth and Heinemann.

NRI (2002) *Harnessing Tourism for Poverty Elimination: A Blueprint from The Gambia. Final Report to the Department for International Development*. Chatham: Natural Resources Institute. Available from www.nri.org/NRET/GambiaFinalSummaryReport2.pdf.

21 Managing the heritage enterprise for liveable host communities

Frank Go, Ronald M. Lee and Antonio Paolo Russo

Chapter objectives

The purpose of this chapter is to explore the concepts of heritage enterprise and cultural tourism from a host community perspective in the context of the global threats and opportunities, national policy and regional inputs and system innovation initiatives, as an effective framework for managing regional growth. Having completed this chapter, the reader will be able to:

- identify the challenges inherent in managing regional (local) tourism in the age of globalisation
- examine the relationship between the 'heritage enterprise' and a host community within an approach that integrates cultural tourism with other development agents, agendas and spheres
- debate the role that the heritage enterprise approach can play in strategic decision-making and the potential, subsequent co-ordination and control of cultural tourism inputs, processes and outputs
- contribute to a regional innovation system inspired by host community 'need-led' strategies as opposed to 'market-led' strategies that aim for economic growth only

Chapter contents

Introduction: tourism in the age of globalisation

The evolving New World Economic Order is characterised by an increasing mobility of capital, a growing diffusion of transnational corporations, and the extension of industrial, banking, and travel and tourism principles and practices from the First World towards marginal and transitional regions. Since the 'Battle of Seattle' in 1999, the outbreaks of violence at various meetings involving the World Trade Organisation and the European Union, and the G8 meeting in Genoa, would lead one to assume that the world economy is in crisis. While the anti-globalist activists have diverse interests, they have developed numerous protest links on the Internet to influence public opinion on the conduct of multinationals and corporate leaders in relation to pressing world issues (among the most popular of these are www.mcspotlight.org, www.urban75.com and www.they rule). According to the 'anti-globalist' movement, two major problems need immediate attention. First, the challenge to economic expansion posed by the environmental constraints of energy supplies, resources and pollution. Secondly, the explosive issue of inequality in the distribution of wealth between rich and poor countries. Gobalisation is 'the intensification of worldwide social relations which link distant realities in such a way that local happenings are shaped by events occurring many miles away and vice versa' (Giddens, 1990: 64, cited by Gray, 1998: 57). It has caused the rapid rise of the global economy, the privatisation of property and electronically-mediated commercial and social networks, and implies that the right not to be excluded – the right of access – becomes more and more important (Rifkin, 2000: 239). The level of economic development differs vastly among regions across the world. The institutional and cultural contexts crucially affect the capacity to enhance the value of the local development assets. Today we see a more disconnected world than before, one in which the poor, the marginal and the unskilled have even fewer possibilities to cross the gap that separates them from the wealthy few. Failing to connect communities in the 'disconnected' Second and Third Worlds will lead to the widening of the 'digital divide'.

The United Nations and national governments are increasingly confronted with the challenge of how to spread the benefits brought by technological progress and the mobility of capital and human resources among sectors of society and between regions. The numerous regional conflicts of the last decade suggest that the incapacity to govern and steer globalisation towards the 'common welfare' places at risk the very conditions for sustainable economic growth that benefits all, instead of the 'happy few'. Cultural tourism is, in part, a host–guest encounter, 'through which social change is experienced, contested and constituted' (Cosgrove and Jackson, 1987: 95, cited in Squire, 1994: 116).

The purpose of this chapter is to present a host community logic that integrates cultural tourism with other development agents, agendas and spheres (Moulaert and Nussbaumer, 2004) and explore, in the context of the 'host–guest' encounter, how to bridge the multiple 'gaps' or differences in culture, distance, infrastructure and governance by managing the co-ordination and control of information management (Kumar and Fenema, 1997). Moreover, it examines the process of elicitation of cultural contents – the selection and co-ordinated development of themes, symbol values and media for dissemination by the 'heritage enterprise'. The latter is viewed as a potential tool to deconstruct mass tourism and translate local narratives into compelling eContent, which empowers local stakeholders to share the richness of their heritage with the global market. Despite the great differences between host communities, they share a confrontation with complexity born out of the 'uneasy' relationship between tourism, culture and the host community. The present lack of synthesis between the three domains hinders effective decision-making and their conversion of heritage assets into resource-supporting functions that contribute to bridging the multiple 'gaps'.

Tourism, culture and host community: a complex relationship

More than any other sector, perhaps with the exception of education, tourism has a strong effect on local culture. From the standpoint of cultural life, tourism that is both 'need-led' and 'demand-led' stands the best chance of benefiting the host culture. It builds on local uniqueness and seeks solutions that are compatible to the 'sense of place' and responsive to the needs of the local community. It generates the resources that are needed to keep cultures alive. What is more important, in the context of this chapter, is that it allows 'marginal' players in the globalisation process to become relevant again, using their 'uniqueness', 'distinction' and 'knowledge' for their own advantage. They can be conceived as the *heritage industry*, whose operators are in charge of preserving, transmitting, processing and accumulating cultural capital.

The heritage industry, small in size, information-intensive and creative, is made up of 'heritage entrepreneurs' who are deeply embedded in the very social fabric of host communities that have accumulated cultural capital over the ages. For Richards and Hall (2000: 1), 'the rationale of sustainable tourism development (…) rests on the assurance of renewable economic, social and cultural benefits to the community and its environment'. In this context, cultural tourism represents a sustainable and powerful tool in bringing together different cultures and systems of values, recreating *cultural empathy* between guest and host communities and leading to greater understanding and tolerance.

However, this rarely happens and, in the eyes of international organisations, tourism remains a 'problem area', something to constrain and regulate, rather than a potential solution. Some challenges that host communities share are as follows:

- *Displacement and exclusion*. Despite the efforts of tourist planners, geographers and business specialists, tourism remains the stereotype of the 'irrational', heterogeneous, rent-exploiting, partially-industrialised sector, that is difficult to co-ordinate, let alone to govern (see Leiper, 1990a; Britton, 1991; Ioannides and Debbage, 1998; Tremblay, 1998). Just as heavy industry creates chemical pollution, tourism causes displacement and exclusion according to the critics of globalisation.
- *Increased pressure on local resources*. Efficient modes of transportation contribute to the growth of cities and tourism through the reduction of travel time and relative distance (Souza and Stutz, 1994: 234–6). However, increased accessibility – both *external* (the ease of

getting to the destination) and *internal* (being close to assets) – and the growing number of tourists have resulted, in the generality of cases, in greater pressure on local resources.

■ *Limited contribution to the elevation of economic status in host communities.* The critics of globalisation view the world through the eyes of the exploited population, that is the homeless, the unemployed, refugees and undocumented temporary workers (Souza and Stutz, 1994: 22). Choy (1995) and Willams and Shaw (1988) have argued that tourism contributes relatively little in terms of job quality, protection and wages that can help to elevate the economic status of host communities.

■ *Conflict and exclusion within the host community.* Cultural tourism development presents some very definite imbalances. On one side, it depends on localised and scarce resources. On the other, it is governed by an industry that is increasingly 'global' and, as such, disconnected from the sources of cultural capital. Moreover, conflict and exclusion result, even *within* the host community, in those who 'pilfer' from tourist growth for personal interests, for example, speculators and rent-seekers, and those who bear the costs from tourism pressure.

■ *Incapacity to achieve a reconciliation of inherent conflict.* Like any industry, tourism needs profit and investment incentives to grow. However, neither commercial interests nor government entities have the capacity to achieve a reconciliation of the inherent conflict between heritage and tourism. It is the old story of the destination life cycles. Indeed, authors such as Haywood (1998) and Ioannides (1992) are inclined to link the performance pattern of destinations to the strategies of multinational companies.

This list is, of course, far from exhaustive, but rather is indicative of the need to change the very foundations of 'mass tourism', at least from a host community perspective. In this context, Richards and Hall (2000: 7) imply that top-down, distributive empowerment models create more tensions between the actors involved and tend to be largely unsuccessful.

Information and communications technology and tourism

In this section we investigate if strategies based on information and communications technologies can contribute towards achieving peace and sustainable host community development through cultural tourism. In particular, we shall examine some key issues arising from the impact of the relationship between information and communications technologies and cultural tourism:

■ Why should information technology experts and social scientists be interested in issues of 'access' and 'inequality'?
■ What concepts illuminate issues of resource-use inequalities and problems of inequality?
■ How can the skills of information technology and tourism (ITT) experts be used to help resolve these challenges?

1.   Managing access and inequality

Globalisation has profound implications for competitiveness, trade and tourism policy, and the quality of life. Two opposing trends seem apparent. On the one hand, we witness increasing economic interdependence and multilateral global agreements. On the other, a growing political fragmentation and the emergence of multiculturalism and regionalism can be observed. At the same time the 'digital divide' has become a reality. Within this context, the relationship between cultural tourism and information and communications technologies (ICT) represents an almost unrivalled opportunity to enhance access to other cultures, tourist business performance and host community liveability.

However, 'bridge building' to achieve the effective and equitable functioning of systems is a very complex and long-term process. It involves a cast of diverse players, from public sector departments and the political forces that dictate them, to private professionals and non-governmental organisations. Host communities, especially in poor regions, largely lack the education and skills that are needed to control their destiny. It implies that outsiders are likely to institutionalise the host function.

2.   Concepts that illuminate issues of resource-use inequalities and problems of inequality

Cities and regions that are unable to control the change process and their own destiny are likely to find their indigenous culture withering, and its two most important 'products' – social trust and empathy – declining. Typically, as a result, such places become less attractive to live, work, visit and invest in. From a sustainability perspective, urban change may be short-lived and contentious.

Globalisation tends to impose its own signs, symbols and values that lead to both cultural convergence and divergence, and a reorganisation of trade and tourism. It is 'most visible in three basic shifts in the sources of cultural identity: from local to global images, from public to private institutions, and from ethnically and racially homogeneous communities to those that are more diverse' (Zukin, 1995: 24). The global culture of today is epitomised by the urban symbolism of the McDonald's restaurant and Sheraton hotels, that more often than not rise at the expense (if not, physically, in the place) of the local, traditional heritage. Youngsters all over the world are more keen to keep up with global trends and fashions, when they have the means, than in reviving local traditions and languages. In such conditions, one of the pillars of societies, cultural identity, may be wasted.

Furthermore, globalisation has caused a power shift from public to private institutions. The capacity of cities to sustain and govern the transformation process is crucial. 'Traditional' decision-makers are in search of new models of governance, both local and transregional, which sustain the development process, mediated through different and possibly diverging stances, and guarantee the necessary political and social support

(Van den Berg et al., 1997). Strategic networks replicate the complexity and spatial articulation of the 'globalisation engine'. At the local level, the formation of such networks may be seen as a matter of building trust (Ganzaroli, 2002).

Finally, there is a noticeable shift from ethnically and racially homogeneous communities to more diverse ones. Traditionally, heritage was conceived as a bridge between the past and the future of a community, a reflection of founding values, history and identity (Graham et al., 1998). The 'cultural capital' embodied in buildings, artifacts, sights, songs and rites favours the transmission of the cultural expression of a people through time and space. In origin, the objects that we now recognise as 'heritage' were the embodiment of the social-economic circumstances of the respective ages. Only in thriving and culturally active communities could such cultural stock be accumulated (Bendixen, 1997). The emerging heterogeneity of society causes a dramatic change. It implies a breaking of tourism business rules, which traditionally (e.g., in Europe) depended for their success on cultural heritage. Waves of cultural diversity require new ways of thinking and greater flexibility in terms of acting, both on the demand and supply sides. The rise of cultural diversity, coupled with the growing significance and diffusion of e-content, is likely to result in the potential deconstruction of the modern tourism business. However, it also offers new opportunities, for example, when adopting e-government (Economist, 2000).

3. Applying the skills of ITT experts to resolve issues

Computer network technology has revolutionised the management and control of distributed locations of labour over a greater geographic area for transnational corporations (Souza and Stutz, 1994: 255). The ILO *World Employment Report, 2001: Life at Work in the Information Economy* (2001b) indicates how the high mobility of capital and its inherently knowledge-based nature allows lower-income cities and regions to 'leapfrog' stages in traditional economic development, via investment in human resources. It implies the need to foster connections between individuals and organisations – what is often referred to as 'social capital' or 'social trust'. Bridging the digital divide requires, above all, abandoning traditional thinking and acting. It demands the embrace of a new humanism based on a *right of access*, which depends on the availability of social trust and empathy. Both social trust and empathy, in turn, rely for their existence on culture (Rifkin, 2000: 247). Many businesses fail in places that lack trust, and 'the World Bank is beginning to understand the relationship between culture and commerce' (Rifkin, 2000: 245).

So far, there has not been any systematic attempt to develop more thorough knowledge and methods – and hardly any tools – to use culture and commerce as the foundation to turn heritage entrepreneurship into a profession. ICT experts and social scientists dedicated to cultural tourism development should be interested in access issues because:

- they represent a reason for being, that is, allowing individuals and communities an opportunity to be included and 'connected';

- the use and development of tools, technologies and methodologies to facilitate the efficient netting of information and communications systems in tourism are today more clearly defined (see Buhalis, 1999);
- the long-term success of this field of inquiry depends largely on its ability to bring about integration at the host community level. The co-operation of the public and private sectors within a regional alliance is needed if local resources are to be used more efficiently for development.

The realisation of a positive, symbiotic relationship between heritage and tourism is a prerequisite for host community development and revitalisation. However, for the most part, a gap remains between the various decision-makers that is, the host community, industry and the visitors, a gap which, as this chapter now goes on to suggest, is caused primarily by the complex decision-making process involving insiders, local agents of change, who possess 'fine-grained' knowledge of the host community environment, and outsiders (corporate boardroom), who usually lack such knowledge.

The deconstruction of mass tourism

As Orbasli (2001) indicates, the relations between the tourism players are both very complex and differ from country to country,

> particularly in respect of the location of power, control and decision-making. The total cast of host community management involves numerous players in a variety of roles, from a wide range of disciplines and practices and often with conflicting interests and agendas. (…) The relationships between individual or collective decision-makers can turn to one of conflict or tension. Conflicts originate from known dichotomies and from differing objectives often closely linked to accountability structures. (Orbasli, 2001: 99)

The decision-making process involves outsiders (boardroom) and insiders, local agents of change with an understanding of the local environment. A delicate balance has to be established between insiders and outsiders for effective management, in order to maximise the benefits from development. Achieving such balance requires coming to terms with two main issues (Russo et al., 2001). First, the establishment of a participatory relationship between the initiators and the recipients of development – potential legislative gaps and cultural differences need to be bridged. Secondly, the recognition that 'if there is an Achilles heel to the new age, it probably lies in the misguided belief that commercially directed relationships and electronically mediated networks can substitute for traditional relationships and communities' (Rifkin, 2000: 241).

Therefore, host communities that aim to capitalise on tourism must first assess their own identity, lifestyles and environments. Each community ought to recognise its potential as a desirable place in which to live, work and visit by developing assets based on its unique character. It requires nothing short of the deconstruction of cultural tourism, and must address all the stages in which cultural contents are elicited, processed and brought to the public. To pass from principles to practice, the relations

Figure 21.1 Inspire confidence through clear host community identity

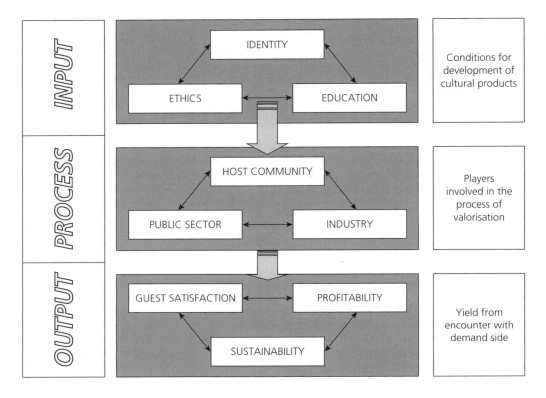

between the various actors have been modelled for the sake of analysis (Figure 21.1). It identifies three dimensions of development (input, process, output), each involving a number of issues and reasons for entering into partnerships (Go and Williams, 1993).

Inputs

Cultural identity is a key asset because development depends crucially on the establishment of a 'heritage ethics', one that recognises cultural assets (both tangible and intangible) as largely non-reproducible resources. The cultural capital stock is heterogeneous in nature. It depends on environmental and organisational factors (e.g., accessibility, landscape, visitor-friendliness). It must be reconstituted with appropriate actions.

Education is another fundamental factor that stimulates and empowers host communities in the 'wise' use of heritage. Only 'insiders' can be fully aware of the risks of an unbalanced use of cultural assets. At the same time, the cultural empathy that is implied by cultural tourism needs to be expressed. Knowledge and pride of one's heritage, as well as the recognition of opportunities that the host–guest encounter offers, are also a product of discourse and self-recognition. Information is an underlying factor both for education and ethics in constructing the identity of a place for visitors.

The way in which tourist information is put together and brought to the visitor is crucial, especially in relation to building a trustworthy image. Increasingly, visitors wish to be part of the process of elicitation and elaboration of contents, rather than being told what they have to see or like. Interactivity – or the involvement of visitors and locals in the co-determination and appreciation of culture as a living process, and not a sterile identification of the present with the past, as most of the time heritage tourism is (mis)understood (Trotter, 2001) – is then an important requirement for a holistic, sustainable tourist experience. Insiders and outsiders express a variety of interests that are often hard to reconcile, with the consequence that more adaptive, connected and culturally cohesive organisations impose their own strategies. However, cultural empathy, resulting from an ethical, informed use of heritage assets, has a tendency to get the needed attention of private organisations.

Quality is the dimension on which the big 'quantities' of mass tourism become unnecessary even to the 'greediest operator'. The process of packaging and delivering high cultural services is one that requires a considerable degree of skills and local, fine-grained knowledge. The local operator who embraces the heritage enterprise vision, and puts it into practice, has an advantage over the anonymous, ubiquitous tour packager because he is *a member* of the host community culture that is being reproduced (Shaw and Williams, 1998). He takes responsibility for integrating cultural contents with the economic production, marketing and delivery of an 'authentic' cultural tourism service experience. In this way, local culture is kept alive and generates value. However, as Dahles (2000) points out, to identify the conditions under which the small and medium-sized operators become real engines of local development requires a deeper understanding of the social meanings embodied in the production, exchange and consumption through the host–guest encounter or 'hospitality' extended to visitors. While complex in nature, hospitality represents an 'institutional device to cut down the time needed to merge cultures, and to integrate alien mindsets and costumes' (Ciborra and Lanzara, 1999). The age of 'dynamic efficiency' requires a new language to frame the relationship between information technology and cultural organisations (Ciborra and Lanzara, 1999).

The publicly available resources described above can also be incorporated into more structured educational programmes. The objective would be to provide a tool for educating local stakeholders and tourists in the field of heritage valorisation and cultural exchange. E-learning and training will achieve generalised awareness, education and knowledge development on the theme of sustainable cultural growth. The architecture of e-learning programmes can be made available to host communities that bear the responsibility to elicit cultural content. Stakeholders participating in the heritage enterprise aiming to develop a liveable host community need training in how to utilise and share cultural resources most effectively.

Process

Through education and ethics, cultural identity, as embodied in heritage and local skills, becomes an asset for cultural tourism development. Its valorisation process involves dealing with three major stakeholders: residents, visitors and the travel and hospitality industry, who have opposing interests. *Residents* want to raise their standard of living through economic growth and safeguard their quality of life through environmental and heritage preservation. *Visitors* seek an amenable experience, mainly for recreational purposes. And the *travel and hospitality industry* aims to maximise profits.

As previously mentioned, the stakeholders can be categorised as either 'outsiders' or 'insiders'. The host community represents the natural 'insider', who bears the effects, direct and indirect, positive and negative, of the tourism development process. Transnational corporations, national governments and supranational bodies may be categorised as outsiders, albeit in different degrees, and are less concerned with the local as opposed to the potential contribution of tourism activity to national interests and corporate performance. However, if the tourism industry is dominated by outside interests and is therefore disconnected or not 'anchored' in the host community culture, its direct benefits in terms of revenue and job generation will be severely limited. The latter scenario is a typical case of remote, fast-growing, tourist destination regions in relatively unexploited areas. The issues raised by the growth of cultural tourism are the host community's reflection of local traditions, identity and social composition. The model sketched in Figure 21.1 suggests the need for a synthesis in host community logic whereby:

- a vision, opportunities and threats are formulated and communicated;
- an agenda is set and the developmental process facilitated through a realistic strategy and operational plan;
- development agents are identified who show potential to become compatible partners; and
- a sphere can be created that enables partners to co-ordinate and control their responsibilities and activities.

We will refer to the latter as the 'heritage enterprise'.

Output

The multifaceted cultural valorisation process is expected to yield results that we can group as 'guest satisfaction', 'profitability' and 'sustainability'. These yield dimensions result from the host–guest encounter. On the demand side, the tourists seek a cultural experience resulting from the encounter with the host community, its residents and industry, supported by the public sector. At the centre of the virtuous circle there is the tourist. However, he/she is no longer a passive recipient of strategies formulated above his/her head, but rather an empowered, active player in search of his/her roots, of authentic heritage and 'quality experience'.

Guest satisfaction, in the cultural tourism context, results from the intensity and quality of a cultural experience and is rooted in personal, social and cultural values. At these levels it is also clearly connected with stories. For instance, the Beatrix Potter stories have been appropriated symbolically as starting points for another sphere of values about happy childhood 'and nostalgia for English country life, ideas about the rural and the urban, and authenticity and heritage preservation' (Squire, 1994: 117).

Profitability results from the operators' ability to generate revenues that exceed their business costs. Enlarging the range and 'depth' of service experiences available to visitors, and their empowerment, does not necessarily imply a reduction of business profitability. Rather it requires the (re)designing of the system of valorisation and commercialisation of relevant tourist assets. Such restructuring within the value chain provides an opportunity to offer clients 'authentic' cultural content (e.g., the Beatrix Potter stories) and achieve greater efficiency and equity at the local scale.

Sustainability hinges on the perception of both cultural identity and environment as 'constraints' to growth. But the reproduction of heritage is only one dimension of tourist attractiveness, as stressed above. The awareness of the environment as an integral part of a local culture can be strengthened through education. Employment generation resulting from sustainable tourism development represents a dynamic feature of cultural empathy between host and guest. If the host community succeeds, jointly, in communicating the true value of their heritage and cultural assets to guests, supported by ICT applications, it will trigger a virtuous cycle of growth. The adoption of a new heritage enterprise business model can help transform host–guest encounters that contribute to 'client life value', that is potentially lasting client–vendor relationships.

The heritage enterprise: managing confidence

The host community of tomorrow is taking shape as an electronic exchange of information and content, with artists, traders, visitors and scientists connected via satellite, computer networks and telecommunications. At least three ideas have come together to create this entity.

First, the application of electronics, the technology that enables a co-operative, global exchange of information, content and educational courses. E-business and e-learning have enabled new kinds of (globally)-distributed project, with business corporations and 'distance-education' exchange and global-scale research projects between universities.

Secondly, the global nature of society. Both cultural heritage conservationists and businesses at the local level still fail to recognise fully how to integrate their efforts on the global level. Therefore, tourism industry objectives often impinge on heritage resources, and vice versa. Astute conservationists and small and medium-sized entrepreneurs will understand that the cultural heritage is just as important as the development of roads and power lines. They will plan their agendas to deal with global issues and experiment within co-operative programmes among universities.

Thirdly, the available technologies stimulate networking and new kinds of co-operation among individuals and institutions that are less formal and bureaucratic. Electronic and social networks have the potential to unite groups of people within a global network to solve fundamental problems. The heritage host community of tomorrow will be inextricably integrated in the network context, and interfacing with a myriad of both 'global' and local stakeholders. The Internet may be viewed as a means to co-ordinate their interfacing. It derives its strength from the principle of connectivity, for example, between vendors and users. As Squire (1994: 116) indicates: 'Tourism is about meanings.' Therefore, it should be viewed as a 'confidence good', that is until it is consumed the client must be confident that the actual experience will materialise and satisfy expectations (Werthner and Klein, 1999). 'While price and customer service are key competitive factors during the booking procedure, suppliers and intermediaries are increasingly competing on the confidence inspired in the customer directly through the quality of information provided' (UN, 2000).

With few exceptions the traditional destination marketing organisations (DMOs) are among the least developed actors in the online tourism sector. There may be various explanations for their performance. One may be the opposing needs and interests of actors within a complex process of creating relationships to achieve cultural, social and economic objectives. It reflects the need for the appropriate co-ordination and control of a myriad of stakeholders who are active – either directly or indirectly – in managing and planning cultural tourism development.

In the sections that follow we will investigate how the Internet can contribute to the trade and tourism competitiveness of host communities, especially those in emerging countries, and how heritage through cultural tourism can be linked to the Internet so as to benefit, at the host community level, both the host community and commercial enterprises. We shall look, particularly, at how business-to-business and business-to-consumer electronic commerce can be managed to improve customer service, reduce transaction costs and promote market expansion.

The role of the heritage enterprise

Partnerships between heritage organisations, enterprises, intermediaries and government are important because tourism is becoming more international and most destinations have to compete at the global level. Both producers and intermediaries are increasingly using information technology to increase their knowledge and relationship with customers (Riege et al., 2001: 59). The model proposed in Figure 21.1 exposes the networking potential of IT and social clusters within host communities. The latter need to position the heritage enterprise within the global network, that is placing one's host community identity in the consumer's mind. A sound heritage strategy contributes to local economic development and is founded on social and cultural partnership. It should be aimed at a particular visitor profile and have a clear objective, for instance, increasing the length of stay or improving visit frequency. For example, the Lake District in the UK could target guests interested in children's stories and pinpoint the real benefit, namely that there is only one area on Earth that can be called 'home' to the famous English children's author Beatrix Potter (Squire, 1994). Visitors need reasons to believe in such benefits, which require a heritage enterprise to co-ordinate the 'telling of its feature story' and subsequent 'service delivery' so that the 'promises made' are kept. A host community that meets the expectations it raises is typically perceived as 'credible'. The expectations are anchored in the tone and style of the various products and services on offer, which are representations of the host community's identity. In short, the mission of the heritage enterprise is to provide access to a story that inspires confidence in the host community by projecting a clear identity and providing trustworthy tourist information. A heritage enterprise can be compared to a map that helps the host community to reach its objectives. It is important to check that strategy on the 'business-to-consumer' and 'business-to-business' levels is consistent with the host community's brand personality.

Business-to-consumer

Mobile telephone technology, it is believed, creates an advantage by realising a 'security blanket' for tourists during their travel activities. Tourists travelling by car, train and bus, and those already in the host city, can have constant access to information, including hotels, maps, telephone directories and bulletin boards listing the city's current attractions. In its most effective stage, mobile telephone technology can be a hand-held tour guide. This feature enables tourists to find alternative routes through a city and gain a deeper appreciation of its heritage. The recent developments in the field of virtual reality have the potential to bring virtual cities and museums to Internet users. But there are also challenges. First, who will provide a co-ordinated mechanism that facilitates the authentic, virtual 'touring' of distant cultures, both geographically and historically? Secondly, who will take responsibility for the appropriate support to implement the new technology within a host community (See Case Study 21.1)?

Case Study 21.1 Venice and Bologna, Italy

Venice, Italy, is an example of a city famous for its art facing the pressure of mass tourism. Both its socio-cultural fabric and the preservation of its cultural assets are at stake. A museum in Venice, for instance, transmits information to mobile telephones that are in the museum's vicinity. Through the mobile device, a tourist gets information about the artifacts and guidance for visiting different parts of the museum. Such 'real-time, real-place' mobile technology supports not only multiple perspectives, but also multiple contexts of use.

The experience of the 'virtual theatre' realised by CINECA in Bologna (documented by Bonfigli et al., 2000) is a good example of how 4-D technology can be used to incorporate a visual chronology of a city. It allows users to see Bologna's growth and development over time from a multitude of angles. Virtual reality applications can be used to combine historical evolution and cultural identity with the information society, which can enhance the dissemination of cultural heritage. The transmission of the heavy graphic files over the Internet can be improved by installing custom-made hardware.

Business-to-business

A myriad of organisations and businesses are, of course, concerned with the commercial exploitation of the heritage resource through the provision of tourism services. Together, they are increasingly influenced by a dominant 'commercial' ideology, which, in comparison to the conservation ideology, is driven principally by the concerns of both the public and private sector with a vested tourism business-centric interest in development. In an increasingly global and competitive market, it has led to mass tourism characterised by standardisation. It may result in cultural crisis, environmental pollution and a type of tourism development that can become not only counterproductive but, in the worst case scenario, self-destructive.

Hence, the challenge for the host community is to empower 'heritage' to 'escape' from the subordination of exploitation in order to respond to new and emerging social demands. In that sense, host community tourism is about business-to-business co-ordination – in particular, the matching of a federation of specialised and culture-related vendors. Tourism businesses should be organised to integrate a comprehensive information infrastructure and make full use of national and regional resources. Tourismus & Congress GMbH is an example of how to connect regional and nation-wide actors online (see Case Study 21.2). The co-ordination of tourism service provision, combined with the utilisation of the ICT infrastructure, is the first step that a host community takes to becoming a creative learning organisation. The second step is to support its further evolution through a 'heritage enterprise' context. The latter should link the worlds of literature, education and host community (perhaps represented by the arts and/or tourist office) and possibly be supported by business and government in a public–private partnership construction. A number of stakeholders in the host community can be trained in utilising and sharing cultural resources in the most effective way, and thus participate in local development. Training begins as soon as local actors experience learning by going through the starting process. The public element involves the training space and the creation of an Internet café or similar workspace.

Case Study 21.2   Tourismus & Congress GMbH & The BONNTICKET system, Germany

Tourismus & Congress GMbH offers complete travel packages which integrate concerts into a cultural programme and respond to consumer demands. 'Last minute' decision-making as a phenomenon can also affect city and culture visitor flows and therefore it is important to anticipate this. It is necessary from the beginning to build links and develop networks, and to do this, a central ticket reservation system is required which functions effectively. Tourismus & Congress GMbH make use of the existing infrastructure in the city of Bonn. The BONNTICKET system has 80 regional pre-sale agencies and more than 600 agencies nationwide connected online. Having online information means that, for example, a bus tour operator can offer a package including food, accommodation and an evening event, with the entrance tickets reserved or purchased in advance. To 'package' means to increase effectiveness and establish confidence by professional handling. The next step in regional marketing is to provide a ticket system, which can provide decentralised access to the complete tourist offer.

Source: Schild (1997: 97)

Conclusion

The 'competition–collaboration' paradox (Go and Williams, 1993) that exists between the myriad of interests shown in Figure 21.1 provides a useful arena in which to reconcile heritage and tourism and a basic model for the reconstruction of the tourist business. As this chapter proposes, the heritage enterprise can help host communities to move beyond a single economic perspective to a host community logic that resides in the communicative integration of cultural, social and economic agents.

The heritage enterprise can serve a crucial threefold role in managing the process of creating and sustaining a liveable host community. First, it can contribute to the shaping of alternative visions or designs for the desired future of the host community. Secondly, it can facilitate knowledge transfer to and between developmental agents to enable them to benefit from the potential 'heritage content' – 'new technology' interface. Thirdly, it can stimulate the elicitation of cultural content, strengthening the distribution of a coherent host community heritage identity that can be successfully profiled in 'a global ocean of symbols'. The heritage enterprise can be viewed as an 'incubator' that links 'back-office' and 'front-office' functions. The back office makes possible easy cloning, the sharing of ideas with communities of practice across the world, yielding cost savings and enhancing efficiency. The e-content derived from local heritage functions as 'front-office' and a means to strengthen cultural identity and the image-building process.

The application of a host community logic enables one to view regional physical space and virtual space as 'a single structure'. It is a vision enabling a host community to profile its identity in a coherent way through the creation and sustenance of a 'heritage enterprise'. The heritage enterprise seeks to establish integrative communications between various, divergent developmental agents, heritage, tourism, business and government. Thus far, these fields have developed largely independently of each other. Therefore, the major system innovation of the heritage enterprise lies in the capacity to bridge the gaps that divide three fields of knowledge and planning – governance, organisational culture and technology – by the diffusion of a narrative bound by a 'brand identity'. Its main asset is the cultural richness of locality, which 'feeds' the heritage enterprise 'incubation process' designed to motivate the talent and mobilise the means to systematically 'explore' and 'exploit' regional heritage in a sustainable manner. In that sense its prime responsibility is to create a shared vision within the nodes of existing and divergent networks, particularly identifying the creative potential for 'need-led' host community growth, through export to clients who reside outside a particular region. Finally, take precautions to mitigate the negative effects of tourism on the host community, such as the danger of physical erosion, vandalism, civil disturbance and social exclusion from wealth creation options and the common welfare.

In summary, cultural tourism may truly contribute to the achievement of world peace through sustainable, equitable development, especially in marginal but culture-rich regions. We hope that the heritage enterprise vision may guide transnational corporations, international governmental organisations and NGOs when planning for a sustainable future. Of course, it requires time to learn each other's language, to anchor processes and projects within a host community's social fabric and transform the incidental nature of host–guest 'encounters' into lasting relationships. Heritage, through cultural tourism, offers host communities a formidable opportunity to 'put right', at least in part, some of the negative consequences of an unbridled, imposed globalisation. Utilising the strategies indicated in this chapter, host communities can begin to empower their stakeholders to capitalise on their heritage assets *pro bono unico*, for the common welfare.

Discussion questions

1. What are the implications of changing lifestyles, travel patterns and existing international destination trends on the competitiveness of European Union member states?
2. What are the potential costs and benefits of a heritage enterprise approach from both a private and public sector perspective?
3. How realistic is the achievement of a 'heritage enterprise' when considering the opposing cultural and commercial interests that seem dominant in the host community tourism management decision-making context?

Suggested further reading

Ashworth, G.J. and Tunbridge, J.E. (1990) *The Tourist-Historic City*. London: Belhaven Press.
Orbasli, A. (2001) *Tourists in Historic Towns: Urban Conservation and Heritage Management*. London and New York: E&FN Spon.
Schild, H.-H. (1997) In D. Dodd and A. van Hemel (eds), *Planning Cultural Tourism in Europe: A Presentation of Theories and Cases*. Amsterdam: Boekman Stichting, pp. 91–100.
Urry, J. (1990) *The Tourist Gaze: Leisure and Travel in Contemporary Societies*. London: Sage.

This short concluding section aims to highlight the key factors identified in the text in relation to the management of tourism. Clearly both tourism and management are broad areas about which it is impossible to generalise. Indeed, the focus of the different chapters serves to highlight this diversity. It is, however, possible to identify some key themes that are impacting upon the management of tourism. These are recurring themes throughout much of the text and so the intent here is merely to summarise them and their importance. The key issues are globalisation, integration, sustainable development, technological developments, and the extent and impact of disasters and crisis in tourism. Other smaller issues include quality and cost management.

Globalisation

Chapter 21 considers issues in relation to tourism in the age of globalisation. The impact of globalisation on HRM was also considered in Chapter 6, as was the importance of cultural contexts. While it is evident throughout much of the text that tourism managers now operate in a global environment, it is also important to note that this has far less relevance for many small businesses involved in tourism. It was noted in Chapter 1 that significant barriers to globalisation exist for international airlines, and reasons for this are considered in Chapter 3.

Integration

Integration is a strong theme, recurring as it does throughout the industry chapters. In particular, horizontal integration is explained in detail in relation to the scheduled airline industry in Chapter 3. The Oneworld case study in this chapter illustrates this aspect of contemporary business well. Vertical integration is examined in relation to the travel trade or, in other words, between travel agents and tour operators. The implications of such integration have an enormous impact on mass market tourism and yet this is often a feature of the industry that is poorly understood by consumers.

Sustainable development

The environmental impacts of tourism are only one of the components of sustainability to be examined by this text. Negative impacts of tourism are highlighted in many chapters. Indeed, the point is made in Chapter 20 that there are inevitable costs to tourism that have to be expected, and in many cases accepted, in exchange for the tourist dollar. Evidence of this is provided in a number of chapters. There are clear implications of such costs for tourism managers. A variety of approaches to meet the management challenges posed by these implications are proposed within the book.

Sustainable development featured in many chapters. Chapter 20 described the Commission on Sustainable Development meeting in New York in April 1999 – the first to address tourism – as having a marked impact on social and economic issues. This represented a movement beyond the relatively narrow green agenda. It was argued that an ethical approach requires poverty reduction to be given a higher priority. Chapter 20 concludes that responsible and ethical tourism is a business and consumer response to some of the major economic, social and environmental issues which affect our world. It is about travelling in better ways, taking responsibility for the effects which our impacts have socially and economically on others and on their social, cultural and natural environment.

Technological developments

Technology is a strong theme throughout the book and is the subject of Chapter 16 by Buhalis. Following on from this general examination of the use of ICTs in tourism, including how ICTs can support the profitability and effectiveness of organisations, Ryan, in Chapter 17, looks in detail at the application of web-based data mining to the marketing of destination. Chapter 17 therefore provides an applied look at the use of technology by destinations. At the same time, this chapter illustrates many of the inhibiting factors. Chapter 6 considers the impact of ICTs on the HRM function.

Buhalis makes the point that ICTs are gradually being centrally placed as one of the most critical factors for both the operational and strategic management of the industry. Chapters 5 and 16 both highlight the importance of information to tourism and the resultant suitability of technology to the industry. However, ICTs are not presented as a panacea. Indeed, a restructuring of several management practices is required so that organisations can achieve their strategic objectives when using ICTs.

Technology is viewed in two different lights in Chapter 5. First, disintermediation in relation to travel distribution is explained by the growth of technological means of reaching consumers. Secondly, the growth of new virtual intermediaries is outlined.

Disasters and crises

Tourism, as an activity, has an inherent fragility and vulnerability, making it highly susceptible to crises. A number of chapters refer, for example, to September 11, 2001 and the effect that it had on tourism. The management of crises was covered fully in Chapter 19. The importance of appropriate management responses to crises cannot be over-emphasised as management failures at such times can greatly aggravate problems. However, it is also important to note the resilience of the industry. Chapter 3, in its examination of the aftermath of September 11, 2001 for the airline industry, illustrated this resilience very well.

ow-cost strategies

The recurring use of low-cost business models as examples across the chapters clearly indicates the importance of this growing form of business. It is particularly interesting to note the extent to which easyJet was used as an example. Cost-cutting exercises in general were seen to be important in the current business climate, as evidenced by the discussion of commission cutting in Chapter 5.

Quality management

Quality is another area of importance currently. Chapter 2 focused heavily on this aspect in relation to the accommodation sector. Given the importance accorded to this aspect of management in the services management literature generally, this aspect would have received more attention in this text if space had allowed.

Conclusion

While the above themes were the predominant ones in terms of their breadth of applicability across the many areas covered in the book, other relevant aspects can be identified, including the importance of the changing structure of the industry, the extent to which relationship marketing techniques and loyalty schemes are used within the industry, the applicability of value chain approaches in certain areas and the relevance of systems theory. The suggestions for further reading provided at the end of each chapter should enable readers to develop further any interest in these and the many other theoretical perspectives mentioned in the chapters.

References

Access Economics (1997) *The Economic Significance of Travel & Tourism: Is There a Case for Government Funding for Generic Tourism Marketing?* Canberra: Tourism Council Australia, Property Council of Australia and Tourism Task Force.

Adler, J. (1989) Origins of sightseeing. *Annals of Tourism Research*, 16(1): 7–29.

Air Transport World (1997) Bilateral ballistics. 34(2): 53–61.

Airey, D. (1983) European government approaches to tourism. *Tourism Management*, 4: 234–44.

Akama, J. (2002) The role of government in the development of tourism in Kenya. *International Journal of Tourism Research*, 4(1): 1–13.

Albrecht, K. (1992) *The Only Thing that Matters*. New York: Harper Business.

Albright, H. and Cahn, R. (1985) *The Birth of the National Park Service*. Salt Lake City, UT: Howe Brothers.

Alford, P. (1998) Database marketing in travel and tourism. *Travel & Tourism Analyst*, 1(1): 87–104.

Ampadu-Agyei, O. (1999) Central region project, Ghana: a case study. Paper presented at 'Changing Tastes, Changing Places' Conference. London: Royal Geographical Society.

Anderssen, P. and Colberg, R.T. (1973) Multivariate analysis in travel research: a tool for travel package design and market segmentation. *Proceedings of the 4th Annual Conference, Travel Research Association*. Idaho.

Andress, M. (2002) Prague makes a premier-class pitch. *Financial Times*, 29 October: 15.

Apostolides, P. (1996) Tourism development policy and environmental protection in Cyprus. In *Sustainable Tourism Development*. Environmental Encounters No. 32. Strasbourg: Council of Europe, pp. 31–40.

Arnold, G. (1998) *Corporate Financial Management*. London: Financial Times/Pitman Publishing.

Arnold, G.C. and Hatzopoulos, P.D. (2000) The theory–practice gap in capital budgeting: evidence from the United Kingdom. *Journal of Business Finance & Accounting*, 27(5–6): 603–26.

Ascher, B. (1984) Obstacles to international travel and tourism. *Journal of Travel Research*, 22(3): 2–15.

Ashton, T. and Green, F. (1996) *Education, Training and the Global Economy*. Cheltenham: Edward Elgar.

Ashworth, G. (1989) Urban tourism: an imbalance in attention. In C. Cooper (ed.), *Progress in Tourism, Recreation and Hospitality Management* (Vol. I). London: Belhaven Press, pp. 33–54.

Ashworth, G. (1992) Is there an urban tourism? *Tourism Recreation Research*, 17(2): 3–8.

Ashworth, G. and Tunbridge, J. (1990) *The Tourist-Historic City*. London: Belhaven Press.

Ashworth, G. and Voogd, H. (1988) Marketing the city: concepts, processes and Dutch applications. *Town Planning Review*, 59: 65–79.

Athiyamen, A. and Robertson, R. (1995) Strategic planning in large tourism firms: an empirical analysis. *Tourism Management*, 16(6): 447–53.

Atkinson, H., Berry, A. and Jarvis, R. (1995) *Business Accounting for Hospitality and Tourism*. London: International Thomson Business Press.

Australia Tourism Forecasting Council (1998) *Inbound Tourism Short-term Scenarios*. Special Report – Tourism Forecasting Council, No. 2, pp. 24.

Aviation Week and Space Technology (1999) Europe assesses deregulation. 13 December: 44.

Aviation Week and Space Technology (2002) EC Vice President advocates transatlantic deregulation. 18 February: 47.

Bah, A. and Goodwin, H. (2003) *Improving Access for the Informal Sector to Tourism in The Gambia*. London: Pro-Poor Tourism. Available at www.propoortourism.org.uk.

Bailey, E.E. and Baumol, W.J. (1984) Deregulation and the theory of contestable markets. *Yale Journal of Regulation*, 2: 111–37.

Barnett, M. and Standing, C. (2001) Repositioning travel agencies on the Internet. *Journal of Vacation Marketing*, 7(2): 143–52.

Basu, K. (2001) On the goals of development. In G. Meier and J. Stiglitz (eds), *Frontiers of Development Economics: The Future in Perspective*. Oxford: Oxford University Press, pp. 61–87.

Bateson, J.E.G. (1991) *Managing Services Marketing: Text and Readings*. London: The Dryden Press.

Bateson, J.E.G. and Hoffman, D.K. (1996) *Managing Services Marketing: Texts and Readings*

(4th edition). Fort Worth, TX: Harcourt Brace College Publishers.

Baum, T. (1993) *Human Resource Issues in International Tourism*. Oxford: Butterworth Heinemann.

Baum, T. (1995) *Managing Human Resources in the European Tourism and Hospitality Industry: A Strategic Approach*. London: Chapman & Hall.

Baum, T. (1997) Making or breaking the tourist experience: the role of human resource management. In C. Ryan (ed.), *Tourist Experience: A New Introduction*. London: Cassell, pp. 92–111.

Baum, T. (2002) Skills and training for the hospitality sector: a review of issues. *Journal of Vocational Education and Training*, 54(3): 343–63.

Baum, T. and Lundtorp, S. (2001) *Seasonality in Tourism*. London: Elsevier.

Baumol, W.J., Panzar, J.C. and Willig, R.D. (1982) *Contestable Markets and the Theory of Industrial Structure*. New York: Harcourt Brace Jovanovich.

Baumol, W.J. and Willig, R.D. (1986) Contestability: developments since the book. *Oxford Economic Papers*, 38: 9–36.

Becherel, L. and Cooper, C. (2002) The impact of globalisation on HR management in the tourism sector. *Tourism Recreation Research*, 27(1): 3–16.

Bendixen, P. (1997) Cultural tourism: economic success at the expense of culture? *The International Journal of Cultural Policy*, 4(1): 21–46.

Bergquist, W. (1993) *The Post-modern Organisation: Mastering the Art of Irreversible Change*. San Francisco: Jossey-Bass.

Berry, L. (1995) *On Great Service: A Framework for Action*. New York: The Free Press.

BHA (2001) *British Hospitality: Trends and Statistics*. London: British Hospitality Association.

Bianchi, R. (2002) Towards a new political economy of global tourism. In R. Sharpley and D.J. Telfer (eds), *Tourism and Development: Concepts and Issues*. Clevedon: Channel View Publications, pp. 265–99.

Blackwood, T. and Mowl, G. (2000) Expatriate-owned small businesses: measuring and accounting for success. *International Small Business Journal*, 18(3): 60–73.

Blair, J. (1995) *Local Economic Development: Analysis and Practice*. London: Sage.

Blank, U. (1996) Tourism in United States cities. In C. Law (ed.), *Tourism in Major Cities*. London: International Thomson Business Press, pp. 206–32.

Blois, K. (ed.) (2000) *The Oxford Textbook of Marketing*. Oxford: Oxford University Press.

Boberg, K. and Collison, F. (1985) Computer reservation systems and airline competition. *Tourism Management*, 6(3): 174–83.

Boella, M., Crozet, C. and Pagnon-Maudet, C. (2001) Hotel law: aspects of English, French and Spanish Law compared. *International Travel Law Journal*, 1: 34–9.

Bonfigli, M.E., Calon, L. and Guidazzoli, A. (2000) Nu.M.E.: a www virtual historic museum of the city of Bologna. In J. Carrol et al. (eds), *Proceedings of SAC, 2000: ACM Symposium of Applied Computing* (Vol. 2). Como: Villa Olmo, pp. 956–61.

Booms, B.H. and Bitner, M.J. (1981) Marketing strategies and organisational structures for service firms. In J.H. Donnelly and W.R. George (eds), *Marketing of Services*. Chicago: American Marketing Association, pp. 47–51.

Booth, S. (1993) *Crisis Management Strategy: Competition and Change in Modern Enterprises*. New York: Routledge.

Bowman, C. (1992) Charting competitive strategy. In D. Faulkner and G. Johnson (eds), *The Challenge of Strategic Management*. London: Kogan Page.

Bramwell, B. (1998) User satisfaction and product development in urban tourism. *Tourism Management*, 19(1): 35–47.

Bramwell, B. and Lane, B. (1993) Sustainable tourism: an evolving global approach. *Journal of Sustainable Tourism*, 1(1): 1–5.

Bramwell, B. and Lane, B. (2000) Collaboration and partnerships in tourism planing. In B. Bramwell and B. Lane (eds), *Tourism Collaboration and Partnerships: Politics, Practice and Sustainability*. Clevedon: Channel View Publications, pp.1–20.

Bramwell, B. and Rawding, L. (1996) Tourism marketing images of industrial cities. *Annals of Tourism Research*, 23(1): 201–21.

Brealey, R.A. and Myers, S.C. (2003) *Principles of Corporate Finance* (international edition). New York: McGraw-Hill.

Brenner, M.A., Leet, J.O. and Schott, E. (1985) *Airline Deregulation*. Westport, CT: Eno Foundation for Transportation.

Bridge, J. and Moutinho, L. (2000) Financial management in tourism. In L. Mouthino (ed.), *Strategic Management in Tourism*. Wallingford: CABI Publishing.

Britton, S.G. (1982) The political economy of tourism in the Third World. *Annals of Tourism Research*, 9(3): 331–58.

Britton, S. (1991) Tourism, capital, and place: towards a critical geography of tourism. *Environment and Planning D: Society and Space*, 9(4): 451–78.

Broadhurst, R. (2001) *Managing Environments for Leisure and Recreation*. London: Routledge.

Brogowicz, A., Delene, L. and Lyth, D. (1990) A synthesized service quality model with managerial implications. *International Journal of Service Industry Management*, 1(1): 27–45.

Bronner, F. and de Hoog, R. (1985) A recipe for fixing decision ingredients. *European Research*, July: 109–15.

Brown, S. (1993) Postmodern marketing? *European Journal of Marketing*, 27(4): 19–34.

Brown, S. (1995) *Postmodern Marketing*. London: Routledge.

Brown, S. (2001) *Marketing: The Retro Revolution*. London: Sage.

Brown, S.W., Fisk, R.P. and Bitner, M.J. (1994) The development and emergence of services marketing thought. *International Journal of Service Industry Management*, 5(1): 21–48.

Brunet, S., Bauer, J., De Lacy, T. and Tshering, K. (2001) Tourism development in Bhutan: tensions between tradition and modernity. *Journal of Sustainable Tourism*, 9(3): 243–63.

Budowski, G. (1976) Tourism and environmental conservation: conflict, coexistence or symbiosis? *Environmental Conservation*, 3(1): 27–31.

Buhalis, D. (1993) Regional integrated computer information reservation management systems as a strategic tool for the small and medium tourism enterprises. *Tourism Management*, 14(5): 366–78.

Buhalis, D. (1994) Information and telecommunications technologies as a strategic tool for small and medium tourism enterprises in the contemporary business environment. In A. Seaton, R. Wood, P. Dieke and C. Jenkins (eds), *Tourism: The State of the Art (the Strathclyde Symposium)*. Chichester: J. Wiley & Sons, pp. 254–75.

Buhalis, D. (1997) Information technologies as a strategic tool for economic, cultural and environmental benefits enhancement of tourism at destination regions. *Progress in Tourism and Hospitality Research*, 3(1): 71–93.

Buhalis, D. (1998) Strategic use of information technologies in the tourism industry. *Tourism Management*, 19(3): 409–23.

Buhalis, D. (1999) Information technology for small and medium-sized tourism enterprises: Adaptation and Benefits. *Information Technology and Tourism*, 2(1): 79–95.

Buhalis, D. (2000) Information technology in tourism: the state of the art. *Tourism Recreation Research*, 25(1): 41–58.

Buhalis, D. (2001) Tourism in Greece: strategic analysis and challenges. *Current Issues in Tourism*, 4(5): 440–80.

Buhalis, D. (2002) *eTourism: Information Technology for Strategic Tourism Management*. London: Pearson Education.

Buhalis, D. and Laws, E. (2001) *Tourism Distribution Channels: Practices, Issues and Transformations*. London: Continuum.

Buhalis, D. and Licata, C. (2002) The eTourism intermediaries. *Tourism Management*, 23(3): 207–20.

Buhalis, D. and Main, H. (1998) Information technology in small and medium hospitality enterprises: strategic analysis and critical factors. *International Journal of Contemporary Hospitality Management*, 10(5): 198–202.

Burgess, L. and Cooper, J. (2000) Extending the viability of MICA (Model of Internet Commerce Adoption) as a metric for explaining the process of business adoption of Internet commerce. Paper presented at the International Conference on Telecommunications and Electronic Commerce, Dallas, November.

Burns, P. (1999) Paradoxes in planning. *Annals of Tourism Research*, 26(2): 329–48.

Burns, P.M. and Holden, A. (1994) *Tourism: A New Perspective*. Hemel Hempstead: Prentice Hall.

Busby, G. (2001) Vocationalism in higher-level tourism courses: the British perspective. *Journal of Further and Higher Education*, 25(1): 29–43.

Butcher, J. (2003) *The Moralization of Tourism*. London: Routledge.

Butler, R. (1980) The concept of the tourist area cycle of evolution: implications for management of resources. *Canadian Geographer*, 24(1): 5–12.

Butler, R. (1985) Evolution of tourism in the Scottish Highlands. *Annals of Tourism Research*, 12(3): 371–91.

Butler, R. (1998) Sustainable tourism: looking backwards in order to progress? In C.M. Hall and A. Lew (eds), *Sustainable Tourism: A Geographical Perspective*. Harlow: Longman, pp. 25–34.

Butler, R. and Hall, C.M. (1998) Conclusion: the sustainability of tourism and recreation in rural areas. In R. Butler, C.M. Hall and J. Jenkins (eds), *Tourism and Recreation in Rural Areas*. Chichester: John Wiley & Sons, pp. 249–58.

Buttle, F. (2001) The CRM value chain. *Marketing Business*, 96: 52–5.

Button, K. (1989) The deregulation of US interstate aviation: an assessment of causes and consequences (Parts 1 & 2). *Transport Reviews*, 9(2): 99–118 and 9(3): 189–215.

Button, K. (1996) Liberalizing European aviation: is there an empty core problem? *Journal of Transport Economics and Policy*, September: 275–91.

Button, K. and Gillingwater, K. (eds) (1983) *Future Transport Policy*. London: Routledge.

Button, K., Haynes, K. and Stough, R. (1998) *Flying into the Future: Air Transport Policy in the European Union*. Cheltenham: Edward Elgar.

CAA (2002) *Consultation on Proposed Amendments to ATOL Regulations: 'Contract Splitting' in Holiday Sales*. London: Civil Aviation Authority.

Callan, R.J. (1998) An attributional approach to hotel selection. Part 2: The customers' perceptions. *Progress in Tourism and Hospitality Research*, 4(1): 67–84.

Campbell, C.K. (1967) An approach to research in recreational geography. In *B.C. Occasional Papers No. 7*, Department of Geography, University of British Columbia, Vancouver, pp. 85–90.

Carey, S. and Gountas, Y. (1999) Changing attitudes to 'mass tourism' products: the UK outbound market perspective. *Journal of Vacation Marketing*, December: 69–75.

Carlzon, J. (1987) *Moments of Truth*. Cambridge, MA: Ballinger.

Cater, E. (1995) Environmental contradictions in sustainable tourism. *The Geographical Journal*, 161(1): 21–8.

Cavaco, C. (1995) Rural tourism: the creation of new tourist spaces. In A. Montanari and A. Williams (eds), *European Tourism: Regions, Spaces and Restructuring*. Chichester: John Wiley & Sons, pp. 129–49.

Caves, R.E. (1997) European airline networks and their implications for airport planning. *Transport Reviews*, 17(2): 121–44.

Chadwick, R. (1994) Concepts, definitions and measures used in travel and tourism research. In J.R.B. Ritchie and C.R. Goeldner (eds), *Travel Tourism and Hospitality Research: A Handbook for Managers and Researchers* (2nd edition) New York: John Wiley and Sons, pp. 65–80.

Child, J. (1977) *Organisation: A Guide to Problems and Practice*. London: Harper & Row.

Chisnall, P.M. (1985) *Marketing: A Behavioural Analysis* (2nd edition). London: McGraw-Hill.

Chon, K. (1990) The role of destination image in tourism: a review and discussion. *The Tourist Review*, 45(2): 2–9.

Choy, D.J.L. (1995) The quality of tourism employment. *Tourism Management*, 16(2): 129–39.

Christopher, M. (1992) *The Strategy of Distribution Management*. Oxford: Butterworth-Heinemann.

Ciborra, C.U. and Lanzara, G.F. (1999) Hospitality and IT. In F. Ljunberg (ed.), *Informatics in the Next Millennium*. Lund: Studentlitteratur.

City of Niagara Falls (2000) *City of Niagara Falls Business News*, Fall/Winter edition. Available at: http://www.city.niagarafalls.on.ca/economicoutreach/newsletter/volume9/#casino

City of Niagara Falls (2001) *City of Niagara Falls Business News*, Fall/Winter edition. Available at: http://www.city.niagarafalls.on.ca/economicoutreach/newsletter/volume11/#casino

Clark, G., Darrall, J., Grove-White, R., Macnaghten, P. and Urry, J. (1994) *Leisure Landscapes – Leisure, Culture and the English Countryside: Challenges and Conflicts*. London: Campaign for the Protection of Rural England.

Clarke, J. (2000) Tourism brands: an exploratory study of the brands box model. *Journal of Vacation Marketing*, 6(4): 329–45.

Clarke, M. (2002) *Contracts of Carriage by Air*. London: Lloyd's of London Press.

Clarke, J. and Elwin, J. (2002) Final Report to the Thames Valley Museums Group. OCTALS at Oxford Brookes University (unpublished).

Clift, S. and Grabowski, P. (1997) *Tourism and Health: Risks, Research and Responses*. London: Pinter.

Cooper, C., Fletcher, J., Gilbert, D., Wanhill, S. and Shepherd, R. (1998) *Tourism Principles and Practice* (2nd edition). London: Addison-Wesley Longman.

Cooper, D.E. (1997) *Ethics: The Classical Readings*. New York: Longman.

Copeland, D. (1991) So you want to build the next SABRE System. *Business Quarterly*, 55(33): 56–60.

Copeland, D. and McKenney, J. (1988) Airline reservation systems: lessons from history. *MIS Quarterly*, 12: 535–70.

Cosgrove, D. and Jackson, P. (1987) New directions in cultural geography. *Area*, 19: 95–101.

Coshall, J. (2003) The threat of terrorism as an intervention on international travel flows. *Journal of Travel Research*, 42(1): 4–12.

Countryside Commission (1995) *Sustainable Rural Tourism: Opportunities for Local Action*. CCP483. Cheltenham: Countryside Commission.

Crick, M. (1992) Life in the informal sector: street guides in Kandy, Sri Lanka. In D. Harrison (ed.), *Tourism and the Less Developed Countries*. London: Belhaven Press, pp. 135–47.

Croall, J. (1995) *Preserve or Destroy: Tourism and the Environment*. London: Calouste Gulbenkian Foundation.

Cronin, L. (1990) A strategy for tourism and sustainable developments. *World Leisure and Recreation*, 32(3): 12–18.

Crossland, D. (1998) *Airtours plc Annual Report and Accounts*. Manchester: Airtours plc.

D'Amore, L.J. (1993) A code of ethics and guidelines for socially and environmentally responsible tourism. *Journal of Travel Research*, 31(3): 64–6.

Dahles, H. (2000) Tourism, small enterprises and community development. In G. Richards and D. Hall (eds), *Tourism and Sustainable Community Development*. London and New York: Routledge.

Dahles, H. (2001) The politics of tourism in Indonesia: modernization, national unity, and cultural diversity. In H. Dahles (ed.), *Tourism, Heritage and National Culture in Java: Dilemmas of a Local Community*. Richmond: Curzon Press, pp. 26–52.

Daily Mail (2002) Big plane order helps easyJet reach for the stars. *Daily Mail* (City and Finance section), 16 October, p. 76.

Daniels, S.E. and Krannich, R.S. (1990) The recreational opportunity spectrum as a conflict management tool. In J. Vining (ed.), *Social Science and Natural Resource Recreation Management*. Boulder, CO: Westview Press, pp. 165–79.

Dann, G.M.S. (2000a) Differentiating destinations in the language of tourism: harmless hype or promotional irresponsibility? *Tourism Recreation Research*, 25(2): 63–75.

Dann, G.M.S. (2000b) National tourist offices and the language of differentiation. In W.C. Garner and D.W. Lime (eds), *Trends in Outdoor Recreation, Leisure and Tourism*. Wallingford: CABI Publishing, pp. 335–45.

Dann, G.M.S. (2001) The self-admitted use of cliché in the language of tourism. *Tourism Culture and Communication*, 3(1): 1–14.

David, F. (1989) How companies define their mission. *Long Range Planning*, 22(1): 90–7.

Davidson, H. (1997) *Even More Offensive Marketing. An Exhilarating Action Guide to Winning in Business*. Harmondsworth: Penguin.

Davidson, R. (2001) Distribution channel analysis for business travel. In D. Buhalis and E. Laws (eds), *Tourism Distribution Channels: Practices, Issues and Transformations*. London: Continuum, pp. 73–86.

Davidson, R. and Maitland, R. (1997) *Tourism Destinations*. London: Hodder and Stoughton.

Davis, G., Wanna, J., Warhurst, J. and Weller, P. (1993) *Public Policy in Australia*. St Leonards: Allen and Unwin.

de Kadt, E. (ed.) (1979) *Tourism: Passport to Development?* Oxford: Oxford University Press.

DEAT (1996) *Development and Promotion of Tourism in South Africa*. Pretoria: Department of Environmental Affairs and Tourism, Government of South Africa.

DEAT (2002) *Guidelines for Responsible Tourism*. Pretoria: Department of Environmental Affairs and Tourism. Available at http://www.icrtourism.org.

Debbage, K. (1994) US airport market concentration and deconcentration. *Transportation Quarterly*, 47(1): 115–36.

Debbage, K. (2000) Air transportation and international tourism: the regulatory and infrastructural constraints of aviation bilaterals and airport landing slots. In M. Robinson, N. Evans, P. Long, R. Sharpley and J. Swarbrooke (eds), *Management, Marketing and the Political Economy of Travel and Tourism*. Sunderland: Business Education Publishers, pp. 67–83.

Debbage, K. (2002) Airport runway slots: limits to growth? *Annals of Tourism Research*, 29(4): 933–51.

Decrop, A. (1999) Tourists' decision-making and behaviour processes. In A. Pizam and Y. Mansfeld (eds), *Consumer Behaviour in Travel and Tourism*. Oxford: Haworth Hospitality Press, pp. 103–32.

DEFRA (1999) *Appraisal of Options on Access to the Open Countryside of England and Wales*. London: Department for Environment, Food and Rural Affairs.

Deutsch, K. (1970) *Politics and Government: How People Decide Their Fate*. Boston, MA: Houghton Mifflin.

Dick, A.S. and Basu, K. (1994) Customer loyalty: toward an integrated conceptual framework. *Journal of the Academy of Marketing Science*, 22(2): 99–114.

Dixit, A.K. and Pindyck, R.S. (1995) The options approach to capital investment. *Harvard Business Review*. May–June: 105–15.

Doolin, B., Burgess, L. and Cooper, J. (2002) Evaluating the use of the Web for tourism marketing: a case study from New Zealand. *Tourism Management*, 23(5): 557–61.

Dowling, R. (1992) Tourism and environmental integration: the journey from idealism to realism. In C. Cooper and A. Lockwood (eds), *Progress in Tourism, Recreation and Hospitality Management* (Vol. 4) London: Belhaven Press, pp. 33–46.

Doyle, P. (1997) Go for robust growth. *Marketing Business*, April: 53.

Dredge, D. (2001) Leisure lifestyles and tourism: socio-cultural, economic and spatial change in Lake Macquarie. *Tourism Geographies*, 3(3): 279–99.

Dror, Y. (1973) The planning process: a facet design. In A. Faludi (ed.), *A Reader in Planning Theory*. Oxford: Pergamon Press, pp. 323–43.

Dwyer, L., Forsyth, P. and Prasada, R. (2000) Price competitiveness of tourism packages to Australia: beyond the 'Big Mac' index. *Asia Pacific Journal of Tourism Research*, (5)2: 50–6.

Eagles, P.F.J. (2001) Evolution of the concept of visitor use management in parks. *Industry and Environment*, 24(3/4): 65–7.

Eagles, P.F.J. (2002) Trends in park tourism: economics, finance and management. *Journal of Sustainable Tourism*, 10(2): 132–53.

easyJet (2001) *Annual Report and Accounts 2001*. Luton: easyJet.

Eber, S. (ed.) (1992) *Beyond the Green Horizon: Principles for Sustainable Tourism*. Godalming: Worldwide Fund for Nature.

EC (1993) *Taking Account of Environment in Tourism Development*. DG XXIII Tourism Unit, Luxembourg: European Commission.

Economic Report of the President (1988) Annual Report of the Council of Economic Advisors. Washington, DC: US Government Printing Office.

Economist (2000) Survey: government and the Internet. The next revolution. *The Economist*, 24 June.

Economist (2001) Survey: air travel. *The Economist*, 10 March.

Edgell, D.L. (1990) *International Tourism Policy*. New York: Van Nostrand Reinhold.

Edgell, D., Ruf, K. and Agarwal, A. (1999) Strategic marketing planning for the tourism industry. *Journal of Travel & Tourism Marketing*, 8(3): 111–20.

Elliott, J. (1997) *Tourism: Politics and Public Sector Management*. London: Routledge.

Embacher, H. (1994) Marketing for agri-tourism in Austria: strategy and realisation in a highly developed tourist destination. *Journal of Sustainable Tourism*, 2(1–2): 61–76.

Emmer, R., Tauck, C., Wilkinson, S. and Moore, R. (1993) Marketing hotels using global distribution systems. *The Cornell Hotel Restaurant Administration Quarterly*, 34(6): 80–9.

Engel, J.F., Blackwell, R.D. and Miniard, P.W. (1993) *Consumer Behaviour* (7th edition). New York: Dryden Press.

Enright, M. (2002) Marketing and conflicting dates for its emergence: Hotchkiss, Bartels, the 'Fifties School' and alternative accounts. *Journal of Marketing*, 18(5–6): 445–61.

ETB (1991) *Tourism and the Environment: Maintaining the Balance*. London: English Tourist Board.

e-tid (2003) Dynamic start for lastminute.com's packaging product. Available at: http://www.e-tid.com/viewarticle.asp?id=19482 (accessed on 22.01.03).

EuroBarometer (1998) *Facts and Figures on the Europeans' Holiday*. EuroBarometer for DG XXIII. Brussels: European Commission.

Faulkner, B. (2001) Towards a framework for tourism disaster management. *Tourism Management*, 22(2): 135–47.

Faulkner, B. and Vikulov, S. (2001) Katherine: washed out one day, back on track the next. A post-mortem on a tourism disaster. *Tourism Management*, 22(4): 331–44.

Federal Aviation Administration (2000) *Airport Activity Statistics*. Washington, DC: US Government Printing Office.

Feldman, J.M. (1997) Easy does it on easyJet. *Air Transport World*, 1: 64–5.

Feldman, J. (1987) CRS in the USA: determining future levels of airline competition. *Travel and Tourism Analyst*, 3: 3–14.

Fennell, D. (1999) *Ecotourism: An Introduction*. London: Routledge.

Fennell, D.A. and Malloy, D.C. (1999) Measuring the ethical nature of tour operations. *Annals of Tourism Research*, 26(4): 928–43.

Financial Times (2001) Ryanair continues to escape turbulence. *Financial Times*, 6 November, p. 28.

Fleischer, A. and Felenstein, D. (2000) Support for rural tourism: does it make a difference? *Annals of Tourism Research*, 27(4): 1007–24.

Forsyth, T. (1995) Business attitudes to sustainable tourism: self-regulation in the UK outgoing tourism industry. *Journal of Sustainable Tourism*, 3(4): 210–31.

Fournier, S. and Mick, D.G. (1999) Rediscovering satisfaction. *Journal of Marketing*, 63: 5–23.

France, L. (1994) Tourism and tourists. In P. Callaghan, P. Long and M. Robinson (eds), *Travel and Tourism* (2nd edition). Sunderland: Business Education Publishers, pp. 1–6.

France, L., Towner, J., Evans, H. and Sowden, C. (1994) The importance of tourism. In P. Callaghan, P. Long and M. Robinson (eds), *Travel and Tourism*, (2nd edition). Sunderland: Business Education Publishers, pp. 25–49.

Frechtling, D. (2001) *Forecasting Tourism Demand*. Oxford: Butterworth Heinemann.

Freeman, R. (1984) *Strategic Management: A Stakeholder Approach*. London: Pitman Publishing.

Gamble, P. and Jones, P. (1991) Quality as a strategic issue. In R. Teare and A. Boer (eds), *Strategic*

Hospitality Management. London: Cassell, pp. 72–82.

Gannon, A. (1994) Rural tourism as a factor in rural community economic development for economies in transition. *Journal of Sustainable Tourism*, 2(1–2): 51–60.

Ganzaroli, A. (2002) *Creating Trust Between Local and Global Systems: Information and Communication Technologies and New Forms of Intermediation Between Local and Global Systems.* Rotterdam: EURIDIS and Faculty of Business Erasmus University.

Garner, J. and Jones, B. (1997) *Countryside Law* (3rd edition). London: Shaw & Sons.

Garrod, B. and Fyall, A. (1998) Beyond the rhetoric of sustainable tourism? *Tourism Management*, 19(3): 199–212.

Gartner, W. (1989) Tourism image: attribute measurement of state tourism products using multidimensional scaling techniques. *Journal of Travel Research*, 28(2): 15–19.

Getz, D. and Page, S. (1997) Conclusions and implications for rural business development. In S. Page and D. Getz (eds), *The Business of Rural Tourism: International Perspectives.* London: International Thomson Business Press, pp. 191–205.

Giddens, A. (1990) *The Consequences of Modernity.* Cambridge: Polity Press.

Gilbert, D.C. (1991) An examination of the consumer behaviour process related to tourism. In C. Cooper (ed.), *Progress in Tourism, Recreation, and Hospitality Management* (Vol. 3). London: Belhaven Press, pp. 78–105.

Gilbert, D. and Joshi, I. (1992) Quality management in the tourism and hospitality industry. In C. Cooper and A. Lockwood (eds), *Progress in Tourism, Recreation and Hospitality Management* (Vol. IV). London: Belhaven Press, pp. 149–68.

Gilbert, E.W. (1939) The growth of inland and seaside health resorts in England. *The Scottish Geographical Magazine*, 55(1): 16–35.

Gillespie, C.H. and Baum, T. (2000) Innovation and creativity in professional higher education: the development of a CD-Rom to support teaching and learning in food and beverage management. *The Scottish Journal of Adult and Continuing Education*, 6(2): 147–67.

Glaesser, D. (2003) *Crisis Management in the Tourism Industry.* Oxford: Butterworth Heinemann.

Go, F. and Pine, R. (1995) *Globalization Strategy in the Hotel Industry.* London: Routledge.

Go, F.M. and Williams, A.P. (1993) Competing and co-operating in the changing tourism channel system. *Journal of Travel & Tourism Marketing*, 2(2/3): 229–48.

Godfrey, K. (1996) Towards sustainability? Tourism in the Republic of Cyprus. In L. Harrison and W. Husbands (eds), *Practising Responsible Tourism: International Case Studies in Tourism Planning, Policy and Development.* Chichester: John Wiley & Sons, pp. 58–79.

Godfrey, K. and Clarke, J. (2000) *The Tourism Development Handbook: A Practical Approach to Planning and Marketing.* London: Cassell.

Gold, J. and Ward, S. (eds) (1994) *Place Promotion: The Use of Publicity and Marketing to Sell Towns and Regions.* Chichester: John Wiley & Sons.

Goodwin, M. (1998) The governance of rural areas: some emerging research issues and agendas. *Journal of Rural Studies*, 14(1): 5–12.

Goodwin, H. (2002) The case for responsible tourism. In T. Jenkins et al. (eds), *Ethical Tourism: Who Benefits?* London: Hodder & Stoughton.

Gospodini, A. (2001) Urban design, urban space morphology, urban tourism: an emerging new paradigm concerning their relationship. *European Planning Studies*, 9(7): 925–34.

Grabowski, P. and Chatterjee, S. (1997) The Indian plague scare of 1994: a case study. In S. Clift and P. Grabowski (eds), *Tourism and Health: Risks, Research and Responses.* London: Pinter, pp. 80–96.

Graham, B., Ashworth, G.J. and Tunbridge, J.E. (1998) *A Geography of Heritage: Power, Culture and Economy.* London: Arnold.

Grant, D. and Mason, S. (2003) *Holiday Law* (3rd edition). London: Sweet & Maxwell.

Grant, D. and Mason, S. (1998b) Tourism and the law. In R. Sharpley (ed.), *The Tourism Business: An Introduction.* Sunderland: Business Education Publishers, pp. 313–44.

Grant, D. and Sharpley, J. (2001) No room at the inn: the hotelkeeper's right to reject or eject guests. *International Travel Law Journal*, 1: 53–61.

Gratton, C. and Dobson, N. (1999) The economic benefits of hosting major sporting events. *Insights*, 11: A31–36.

Gray, J. (1998) *False Dawn: The Delusions of Global Capitalism.* New York: The New Press.

Greer, T. and Wall, G. (1979) Recreational hinterlands: a theoretical and empirical analysis. In G. Wall (ed.), *Recreational Land Use in Southern Ontario.* Department of Geography Publication Series No.14, University of Waterloo, Ontario, 227–45.

Gretzel, U., Yuan YuLan and Fesenmaier, D. (2000) Preparing for the new economy: advertising strategies and change in destination marketing organizations. *Journal of Travel Research*, 39(2): 146–56.

Grönroos, C. (1983) *Strategic Management and Marketing in the Service Sector*. London: Chartwell Brat.

Grönroos, C. (1988) Service quality: the six criteria of good perceived service quality. *Review of Business*, 9(3): 10–13.

Grönroos, C. (2000) *Service Management and Marketing: A Customer Relationship Management Approach*, (2nd edition). Chichester: John Wiley and Sons.

Groth, J.C. and Anderson, R.C. (1997) Capital structure: perspectives for managers. *Management Decision*, 35(7): 552–61.

Guerra, D. and Peroni, G. (1991) *Occupations within the Hotel Tourist Sector within the European Community*. Berlin: CEDEFOP (The European Centre for the Development of Vocational Training).

Gunn, C. (1972) *Vacationscape*. Austin, TX: Bureau of Business Research.

Gunn, C. (1988) *Vacationscape: Designing Tourist Regions* (2nd edition). Austin, TX: Bureau of Business Research, University of Texas.

Gunn, C.A. (1994) *Tourism Planning*. Washington, DC: Taylor and Francis.

Hall, C.M. (1994) *Tourism and Politics: Policy, Power and Place*. Chichester: John Wiley & Sons.

Hall, C.M. (1998) *Introduction to Tourism: Development, Dimensions and Issues* (3rd edition). South Melbourne: Addison-Wesley Longman.

Hall, C.M. (1999) Rethinking collaboration and partnership: a public policy perspective. *Journal of Sustainable Tourism*, 7(3/4): 274–89.

Hall, C.M. (2000) *Tourism Planning: Policies, Processes and Relationships*. Harlow: Prentice Hall.

Hall, C.M. (2001) The development of rural wine and food tourism clusters and networks: factors and issues. Conference Proceedings, *New Directions in Managing Rural Tourism and Leisure: Local Impacts, Global Trends*. Ayr: Scottish Agricultural College.

Hall, C.M. (2002) *Introduction to Tourism: Development, Dimensions and Issues* (4th edition). South Melbourne: Pearson Education.

Hall, C.M. and Jenkins, J. (1995) *Tourism and Public Policy*. London: Routledge.

Hall, C.M. and Jenkins, J. (1998) Rural tourism and recreation policy dimensions. In R. Butler, C.M. Hall and J. Jenkins (eds), *Tourism and Recreation in Rural Areas*. Chichester: John Wiley & Sons.

Hall, C.M. and Kearsley, G.W. (2001) *Tourism in New Zealand: An Introduction*. Melbourne: Oxford University Press.

Hall, C.M. and O'Sullivan, V. (1996) Tourism, political stability and violence. In A. Pizam and Y. Mansfeld (eds), *Tourism, Crime and International Security Issues*. Chichester: John Wiley & Sons, pp. 105–21.

Hall, D. (1999) Destination branding, niche marketing and national image projection in Central and Eastern Europe. *Journal of Vacation Marketing*, 5(3): 227–37.

Hall, R. (1992) The strategic analysis of intangible resources. *Strategic Management Journal*, 13: 135–44.

Hammer, M. and Champy, J. (1993) *Reengineering the Corporation: A Manifesto for Business Revolution*. London: Nicholas Brearley.

Hannigan, J. (1998) *Fantasy City: Pleasure and Profit in the Postmodern Metropolis*. London: Routledge.

Hardin, G. (1968) The tragedy of the commons. *Science*, 162: 1243–8.

Harrington, D. and Lenehan, T. (1998) *Managing Quality in Tourism: Theory and Practice*. Dublin: Oak Tree Press.

Harrington, D. and Power, J. (2001) Quality issues in tourism distribution: practices and prospects. In D. Buhalis and E. Laws (eds), *Tourism Distribution Channels: Practices, Issues and Transformations*. London: Continuum, pp. 103–18.

Harris, Kerr, Forster & Co. and Stanton Robbins & Co. (1966) *Australia's Travel and Tourism Industry 1965*. Sydney: Australian National Travel Association.

Harrison, C. (1991) *Countryside Recreation in a Changing Society*. London: TMS Partnership.

Harvey, D. (1989) From managerialism to entrepreneurialism: the transformation in urban governance in late capitalism. *Geografiska Annaler*, 71: 3–17.

Hashimoto, A. (2002) Tourism and sociocultural development issues. In R. Sharpley and D.J. Telfer (eds), *Tourism and Development: Concepts and Issues*. Clevedon: Channel View Publications, pp. 202–30.

Haulot, A. (1981) Social tourism: current dimensions and future developments. *Tourism Management*, 2: 207–12.

Haywood, K.M. (1998) Economic business cycles and the tourism life-cycle concept. In D. Ioannides and K.G. Debbage (eds), *The Economic Geography of the Tourism Industry*. London and New York: Routledge, pp. 273–84.

Haywood, M. (1988) Responsible and responsive tourism planning in the community. *Tourism Management*, 9(2): 105–18.

Henderson, J. (1994) The structure of the travel and tourism industry. In P. Callaghan, P. Long and M. Robinson (eds), *Travel and Tourism* (2nd edition). Sunderland: Business Education Publishers, pp. 51–8.

Henderson, J. (2002) Managing a tourism crisis in Southeast Asia: the role of national tourism organisations. *International Journal of Hospitality and Tourism Administration*, 3(1): 85–105.

Henderson, J. (2003) Communicating in a crisis: flight SQ 006. *Tourism Management*, 24(3): 279–87.

Hettne, B. (1995) *Development Theory and the Three Worlds*. New York: Longman.

Hjalager, A. (1996) Agricultural diversification into tourism: evidence of a European Community development programme. *Tourism Management*, 17(2): 103–11.

HMSO (2000) *The Countryside and Rights of Way Act 2000*. London: Her Majesty's Stationery Office.

Ho, S.S.M. and Pike, R.H. (1992) The use of risk analysis techniques in capital investment appraisal. In J. Rutteford (ed.), *Financial strategy: Adding Shareholder Value*. Chichester: John Wiley & Sons, pp. 125–43.

Hofmeyr, K. (1997) Employee attitudes: a key dimension in organisational success. *People Dynamics*, 15(8): 30–5.

Hoggart, K., Buller, H. and Black, R. (1995) *Rural Europe: Identity and Change*. London: Arnold.

Hogwood, B. and Gunn, L. (1984) *Policy Analysis for the Real World*. New York: Oxford University Press.

Hogwood, B. and Guy Peters, B. (1985) *Policy Dynamics*. Brighton: Harvester Wheatsheaf.

Holcomb, B. (1993) Revisioning place: de- and re-constructing the image of the industrial city. In G. Kearns and C. Philo (eds), *Selling Places: The City as Cultural Capital, Past and Present*. London: Pergamon Press, pp. 133–43.

Holcomb, B. (1994) City make-overs: marketing the post-industrial city. In J.R. Gold, and S.V. Ward (eds), *Place Promotion: The Use of Publicity and Marketing to Sell Towns and Regions*. Chichester: John Wiley and Sons, pp. 115–31.

Holden, A. (2000) *Environment and Tourism*. London: Routledge.

Hollinger, R. and Schiebler, S. (1995) Crime and Florida's tourists. In *Security and Risks in Travel and Tourism*, Proceedings of the Talk at the Top Conference. Östersund: Mid-Sweden University, pp. 183–215.

Holloway, J.C. (1989) *The Business of Tourism*. London: Pitman Publishing.

Holloway, J.C. (1994) *The Business of Tourism* (4th edition). London: Longman.

Holloway, J.C. (1998) *The Business of Tourism* (5th edition). Harlow: Longman.

Holloway, J.C. (2002) *The Business of Tourism* (6th edition). London: Longman.

Hooley, G.J., Saunders, J.A. and Piercy, N.F. (1998) *Marketing Strategy and Competitive Positioning* (2nd edition). London: Financial Times/Prentice Hall.

Hope, C. and Mühlemann, A. (1998) Total quality, human resource management and tourism. *Tourism Economics*, 4(4): 367–86.

Hopper, L. (1990) Ratting SABRE: new ways to compete on information. *Harvard Business Review*, 68(3) May–June: 118–25.

Horney, N. (1996) Quality and the role of human resources. In M. Olsen, R. Teare and E. Gummesson (eds), *Service Quality in Hospitality Organisations*. London: Cassell, pp. 69–116.

Hosni, E. (2000) *Strategy for Sustainable Tourism Development in the Sahara*. Paris: United Nations Educational Scientific and Cultural Organisation.

Howard, J.A. and Sheth, J.N. (1969) *The Theory of Buyer Behavior*. New York: John Wiley & Sons.

Huang, J. and Min, J. (2002) Earthquake devastation and recovery in tourism: the Taiwan case. *Tourism Management*, 23(2): 145–54.

Hudson, S. (1999) Consumer behaviour related to tourism. In A. Pizam and Y. Mansfeld (eds), *Consumer Behaviour in Travel and Tourism*. Oxford: Haworth Hospitality Press, pp. 7–32.

Hudson, S., Snaith, T., Miller, G.A. and Hudson, P. (2001) Distribution channels in the travel industry: using mystery shoppers to understand the influence of travel agency recommendations. *Journal of Travel Research*, 40 (Nov.): 148–54.

Hughes, H.L. (1984) Government support for tourism in the UK: a different perspective. *Tourism Management*, 5(1): 13–19.

Hunt, J.D. (1975) Image as a factor in tourism development. *Journal of Travel Research*, Winter: 1–7.

Hunter, C. and Green, H. (1995) *Tourism and the Environment: A Sustainable Relationship?* London: Routledge.

ILO (2001a) *Human Resources Development, Employment and Globalisation in the Hotel, Catering and Tourism Sector*. Geneva: International Labour Organisation, Bureau of Publications.

ILO (2001b) *World Employment Report, 2001: life at work in the information economy* (June). Geneva: International Labour Organisation, Bureau of Publications.

Ingham, B. (1993) The meaning of development: interactions between new and old ideas. *World Development*, 21(11): 1803–21.

Ingold, A., McMahon-Beattie, U. and Yeoman, I. (2000) *Yield Management* (2nd edition). London: Continuum.

Inkpen, G. (1998) *Information technology for travel and tourism* (2nd edition). London: Addison-Wesley Longman.

Inskeep, E. (1991) *Tourism Planning: An Integrated and Sustainable Development Approach*. New York: Van Nostrand Reinhold.

Ioannides, D. (1992) Tourism development agents: the Cypriot resort cycle. *Annals of Tourism Research*, 19(4): 711–31.

Ioannides, D. and Debbage, K.G. (eds) (1998) *The Economic Geography of the Tourism Industry*. London and New York: Routledge.

Jansen-Verbeke, M. (1986) Inner-city tourism: resources, tourists and promoters. *Annals of Tourism Research*, 13(1): 79–100.

Jenkins, D. (2000) Getting the measure of London: a personal view from The Eye. *Locum Destination Review*, 1: 17–19.

Jenkins, J. (2001) Statutory authorities in whose interests? The case of Tourism New South Wales, the bed tax, and 'the Games'. *Pacific Tourism Review*, 4(4): 201–18.

Jenkins, J.M. and Hall, C.M. (1997) Tourism planning and policy in Australia. In C.M. Hall, J. Jenkins and G. Kearsley (eds), *Tourism Planning and Policy in Australia and New Zealand: Cases, Issues and Practice*. Sydney: Irwin, pp. 37–48.

Jenkins, J., Hall, C.M. and Troughton, M. (1998) The restructuring of rural economies: rural tourism and recreation as a government response. In R. Butler, C.M. Hall and J. Jenkins (eds), *Tourism and Recreation in Rural Areas*. Chichester: John Wiley & Sons, pp. 43–67.

Jim, C. (1989) Visitor management in recreation areas. *Environmental Conservation*, 16(1): 19–34.

Jithendran, K.J. and Baum, T. (2000) Human resource development and sustainability: the case of India. *International Journal of Tourism Research*, 2(6): 403–36.

Johns, N. (1996) The developing role of quality in the hospitality industry. In M. Olsen, R. Teare and E. Gummesson (eds), *Service Quality in Hospitality Organisations*. London: Cassell, pp. 9–26.

Johnson, G. and Scholes, K. (2001) *Exploring Corporate Strategy*. Hemel Hempstead: Prentice Hall.

Jones, P. (1996) *Introduction to Hospitality Operations*. London: Cassell.

Jones, P. and Lockwood, A. (1989) *The Management of Hotel Operations*. London: Cassell.

Jones, P. and Pizam, A. (eds) (1993) *The International Hospitality Industry: Organisational and Operational Issues*. London: Pitman Publishing.

Judd, D. and Fainstein, S. (1999) *The Tourist City*. New Haven, CT: Yale University Press.

Kahn, A.E. (1988) Airline deregulation – a mixed bag, but a clear success nevertheless. *Transportation Law Journal*, 16: 229–51.

Kandampully, J. (1997) Quality service in tourism. In M. Foley, J. Lennon and G. Maxwell (eds), *Hospitality, Tourism and Leisure Management*. London: Cassell, pp. 3–20.

Kandampully, J. and Duddy, R. (2001) Service system: a strategic approach to gain a competitive advantage in the hospitality and tourism industry. *International Journal of Hospitality & Tourism Administration*, 2(1): 27–48.

Kärcher, K. (1996) The four Global Distribution Systems in the travel and tourism industry. *Electronic Markets*, 6(2): 20–4.

Kärcher, K. (1997) *Reinventing Package Holiday Business*. Berlin: Deutscher Universitäts Verlag.

Kearns, G. and Philo, C. (1993) Culture, history, capital: a critical introduction to the selling of places. In G. Kearns and C. Philo (eds), *Selling Places: The City as Cultural Capital, Past and Present*. London: Pergamon Press, pp. 1–32.

Key Note Market Review (1998) *Travel Agents and Overseas Tour Operators*. Middlesex: Key Note Market Review.

Kilbourne, W.E. (1995) Green advertising: salvation or oxymoron? *Journal of Advertising*, 24(2): 7–19.

Knowles, T. (1996) *Corporate Strategy for Hospitality*. Harlow: Longman.

Knowles, T. (1998) *Hospitality Management* (2nd edition). Harlow: Longman.

Knowles, T. and Egan, D. (2001) Recession and its implications for the international hotel industry. *Travel and Tourism Analyst*, 6: 59–76.

Kotas, R., Teare, R., Logie, J., Jayawardena, C. and Bowen, J. (eds) (1996) *The International Hospitality Business*. London: Cassell.

Kotler, P. (1988) *Marketing Management*. Hemel Hempstead: Prentice Hall.

Kotler, P. (1991) *Marketing Management: Analysis, Planning, Implementation and Control* (7th edition). London: Prentice Hall.

Kotler, P. and Armstrong, G. (1999) *Principles of Marketing* (8th edition). Hemel Hempstead: Prentice Hall.

Kotler, P., Haider, D.H. and Rein, I. (1993) *Marketing Places: Attracting Investment, Industry and Tourism to Cities, States and Nations*. New York: The Free Press.

Krajewski, L. and Ritzman, L. (1996) *Operations Management: Strategy and Analysis*. Reading, MA: Addison-Wesley.

Krippendorf, J. (1987) *The Holiday Makers: Understanding the Impact of Leisure and Travel*. Oxford: Butterworth Heinemann.

Kumar, K. and Fenema, P.C. van (1997) Barrier Model: Towards a Theory of Managing Geographically Distributed Projects. Working Paper. Rotterdam: Rotterdam School of Management.

Lane, J.E. (1993) *The Public Sector: Concepts, Models and Approaches*. London: Sage.

Langer, M. (1997) *Service Quality in Tourism: Measurement Methods and Empirical Analysis*. Frankfurt: Peter Lang.

Law, C. (1993) *Urban Tourism: Attracting Visitors to Large Cities*. London: Mansell.

Law, C. (ed.) (1996) *Tourism in Major Cities*. London: International Thomson Business Press.

Law, C. (2002) *Urban Tourism: The Visitor Economy and the Growth of Large Cities* (2nd edition). London: Continuum.

Lea, J. (1988) *Tourism and Development in the Third World*. London: Routledge.

Leiper, N. (1979) The framework of tourism. *Annals of Tourism Research*, 6(4): 390–407.

Leiper, N. (1990a) Partial industrialization of tourism systems. *Annals of Tourism Research*, 17: 600–5.

Leiper, N. (1990b) *Tourism Systems*. Occasional Paper 2. Auckland: Massey University, Department of Management Systems.

Lickorish, L.J. and Jenkins, C.L. (1997) *An Introduction to Tourism*. Oxford: Butterworth Heinemann.

Lockwood, A., Baker, M. and Ghillyer, A. (eds) (1996) *Quality Management in Hospitality*. London: Cassell.

Lovelock, C.H. and Yip, G.S. (1999) Developing global strategies for service businesses. In J.E.G. Bateson, and K.D. Hoffman (eds), *Managing Services Marketing: Text and Readings* (4th edition). Fort Worth, TX: Harcourt Brace, pp. 365–78.

Lowe, P. and Rüdig, W. (1986) Review article: political ecology and the social sciences. *British Journal of Political Science*, 16: 513–50.

Lubbers, R. (1998) *The Dynamic of Globalization and Nation State and Democracy in the Globalizing World*. Available at: http://www.globalize.org/dynamic.htm (accessed on 30.10.02).

Lubetkin, M. (1999) Bed-and-breakfasts: advertising and promotion. *The Cornell Hotel and Restaurant Administration Quarterly*, 40(4): 84–90.

Luloff, A., Bridger, J., Graefe, A., Sayler, M., Martin, K. and Gitelson, R. (1994) Assessing rural tourism efforts in the United States. *Annals of Tourism Research*, 21(1): 46–64.

Lundgren, J.O. (1982) The tourist frontier of Nouveau Quebec: functions and regional Linkages. *Tourist Review*, 37(2): 10–16.

Lussier, R.N. (1985) Start-up business advice from business owners to would-be entrepreneurs. *SAM Advanced Management Journal*, Winter: 10–13.

MacLeod, G. (2002) From urban entrepreneurialism to a 'revanchist city'? On the spatial injustices of Glasgow's renaissance. *Antipode*, 34(3): 602–24.

Macnaghten, P. and Urry, J. (1998) *Contested Natures*. London: Sage.

Mahesh, V.S. (1993) Human resource planning and development: a focus on service excellence. In T. Baum (ed.), *Human Resource Issues in International Tourism*. Oxford: Butterworth Heinemann, pp. 22–9.

Malecki, E.J. (1997) *Technology and Economic Development: The Dynamics of Local Regional and National Competitiveness* (2nd edition). Harlow: Longman.

Marsden, T. and Murdoch, J. (1998) The shifting nature of rural governance and community participation. *Journal of Rural Studies*, 14(1): 1–4.

Mason, P. and Mowforth, M. (1995) *Codes of Conduct in Tourism*. Occasional Papers in Geography No. 1. Plymouth: University of Plymouth, Department of Geographical Sciences.

Matejka, J.K. (1973) Critical factors in vacation area selection. *Arkansas Business and Economic Review*, 6(1): 17–19.

Mathieson, A. and Wall, G. (1982) *Tourism: Economic, Physical and Social Impacts*. Harlow: Longman.

Mayo, E.J. (1973) Regional images and regional travel behavior. *Proceedings of the 4th Annual Conference, Travel Research Association*. Idaho.

Mazanec, J. (ed.) (1997) *International City Tourism: Analysis and Strategy*. London: Pinter.

McCarthy, E.J. (1960) *Basic Marketing*. Homewood, IL: Irwin.

McCormick, J. (1995) *The Global Environmental Movement* (2nd edition). Chichester: John Wiley & Sons.

McDonald, M.H.B. (1999) *Marketing Plans: How to Prepare Them, How to Use Them* (4th edition). Oxford: Butterworth Heinemann.

McKercher, B. (1993) Some fundamental truths about tourism: understanding tourism's social and environmental impacts. *Journal of Sustainable Tourism*, 1(1): 6–16.

McKercher, B. (2003) Communication. Available at: http://www.trinet-l@hawaii.edu.

McMahon, R.G.P. and Stanger, A.M.J. (1995) Understanding the small enterprise financial objective function. *Entrepreneurship: Theory and Practice*, Summer: 22.

Meethan, K. (2002a) Selling the difference: tourism marketing in Devon and Cornwall, South-west England. In R. Voase (ed.), *Tourism in Western Europe: A Collection of Case Histories*. Wallingford: CABI Publishing, pp. 23–42.

Meethan, K. (2002b) *Tourism in Global Society: Place, Culture, Consumption*. Basingstoke: Palgrave.

Mercer, D. (1979) Victoria's land conservation council and the alpine region. *Australian Geographical Studies*, 17(1): 107–30.

Metaxas, T. (2002) Place/city marketing as a tool for local economic development and city's competitiveness: a comparative evaluation of place marketing policies in European cities. Paper presented at the EURA Conference 'Urban and Spatial European Policies: levels of Territorial Government', 18–20 April, Turin.

Meyer-Cech, K. (2001) Regional co-operation in rural theme trails – lessons learned from the 'Cheese Trail Bregenzerwald' and other Austrian examples. Conference Proceedings, *New Directions in Managing Rural Tourism and Leisure: Local Impacts, Global Trends*. Ayr: Scottish Agricultural College.

Middleton, V.T.C. (1988) *Marketing in Travel and Tourism*. Oxford: Butterworth Heinemann.

Middleton, V.T.C. with Clarke, J. (2001) *Marketing in Travel and Tourism* (3rd edition). Oxford: Butterworth Heinemann.

Mieczkowski, Z. (1995) *Environmental Issues of Tourism and Recreation*. Lanham, MD: University Press of America.

Mihalič, T. (1996) Tourism and warfare – the case of Slovenia. In A. Pizam and Y. Mansfeld (eds), *Tourism, Crime and International Security Issues*. Chichester: John Wiley & Sons, pp. 231–46.

Mihalič T. (2002) Tourism and economic development issues. In R. Sharpley and D. Telfer (eds), *Tourism and Development: Concepts and Issues*. Clevedon: Channel View Publications, pp. 81–111.

Mill, R.C. (1992) *Tourism: The International Business*. Englewood Cliffs, NJ: Prentice-Hall.

Mill, R.C. and Morrison, A.M. (1985) *The Tourism System: An Introductory Text*. Englewood Cliffs, NJ: Prentice-Hall International.

Mill, R. and Morrison, A. (1998) *The Tourism System: An Introductory Text* (3rd edition). Dubuque, IA: Kendell/Hunt Publishing Co.

Mintel (2000) *International Business Travel*. September. London: Mintel.

Mintel (2001) *Ethical Tourism*. October. London: Mintel.

Mintzberg, H., Quinn, J. and Ghoshal, S. (1998) *The Strategy Process*. Hemel Hempstead: Prentice Hall.

Miossec, J.M. (1976) *Elements pour une théorie de l'Espace touristique*. Les Cahiers du Tourisme, C-36. Aix-en-Province: Centre des Hautes Etudes Touristiques.

Mishan, E. (1969) *The Costs of Economic Growth*. Harmondsworth: Penguin.

Mitchell, B. (1997) *Resource and Environmental Management*. Harlow: Longman.

Mitroff, I. (1983) *Stakeholders of the Organisational Mind*. San Fransisco: Jossey-Bass.

Money, R. and Crotts, J. (2003) The effect of uncertainty avoidance on information search, planning and purchases of international travel vacations. *Tourism Management*, 24(2): 191–202.

Morrison, A.M., Mills, J.E., Chuvessiriporn, S. and Ismail, J.A. (2002) Where are we now? An initial analysis of web-based marketing issues affecting travel and tourism. In K. Wöber, A.J. Frew and M. Hitz (eds), *Information and Communication Technologies in Tourism 2002: Proceedings of the International Conference in Innsbruck, Austria, 2002*. Vienna: Springer, pp. 375–86.

Morrison, S.A. and Winston, C. (1995) *The Evolution of the Airline Industry*. Washington, DC: Brookings Institution.

Moscardo, G. (1991) Museum scripts: an example of the application of social cognitive research to tourism. *Australian Psychologist*, 26(3): 158–65.

Moscardo, G. (1999) *Making Visitors Mindful: Principles for Creating Quality Sustainable Visitor Experiences through Effective Communication*. Champaign, IL: Sagamore Publishing.

Moulaert, F. and Nussbaumer, J. (2004) Beyond the learning region: the dialectics of innovation and culture in territorial development. In R.A. Boschama and R. Kloosterman (eds), *Clustering, Learning and Regional Development*. Dordrecht: Kluwer.

Moutinho, L. (1987) Consumer behaviour in tourism. *European Journal of Marketing*, 21(10): 5–44.

Mowforth, M. and Munt, I. (1998) *Tourism and Sustainability: New Tourism in the Third World*. London: Routledge.

Mowl, G. (2002) Tourism and the environment. In R. Sharpley (ed.), *The Tourism Business: An Introduction*. Sunderland: Business Education Publishers, pp. 219–42.

Murphree, M. and Hulme, D. (1998) Communities, wildlife and the 'new conservation' in Africa. *Journal of International Development*, 11(2): 277–85.

Murphy, P. (1985) *Tourism: A Community Approach*. London: Routledge.

Murphy, P. (1988) Community-driven tourism planning. *Tourism Management*, 9(2): 96–104.

Narayan, P. (2000) Fiji's tourism industry: a SWOT analysis. *The Journal of Tourism Studies*, 11(2): 15–24.

Nielsen, A.C. (2002) How New Zealand is perceived by tourist markets. Unpublished report commissioned by Tourism New Zealand, Wellington.

Newsome, D., Moore, S. and Dowling, R. (2002) *Natural Area Tourism: Ecology, Impacts and Management*. Clevedon: Channel View Publications.

Nightingale, M. (1985) The hospitality industry: defining quality for a quality assurance programme – a study of perceptions. *Service Industries Journal*, 5(1): 9–22.

Nordlinger, E. (1981) *On the Autonomy of the Democratic State*. Cambridge, MA: Harvard University Press.

NRI (2002) *Harnessing Tourism for Poverty Elimination: A Blueprint from The Gambia Final Report to DFID*. Chatham: Natural Resources Institute.

Nylander, M. (2001) National policy for rural tourism: the case of Finland. In L. Roberts and D. Hall (eds), *Rural Tourism and Recreation: Principles to Practice*. Wallingford: CABI Publishing, pp. 77–81.

O'Connor, P. (1999) *Electronic Information Distribution in Tourism and Hospitality*. Wallingford: CABI Publishing.

O'Connor, P. (2001) The changing face of hotel electronic distribution. *Travel and Tourism Analyst*, 5: 61–78.

O'Connor, P. and Frew, A. (2000) Evaluating electronic channels of distribution in the hotel sector: a Delphi study. *Information Technology and Tourism*, 3(3/4): 177–93.

O'Connor, P. and Horan, P. (1999) An analysis of web reservations facilities in the top 50 international hotel chains. *International Journal of Hospitality Information Technology*, 1(1): 77–87.

OECD (1974) *Government Policy in the Development of Tourism*. Paris: Organisation for Economic Co-operation and Development.

OECD (1981) *The Impact of Tourism on the Environment*. Paris: Organisation for Economic Co-operation and Development.

Olmeda, I. and Sheldon, P.J. (2001) Data mining techniques and applications for tourism Internet marketing. *Journal of Travel and Tourism Marketing*, 11(2/3): 1–20.

Olsen, M. (1991) *Strategic Management in the Hospitality Industry: A Literature Review*. London: Belhaven Press.

Olsen, M., Teare, R. and Gummesson, E. (eds) (1996) *Service Quality in Hospitality Organisations*. London: Cassell.

O'Neill, M. and Fitz, F. (1996) Northern Ireland tourism: what chance now? *Tourism Management*, 17(2): 161–3.

Opperman, M. (1996) Rural tourism in southern Germany. *Annals of Tourism Research*, 23(1): 86–102.

Opperman, M. and Chon, K. (1997) *Tourism in Developing Countries*. London: International Thomson Business Press.

Orbasli, A. (2001) *Tourists in Historic Towns: Urban Conservation and Heritage Management*. London and New York: E & FN Spon.

O'Toole, K. (2002) Open channels. *Airline Business*, January: 56–8.

Oum, T.A. and Zhang, A. (2001) Key aspects of global strategic alliances and the impacts on the future of Canadian airline industry. *Journal of Air Transport Management*, 7: 287–301.

Padgett, M. and Hall, C.M. (2001) Tourism at the polls. In C.M. Hall and G. Kearsley (eds), *Tourism in New Zealand: An Introduction*. Melbourne: Oxford University Press, pp. 99–104.

Page, S. (1995) *Urban Tourism*. London: Routledge.

Page, S.J. (1999) *Transport and Tourism*. Harlow: Addison-Wesley Longman.

Page, S. (2000) Urban tourism. In C. Ryan and S. Page (eds), *Tourism Management: Towards the New Millennium*. Oxford: Pergamon Press, pp. 197–202.

Page, S. and Getz, D. (eds) (1997) *The Business of Rural Tourism: International Perspectives*. London: International Thomson Business Press.

Page, S. and Hall, C.M. (2003) *Managing Urban Tourism*. Harlow: Pearson Education.

Pannett, A. and Boella, M. (1999) *Principles of Hospitality Law* (2nd edition). London: Cassell.

Parasuraman, A., Zeithaml, V. and Berry, L. (1985) A conceptual model of service quality and its implications for future research. *Journal of Marketing*, 49(4): 41–50.

Parasuraman, A., Zeithaml, V. and Berry, L. (1988) SERVQUAL: a multi-item scale for measuring consumer perceptions of quality service. *Journal of Retailing*, 64(1): 12–40.

Parviainen, J., Pöysti, E. and Kehitys, S. (1995) *Towards Sustainable Tourism in Finland*. Helsinki: Finnish Tourism Board.

Payne, D. and Dimanche, F. (1996) Towards a code of conduct for the tourism industry: an ethics model. *Journal of Business Ethics*, 15: 997–1007.

Peacock, M. (1995) *Information Technology in Hospitality*. London: Cassell.

Pearce, D. (1989) *Tourist Development* (2nd edition). Harlow: Longman.

Pearce, D. (1992) *Tourist Organizations*. Harlow: Longman Scientific and Technical.

Pender, L.J. (ed.) (1999) *Marketing Management for Travel and Tourism*. Cheltenham: Stanley Thornes.

Pender, L.J. (2001) *Travel Trade and Transport: An Introduction*. London: Continuum.

Pigram, J. (1983) *Outdoor Recreation and Resource Management*. London: Croom Helm.

Pigram, J. (1990) Sustainable tourism – policy considerations. *Journal of Tourism Studies*, 1(2): 2–9.

Pigram, J. (1993) Planning for tourism in rural areas: bridging the policy implementation gap. In D. Pearce and R. Butler (eds), *Tourism Research: Critiques and Challenges*. London: Routledege, pp. 156–74.

Pike, S. (2002a) Destination image analysis – a review of 142 papers from 1973 to 2000. *Tourism Management*, 23(5): 541–9.

Pike, S. (2002b) ToMA as a measure of competitive advantage for short break holiday destinations. *Journal of Tourism Studies*, 13(1): 9–19.

Pike, S. and Ryan, C. (2003) Dimensions of short break destination attractiveness: a comparison of cognitive, affective and conative perceptions. In D. Braithwaite and P. Hobson (eds), *Riding the Wave of Tourism and Hospitality*. Refereed papers presented at the 2003 Conference, 'Riding the Wave of Tourism and Hospitality', Council of Australian Universities in Tourism and Hospitality Education, Southern Cross University, Lismore, NSW.

Pizam, A. and Mansfeld, Y. (eds) (1996) *Tourism, Crime and International Security Issues*. Chichester: John Wiley & Sons.

Pollock, A. (1998) Creating intelligent destinations for wired customers. In D. Buhalis, A.M. Tjoa and J. Jafari, (eds), *Information and Communications Technologies in Tourism* (ENTER 1998 Proceedings). Vienna: Springer-Verlag, pp. 235–48.

Poon, A. (1993) *Tourism, Technology and Competitive Strategies*. Wallingford: CABI Publishing.

Poon, A. (2001) The future of travel agents. *Travel and Tourism Analyst*, 3: 57–80.

Porter, M. (1980) *Competitive Strategy: Techniques for Analyzing Industries and Competitors*. New York: The Free Press.

Porter, M. (1987) From competitive advantage to corporate strategy. *Harvard Business Review*, May 1: 43–59.

Porter, M. (1998) *On Competition: A Harvard Business Review Book*. Boston, MA: Harvard Business School Publishing.

Preble, J.F., Reichel, A. and Hoffman, R.C. (2000) Strategic alliances for competitive advantage: evidence from Israel's hospitality and tourism industry. *International Journal of Hospitality Management*, 19(3): 327–41.

Pride, W., Hughes, R., Kapoor, J., Canzer, B. and Powers, R. (1999) *Business* (Canadian edition). Scarborough, ON: International Thomson Publishing.

Prideaux, B. (1993) Possible effects of new transport technologies on the tourism industry in the 21st Century. *Papers of the Australasian Transport Research Forum* (University of Queensland), 18: 245–58.

Prideaux, B. (1999) Tourism perspectives of the Asian financial crisis: lessons for the future. *Current Issues in Tourism*, 2(4): 279–93.

Prideaux, B. (2000) The role of the transport system in destination development. *Tourism Management*, 21(1): 53–63.

Prideaux, B., Wei, S. and Ruys, H. (2001) The senior drive tour market in Australia. *Journal of Vacation Marketing*, 7(3): 209–20.

Pustay, M.W. (1993) Towards a global airline industry: prospects and impediments. *Logistics and Transportation Review*, 23(1): 103–28.

QAA (2000) *Hospitality, Leisure, Sport and Tourism: Subject Benchmark Statement*. Gloucester: Quality Assurance Agency.

Rachman, Z.M. and Richins, H. (1997) The status of New Zealand tour operator Web sites. *Journal of Tourism Studies*, 8(2): 62–77.

Radisson Hotels and Resorts (2002) *Responsible Business Report*.

Rapert, M.I. and Wren, B.M. (1998) Service quality as a competitive opportunity. *The Journal of Services Marketing*, 12(3): 223–35.

Redclift, M. (1987) *Sustainable Development: Exploring the Contradictions*. London: Routledge.

Reid, D. (1995) *Sustainable Development: An Introductory Guide*. London: Earthscan.

Renshaw, M.B. (1997) *The Travel Agent* (2nd edition). Sunderland: Business Education Publishers.

Richards, G. (1995) Retailing travel products: bridging the information gap. *Progress in Tourism and Hospitality Research*, 1: 17–29.

Richards, G. and Hall, D. (2000) The community: a sustainable concept in tourism development? In G. Richards and D. Hall (eds), *Tourism and Sustainable Community Development*. London and New York: Routledge. pp. 1–14.

Richter, L. (1980) The political uses of tourism: a Phillippine case study. *The Journal of Developing Areas*, 14: 237–57.

Richter, L. (1989) *The Politics of Tourism in Asia*. Honolulu: University of Hawaii Press.

Richter, L. (1992) Political instability and tourism in the Third World. In D. Harrison (ed.), *Tourism and the Less Developed Countries*. London: Bellhaven Press, pp. 35–46.

Richter, L. and Waugh, W. (1983) Tourism, politics and political science: a case of not so benign neglect. *Annals of Tourism Research*, 10: 313–15.

Richter, L. and Waugh, W. (1986) Terrorism and tourism as logical companions. *Tourism Management*, 7(4): 230–8.

Riege, A.M., Perry, C. and Go, F.M. (2001) Partnerships in international travel and tourism marketing: a systems-oriented approach between Australia, New Zealand, Germany and the United Kingdom. *Journal of Travel and Tourism Marketing*, 11(1): 59–77.

Ries, A. and Trout, J. (1986) *Positioning: The Battle for Your Mind*. New York: McGraw-Hill.

Rifkin, J. (2000) *The New Culture of Hypercapitalism: Where All of Life is a Paid for Experience*. New York: Putnam.

Roberts, L. and Hall, D. (2001) *Rural Tourism and Recreation: Principles to Practice*. Wallingford: CABI Publishing.

Robinson, H. (1976) *A Geography of Tourism*. London: MacDonald and Evans.

Rosenbloom, B. (1987) *Marketing Channels: A Management View* (3rd edition). London: The Dryden Press.

Ross, S.A., Westerfield, R.W. and Jordan, B.D. (2003) *Fundamentals of Corporate Finance*. (international edition). New York: McGraw-Hill.

Rounce, J. (1987) International hotel product branding: segmenting the market place. *Travel & Tourism Analyst*, 1: 13–22.

Russo, A.P., Boniface, P. and Shoval, N. (2001) Tourism management in heritage cities. *Annals of Tourism Research*, 28(3): 824–6.

Ryan, C. (1991) Tourism, terrorism and violence: the risks of wider world travel. *Conflict Studies 244*. London: Research Institute for the Study of Conflict and Terrorism.

Ryan, C. (1994) The motivations of holiday makers. Unpublished PhD thesis. Birmingham: Aston Management School, Aston University of Birmingham.

Ryan, C. (2000) Web pages and tourism, 2000. Paper presented at PATA Internet Marketing Seminar, organised by PATA Korea Chapter, PATA Asia Division, KOFTA, CO-EX International Conference Center, Seoul, Korea. *PATA Internet Marketing Seminar*. Seoul: PATA Asian Division, pp. 63–75.

Ryan, C. (2002) The politics of branding cities and regions: the case of New Zealand. In N. Morgan, A. Pritchard and R. Pride (eds), *Destination Branding: Creating the Unique Destination Proposition*. Oxford: Butterworth Heinemann, pp. 66–86.

Santana, G. (2001) Globalisation, safety and national security. In S. Wahab and C. Cooper (eds), *Tourism in the Age of Globalisation*. London: Routledge, pp. 213–41.

Sautter, E. and Leisen, B. (1999) Managing stakeholders. A tourism planning model. *Annals of Tourism Research*, 26(2): 312–28.

Schild, H.-H. (1997) *Planning Cultural Tourism in Europe: A presentation of Theories and Cases*. In D. Dodd and A. van Hemel (eds). Amsterdam: BoekmanStichting.

Schwella, E. (2000) Globalisation and human resource management: context, challenges and change. *Administratio Publica*, 10(2): 88–105.

Selbst, P. (1978) *The Containment and Control of Organizational Crisis*. New York: Van Nostrand Reinhold.

Self, P. (1977) *Administrative Theories and Politics* (2nd edition). London: George Allen & Unwin.

Sen, A. (1999) *Development as Freedom*. New York: Anchor Books.

Sharpe, W. (1964) Capital asset prices: a theory of market equilibrium under conditions of risk. *Journal of Finance*, 19: 768–83.

Sharpley, J. and Grant, D. (2000) From pack horse to package holidays: who is a traveller? *International Travel Law Journal*, 3: 159–83.

Sharpley, R. (1996) *Tourism and Leisure in the Countryside* (2nd edition). Huntingdon: Elm Publications.

Sharpley, R. (2000) Tourism and sustainable development: exploring the theoretical divide. *Journal of Sustainable Tourism*, 8(1): 1–19.

Sharpley, R. (2001a) Sustainability and the political-economy of tourism in Cyprus. *Tourism*, 49(3): 241–54.

Sharpley, R. (2001b) Tourism in Cyprus: challenges and opportunities. *Tourism Geographies*, 3(1): 64–85.

Sharpley, R. (2002) Sustainability: a barrier to tourism development. In R. Sharpley and D.J. Telfer (eds), *Tourism and Development: Concepts and Issues*. Clevedon: Channel View Publications, pp. 319–37.

Sharpley, R. and Craven, B. (2001) The 2001 foot and mouth crisis – rural economy and tourism policy implications: a comment. *Current Issues in Tourism*, 4(6): 527–37.

Sharpley, R., Sharpley, J. and Adams, J. (1996) Travel advice or trade embargo? The impacts and implications of official travel advice. *Tourism Management*, 17(1): 1–7.

Shaw, G. and Williams, A.M. (1998) Entrepreneurship, small business culture and tourism development. In D. Ioannides and K.G. Debbage (eds), *The Economic Geography of the Tourism Industry*. London and New York: Routledge, pp. 235–55.

Shaw, G. and Williams, A. (2002) *Critical Issues in Tourism: A Geographical Perspective* (2nd edition). Oxford: Blackwell.

Sheen, L. (1998) Is consumers' money really safe in a trust? *International Travel Law Journal*, 1: 57.

Sheldon, P. (1993) Destination information systems. *Annals of Tourism Research*, 20(4): 633–49.

Sheldon, P. (1997) *Information Technologies for Tourism*. Wallingford: CABI Publishing.

Sheldon, P.J., Wöber, K.W. and Fesenmaier, D.R. (eds) (2001) *Information and communication technologies in tourism 2001: Proceedings of the International Conference in Montreal, Canada, 2001*. Vienna: Springer.

Sherry, J. (1993) *The Laws of Innkeepers* (3rd edition). Ithaca, NY: Cornell University Press.

Sheth, J.N., Mittal, B. and Newman, B.I. (1999) *Customer Behaviour: Consumer Behaviour and Beyond*. London: The Dryden Press.

Short, J. (1991) *Imagined Country: Society, Culture and Environment*. London: Routledge.

Sickle, K. van and Eagles, P.F.J. (1998) Budgets, pricing policies and user fees in Canadian parks' tourism. *Tourism Management*, 19(3): 225–35.

Sigala, M. (2002) Internet and the virtual marketspace: implications for building competitive e-commerce strategies in the hospitality industry. *Journal of Hospitality and Tourism Management*, 9(2): 207–16.

Silver, I. (1993) Marketing authenticity in Third World countries. *Annals of Tourism Research*, 20(2): 302–18.

Simpson, F. and Chapman, M. (1999) A comparison of urban governance and planning policy: East looking West. *Cities*, 16: 353–64.

Slattery, P. (1991) Hotel branding in the 1990s. *Travel & Tourism Analyst*, 1: 23–35.

Smith, C. and Jenner, P. (1998) Tourism and the Internet. *Travel and Tourism Analyst*, 1: 62–81.

Smith, C. and Jenner, P. (1999) Barcelona. *TTI City Reports*, No. 4: 1–17.

Smith, V. (ed.) (1977) *Hosts and Guests: The Anthropology of Tourism*. Philadelphia: University of Pennsylvania Press.

Smith, V. (1989) Preface. In V. Smith (ed.), *Hosts and Guests: The Anthropology of Tourism* (2nd edition). Philadelphia: University of Pennsylvania Press, pp. ix–xi.

Snipes, R. (1999) A re-examination of the significance of employee job attitudes on customer satisfaction in the services sector. Proceedings of the Annual Meeting – Western Decision Sciences Institute. Puerto Vallarta, Mexico, pp. 502–5.

Sofield, T. and Getz, D. (1997) Rural tourism in Australia: the Undara experience. In S. Page and D. Getz (eds), *The Business of Rural Tourism: International Perspectives*. London: International Thomson Business Press, pp. 143–61.

Sönmez, S. (1998) Tourism, terrorism and political instability. *Annals of Tourism Research*, 25(2): 416–56.

Sönmez, S. and Graefe, S. (1998a) Influence of terrorism risk on foreign tourism decisions. *Annals of Tourism Research*, 25(1): 112–44.

Sönmez, S. and Graefe, S. (1998b) Determining future travel behaviour from past travel experience and perceptions of risk and safety. *Journal of Travel Research*, 37(2): 172–7.

Sönmez, S., Apostolopoulos, Y. and Tarlow, P. (1999) Tourism in crisis: managing the effects of terrorism. *Journal of Travel Research*, 38(1): 13–18.

Southgate, C. and Sharpley, R. (2002) Tourism, development and the environment. In R. Sharpley and D. Telfer (eds), *Tourism and Development: Concepts and Issues*. Clevedon: Channel View Publications, pp. 231–62.

Souza, A.R. and Stutz, F.P. (1994) *The World Economy Resources: Location, Trade and Development*. New York: Macmillan.

Spann, R.N. (1979) *Government Administration in Australia*. Sydney: George Allen & Unwin.

Sparkes, R. (1995) *The Ethical Investor*. London: Harper Collins.

Spearritt, P. (2002) *Marketing Cities: Icons, Brands and Slogans*. Brisbane: Social Change Online, The Brisbane Institute. Available at: http://www.brisinst.org.au/resources/spearritt_peter_cities.html.

Squire, S. (1994) The cultural values of literary tourism. *Annals of Tourism Research*, 21: 103–20.

Stern, L., El-Ansary, A. and Cougwas, A. (1996) *Marketing Channels* (5th edition). Englewood Cliffs, NJ: Prentice-Hall.

Stoker, G. (1997) Public–private partnerships and urban governance. In G. Stoker (ed.), *Partners in Urban Governance: European and American Experiences*. Basingstoke: Macmillan, pp. 1–21.

Stone, P. (2000) Countryside ideologies and rural governance: the case study of the Lake District. Unpublished MSc thesis, University of Northumbria.

Su WenYu and Bowen, J.T. (2000) Restaurant customer complaint behavior. *Journal of Restaurant & Foodservice Marketing*, 4(2): 35–65.

Sull, D. (1999) Case study: easyJet's $500 million gamble. *European Management Journal*, 17(1), February: 20–38.

Swarbrooke, J. (1999) *Sustainable Tourism Management*. Wallingford: CABI Publishing.

Swarbrooke, J. (2000) Tourism, economic development and urban regeneration: a critical evaluation. In M. Robinson, R. Sharpley, N. Evans, P. Long and J. Swarbrooke (eds), *Reflections on International Tourism: Developments in Urban and Rural Tourism*. Sunderland: Business Education Publishers, pp. 269–85.

Synergy (2000) *Tourism Certification: An Analysis of Green Globe 21 and other Tourism Certification Programmes*. London: Synergy for WWF-UK.

Taylor, G. (1995) The community approach: does it really work? *Tourism Management*, 16(7): 487–9.

Taylor, P. (1998) Mixed strategy pricing behaviour in the UK package tour industry. *International Journal of the Economics of Business*, 5(1): 29–46.

Teare, R. and Olsen, M. (eds) (1992) *International Hospitality Management: Corporate Strategy in Practice*. London: Pitman Publishing.

Tearfund (2000a) *Tourism an Ethical Issue: Market Research Report*. London: Tearfund.

Tearfund (2000b) *Don't Forget Your Ethics!* London: Tearfund.

Tearfund (2001) *Tourism: Putting Ethics into Practice*. London: Tearfund.

Tearfund (2002) *Worlds Apart*. London: Tearfund.

Telfer, D.J. (1996) Food purchases in a five-star hotel: a case study of the Aquila Prambanan Hotel, Yogyakarta. *Tourism Economics*, 2(4): 321–38.

Telfer, D.J. (2000) Agritourism: a path to community development? The case of Bangunkerto, Indonesia. In G. Richards and D. Hall (eds), *Tourism and Sustainable Community Development*. London: Routledge, pp. 242–57.

Telfer, D.J. (2002a) The evolution of tourism and development theory. In R. Sharpley and D.J. Telfer (eds), *Tourism and Development: Concepts and Issues*. Clevedon: Channel View Publications, pp. 35–78.

Telfer, D.J. (2002b) Tourism and regional development issues. In R. Sharpley and D.J. Telfer (eds), *Tourism and Development: Concepts and Issues*. Clevedon: Channel View Publications, pp. 112–48.

Testoni, L. (2001) Planning for sustainable tourism. *Pacific Tourism Review*, 4: 191–9.

The Economist (2001) A survey of air travel. *The Economist*, 10 March: 1–22.

The Independent (2002) Anger over package holiday 'extras'. *The Independent*, 11 July.

Thomas, R. and Long, J. (2001) Tourism and economic regeneration: the role of skills development. *International Journal of Tourism Research*, 3(3): 229–40.

Thompson, R.J. and Cooper, P.D. (1979) Additonal evidence on the limited size of evoked and inept sets of travel destination. *Journal of Travel Research*, 17(3): 23–5.

Thurlby, B. (1998) Competitive forces are also subject to change. *Management Decision*, 36(1): 19–24.

Thurot, J.M. (1980) *Capacité de charge et production touristique*. Etudes et Mémoires No. 43, Aix-en-Province: Centre des Hautes Etudes Touristiques.

Towner, J. (1996) *An Historical Geography of Recreation and Tourism in the Western World, 1540–1940*. Chichester: John Wiley & Sons.

Tremblay, P. (1998) The economic organization of tourism. *Annals of Tourism Research*, 25(4): 837–59.

Tribe, J. (1997) *Corporate Strategy for Tourism*. London: Thomson Learning.

Tribe, J. (1999) *The Economics of Leisure and Tourism*. Oxford: Butterworth Heinemann.

Tribe, J. and Snaith, T. (1998) From SERVQUAL to HOLSAT: holiday satisfaction in Varadero, Cuba. *Tourism Management*, 19(1): 25–34.

Tribe, J., Font, X., Griffiths, N., Vickery, R. and Yale, K. (2000) *Environmental Management for Rural Tourism and Recreation*. London: Cassell.

Trotter, R. (2001) Heritage tourism. In N. Douglas, N. Douglas and R. Derrett (eds), *Special Interest Tourism*. Brisbane and New York: John Wiley & Sons, pp. 140–64.

Truitt, L., Teye, V. and Farris, M. (1991) The role of computer reservation systems: international implications for the tourism industry. *Tourism Management*, 12(1): 21–36.

TTI (2000) *City Reports* (No.1). London: Travel and Tourism Intelligence.

TTI (2001) *The International Hotel Industry* (3rd edition). London: Travel & Tourism Intelligence.

Turner, L. and Ash, J. (1975) *The Golden Hordes: International Tourism and the Pleasure Periphery*. London: Constable.

Tyler, D. (2000) A framework for analysing urban tourism. In M. Robinson, R. Sharpley, N. Evans, P. Long and J. Swarbrooke (eds), *Reflections on International Tourism: Developments in Urban and Rural Tourism*. Sunderland: Business Education Publishers, pp. 287–99.

Tyler, D., Guerrier, Y. and Robertson, M. (1998) *Managing Tourism in Cities: Policy, Process and Practice*. Chichester: John Wiley & Sons.

Ujma, D. (2001) Distribution channels for tourism: theories and issues. In D. Buhalis and E. Laws (eds), *Tourism Distribution Channels: Practices, Issues and Transformations*. London: Continuum, pp. 33–52.

UK Civil Aviation Authority (1998) *The Single European Aviation Market: The First Five Years*. CAP 685. London: CAA.

Um, S. and Crompton, J.L. (1990) Attitude determinants in tourism destination choice. *Annals of Tourism Research*, 25(3): 551–78.

Urry, J. (1990) *The Tourist Gaze: Leisure and Travel in Contemporary Societies*. London: Sage.

US General Accounting Office (1990) *Airline Competition: Higher Fares and Reduced Competition at Concentrated Airports*. Washington, DC: GAO.

US General Accounting Office (1993) *International Aviation: Measures by European Community Could Limit US Airlines Ability to Compete Abroad*. Washington, DC: GAO.

US General Accounting Office (1996) *Airline Deregulation: Changes in Airfares, Service, and Safety at Small, Medium-sized, and Large Communities*. Washington, DC: GAO.

US General Accounting Office (1999) *Airline Deregulation: Changes in Airfares, Service Quality, and Barriers to Entry*. Washington, DC: GAO.

van Dam, Y.K. and Apeldoorn, P.A.C. (1996) Sustainable marketing. *Journal of Macromarketing*, 16(2): 45–56.

Van den Berg, L., Braun, E. and Van der Meer, J. (1997) *Metropolitan Organising Capacity: Experiences with Organising Major Projects in European Cities*. Aldershot: Ashgate.

Vellas, F. and Becherel, L. (1995) *International Tourism*. London: Macmillan.

Vernon, R. (1966) International investment and international trade in the product cycle. *Quarterly Journal of Economics*, 80: 190–207.

Vernon, R. (1979) The product cycle hypothesis in a new international environment. *Oxford Bulletin of Economics and Statistics*, 41: 255–67.

Vrancken, P. (2000) Travel agency liability in South Africa. *International Travel Law Journal*, 4: 203–6.

Wahab, S. (1996) Tourism and terrorism: synthesis of the problem with emphasis on Egypt. In A. Pizam and Y. Mansfeld (eds), *Tourism, Crime and International Security Issues*. Chichester: John Wiley & Sons, pp. 175–86.

Walker, O.C., Boyd, A.W. and Larreche, J.C. (1999) *Marketing Strategy: Planning and Implementation*. New York: Irwin McGraw Hill.

Wall, G. (1996) Terrorism and tourism: an overview and Irish example. In A. Pizam and Y. Mansfeld (eds), *Tourism, Crime and International Security Issues*. Chichester: John Wiley & Sons, pp. 143–58.

Wall, G. (1997) Sustainable tourism – unsustainable development. In S. Wahab and J. Pigram (eds), *Tourism, Development and Growth: The Challenge of Sustainability*. London: Routledge, pp. 33–49.

Walrond, C. (2000) Encounter norms for backcountry trout anglers in New Zealand. *International Journal of Wilderness*, 6(2): 29–33.

Walrond, C.W. (2001) Encounter levels: a study of backcountry river trout anglers in Nelson–Marlborough and Otago. Unpublished PhD thesis, Centre for Tourism Research, Otago University, Dunedin, New Zealand.

Wanhill, S.R.C. (1987) UK – politics and tourism. *Tourism Management*, 8(1): 54–8.

Wanhill, S. (1998) Intermediaries. In C. Cooper, J. Fletcher, D. Gilbert, R. Shepherd, and S. Wanhill (eds), *Tourism: Principles and Practice* (2nd edition). London: Longman, pp. 423–46.

Wardell, D. (1987) Airline reservation systems in the USA: CRS agency dealerships and the gold handcuff. *Travel and Tourism Analyst*, 1(January): 45–56.

Wardell, D. (1998) The impact of electronic distribution on travel agents. *Travel and Tourism Analyst*, 2: 41–55.

Warhurst, C., Nickson, D., Witz, A. and Cullen, A.M. (2000) Aesthetic labour in interactive service work: some case study evidence from the 'New' Glasgow. *Service Industries Journal*, 20(3): 1–18.

WCED (World Commission on Environment and Development) (1987) *Our Common Future*. New York: Oxford University Press.

Weaver, D. (2000) Sustainable tourism: is it sustainable? In B. Faulkner, G. Moscardo and E. Laws (eds), *Tourism in the 21st Century: Lessons from Experience*. London: Continuum, pp. 300–11.

Weaver, D. and Opperman, M. (2000) *Tourism Management*. Brisbane: John Wiley & Sons.

Webster, F.E. (1997) The future role of marketing in the organization. In D.R. Lehmann and K.E. Jocz (eds), *Reflections on the Futures of Marketing*. Cambridge, MA: Marketing Science Institute.

Wells, W. and Gubar, G. (1966) Life cycle concepts in marketing research. *Journal of Marketing Research*, November: 355–63.

Werthner, H. and Klein, S. (1999) *Information Technology and Tourism: A Challenging Relationship*. Vienna and New York: Springer Verlag.

Wheatcroft, S. (1994) *Aviation and Tourism Policies: Balancing the Benefits*. London: Routledge.

Wheeler, B. (1994) Egotourism, sustainable tourism and the environment: a symbiotic, symbolic or shambolic relationship. In A.V. Seaton (ed.), *Tourism: the State of the Art*. Chichester: John Wiley & Sons.

Wight, P. (1998) Tools for sustainability analysis in planning and managing tourism and recreation in the destination. In C.M. Hall and A. Lew (eds), *Sustainable Tourism: A Geographical Perspective*. Harlow: Longman, pp. 75–91.

Williams, A. and Shaw, G. (1998a) *Tourism and Economic Development: European Experiences* (3rd edition). Chichester: John Wiley & Sons.

Williams, A. and Shaw, G. (1998b) Tourism and the environment: sustainability and economic restructuring. In C.M. Hall and A. Lew (eds), *Sustainable Tourism: A Geographical Perspective*. Harlow: Longman, pp. 49–59.

Williams, A.M. and Shaw, G. (1988) Tourism: candyfloss industry or job generator. *Town Planning Review*, 59(1): 81–103.

Williams, H. and Watts, C. (2002) *Steps to Success: Global Good Practices in Tourism Human Resources*. Toronto: Prentice-Hall.

Wilson, S., Fesenmaier, D., Fesenmaier, J. and van Es, J. (2001) Factors for success in rural tourism development. *Journal of Travel Research*, 40(2): 132–8.

Witt, C. and Mühlemann, A. (1994) The implementation of total quality management in tourism: some guidelines. *Tourism Management*, 15(6): 416–24.

de Witt, R. and Meyer, R. (1998) *Strategy: Process, Content, Context*. London: Thomson International Press.

Witt, S., Brooke, M. and Buckley, P. (1992) *The Management of International Tourism* (2nd edition). London: Routledge.

Witt, S. and Mouthino, L. (1995) *Tourism Marketing and Management Handbook*. Hemel Hempstead: Prentice Hall.

Wöber, K. (2000) Standardising city tourism statistics. *Annals of Tourism Research*, 27(1): 51–68.

Wöber, K., Frew, A.J. and Hitz, M. (eds) (2002) *Information and communication technologies in tourism 2002: Proceedings of the International Conference in Innsbruck, Austria, 2002*. Vienna: Springer.

Wood, K. and House, S. (1991) *The Good Tourist: A Worldwide Guide for the Green Traveller*. London: Mandarin.

Wood, R.C. (1997) *Working in Hotels and Catering* (2nd edition). London: Routledge.

Woodside, A.G. and King, R.I. (2001) An updated model of travel and tourism purchase-consumption systems. *Journal of Travel and Tourism Marketing*, 10(1): 3–27.

Woodside, A.G. and Lyonski, S. (1989) A general model of traveller destination choice. *Journal of Travel Research*, 27(4): 8–14.

Woodside, A.G. and Sherrell, D. (1977) Traveler evoked, inept and inert sets of vacation destinations. *Journal of Travel Research*, 16: 14–18.

WTO (1988) *Guidelines for the Transfer of New Technologies in the Field of Tourism*. Madrid: World Tourism Organisation.

WTO (1993) *Sustainable Tourism Development: A Guide for Local Planners*. Madrid: World Tourism Organisation.

WTO (1995) *Global Distribution Systems in the Tourism Industry*. Madrid: World Tourism Organisation.

WTO (1997) *Tourism 2020 Vision: Executive Summary*. Madrid: World Tourism Organisation.

WTO (1999a) *Changes in Leisure Time*. Madrid: World Tourism Organisation.

WTO (1999b) *Global Code of Ethics*. Available at: http://www.world-tourism.org.

WTO (2000) *Marketing Tourism Destinations Online: Strategies for the Information Age*. Madrid: World Tourism Organisation.

WTO (2001a) *eBusiness for Tourism: Practical Guidelines for Destinations and Businesses*. Madrid: World Tourism Organisation.

WTO (2001b) *Tourism after 11 September 2001: Analysis, Remedial Actions and Prospects*. Madrid: World Tourism Organisation.

WTO (2002a) *Special Report Number 21–2002: Climbing Towards Recovery?* Madrid: World Tourism Organisation.

WTO (2002b) *Tourism and Poverty Alleviation*. World Tourism Organisation. Madrid: Also available at: http://www.world-tourism.org/cgi-bin/infoshop. storefront/EN/product/1267-1

WTO and UNSTAT (1994) *Recommendations on Tourism Statistics*. Madrid: World Tourism Organisation, and New York: United Nations.

WTO Business Council (2001) *E-Business for Tourism: Practical Guidelines for Destinations and Businesses*. Madrid: World Tourism Organisation Business Council.

WTO/WTTC (1996) *Agenda 21 for the Travel and Tourism Industry: Towards Environmentally Sustainable Development*. Madrid: World Tourism Organisation/World Travel and Tourism Council.

WTTC (2002a) *Corporate Social Leadership in Travel and Tourism*. London: World Travel and Tourism Council.

WTTC (2002b) HR Opportunities and Challenges: A Report by the WTTC Human Resource Task Force. Available at: http://www.wttc.org/communicate/pdf/6675HROppsEndChallenges.pdf (accessed on 30.10.02).

WTTC (2002c) *World Travel and Tourism Council Year 2002: End of Year Update*. TSA Research Summary and Highlights.www.wttc.org. Madrid: World Travel and Tourism Council.

WTTC (2003) *SARS Economic Impact: Hong Kong*. Brussels: World Travel and Tourism Council. Also available at: http://www.wttc.org.

Yale, P. (1995) *The Business of Tour Operations*. Harlow: Longman.

Yokeno, N. (1974) The general equilibrium system of 'space-economics' for tourism. *Reports for the Japan Academic Society of Tourism*, 8: 38–44.

Young, C. (nd) *Hadrian's Wall: Striking the Balance*. Centre for Travel and Tourism. Northumberland: The University of Northumbria.

Young, Sir G. (1973) *Tourism: Blessing or Blight?* Harmondsworth: Penguin.

Zeithaml, V.A. and Bitner, M.J. (2000) *Services Marketing: Integrating Customer Focus Across the Firm* (2nd edition). London: Irwin McGraw-Hill.

Zhang, Chun Ming (1999) Division and development strategy of tourism in Altay prefecture, Xinjiang. *Arid Land Geography*, 22(1): 20–6.

Zukin, S. (1995) *The Cultures of Cities*. Cambridge, MA: Blackwell.

Useful websites

Association of Independent Tour Operators:	http://www.aito.co.uk
Civil Aviation Authority ATOL Business:	http://www.caa.co.uk
Federation of Tour Operators:	http://www.fto.co.uk
First Choice plc:	http://www.firstchoice.co.uk
My Travel Group plc:	http://www.mytravelgroup.com
Thomas Cook AG:	http://www.thomascook.info
Travel Weekly	http://www.travelweekly.co.uk
Trading Standards Institute:	http://www.tradingstandards.gov.uk
Tui AG:	http://www.tui.com

Ethical Trading Initiative www.ethicaltrade.org

Fair Trade in Tourism South Africa www.fairtourismsa.org.za

International Centre for Responsible Tourism www.icrtourism.org

Pro-Poor Tourism Partnership www.propoortourism.org.uk

Red Card for Tourism www.akte.ch

responsibletravel Ltd www.responsibletravel.com

Responsible Tourism Partnership www.theresponsibletourismpartnership.com

Tearfund www.tearfund.org

Tourism Concern www.tourismconcern.org.uk

World Tourism Organization www.world-tourism.org